An Introduction to

Requirements Engineering

An Introduction to
Requirements Engineering

Ian K Bray

An imprint of **Pearson Education**

Harlow, England · London · New York · Reading, Massachusetts · San Francisco · Toronto · Don Mills, Ontario · Sydney
Tokyo · Singapore · Hong Kong · Seoul · Taipei · Cape Town · Madrid · Mexico City · Amsterdam · Munich · Paris · Milan

Pearson Education Limited
Edinburgh Gate
Harlow
Essex CM20 2JE
United Kingdom

and Associated Companies throughout the world

Visit us on the World Wide Web at:
www.pearsoneduc.com

_____

First published 2002

© Pearson Education Limited 2002

ISBN 0201 767929

British Library Cataloguing-in-Publication Data
A catalogue record for this book is available from the British Library

Library of Congress Cataloging-in-Publication Data
A catalog record for this book is available from the Library of Congress

Transferred to digital print on demand, 2008

Typeset in 9/12pt Stone Serif by 35
Printed and bound by CPI Antony Rowe, Eastbourne

Brief Contents

Part 3 – Case studies   335

Contents

Acknowledgements

Some of the ideas presented in this book are my own but, as with any book of this nature, much of it comprises a selection and presentation of the ideas of others. Within reason, I have attempted to give due credit to the originators of those ideas and this accounts for many of the references that are included.

There is a debt owed to past students of Bournemouth University, particularly those who have taken the BSc in Software Engineering Management. Since 1989 I have taught a Requirements Engineering unit on that course and students have, perhaps unwittingly, provided much feedback that has helped shape this book.

I would also like to thank colleagues at the University; Karl Cox for his many useful comments upon drafts of the work and Gordon Hukins for introducing me to some of the niceties of formal methods.

Part 1

The topics

Introduction **1**

1.1 Is this book for you?

This book is intended for the novice, in particular the undergraduate novice who, as part of a wider course, is being introduced to software requirements engineering. It might have been called 'a duffer's guide to requirements engineering' except that requirements engineering will forever remain beyond the grasp of duffers. It is a hard subject to which there is no formulaic approach.

In part, this is because it is a surprisingly large subject. This book omits far more than it includes and any readers with prior expertise may object to their pet topic being glossed over or omitted entirely. But this *is* only an introduction; you have to start somewhere and the aim here is to establish a firm foundation. Many readers may never need to know more but, for those who do, pointers are provided and further study of more advanced and subtle topics will, hopefully, have been facilitated. By assuming little prior knowledge and by carefully structuring the material, it is hoped that this book will make the subject reasonably accessible.

Whilst there are some good books on the subject, few are targeted at the undergraduate and most focus upon particular facets rather than offering a broad introduction. In many, there is a tendency to concentrate upon system modelling techniques and the minutiae of notations. Whilst some mastery of these techniques is required, it is far from being adequate in itself. It would be rather like teaching would-be surgeons to dissect and stitch and then expecting them to be able to perform operations. Dissection and stitching are essential skills but, without a detailed knowledge of anatomy, disease and so on they are of very limited use. So it is with requirements engineering; knowing how to model, say, a system's data structure is necessary but far from adequate.

Of course, no book is a substitute for experience and whilst the bare bones of the knowledge are provided here, skills and expertise are developed through practice and exposure to good example. This, in itself, presents something of a problem. Requirements engineering really comes into its own in the larger, more complex projects. These are hardly a good starting point for the novice and, in any case, examples of such material simply would not fit into a book like this. Therefore, we must start with small, relatively simple, case studies and rely on your coursework and, ultimately, industry and commerce to provide the opportunities to develop and scale up your expertise. (That said, despite the limits to what can be covered in an undergraduate programme, over the years, several of my students have reported back from their third year work experience that they already knew more about requirements engineering than anyone else in their placement companies!)

A small, but varied, selection of case studies is provided here:

- the lift control system;
- the racing results program;
- the drill file transformation program;
- the Petri net diagram tool.

These are all relatively simple, but they serve to illustrate points and provide examples. By demonstrating the application of relevant technology, they also help to bridge the gap between 'theory' and practice; a gap which, according to many (e.g. Potts, 1993), has been all too evident in this subject area to date.

The book is in three parts: the first provides a guide to all the important requirements engineering topics, the second gives more detail on useful techniques (for definition, modelling and so on) and the third part contains examples of requirements documentation for the case studies (extracts from which are used to illustrate points in parts one and two). The jargon of requirements engineering cannot be ignored and specialised terms are explained when they first arise, but there is also an extensive glossary (see p. 394).

It may be helpful to also make clear what is excluded. The more advanced requirements engineering topics are not pursued in depth (although numerous pointers for further study are provided). Whilst the book is concerned with software it has little, if anything, to say about computers. Programming and the structural design of software are also left aside as are project management, configuration management and, to a large extent, software testing.

1.2 Know the beast

Engineering concerns the building of useful artefacts, often describable as machines. It is the utility, or purpose, of the end product, rather than any lack of creativity, that distinguishes engineering from art[1]. Engineering may be further distinguished from that other producer of useful artefacts, craft, largely by the matter of scale. Engineering produces the larger, more complex, useful artefacts and, in order to succeed, it requires a particular technology.

Software engineering is special in that it concerns the configuration of a general-purpose machine (the computer) to fulfil a specific purpose. The software that performs the configuration may itself be regarded as a machine but it differs from all other machines in that it is intangible. As Michael Jackson

---

[1] As Oscar Wilde wrote in the Preface to *The Picture of Dorian Gray*, 'all art is quite useless'.

elegantly puts it, 'To develop software is to build a machine simply by describing it' (Jackson, 1995, p. 1).

Before constructing any machine or artefact to fulfil a particular purpose it is, naturally, a very good idea to decide, in some detail, what that purpose is. Thus we are led to requirements engineering; that part of software engineering that concerns how we decide what system we are going to build.

It may seem a little odd that other engineering disciplines do not each have their own version of requirements engineering. In fact, they do, they just do not call it that. It may also be the case that less emphasis is placed upon it and that, in turn, may be because in the tangible, physical, mechanical world, the relationship between the purpose of a system (the problem it is required to solve) and the nature of the system itself (the solution) is more obvious to us.

For example, it you were to present a bicycle to someone who had never seen one before, they would probably figure out quite quickly what it was for. And it works the other way around; ask someone how to cross a river without getting wet and they could probably sketch a design for a raft or a bridge without too much trouble.

In some respects, software is more difficult. Partly it is a matter of complexity; software problems tend to include the most complex problems (sometimes referred to as 'wicked' problems), but it is also the case that reality imposes no physical constraints to limit the imagination and that it is harder to picture the abstract (it is pure 'thought stuff').

1.3   Does requirements engineering really matter?

The chances are that you have already written several pieces of software and you probably have not had to do much in the way of requirements engineering. The starting point may well have been a brief problem description, for example 'write a program that will simulate a simple, four function pocket calculator'.

It is possible to 'get away' with such a simple approach because:

- the problem is small and simple;
- it is widely familiar;
- and, to be blunt, it does not really matter if you get it wrong.

For a fair bit of commercial software, all these conditions still apply; but for a larger chunk of it, they do not, and then you ignore or downplay requirements engineering at your peril.

Partly, the seriousness of the hazard arises from the fact that requirements engineering comes at, or near, the beginning of the software engineering process. It provides the foundations upon which the rest of the project is built. If you make a mistake in the later stages of development, it is only those later stages that are affected and it is usually a relatively simple matter to rectify the error. However, if the mistake is made near the beginning, and not fixed fairly

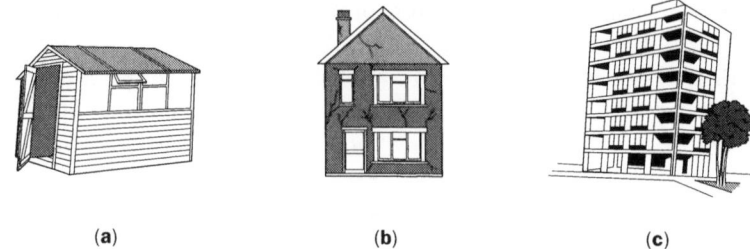

(a)   (b)   (c)

Figure 1.1

promptly, all that follows elaborates upon that mistake. The costs of fixing the fault escalate and it is often the case that it would be cheaper to start all over again.

That said, size still matters. To draw an analogy with building, if your garden shed starts to lean (Figure 1.1 (a)) it costs next to nothing to lever it up and slip in a few bricks. If a house has inadequate foundations and is subject to subsidence (b) it can, at considerable cost, be under-pinned. But if a tower block starts to lean (c)? Well, it is worth making quite sure that it just does not happen!

One way of gauging the necessity of good requirements engineering is to look at what can happen when it does go wrong. It is certainly the case that insufficient emphasis was placed upon software requirements engineering in the past and this has led to many difficulties. Whilst they represent only the tip of the iceberg, it is the major fiascos that catch the headlines; and, if the detailed reports are examined, it is often found to be the case that the problems have their roots in the requirements engineering. Unfortunately, it is not all in the distant past; serious problems and cancelled projects are still with us. For example[2]:

- Performing Rights Society, PROMS project. Abandoned in 1992 after spending £11 million. Poor requirements engineering was a prominent factor. It was reported that they failed to set out the requirements in a form that could be understood and checked by ordinary people and that the specifications were ill-conceived.

- Wessex Regional Information Systems Plan (RISP). Abandoned in 1990 after spending £43 million. Major problems included 'lack of a clear definition of the scope of RISP' (Flowers, 1991, p. 136).

- London Stock Exchange TAURUS project. Cancelled in 1993 after spending £75 million (total costs of failure estimated at up to £480 million). Many problems originated in failures to reconcile conflicting requirements.

- London Ambulance Service despatch system. Closed down in 1992 after two days operation. Sutcliffe writes of 'poor requirements analysis within the social domain' (Sutcliffe, 1998, p. 63).

---

[2] For more detail on several of these, and other, failed projects see Flowers (1996).

- Swanick Air Traffic Control. Due for completion in 1998 but as at 2001 (and at an *additional* cost of £180 million) still not completed. The major causes identified by the official enquiry included 'proceeding with system implementation without a robust requirements specification' (HMSO, 1999).

Projects such as these have often been the subject of subsequent enquiry and there are, of course various reasons for failure but, as Robert Glass observes in his excellent book *Software Runaways*:

> There is little doubt that project requirements are the single biggest cause of trouble on the software project front. Study after study has found that, where there is a failure, requirements problems are usually at the heart of the matter.
>
> (Glass, 1998, p. 21)

And others have come to the same conclusion, for example, Hooper and Hsia (1982, p. 88), describe requirements engineering as 'the most critical and problem-prone area'.

Whilst this indicates that good requirements engineering is absolutely essential for large projects, it is also the case that it offers great benefits for medium and even small projects. So, read on!

1.4   The nature of requirements engineering

It is worth emphasising that we include the word 'engineering' in requirements engineering because it is not a case of producing a vague idea of what is required, rather it is a matter of determining *precisely* what is required.

It is often said that requirements engineering concerns *what* the system will do whereas the following stage, design, concerns *how* it will work. This is a useful starting point but it is something of an over-simplification and, as should be made clear, the nature of requirements engineering is rather more subtle and complex.

A slightly different view is that software engineering is about solving problems and the purpose of requirements engineering is to define the problem that requires solution. Clearly, a development project is unlikely to start until a problem has initially been recognised. However, the first perception of a problem is almost invariably poorly defined and so requirements engineering can be seen as the task of converting a poorly defined problem into a well defined problem (for which a solution can be recognised). For example, the problem 'we need to control a lift' is poorly defined; how could one judge if it has been satisfactorily solved? It follows that the satisfactory conclusion of requirements engineering can be assessed (in part) by asking whether or not a good solution to the problem that has been defined could be recognised unambiguously. This closely relates to the notion of quality as 'fitness for purpose'. How can fitness for purpose be achieved (or even adjudged) if the purpose is not clearly defined?

To the novice, it is often surprising that requirements engineering should be such a hard task; surely just finding out what the problem is in the first place is not as difficult as solving the problem? Experience has shown otherwise.

To a large extent, the difficulty is inherent in the task. As will be seen, requirements engineering incorporates a variety of activities and makes great demands upon the practitioner. It is the main point at which problem domain knowledge (i.e. knowledge about the application for which the system is required) is incorporated into the development. This domain knowledge must be superimposed upon the expertise required for requirements engineering itself and so places a double load upon the practitioner. It is also often the case that much domain knowledge must be gathered from other people (such as clients and potential users) and this introduces difficulties of communication and knowledge transfer. In practice, it is not simply a case of transferring pre-existing knowledge; clients' requirements are notoriously ill-formed and much elaboration and refinement is necessary.

The requirements engineering phase is also unique in that there is seldom a pre-existing model or purpose-built documentation to work from. Subsequent phases build upon what went before; models are, at least to a degree, *derived*, but the products of requirements engineering are *created* – something from, virtually, nothing.

These factors conspire to preclude the possibility of any prescriptive method; there is no prospect of automating or even 'dumbing down' the essential elements of requirements engineering.

To some extent, however, the difficulties are self imposed. Knowledge and useful technology *are* available which can provide the foundations upon which expertise is built. Unfortunately, these matters are not widely taught and, hence, not widely appreciated and applied. This is the situation that this book may help to address.

1.5   The problem domain (and other domains)

Just occasionally, we discover the solution to a problem before we are even aware that the problem exists. It may be hard to imagine now, but when the laser was first invented, nobody knew to what purpose it might be put. The easy release glue that is used on those little sticky notelets was discovered by accident when trying to invent a new permanent glue; it was then a case of thinking of something to do with it. A similar situation sometimes arises with software type problems. Electronic text-processing allows almost all imaginable manipulations and there must be many users of word-processors who, upon encountering a text-processing problem, find that a solution has already been provided.

But usually it is the other way around; the problem is recognised first and then we go in search of a solution. It is hard to imagine what problems will arise in the future but here are some examples of software type problems that have arisen in the past:

- An entire feature film will not fit onto one compact disk.
- A control system is needed that will make more efficient use of the lifts in this building.
- We want a way of working out race results that is quicker and less error prone.
- We would like a new email system that is easier to use than the old one.
- The current air traffic control system will not be able to handle the anticipated growth in air traffic.

It is not always obvious that problems such as those listed can best be solved with software but where they involve the manipulation of data, this is a pretty good bet.

The problem domain (sometimes shortened to PD) can be defined as:

that part of the universe within which the problems exist.

For example, in the case of a lift control system, it would include any existing hardware (lifts, motors, buttons, indicators, sensors, etc.), the building characteristics (number of floors and lift-shafts), the anticipated pattern of usage, the characteristics of the users, the lift usage policy of the client (e.g. should users be discouraged from using a lift for short journeys?) and so on.

Within the lift control problem domain, the problem, as stated above, is, 'a control system is needed that will make more efficient use of the lifts in this building'. In practice, we usually refine the problem into a whole set of sub-problems but, for now, just note that in order to solve the problem(s), it is clearly necessary for the solution system to produce some effects within the problem domain. It is these desired effects that constitute the requirements.

So, the problem domain can equally well be regarded as that part of the world within which the new, solution system (sometimes shortened to SS) will operate and will produce the required effects. Since software-based solution systems are often called applications, the problem domain may be called the application domain.

It may also be referred to as the operating environment since it includes the environment within which the new system will operate. However, it is inevitable that the solution system will change the problem domain in some way (otherwise it could not solve the problem) and so really there are differences, albeit subtle perhaps, between the problem domain and the operating environment.

The problem domain is sometimes regarded as being a set of sub-systems, known as terminators[3] or terminals, which will physically interface with the new, solution system. However, as can be seen from the above lift control system example, only *some* parts of the problem domain (e.g. the hardware) will interface with the new system; other parts (e.g. the anticipated pattern of usage) clearly will not. So, if the problem domain is considered as consisting *only* of the set of

---

[3] A term deriving from data flow diagramming, see Section 13.1.1.1.

terminators an impoverished view will result (which, as will be seen, is a weakness with some approaches to analysis).

Whilst the problem domain is the system that is (or should be) the main focus of attention during requirements engineering it is not the only system that is of interest. The solution system (i.e. the one that will be built) will also warrant close consideration, particularly during the later stages of requirements engineering. Reflecting its importance[4], the solution system also goes by various names, including: the application, the machine and the product. Here, it will usually be referred to as the solution system.

Quite often, there is a third system that attracts close scrutiny during requirements engineering; this is any pre-existing solution system. It is not unusual for the new solution system to be replacing an old application or even a non-software based way of performing the task. In the latter case (the replacement of an old, manual or clerical system with a software system) the process is commonly referred to as computerisation.

More will be said of the study of pre-existing systems later, but a couple of points should be emphasised early on. First, there is not always a pre-existing system to study or, if there is, it may bear so little relationship to the way in which the new system will operate that there is little to learn from it. For example, you could learn something, but probably not a great deal, about the problem domain of a new email system by studying the way an internal post system operates. Second, studying a pre-existing (solution) system is not a substitute for studying the problem domain; whilst it might provide some insight, there is always far more to the problem domain.

But to return to the two systems of prime concern, the problem domain and the solution system, these will interact and their relationship can be pictured as shown in Figure 1.2.

The areas delimited by Figure 1.2 do not indicate only the systems and their interaction, they also define the areas of concern of the three principal development activities shown in Figure 1.3.

So, the principal tasks and their domains of interest can be clearly differentiated:

- **Analysis** concerns the problem domain and the problems that exist within it.
- **Specification** concerns the interaction between the problem domain and the solution system.

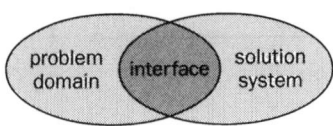

Figure 1.2   (derived from Jackson, 1995)

---

[4] It is alleged that things which we regard with importance tend to have more names, for example, the Inuit have many names for snow!

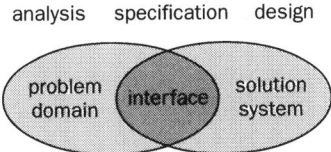

analysis   specification   design

Figure 1.3

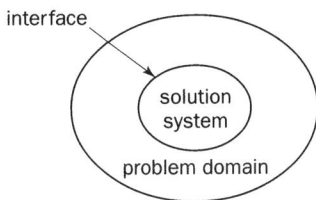

Figure 1.4

- **Design** (which is not part of requirements engineering) concerns the internal workings of the solution system.

(And, as we will explore later, each of these tasks delivers one of the three crucial descriptions.)

There is more than one way of picturing this. Figure 1.4 shows the same thing but, in a slightly less abstract manner, illustrates the fact that the solution system is (or will be) actually contained within the problem domain.

To summarise the plot so far:

- It is a very good idea to decide what a new system should do before you build it.
- We start by studying the problem domain and producing a description of it and a statement of effects that the new, solution system should produce in the problem domain (i.e. the requirements).
- We then specify the behaviour that is required of the new system such that it will produce the required effects in the problem domain.

1.5.1 Types of problem domain

Over the years, there have been various attempts at classifying problem domains. Apart from providing a little intellectual exercise, such efforts can be justified only if they result in methods, guidelines or similar assistance for developing solution systems.

As it happens 'traditional' approaches have, generally, failed to capture the essential characteristics of problem domains in a useful way. For example, they were often classified as:

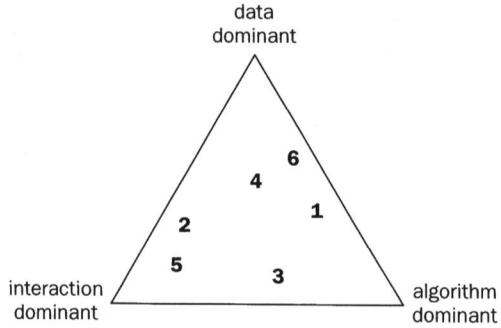

Figure 1.5

- systems software;
- applications software, further classified into:
  - commercial software;
  - engineering software;

or, alternatively (and not entirely orthogonally) as:

- batch/off-line;
- interactive;
- real-time;

or, alternatively again as:

- data dominant;
- interaction dominant;
- algorithm dominant.

Of course, most systems contain elements of all of the last three and the type of chart shown in Figure 1.5 can help characterise a system in terms of their relative weighting. The approximate positions of the following example systems have been suggested:

1. weather forecasting
2. cash machine
3. lift control system
4. payroll
5. word processor
6. file translation

However, this is still a fairly crude and subjective characterisation. It may help to identify where applications are similar but, crucially, it gives but vague guidance as to how to handle the problems. At least as far as requirements engineering is concerned, such classifications have not really led anywhere useful[5].

You will not, for example, find guidance of the kind, 'if the system is of type A then apply version X of the analysis method[6]' or, 'if the system is of type B then it will be necessary to elicit the following details about the problem domain'. In fact, quite the opposite; when the topic of problem domain type arises, most methods claim to be universal.

They might be a little less keen to claim universality were they to consider Jackson's observation that the utility of a method is inversely proportional to its generality (Jackson, 1995). He suggests that the more precisely a problem can be characterised, the more guidance can be provided for tackling the problem. He goes on to suggest a new classification system (which may prove to be one of the most significant advances in software development) based upon the nature of the various sub-domains of the problem domain and the relationships that exist between them.

Whilst recognising that there may be more (this is still early days) Jackson (1995) identifies the following application or problem types:

- **Workpiece** system – where the system must perform directed operations upon realised objects (i.e. that exist only within the solution system). An example would be a word-processor.

- **Control** system – where the system will control the behaviour of part of the problem domain. An example would be a lift control program.

- **Information** system – where the system will have to handle requests for information about the problem domain. An example would be a student records system.

- **Transformation** system – where the system must transform input data in a particular format into output data in a corresponding, particular format. An example would be a program for compiling bank statements from lists of transactions.

- **Connection** system – where the system must maintain correspondence between sub-domains that are not directly connected. An example would be a video-conferencing system.

---

[5] A biological analogy might be the classification of animals upon the basis of where they live. Occasionally there may be some mileage in such a system (for example most marsupials live in Australia) but more often, not. Just because the puma, the llama and the sloth all live in South America does not mean that they have much in common. I can predict far more about their appearance and behaviour if I classify the puma as a cat and the llama as a close relative of the camel.

[6] It may be noted that the term 'method' is used quite loosely within software development. In the formal sense that a method is a procedure that is guaranteed to produce a solution, most software development 'methods' are not methods at all.

(It is the case that real problem domains generally contain elements of more than one type of problem but, as we will see later, that does not invalidate the classification.)

Most development methods and approaches explicitly take little, if any, account of this (or any other) problem domain classification (although, as will be seen, they may be restricted as to which they can handle with any success). However, recent developments have shown how we may exploit this knowledge and Section 4.5 pursues this in some detail; hence this introduction.

1.6 Requirements

As you may have noticed, often there is not a lot of difference between a requirement and a problem. The problem alluded to earlier, 'the current air traffic control system will not be able to handle the anticipated growth in air traffic' is tantamount to the requirement, 'a new air traffic control system is required that will be able to handle the anticipated growth in air traffic'.

However, a definition of requirements may be helpful and here is one:

the effects that the client wishes to be brought about in the problem domain.[7]

A subtly different view regards requirements as the properties that the new system must possess, for example, 'A condition or capability that must be met by the system to solve a problem or achieve an objective' (IEEE, 1984)[8].

The latter definition shifts the focus somewhat from the problem domain (which is not explicitly mentioned but in which, after all, the requirements exist) to the new, solution system. The first definition, therefore, emphasises an important point.

A matter that can cause confusion (and which is further explored later) is the distinction between requirements and facts about the problem domain. For example,

A lift will only reverse direction when stopped at a floor.

is a requirement; it is an effect that the new lift controller system is required to produce. Whereas,

When a lift is within 20 cm vertically (above or below) of the sensor's nominal position the sensor sends a hi signal; otherwise a lo signal.

simply describes a characteristic of the problem domain.

---

[7] Strictly, this only covers *functional* requirements. There is another, relatively rare, class of requirements (see Section 1.6.3) that this definition excludes.
[8] A rather more frivolous definition in this vein could define a requirement as 'anything that the client wants'!

For the moment, I will concentrate only upon requirements but, even here, things are not quite that simple and it soon emerges that there exist various *types* of requirements (and some of them, by the first definition given above, are not really requirements at all!).

1.6.1 Functional requirements

'Ordinary' requirements are often referred to as functional or behavioural requirements. This is presumably because they are requirements that can be met by appropriate behaviour (functionality) on the part of the solution system. For example, a functional requirement for the lift control system (described in Chapter 16) is:

The lift doors are to be cycled every time that a lift stops at a floor.[9]

In order to meet this requirement, the new system (the lift controller) will clearly have to respond to circumstances in the problem domain, in another word, behave, in an appropriate way.

Appropriate behaviour constitutes the functionality of a system and there is often (but not always) a tight correspondence between particular requirements and particular functions of the solution system. So much so, that functions of the solution system are often, loosely, referred to as requirements. For example, the function corresponding to the above requirement could well be:

> The system will cycle the lift doors every time that a lift stops at a floor.

This may well be referred to as a requirement by some. The difference may seem subtle, but it is really a function of the solution system and, whilst loose terminology may often not be of great consequence, it can cause confusion and is not to be encouraged.

The identification of functional requirements is also somewhat complicated by the fact that they may be expressed at various levels of abstraction. For example, for the yacht racing results program (see Chapter 15) you might have the requirement:

All input to the system is to be entered by the user.

This may be fine but it is also possible to be rather more specific and the following might be substituted:

The user can enter and modify boat details,
The user can enter and modify race details,

(and so on).

---

[9] Such a requirement would have to be backed up with descriptions of what is meant by cycling the doors and so on.

Even less abstract versions (but still relating entirely to the behaviour that is required) could be produced. At the lowest level, these may be expressed in terms of the relationships between input to and output from the solution system:

When the user selects the 'modify boat details' option the system will prompt them to enter the boat's name.

The question arises as to which of these levels of functional abstraction represents the 'best bet' when writing requirements. There is no simple answer but some guidance can be given and the examples provided in Part 3 should prove helpful.

The lowest level (sometimes called the input/output level) is clearly into the realm of the interaction between the problem domain and the solution system, and is usually best left to the specification or, where there is one, even to the human machine interface (HMI) specification document.

Partly, however, it depends upon what the client wants. It may be that they have firm ideas about the detail of the interaction with the new system. In this case, such detail may be considered a requirement.

In this rather fuzzy territory you may come across the notion of 'specific' requirements (also known as 'individual' or 'atomic' requirements). The notion may, perhaps, be conveyed by describing them as requirements that may be expressed in one sentence and which are at the lowest level of abstraction short of detailing the physical details of the interaction. They have also been described as functions having just one input (or, by others (Wallace *et al.*, 1987), as having just one output!). Perhaps the terms are best avoided.

1.6.2   Performance requirements

Performance requirements may be regarded as parameters of functionality in that they determine how quickly, how reliably, etc. functions must operate. They are also plagued by dubious terminology. Clearly, performance is observable and performance requirements relate closely to the required functionality. It is, therefore, unfortunate that performance requirements are often referred to by the, arguably, inappropriate label of 'non-functional' or 'non-behavioural' requirements. Be warned.

The separation of performance requirements from the other functional requirements can be justified on the grounds that they tend to be particularly *volatile* requirements. The cost and timescale for development of a system (of given functionality) can be greatly affected by the required performance and so such matters are liable to be traded off. This, in itself, makes it useful to keep them together in a separate section of the documentation; and doing this can also aid in the identification of omitted performance requirements.

Performance requirements are easier to recognise if you keep in mind the sub-categories. Several such categories have been proposed (including safety, security, durability, etc.). Where relevant, they may be critical, but some of these categories are quite rare, and so I will highlight only the most common four:

- speed
- capacity
- reliability
- usability

Speed can be viewed in terms of throughput or in terms of response times. The first is of obvious relevance to off-line (batch) systems, the second to interactive or real-time systems. Either way, it is a straightforward concept but, surprisingly, is often overlooked.

Capacity relates to the quantity of data that can be stored within the system and such matters as the number of users that can be handled simultaneously might also be slotted in here. Data capacity requirements should not be confused with any requirement for the size of the system itself.

It will be possible to store at least 10000 transactions,

is a capacity requirement.

The new system shall occupy no more than 10 Mbytes of RAM,

has nothing to do with functionality, it is a design constraint (see next section).

In the context of software, reliability is a difficult concept. Being entirely abstract, software is not subject to wear and consequent failure in the same way as hardware. It does not develop faults, they were always there; it is simply a matter of how long it is before they are found. Mean time between failure (mtbf) is, nonetheless, often specified for software but frequently a more useful approach is to specify reliability in terms of availability. This is the proportion of the time (within specified periods) that the system is performing correctly (or, at least, usably).

Usability is also difficult to pin down. An exhortation to make the system 'user friendly' may have a place as an objective but does not constitute a testable requirement. The best approach is to consider the way in which usability might be tested and then couch the requirements in those terms. For example:

A computer literate race officer should be able to learn to enter finish times and output race results with an error rate of less than one in twenty boats, with no more than thirty minutes training.

(Depending upon the context, it may also be necessary to explain what is meant by 'computer literate'.)

1.6.3 Design constraints

Design constraints[10] are the true non-functional requirements. They affect (constrain) how the system is built but *not* what it does (at least, not directly). If in

---

[10] Design constraints are often referred to simply as 'constraints'. There are, however, other sorts of constraints and so this shorthand must be used with some caution.

doubt, a useful test is to ask whether, under normal usage, it would be apparent to the eventual users of the system whether the requirement has been met. If it would *not* be apparent, then the requirement is a design constraint.

The ideal situation, from the developer's perspective, is that there are *no* design constraints. The designer is then free to explore all options for building a system that will meet the given functional requirements. However, it does not always work out that way. For various reasons (some good, some bad) clients may wish to impose constraints. (It should only ever be the client who imposes design constraints, not the analyst or requirements engineer.)

Although the distinction is not always clear, two types of design constraint can be identified. The first directly constrains the resultant structure of the system. For example:

The system must be implemented in three main modules, one for each of the main functions; detection, recording and statistical analysis.

The second type affects the structure only indirectly (if at all) by constraining the process or technology used to develop it. For example:

The system must be developed using object oriented design techniques.

Common matters for design constraints include:

- target machine(s) upon which the solution system must operate[11];
- underlying architecture; distributed or local;
- memory size within which it must operate;
- any front-end graphical user interface (GUI) packages that must be employed;
- operating system(s) under which it must operate;
- programming language(s) that must be used;
- other software packages, such as database management systems (DBMS), that must be incorporated
- development standards that must be applied;
- design approaches that must be employed;
- algorithms that must be incorporated.

As indicated earlier, only by delving into the workings of the system could one check whether or not such constraints had been met; the normal user would be blissfully unaware (unless certain types of system failure occur!).

That said, in the extreme, some design constraints *can* impinge upon functionality (for example, there could be insufficient memory to be able to meet

---

[11] This may appear to be an exception to the 'if the user can see it, it is not a constraint' rule. Well, maybe, but often the only clue is the label on the box.

certain capacity requirements) but this is the exception. Where such problems do arise then trade-offs must be discussed and negotiated with the client (see Section 3.4.5).

The recording of non-functional requirements has, generally, received little attention but a relatively rigorous approach is proposed in Mylopoulos *et al.* (1992).

1.6.4 Commercial constraints

Apart from 'what will it do?', the most important questions for many clients are 'when will I get it?' and 'how much will it cost?'. Often they will have firm views upon the answers and any such requirements constitute the commercial constraints.

The relationships between timescale and cost and the eventual functionality, reliability, usability, etc., of the solution system are, to say the least, complex. Such matters are studied under the auspices of project management and software engineering management and so little more will be said about them here. Suffice it to say that commercial constraints are often picked up whilst investigating the other requirements, but they are readily identified; just look out for requirements relating to time (for delivery) and money. List them separately and, until the day that you are the project manager, you can probably leave it at that.

1.6.5 Other types of requirement

You may well find references to other types of requirement in other literature. Sometimes these can be recognised simply as alternative names for the types considered here; at other times they represent rare or even arcane considerations. One is worth brief mention.

Preferences are, in effect, non-mandatory requirements. The implication for the designer is that, if they can be met at little or no cost, then they should be included or the architecture of the system should be designed so as to accommodate them readily in future versions.

1.6.6 Requirements: summary

Requirements may be categorised and an awareness of the differences can assist in structuring the process and the resultant documents. In particular, design constraints should always be recognised for what they are. Table 1.1 summarises the classification described above. The acronym 'SCRU' also seems to serve as a useful mnemonic for the most common varieties of performance requirement. (But remember that performance requirements are frequently referred to as 'non-functional' requirements.)

Table 1.1

Problem domain description (how the world is)	Requirement (what the client wants)						
	Commercial constraint (time and money)	Design constraint (how to build it)	Functional (what it does)				
			'Ordinary'	Performance			
				S p e e d	C a p a c i t y	R e l i a b i l i t y	U s a b i l i t y

1.7 Exercises

1 There follow a number of statements (relating to various systems), each of which describes a problem domain or constitutes a requirement. Classify each according to the table above. (This is actually easier than in 'real life' as you would have far more context to help you.)

a) When the user selects the 'modify boat details' option the system will prompt them to enter the boat's name.

b) The system must be implemented in three main modules, one for each of the main functions; detection, recording and statistical analysis.

c) When a lift is within 20 cm vertically (above or below) of the sensor's nominal position the sensor sends a hi signal; otherwise a lo signal.

d) For each boat, the elapsed time is defined as the difference, in seconds, between the race start time and the boat's finish time.

e) The lift should not be stopped from fast mode but should always be switched to slow mode for at least one second before stopping.

f) A lift's direction may only be reversed when it is stopped at a floor.

g) The system must be developed using the 'XYZ systems method'.

h) The maximum number of lifts is four, the minimum one.

i) Currently, no two users have the same name but some might in the future.

j) The maximum input file size will be two million characters and files of this size should be converted in no more than 60 seconds.

k) The examination entry screen will provide facilities for editing and deleting existing records and will allow the addition of new Subjects for the particular Series entry.

l) A release number consists of four numbers, each of which can be up to three digits long and is separated from the next by a full stop.

m) Maintainability shall be a major goal of the development of the examinations database.

n) The software must be smaller than the existing NCR7116 cash dispenser system.

o) The lift position sensors are switches which close (make circuit) when the lift is within 10 cms (vertically) either side of the sensor position.

p) Confirmation of each action taken, input accepted, or error condition will be displayed after each input.

q) TELLERFAST will have been thoroughly tested at time of delivery so that computational errors will not occur (from Dorfman and Thayer (1990)).

r) TELLERFAST will be written in a modular structure to make modification as easy as possible.

s) AUTOTELLER will be out of operation for servicing no more than 0.001% of its yearly operating time.

t) Tabber will be operated by the existing security personnel who have little or no previous computer system operating experience. After one hour's training, a typical operator should be able to perform the test suite (see Appendix C) with an average user response time of less than five seconds and an error rate of less than 1 in 10.

u) Most subscriptions are received directly from the subscriber; however, the publication also deals with a number of agencies or subscription service bureaux.

v) In order to optimise cash flow, it is important that invoices are printed and despatched within two days of the meter readings being entered.

w) The new system will interface to the boiler via a serial port with the following pin assignations : 0 = flame out detector; 1 = low pressure gas sensor; 2–5 = combustion temperature sensor (high-bit to low bit); 6–9 = flue temperature sensor (high-bit to low bit).

x) The interface to the boiler should be via a separate sub-system so that it can be readily re-programmed for different port configurations

y) As soon as the user enters their name, the system will retrieve their encrypted password from the password file so that it is available by the time they have entered their password.

2 Match the following descriptions to the terms that follow them:

a) that part of the universe within which the problem(s) exist;

b) the requirements engineering task that concerns the interaction between the problem domain and the solution system;

c) an effect that the client wishes to be brought about in the problem domain;

d) the application of a disciplined technology to the development of complex, useful artefacts;

e) the task that concerns the internal workings of the solution system;

f) investigating and describing the problem domain and requirements and designing and documenting the characteristics for a solution system that will meet those requirements;

g)   knowledge about the application area for which a solution system is required;

h)   the system that is intended to bring about the desired effects in the problem domain;

i)   the requirements engineering task that concerns the problem domain and the problems that exist within it;

j)   a solution system that is intended to handle requests for information about the problem domain:

- analysis
- design
- engineering
- information system
- problem domain (application domain)
- problem domain knowledge
- requirement
- requirements engineering
- solution system (application, machine)
- specification

The requirements engineering process

2

Alan Davis defines requirements engineering as: 'all activities up to but not including the decomposition of the software into its actual architectural components' (Davis, 1988b, p. 300). In other words, everything before internal design.

That is essentially true but it perhaps says more about what requirements engineering is *not* rather than what it *is*, so here is a working designation to be going on with:

> **investigating and describing the problem domain and requirements and designing and documenting the characteristics for a solution system that will meet those requirements.**

Ben Kovitz provides a very succinct characterisation of requirements engineering as 'the design of requirements'[12] (Kovitz, 1999, p. 28) which he views as a process of converting an open-ended problem into a well defined problem.

Requirements engineering is, of course, part of a larger process, software engineering. The view of requirements engineering that is presented here makes a few assumptions about that larger process. Fundamentally, it assumes that there *is* a recognisable requirements engineering stage. This is not always the case. Some alternative approaches employ more of a trial and error approach; what has been called the 'you build it and then I'll tell you what's wrong with it' approach. Sometimes (for example, where really novel technology is being investigated and funding is generous or where the application meets the criteria presented in Section 1.3 – small, well known and who cares anyway!) this can be deliberate and justified; more often it stems from ineptitude.

There are many variations on software development process models (or 'life-cycles' as they used to be called). Some of these present an essentially linear process (for example, the 'V' or STARTS model (DTI/NCC, 1986)) whilst others more overtly attempt to show the overlap and iteration that occurs in practice. Some play down the requirements engineering phase but, even where there is implicit doubt as to its nature, most give it due prominence.

---

[12] Design is used here in the sense of external design (i.e. not as in Davis's definition) – see Section 2.7.

There is also widespread agreement that (overlap and iteration aside) requirements engineering comes at or near the beginning and that the principal deliverable or output that feeds from requirements engineering to the subsequent stage (usually 'design') is some form of specification. These features will be assumed here but little more will be said about software engineering in general; that is the subject of other books.

However, requirements engineering is itself a process and it may well help to appreciate the whole by considering the various sub-tasks, their products and the interaction between them. The following sub-tasks may be identified[13]:

- elicitation
- analysis
- specification
- human machine interface (HMI) design
- validation

Each task will be examined in some detail later but, for now, a brief characterisation will be given of each. They are listed above in a (very approximately) sequential order but, to reduce the amount of forward referencing, they are introduced in a slightly different order.

2.1   Analysis

Analysis is a tricky concept, indeed, a tricky term. It carries much baggage from use and misuse over the years and so it is tempting to reject it in favour of a new term. However, applying naming rule 2 (Section 14.2.2.1) dictates that it be (re)designated. That a fully meaningful, short and simple designation is not possible may be deduced from the conspicuous lack of entries in the glossaries of other books on this subject.

However, a basic designation is a start that may be rounded out with further discussion. Analysis:

> **through study of a problem domain, the achievement of understanding of and the documentation of the characteristics of that domain and the problems (requiring solution) that exist within that domain.**

This might be more precisely referred to as '*problem domain* analysis' but elsewhere the term 'analysis' is often compatible with this designation. You are, however, likely to encounter other meanings, such as:

---

[13] Acceptance test planning is sometimes included in such a list. Acceptance tests are a sub-set of functional tests (see Section 6.5) that are intended to demonstrate that the completed system meets its vital requirements; in other words, is acceptable. From the client's perspective this helps ensure a satisfactory product; from the developer's perspective it helps ensure that (the bulk of) payment is received (even if minor faults exist). Acceptance tests are highly recommended and their planning would normally follow on from specification.

- analysis of the documented requirements for a system;
- establishing fundamental, solution system behaviour (as in Yourdon, 1996);
- development of the high level, architectural design for a solution system (as in Jacobson *et al.*, 1996).

The first two of these are more akin to specification (as described here) and the last does not really constitute part of requirements engineering (as described here) at all.

You will also encounter various synonyms or near synonyms, notably 'systems analysis', 'problem analysis' and, possibly, 'requirements analysis' (but the last more often refers to one of the alternatives listed above). Within the context of business applications, 'business modelling' is often tantamount to the same thing as well.

Kovitz (1999, p. 116) divides analysis into two parts:

- 'Learning [about] the problem and the problem domain from the customer; known as *elicitation*.
- Communicating this information to the rest of the development staff by writing a requirements document.'

This emphasises the intimate relationship between elicitation and analysis but, arguably, subsuming elicitation within analysis downplays its separate identity. As Kovitz goes on to say, elicitation has problems and a technology of its own. Since some space is given to these here, it will be treated as a separate, although intimately intertwined, activity.

Kovitz's description also serves to introduce the most important aspect of analysis, the learning. To put the extreme counter-case, information (about a problem domain) can be collected and recorded with no more than a tape recorder or camcorder. There is, however, no sense in which such a machine has achieved any understanding. Learning, in the sense of achieving understanding is currently, for all relevant purposes, a uniquely human activity. The mechanism is poorly understood but appears to centre upon constructing abstractions and creating links between abstractions. It is this that characterises analysis.

Since the mechanism itself is not directly accessible, it is the tangible form of these abstractions upon which we must concentrate. These are the resultant models and descriptions of the problem domain and the effects that must be wrought upon it by the solution system. These models and descriptions must be sufficiently comprehensive to convey all the necessary information but, at the same time, sufficiently abstract to allow comprehension of that information[14].

---

[14] One sometimes hears exhortations for ever 'richer' 'models' (such as unedited video of system users) that, with vast redundancy, capture ever more information about the problem domain. In the extreme, this trend would result in a 'model' that is indistinguishable from reality. This, of course, is not a model at all, simply a duplicate; the whole point of modelling (abstraction to allow comprehension) has been lost. A balance must be struck.

So, to emphasise the vital characteristics of this vital task:

- Analysis concerns (and often models) the problem domain, *not* the solution system.
- The principal goal is to achieve understanding of the nature of the problem domain and the problems that exist within it.
- In essence (despite overlap and iteration), analysis *precedes* specification (of the behaviour of the solution system).

As already implied, the output from analysis is (or should be) a carefully structured description or model of the relevant characteristics of the problem domain, plus a statement of the requirements (i.e. the effects that the solution system should produce in the problem domain in order to solve the problem). This document is sometimes known as the analysis document but the, probably, more common name of requirements document will be adopted here. It should not be confused with the specification document which, not surprisingly, is the output from the specification task, and which defines the required behaviour of the solution system.

It must be recognised that, unfortunately, in many methods and in much of the literature, these documents *are* confused. At best they are combined (which is not necessarily a problem); occasionally the names are interchanged (which is confusing); and, at worst, one or the other is omitted (which can be disastrous).

It is, of course, necessary also to have some *input* to analysis, some information to analyse. For educational purposes, such information is often provided by way of a 'problem description' or 'system description'. Whilst it is easy to get the impression from some texts that such documents are part of the development process, they are simply an educational convenience and have no parallel in the commercial world (other than as a feeble substitute for a proper requirements document!). Relevant information has to be gleaned from primary sources and is seldom found in such a well processed form. This process of information collection is usually termed elicitation and it delivers the, largely unstructured, information that is the raw material for analysis.

2.2 Elicitation

Elicitation concerns the gathering of information and, indeed, it is also known as requirements gathering, requirements capture or, sometimes, requirements acquisition. The three main considerations are:

- What information should be gathered?
- From what sources it can be gleaned?
- By what mechanisms or techniques it may be gathered?

The first question must be approached incrementally since, at first, very little will be known about the problem. We must, therefore, adopt a generalised approach, knowing that, for any system, the characteristics of the problem domain and the problems requiring solution within that domain (the requirements) must be ascertained. Analysis of the early elicited information will characterise the problem domain and, as will be seen, this can then guide the subsequent elicitation. So, there is a feedback loop via analysis (and, as requirements engineering progresses, this feedback loop will extend to include specification).

The available sources of information are largely dictated by the circumstances (but the general possibilities are known) and, together with the essential characteristics of the problem domain, these will guide the selection of elicitation techniques.

Much of the information will be obtained from people who have some interest in the system development and such people are often referred to as stakeholders; they have some stake in the development. It may be that they are the anticipated users of the new system and their daily work experience could be made more or less satisfying. It may be that they own the enterprise that will profit from any increased productivity. It may even be that they will be made redundant by any new system. In every case, a stakeholder has potential losses or gains and this could colour their viewpoint. The astute requirements engineer will be aware of this possibility.

So, the sources of input to the elicitation task are several and varied but well understood. The output, on the other hand, is seldom mentioned, to the extent that there is not even a widely used name. Elicitation output will here be referred to as elicitation notes and, indeed, it often *is* in the form of notes taken during interviews, etc., but it can also encompass audio recordings, video recordings, piles of completed questionnaires and so on. This output is quite distinct from analysis output because it is largely unprocessed, unstructured and may contain many irrelevancies and, initially, omissions.

Elicitation notes are often regarded as temporary documents which, once used, are destined for the bin. This may well be a mistake as, for purposes of tracing the origin of requirements or for understanding the rationale behind requirements, they can prove useful.

2.3 Specification

Specification may be defined as:

> **the invention and definition of a behaviour of a solution system such that it will produce the required effects in the problem domain.**

It is a more creative process than analysis in that the new system does not, as yet, exist and its behaviour must be *invented*. Usually, clients will dictate what problems need to be solved by the new system (what requirements must be met). They will not always, however, dictate the precise system behaviour that will best meet those requirements. Where they do, then specification is simply (!) a matter of documentation; where they do not, then it is up to the requirements engineer to invent, as well as document, a suitable system behaviour. This will, naturally, be taken back to the client for approval, but the invention of the behaviour is part of the specification task. Furthermore, there are generally many different behaviours that would produce the required effects and, with due consideration to various trade-offs, the best that can be devised must be selected.

This is clearly a *design* task; but not an *internal* design task (as occurs after requirements engineering, in the 'design' phase), rather it is an *external* design task; external design being where the externally visible appearance and behaviour of the system are invented. (There is clearly some opportunity for confusion between external and internal (structural) design but the distinction is critical and so is examined further in Section 2.7. If you are the least bit unsure about the distinction, you may care to read that section now.)

Apart from developing the external design for the new system, the specification task is mainly a matter of documentation. The principal output from the specification task is the specification document which, essentially, contains *a definition of the required behaviour of the solution system*. The importance of this document is reflected in its almost bewildering array of names. Common variations include:

- requirements specification;
- system requirements specification;
- requirements definition;
- functional requirements definition;
- etc.

It may well be argued that the specification is *the* most important document in the entire software development process, not least because of its contractual nature. It forms the basis of an agreement between the client and the developer; defining what the client expects to get and what the developer expects to deliver. A well written specification can avoid many problems down the line. One can only guess at how often conversations along these lines have occurred:

Client: 'But I expected that the system would be able to handle that.'
Developer: 'Well, that's not the impression you gave me. I thought that you said that you wanted it to operate like this.'
Client: 'I'd never have said that because without the logging bit the thing is virtually useless.'
Developer: 'Well I can't second guess what you *meant*, I have to work on the basis of what you actually *said*.'

(Let's leave it there before it gets too heated!)

In cases like this, *both* sides often lose out. The client does not get the system that they need and the developer may well have problems getting paid for the work they have done.

It is also worth noting that the specification represents the point of handover of authority. The client has the final say as to what the specification says but the developer has control over the subsequent phases.

A small aside: this book is mostly about requirements engineering 'in the large' and, hence, concentrates upon the specification of *whole applications*.

However, as development proceeds into the subsequent internal design phase and the system's internal structure is determined, specifications can (and should) be developed for the sub-systems at all levels within that structure. At the highest (system) level; there should be no distinction between what will be achieved by software and what will be achieved by other means (since this has yet to be determined); at the lower levels we, as software developers, will produce specifications only for the software components.

Much of what follows is independent of the level of the specification but the emphasis shifts and differences become more apparent as the lowest levels of sub-system are approached. It transpires that the lower levels are less problematical and so, whilst that topic is addressed briefly in Section 5.5, the focus will continue to be on high, 'application' level specification.

2.4 Human to machine interface design

Sometimes, the detailed external design is largely divorced from specification. This almost always corresponds to having a complex HMI (also commonly called the human to computer interface (HCI)). The essential behaviour of the new system is still designed and defined in the specification but the design of the low-level detail (sometimes referred to as the 'look and feel') of the HMI is factored out.

This is partly because the external design and documentation of a sophisticated HMI requires particular expertise. Not only must the HMI expert be able to invent a suitable behaviour but they must also be familiar with the constraints that are imposed by, and the opportunities that are offered by, the available technology. It is rightly regarded as a specialist job.

Another consideration is that the detailed specification of the HMI can be large and, if incorporated into the specification, can mask the essential, 'logical' behaviour of the system.

It is not always the case that a complex external interface to the system is with humans (although they usually are); it is quite possible for the system to have a complex interface to, say, another software system. In this case, exactly the same principle applies but a different sort of expert may be called upon to detail the interface.

2.5 Validation

To err is human and there is no reason to suppose that errors will not be made during requirements engineering. Problems can arise from misunderstanding between elicitor and client, ambiguity in documentation and so on. Unfortunately, as discussed in the introduction, mistakes during this phase are often the most pervasive and expensive. It is, therefore, particularly important that we take steps to minimise errors and to detect and correct any that do occur as soon as is practicable.

Preventing the introduction of errors in the first place is mainly a matter of good engineering practice and this is the subject of the following chapters. Even with best practice, however, it is wise to assume that mistakes will happen and to employ procedures which attempt to detect those mistakes.

So, the requirements engineering process (indeed the whole software engineering process) should be validated. Validation attempts to ensure that the correct functionality for the solution system has been defined and it follows a simple line of reasoning[15]:

- if the problem domain behaves as described (in the requirements document); and
- if the requirements are correctly recorded; and
- if the new system behaves as described (in the specification document); then,
- provided that the invention step (the external design) is correct;

the requirements will be met[16].

This highlights the potential sites of error and, hence, those things that must be tested for correctness:

- Is the description of the problem domain an accurate reflection of its properties?
- Are the requirements (the effects to be produced in the problem domain) accurately recorded?
- Is the external design correct; will the invented behaviour of the new system produce the required effects?
- Is the specification an accurate reflection of the intended external design?

Validation should be built into the requirements engineering process, is accomplished through a variety of testing or checking procedures and can occur at many levels. During an elicitation interview, say, a client's statements can be repeated back to them, in different words, in order to check understanding (e.g. 'so what you saying is that the user can print out results for a whole series of races but not for individual races?'). When a first draft of the requirements document is complete, it can be subjected to a formal review and so on.

An overview of review, and other relevant testing techniques, is presented in Chapter 6.

2.6   A requirements engineering process model

The interactions between the various requirements engineering tasks can be indicated in a process model and one is suggested below (Figure 2.1). As with

---

[15] A very similar line of reasoning can also be applied to the subsequent structural design stage. See Jackson (1995, p. 170) or Kovitz (1999, p. 39).

[16] Some would regard this as an over-simplistic view, based, as it is, on the notion that a program *can* be fully specified; see Lehman and Belady (1985, Chapters 19 and 20).

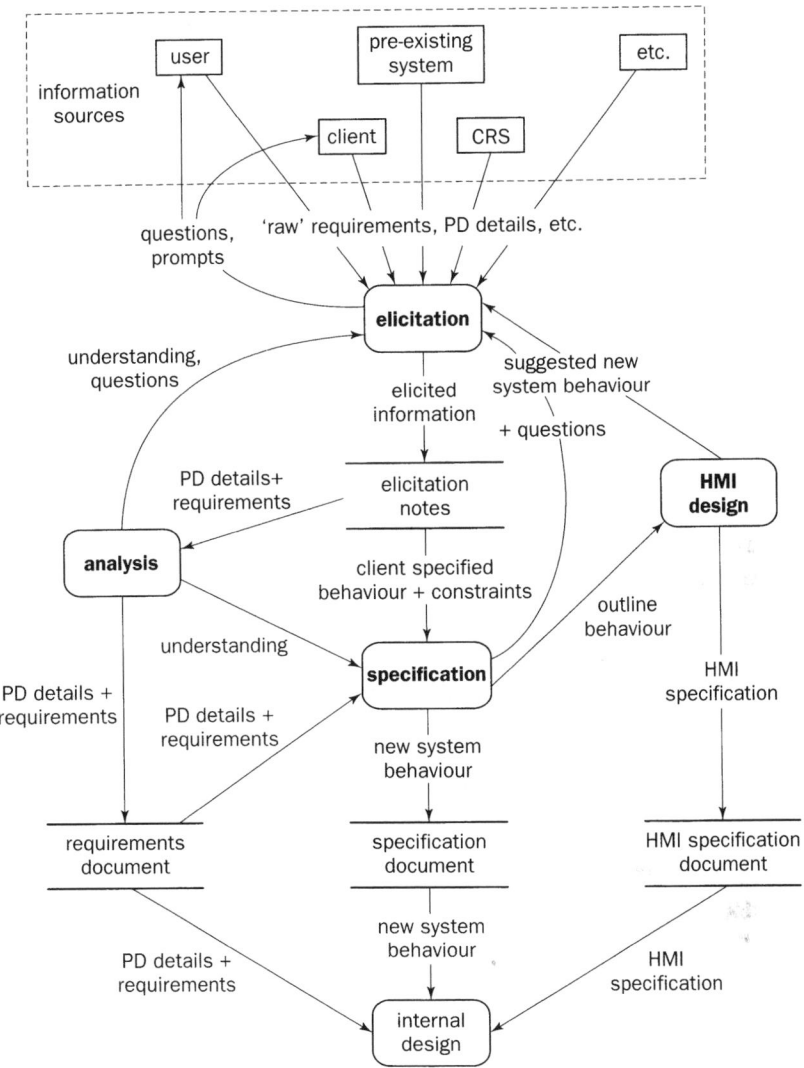

Figure 2.1
Note: CRS – client requirements specification

most data flow diagrams (DFDs), this says little about the sequencing of tasks; but that is outlined in the following discussion.

Validation (testing) is not shown separately in this model because, as previously implied, it permeates the entire process. Note also that this model is somewhat idealised. In practice, there is much variation and the process is inherently more intricate and tortuous than is implied. Nonetheless, for the initiate, such a model will, hopefully, shed more than a little light on a complex issue.

At the top of the diagram there appear some representative sources of information. As indicated, humans are interactive sources and are prompted with questions and suggestions. All the 'raw' information that is collected feeds through an elicitation process.

In the early stages of requirements engineering, most of the elicited information will relate to the problem domain and the fundamental requirements and this will feed into analysis. The analysis will shed light upon the problem domain and this understanding feeds back into elicitation where it prompts further questions and generally guides the elicitation process.

It is likely that specification will commence before analysis is complete. Once the fundamentals of the problem domain and the requirements are established, the behaviour of the solution system can be outlined. This is useful in that suggested system behaviour can be fed back to potential users and clients where it helps elicit yet further information.

If sophisticated external design is required, this process can be triggered towards the end of specification and it will also contribute to the elicitation feedback loop. Ultimately, the requirements document and the specification (and, where appropriate, the external design document) form the main outputs from requirements engineering and the input to the subsequent, structural design phase.

2.6.1   Requirements engineering documentation

Four documents appear in the above requirements engineering process model:

- elicitation notes;
- requirements document (aka analysis document);
- specification;
- HMI design document.

These documents are essentially complementary but there will be some overlap of content. Naturally, the elicitation notes will replicate much of the information in both the requirements document and the specification; however, the elicitation notes are in a 'half-baked', poorly structured form and are not intended to be passed on from the requirements engineering phase. Often, they are soon scrapped but it can be argued that they form part of the traceability trail and should be kept for that purpose.

The bulk of the requirements document consists of a precise description of the characteristics of the problem domain and its sub-domains. It also, of course, includes the requirements themselves but the latter may well be duplicated in the specification document simply as a matter of convenience.

Since the HMI design document elaborates the detail of the external interfaces of the solution system, there is inevitably some overlap with the specification document. This overlap is accepted because of the utility of the more abstract interface specifications within the specification document.

Michael Jackson talks of software development entailing three necessary descriptions; 'the common description, the description that's true only of the machine and the description that's true only of the application domain'

(Jackson, 1995, p. 3). It is the first of these that is embodied in the specification (and, where necessary, elaborated further in the HMI design document). The second is not represented herein because it belongs to the subsequent, structural design phase. The third is embodied in that part of the requirements document that describes the problem domain.

Note that this differentiation of documents may well not be apparent in much of the other literature nor in many of the proprietary methods where it is quite common to combine documents or even omit some documentation. You may care to give such inconsistencies further thought when you have fully considered the view that is presented here.

2.6.2   Shortcuts

The process model presented above is quite comprehensive. For many projects, however, it is not necessary or appropriate to apply the 'whole works'. We have already seen that where problems are small or familiar or failure can be tolerated, the requirements engineering phase, in its entirety, can be largely bypassed.

There are, however, intermediate situations and perhaps the commonest of these is where the problem is not necessarily small, and success is critical, but the problem domain is already well understood. This could occur, for example, where a developer produces a string of applications which address the same problem domain. In such cases, because of the understanding that already exists, problem domain analysis could be greatly curtailed, if not virtually eliminated, and effort would be concentrated upon the remainder.

Specification is not, generally, a step that should be omitted. Even where the problem domain is well understood, there are many good reasons for developing a specification (see Section 5.4.1). However, when working in familiar territory, there are often big savings to be made with the extensive *re-use* of specifications for predecessor systems. It has also been proposed that specifications can be reverse engineered from the user manuals for pre-existing solution systems of similar functionality.

The extent of HMI design that is required is partly determined by the nature of the application (just how extensive and complex are the human interfaces?), partly by the 'fussiness' of the client (are they prepared to leave such 'details' to chance?) and partly by the expertise of the relevant staff (are the programmer(s) who will implement the interfaces sufficiently competent HMI designers?).

One of the most effective shortcuts is to avoid building a solution system at all and, instead, buy (and, probably, configure) some suitable, ready made system. (Such systems are, generally, referred to as 'commercial, off the shelf' (COTS) software.) This strategy does not obviate the need for requirements engineering; it is still important to investigate the problem domain and establish the requirements in order that the suitability of COTS may be assessed. However, devising a specification for a new system to meet those requirements is replaced by the, probably simpler, task of assessing how well an existing system meets them.

It becomes particularly pertinent to grade requirements, and categories such as:

- essential
- highly desirable
- useful

might be adopted in order to aid the selection process. Considerable compromise and trade-off may well ensue. That is beyond the scope of this book but see, for example, Maiden and Ncube (1998).

So, shortcuts are possible and often appropriate, but they should not be taken in ignorance. Just as when travelling across country, shortcuts can lead you astray. You will not always use all of it, but a good understanding of the full picture (as presented here) is the safest preparation for going 'off the beaten track'.

2.7 Design (and 'analysis and design')

There are (at least) two different sorts of design. This is not a matter of great concern in everyday life, but within software engineering, and particularly requirements engineering, it is important to be clear on the distinction.

What we usually refer to as design, as for example in the 'software design phase' is *internal* design. Internal design (also known as structural design[17]) may be defined as:

the decomposition of a system into its actual structural components for the purpose of constructing it.

This is what we do with the solution system after its required behaviour has been specified. Somebody has to devise how it will actually work; they must invent the structure of the solution system by decomposing it into a number of component parts. There is often a levelled decomposition; we start with a high-level decomposition (sometimes called architectural design) and proceed all the way down to executable code statements[18].

The other type of design concerns the system's appearance and behaviour. This, external design, is very much a part of requirements engineering and so it has already been briefly discussed and is considered in more detail later (as part of the specification task).

Here is a hopefully memorable (if frivolous) example of the difference. Suppose that you wanted a humanoid robot (an android). The external design

---

[17] This is not to be confused with *structured* design, a particular design paradigm. Structural (internal) design is the design of the internal structure of the system by any means (e.g. object oriented design).

[18] Note that, in the case of software, there is no clear distinction between design and construction. The design becomes ever more detailed until it is executable. (Remember Jackson's observation that, 'To develop software is to build a machine simply by describing it' (Jackson, 1995, p. 1). This is quite different from other engineering disciplines where once the design is completed, it is still necessary to 'cut metal'.

would specify the appearance and behaviour (actually an impossibly complex task but let us just say that it must look and behave like a human being). The internal design would then determine how it could actually work and (at least in the world of science fiction) there are several possibilities; a model T-800 or a model T-1000 Terminator (as in the film *Terminator 2: Judgement Day*) being just two.

So, be warned, if ever the word 'design' crops up in software development ask yourself, or, if appropriate, the person who said it, which type of design is meant.

Both types of design share the quality of invention but, as far as we are concerned, there the similarity ends. Important though it is, internal design is not part of requirements engineering and so will not be considered in depth here. However, some appreciation of its character is relevant if only to eliminate any confusion that may arise with other requirements engineering activities. And there are reasons why confusion can arise.

Firstly, there is simple terminology. The use of the word 'design' for both external and internal design is unfortunate but, sadly, English provides no good alternative. 'Styling' may be used for external design but scarcely captures the full gravitas of such an important activity. To compound this problem, in other areas of engineering those who perform styling (or external design) are often called 'designers' whereas those who perform internal (or structural) design are more often called engineers. In this book the terms external design and internal design (sometimes abbreviated to 'edesign' and 'idesign') will be used, where necessary, to make the distinction.

Secondly, there is the matter of decomposition. Internal design is not the only activity that involves decomposition. Many definitions of *analysis* will include something along the lines of, 'resolving, separating or decomposing a system into its constituent elements'. But there is a difference and it is a crucial one. Analysis involves *discovering* the composition of a system (such as the problem domain) that *already exists*; whereas internal design involves *inventing* the composition of a system (the solution system) that does *not*, as yet, exist.

That said, the same techniques may be used to *model* the composition in either case. This partly explains why there are so many books whose titles include the phrase 'analysis and design'[19]. This may otherwise be considered curious; why pick on these two development tasks and exclude, say, specification and coding? As discussed earlier, specification may best be considered as the task that sits *between* analysis and idesign, so why omit it?

Sometimes, it is simply the case that specification is subsumed within analysis; but not often. More commonly, specification is virtually omitted and a partial explanation may be postulated in the short shrift that is usually given to specification; but it seems likely that there is more to it yet. If one ignores or downplays the larger picture and concentrates upon the nitty-gritty of the modelling techniques, the common ground can overwhelm the fundamental difference between analysis and design.

---

[19] Design being used in the sense of internal design.

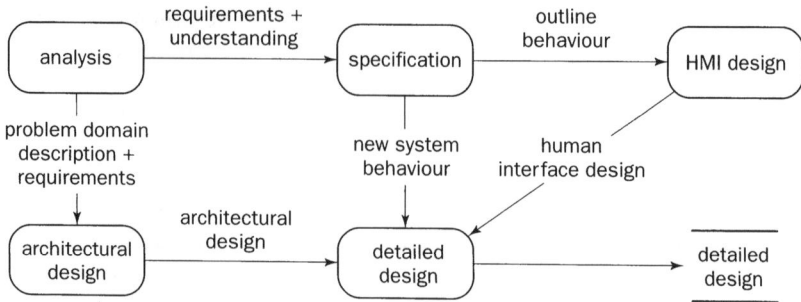

Figure 2.2

(An aside: In fact, there may be more to it yet. It now seems likely that, provided analysis takes account of the particular characteristics of a problem domain (see Sections 1.5.1 and 4.5.1.1) then, a high-level design for the solution system may be derived by a well defined solution method (see Jackson, 2001). The detailed design (which is determined by the specification) can then be 'hung off' the high-level architecture. Omitting most data repositories, this could be represented by a modification of the lower part of the previous process model (Figure 2.1) as shown in Figure 2.2. This is rather speculative but it does no harm to keep one eye on the future!)

2.8 Problem data vs solution data

A subtle, but useful, distinction may be made between problem data (sometimes, for want of a better term, referred to as *real* data) and solution data.

Problem data originate in the problem domain and are central to the problem and its solution. They are the data that must be stored and/or transformed by the solution system if it is to serve a useful purpose. Problem data are very much the subject matter of analysis and should be fully defined within the requirements document. Taking the yacht racing results problem as an example, all the details of boats, races and so on constitute problem data.

By contrast, solution data generally originate in the specification of a particular solution system behaviour. They are the input and output that are required 'merely' to 'drive' the solution system. To pursue the above example, when entering boat details, the user may need to be prompted to 'enter boat name' and will need to enter commands such as 'go to next boat' and 'cancel entry'. In a sense, such solution data are peripheral to the underlying problem but ultimately, will determine if and when particular parts of the application are actually executed.

As a reflection of the last point, solution data are sometimes referred to as 'control data'. But there is the danger of some confusion here, particularly in the case of control systems (see Section 4.5.1.6), where the problem data may also be referred to as control data. For example, the commands that the lift control system sends to the lift motor may well be called control data but the nature of (and very existence of) these data are imposed entirely by the problem domain. The term 'control data' is, therefore, probably best avoided.

2.9 Modelling static data

In the preceding section, the terms problem and solution data are considered within the context of input and output (to and from the solution system). A similar, but if anything more important, distinction can be made within the context of static data.

Most, if not all, problem domains contain significant data in some form. During analysis, it is likely that we will develop models of this problem domain data. It is also likely that the solution system will, eventually, *contain a data model of (part of) the problem domain.* It is easy to confuse the two.

Take, for example, the lift control system. In the problem domain there are the physical buttons that the passenger can press in order to request that the lift goes to a particular floor and these buttons have associated data. Suppose that (as they probably would be) these are the type of switch that makes circuit when pressed and breaks circuit when released. The problem domain data model could reflect this with a button attribute of, say, 'currently pressed'. However, the physical buttons have no memory and would not 'remember' whether or not they had been pressed in the past.

When idesigning the solution system we would almost certainly want to model these buttons but we would probably want to imbue our solution system, *software* buttons with some memory so that they we could check if they *have been* pressed. There is nothing wrong with that *as part of idesign* but many analysts would have no qualms with introducing buttons such as this (with attributes such as 'been pressed' and operations such as 'unpress') during *analysis.* But these are not properties of the problem domain buttons, these are properties of the solution system buttons.

Jackson (1983) goes so far as to give such problem domain entities and solution system entities different, but related, names. For example, in the lift system, the real button entity might be called button-0 and the solution system model of the entity might be called button-1. Both may well have an attribute called 'pressed' but just because the real button is pressed, that does not automatically mean that the solution system model of the button will be pressed; there will inevitably be some delay. Furthermore, it is likely that when the real button is released, the solution system model button will remain pressed until the call is serviced.

Sadly, few others seem to be bothered about this distinction (or even to have noticed it). At least one popular 'analysis and design' book explains how the terminators on a context diagram are the same things as entities in the solution system data model. As we will see, terminators are sub-domains (within the problem domain) that will interact with the solution system, whereas entities, in this sense, are *data models* of selected problem sub-domains within the solution system. One really exists within the problem domain and will actually interact with the system; the other is an intangible data model.

For certain systems it may be possible to 'get away' with ignoring any such distinctions, but this is more a matter of luck than judgement and can hardly be viewed as creating a solid foundation of understanding upon which to build a solution. (And may well be another factor in the spurious blending of analysis into idesign – as was discussed in Section 2.7.)

Even when acknowledging the distinction, it may be tempting to skip the problem domain data model and go straight to the solution system data model but this can be equally hazardous. Indeed, although it is common practice, it is hard to justify developing the solution system data model *at all* during the requirements engineering phase. Even when we get to specification, we can say all we need to say about the solution system behaviour by defining the inputs, the outputs and the required relationships between them. This will certainly imply that some data are stored within the solution system but there is no strong reason to be explicit; we can leave such details to the idesign phase.

In the light of the foregoing, it might be presumed that the requirements engineer could do as good a job, if not better, if they had no knowledge of internal design or programming. There would then be no danger of confusion, omission or premature design because they would not know what was involved in the later stages. As it happens, the counter argument is stronger. In order to perform the requirements engineering satisfactorily, the practitioner really needs to be able to *imagine* what information they *would* need *if* they were to be doing the subsequent implementation. This does not mean that the requirements engineer needs to actually do the implementation but it almost certainly means that they do need previous experience of having built systems. Only then can they fully appreciate the type and level of information that will be required.

2.10   Other activities

There is clearly more to software engineering than just requirements engineering, or even design. Projects are unlikely to succeed without due attention being given to matters such as project management and configuration management.

Particularly closely associated with the requirements engineering phase is the matter of determining feasibility. At various points during a development project it is wise to check that there is likely to be some profit in proceeding. From the outset, it is not always clear that a problem *can* be solved by developing some software-based solution system. Given the power of modern hardware, the sophistication of modern software and our growing collective experience, this is less of a problem than it used to be. However, there very much remains the question of whether or not it is *worth* it. Feasibility determination has therefore become more a matter of economics and is usually based upon some form of cost benefit analysis (CBA).

This is often presented as a 'one off' activity that occurs near the beginning of a project but this is over-simplistic. Clearly, the sooner a 'do not proceed' decision can be made, the greater the potential savings but often, near the beginning of a development, little is known of the potential gains and costs. We can, therefore make only rough estimates and must revisit the question, possibly many times, as development proceeds and we can refine our estimates.

Further discussion of such matters is beyond the scope of this book and reference must be made elsewhere, for example Boehm (1981), Cotterell (1995), DeMarco (1982), Humphrey (1989).

2.11 Exercises

1 Complete the following process model diagram (Figure 2.3) by adding the missing labels.

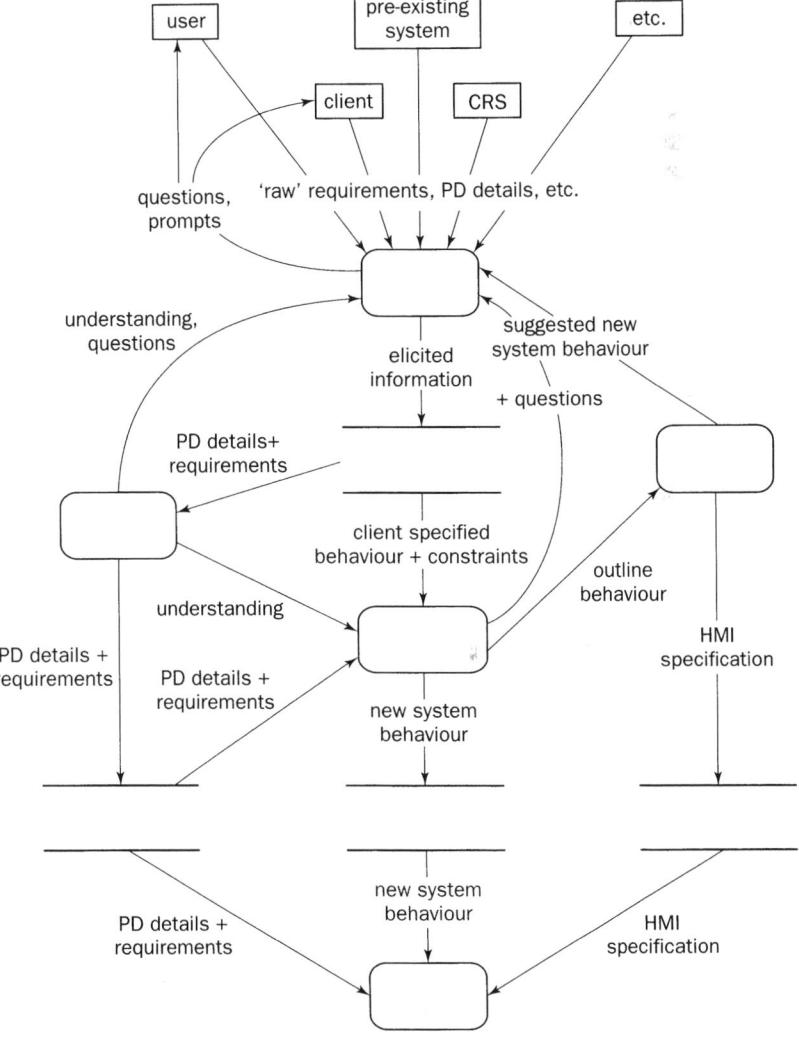

Figure 2.3

2   Explain what shortcuts might be taken during requirements engineering and under what circumstances.

3   Explain the difference between external and internal design.

4   Explain the difference between problem data and solution data.

5   Analysis and internal design both concern the decomposition of systems but there is a crucial difference. Explain what it is.

Elicitation

3

Finding out about a problem domain and the problems that exist within it is not easy. As much as any other software engineering task, it lacks a prescriptive solution and depends largely upon the expertise of the elicitor. This expertise can be built upon a knowledge of the various elicitation techniques and heuristics which are outlined here. However, the skills to phrase questions appropriately, have a feel for a fruitful avenue of enquiry, spot the significance of a throwaway remark and so on, probably owe more to talent and experience than any guidance.

Traditionally, elicitation has often been subsumed within systems analysis and it was the 'common sense', yet expert, approach to information gathering described in systems analysis textbooks that represented the state of the art for many years. More recently, elicitation has attracted renewed attention, not least because of the parallels with knowledge engineering (the elicitation of expertise for incorporation into expert systems) that have become apparent.

Elicitation has now largely replaced the term 'gathering' which had the inappropriate implication that 'ripe' requirements (etc.) are hanging around simply waiting to be 'plucked'. This is seldom the case; 'raw' requirements usually exist only in an incomplete form. In their highly readable examination of this topic, Gause and Weinberg (1989) present the apt metaphor of exploration; one is setting out into, at least partly, uncharted territory in search of information which may well be hidden or only part formed.

So it is not a simple matter of transferring knowledge from one place to another. In the case of problem domain characteristics, the information doubtless exists somewhere but it may be only in the head of a user of some pre-existing system and it may be that said user does not even realise what they do know. The term 'latent knowledge' may be used for such 'hidden knowledge' that is not readily accessible (even to the person who knows it!). An associated notion is 'tacit knowledge'; this refers to information that is well known and accessible to one party but is just considered too obvious to mention to the other.

In the case of requirements, it is more likely that the sought information is in a tenuous form and it is necessary to assist the information provider to rationalise and flesh out relatively vague ideas of what the new system is required to do. This may well be viewed as a process of externalising internal (head) models in order to achieve a common understanding.

Neither can elicitation be readily separated from the other requirements engineering activities. As soon as information starts to be acquired, it must be organised, recorded and fed back to the information provider in order to promote the elicitation of further information.

As indicated in the introduction, there are three strategic considerations that pertain to elicitation in particular:

- what information should be gathered;
- from what sources may it be gleaned;
- and by what mechanisms or techniques may it be gathered.

3.1 The information to elicit

In broad terms, this is determined by the required output from the requirements engineering process as a whole, i.e.:

- a description of the problem domain;
- a list of problems requiring solution (the requirements);
- any client-imposed constraints upon the behaviour or structure of the solution system.

In other words, the information that is required in order to be able to produce the requirements document and the specification document. The descriptions of the general contents of these documents (Sections 4.8.3 and 5.4.3) are clearly relevant.

We can, however, be more specific once the characteristics of the problem domain start to emerge. The section on problem domain oriented analysis (Section 4.5) provides lists of the particular pieces of information that are required for particular types of problem domain. Furthermore, the section on interviewing (Section 9.2.3), provides lists of questions that are widely useful.

3.2 Sources of information

The principal sources of information about problem domains include:

- clients (actual and potential);
- clients' 'specifications';
- any pre-existing solution system (i.e. a system that operates within the problem domain and performs similar functions to the anticipated new solution system) and the documentation pertaining to it;
- users of pre-existing systems;
- potential users of the new solution system;
- predecessor products (i.e. other products of the developer that perform similar functions to that which might be built);

- competitors' products;

- application (problem) domain experts;

- documents defining the characteristics and behaviour of any interfacing systems (terminators);

- relevant technical standards and legislation.

These will not all be available, or indeed relevant, for every development. Clearly, where there is no pre-existing system, there will be no documentation relating to it nor any users of it. Where the new system interfaces only with the user (for example the race results program), there will be no documents defining the behaviour of non-human terminators but for a problem domain such as the lift controller, documentation of the characteristics of the winding motor, etc. is highly pertinent (and should be available).

Perhaps the most significant consideration is whether the client (and, hence, likely users) can be identified in advance. Where they can, there is a 'ready made', single point of authority and the development is usually referred to as custom-built or commissioned. In such cases, it may be easy to identify a pre-existing manual or (partly) computerised system which is to be replaced by the new system. This is often the case for 'commercial' systems (stock control, booking systems, etc.) and may also apply to 'technical' systems such as plant control or draughting applications. Where such a client is external to the development organisation, the development is normally subject to a contract but for a client within the same organisation as the developer, much the same considerations apply regarding elicitation.

The alternative case is where a generic product is developed for a market. Not only are there many potential clients but it is not usually known exactly who they will be. There can be no single pre-existing system for a generic product but there may be predecessor products (i.e. systems fulfilling a similar role) of the developer's and, of course, similar products from other developers could already be on the market.

Whilst, particularly for smaller developments, it is possible for the same person to fill both roles, the distinction between client and user may be significant. The golden rule is that the client is the one who authorises or commissions development (and, usually, payment), whereas users are those who are likely to use the system when it is delivered.

Particularly for generic products, it can be difficult to identify users (or, to be precise, potential users) in advance. It is something of a 'chicken and egg' problem; no system (yet), so no users, so how do you establish what might be wanted? Users of predecessor or other similar systems can be sources where such exist but for novel systems it is even worse. An analogy can be drawn with a proposal to provide a cycleway along a busy highway. If you stand at the side of the highway and ask passers by what they require of a cycleway, at best, the results will be unreliable (because many of those who would use a cycleway will not be using the road) and at worst, you will not find any potential users at all (but this does not mean that they do not exist).

With generic system developments, even when users can be located, there is the problem of their multiplicity. Somehow, their various views have to be amalgamated and this may require the resolution of conflicts (see Section 3.4.5).

This is one of the situations in which one can turn to the application domain expert; someone who will not be an actual user but (it is hoped) can accurately represent the users' point of view. Within the developer's organisation, such an expert is often known as the client representative or (at the risk of forgetting that it is only the *external* design that is their concern) the design authority.

For commissioned developments, clients sometimes produce their own specification (which may be referred to as a client or user requirements specification (CRS/URS)). Such documents can be very useful but, in my experience, are *no substitute* for a properly developed specification and are better viewed as an elicitation source. They usually (if not always) require re-structuring and elaboration. Section 9.9 on requirements stripping examines this in more detail.

3.3 Elicitation techniques

There are about as many techniques for eliciting information as there are potential sources of information. For example:

- background reading
- brain storming
- discourse analysis
- document inspection
- ethnography
- interviewing
- joint application design (JAD)
- questionnaires
- requirements stripping
- sitting with Nellie
- task observation
- use-cases and scenarios

Selection will depend upon the circumstances of the development, as outlined in the previous section, and upon the pre-requisites and utility of each technique. Chapter 9 presents at least an introduction to most of the commonly used techniques including guidance upon when they might be deployed and references to specialist sources so that particular techniques may be studied further if required.

The output from elicitation is seldom given much attention but it is somewhat technique dependent. Interviews, for example, will often produce hand-written notes but they may be audio- or, even, video-taped. These possibilities are also explored in Chapter 9.

3.4   Elicitation strategy

An elicitation plan should be developed which addresses the three considerations:

- What information should be elicited?
- What sources should be used?
- What mechanisms or techniques should be employed?

3.4.1   The information to elicit

As mentioned in the introduction, this matter must be approached incrementally since, at first, very little will be known about the problem and there must be a progression from the general to the specific. If only in outline, it is helpful to decide in advance the objectives for each elicitation session. Matters for early attention will include:

- the basic type of application;
- the identity of the client;
- the main motivation behind the development;
- etc.

In due course, the nature of the problem domain and the requirements will be investigated in greater detail and, eventually, any interface-related detail that the client wishes to specify must be ascertained.

3.4.2   Sources of information

Selection of sources is highly dependent upon the circumstances and, hence, is more variable. At the risk of stating the obvious, for each session, the source must be matched to the elicitation objectives. For example, documentation pertaining to a pre-existing system may well shed light upon the nature of the problem domain but is unlikely to answer any questions about, say, usability requirements.

In general, it is best to aim for the 'horse's mouth'. Seek out the people or other sources from whence the information originates, rather than rely upon second hand relaying of information.

Another useful heuristic is to aim for redundancy; try not to rely upon a single source for any information. Whilst multiple sources introduce the possibility of conflicts (which will need resolution) the end result is likely to be more reliable information.

A problem that can occur is a lack of direct access to the people (often the users) who have the vital expertise about the problem domain and the requirements. Supervisors, commanding officers and so on may be interposed and sometimes act as 'filters and scramblers'. If, after tactful representations, this problem persists, the recommended strategy is to keep asking 'awkward' questions and, if the answers are not forthcoming, flag lots of TBDs (to be determined) in the documentation!

3.4.3 Selection of elicitation techniques

Selection of elicitation techniques depends principally upon the previous two considerations: what sources are available and what information is sought. For example, certain techniques require:

- a pre-existing system;
- user access;
- a client-prepared 'specification';
- etc.

Others have fewer constraints and then the nature of the sought information becomes a greater factor. Some techniques are 'general purpose', others address particular areas; some are useful for gaining a broad perspective, others for filling in detail. Chapter 9 provides an introduction to most of the techniques available; sufficient to allow informed choices to be made. (See also Maiden and Rugg, 1996.)

In practice economics may also be a factor. Some techniques are relatively expensive to apply and there may be a trade-off against the criticality of the project.

3.4.4 Socio-political considerations

Elicitation (indeed, the whole of software development) takes place within a particular socio-political context. Usually, this does not impinge significantly upon the process but sometimes (and possibly more often than we realise) it does.

The people involved may have personal ambitions, vendettas, fears, etc., which contribute to a hidden agenda that, they think, may be advanced on the back of a software development project. At the extreme, this may lead to attempted (possibly very subtle) sabotage.

Detecting and handling such problems is, to say the least, difficult and requires skills that can be developed only through practice. However, an awareness of the problem is the first step and there follow some examples of what may be on the 'hidden agenda':

- fear of redundancy;
- fear of down-skilling;
- attempts to score points in a promotion race;
- a desire to prove themselves right;

- a desire to maintain power through knowledge;
- empire building.

Some of the considerations and techniques presented here can help address these matters and further guidance may be found in Easterbrook and Chechik (2001).

3.4.5 Resolving disagreements and requirements negotiation

Where there is more than one source of information it can happen that, by accident or design, there is some inconsistency between versions of, say, domain characteristics or requirements. Often it will be the case that one version is simply wrong but, in the trickier cases, we are dealing with matters of opinion or preference and resolution may be more difficult.

The first strategy is to attempt to detect any wrong information. Exploring additional sources and analysing the information can usually reveal any such errors. Remaining disagreements should be investigated to ensure that the difference is real. Surprisingly often, apparent disagreements are no more than misunderstandings or different ways of looking at the same thing. Again, analysis of the elicited information should reveal this.

Where genuine disagreement persists there are further options. Perhaps the simplest is to refer to a higher authority. If there is a single client representative with overall authority over, say, requirements, the decision is theirs.

A happier solution may be to develop requirements that represent an acceptable compromise or which introduce greater flexibility so that the solution system can accommodate, say, more than one way of working. Of relevance here is the notion of stakeholder cost benefit analysis (CBA) (see Sutcliffe, 1998). A separate CBA for each stakeholder (rather than one for the entire project) can introduce some objectivity into the process.

Where one of the involved stakeholders is the developer, the resolution of contentious requirements is often known as requirements negotiation. Similar considerations apply as performance may be traded against functionality but there are the additional factors of price (to the client) and cost (to the developer). It is only in recent years that much has been published upon this topic but, see, for example, Boehm and Egyed (1998).

Financial considerations may well extend beyond the remit of the requirements engineer (or analyst) and, in any event, if all else fails, the analyst has little option but to flag the disagreement in the documentation and leave it for later resolution!

3.4.6 Evolving requirements

It is well known that requirements change; indeed, this is often cited as one of the greatest problems in the whole development process. (Since this does affect the whole development process, not just elicitation, the location of this section within this book is fairly arbitrary but sooner rather than later.)

In the past there was talk of handling the problem by getting the requirements right in the first place and then 'freezing' them. This has proved unrealistic. The world changes, often unpredictably and, however attractive the idea might seem, we cannot stop it. If changes *are* predictable then they should be documented so that, where it is cost effective to do so, the design of the solution system can take them into account. But many changes are not predictable and if we then choose simply to ignore them, the resultant solution systems are unlikely to prove satisfactory. So, we must expect changes to occur, both during initial development and subsequent usage of systems. Our only recourse is to accommodate such changes.

As it turns out, problem domains are far less volatile than requirements. It may well happen, for example, that the client requires a new report to be produced or some part of the problem domain to be controlled in a rather different way. However, changes to the underlying problem domain data or the innate behaviour of its various elements are less common. It follows that our first 'line of defence' is a clear separation between problem domain description and requirements. It is then possible to isolate changes and minimise their scope. (As will be seen in the next chapter, some approaches to analysis fare much better than others in this respect.)

Although beyond the scope of this book, this follows through into internal design. If the solution system is well modularised then the 'knock-on' effects of changes are minimised. A particular example is the design of databases; a well designed database will support any conceivable enquiry upon its data set. So if, as suggested above, a requirement arises for a new report, this can be accommodated without any changes to the underlying data model.

Our configuration management must also be designed to control changes to work in progress. This is also somewhat beyond the scope of this book but see, for example, Babich (1986) or Kelly (1996) for more.

Maintainable documentation is another key factor and this can be significantly aided by clear and logical structures that allow the location and extent of changes to be readily identified. Later chapters have more to offer on this topic.

Notwithstanding any of the above, we clearly still want to minimise any unnecessary changes and this is achieved by getting the requirements (and all the rest) near perfect in the first place. The content of this book should help in that respect.

Finally, it may be noted that the longer it takes to develop a system, the more changes will occur during that development. There is, therefore, some incentive to develop systems as rapidly as possible and the next section introduces an elicitation approach that may contribute in that respect.

3.4.7 Approaches to elicitation

In order to try and improve what has often been seen as a not particularly effective elicitation process, more prescriptive approaches to the task have been described. The common theme is to improve communication between the various stakeholders (client representatives, prospective users, developers, etc.) that have an interest in the development. These approaches may have some implications for the elicitation techniques used and may also be part of a wider approach to requirements engineering as a whole. There is also, often, an association with particular types of development (notably business applications) and particular analysis technology.

One such approach is joint application design (JAD) (Hirschheim, 1983, Wood and Silver, 1995). This focuses upon obtaining information from *people* and may therefore be regarded as an alternative to interviews, questionnaires, brainstorming, etc. It may also be regarded as a 'big bang' approach in that rather than, say, an extended series of individual interviews with stakeholders, it compresses elicitation into a few intensive group sessions. The constitution of the groups is prescribed to include representative stakeholders and, under the guidance of a session leader, each session may last a few days (with breaks!). JAD provides fairly prescriptive guidance as to the particular tasks to be accomplished in each session (e.g. 'develop workflow diagram') and these are largely based upon the precepts of structured analysis (although there seems to be no reason why the tasks could not be modified to support alternative approaches).

It is claimed that JAD results in better systems and more satisfied clients and users. This may be supposed to stem from the high level of involvement that is required of a full range of stakeholders plus the chance for stakeholders to intercommunicate and share ideas. It may also be supposed that the intensive approach should reduce overall development timescales which, in itself, should be advantageous as there is simply less time for the problem domain and the requirements to change during the development. Whilst it might be argued that better application of 'traditional' approaches could achieve much the same effect, significant increases in 'productivity' have been reported (Gibson and Jackson, 1987).

Another approach, cooperative requirements capture (CRC), is described by MacAuley (1996). This approach shares the group session idea with JAD but places greater emphasis upon the user.

3.5 Exercises

1 List the three main considerations when developing a requirements elicitation strategy.

2 Explain the difference between latent knowledge and tacit knowledge.

3 Briefly describe the main factors that can compromise the elicitation process.

4 For each of the following scenarios, speculate as to what are likely to be the most useful sources of information during requirements elicitation:

a) The development of a new system to replace an existing sales order processing system.

b) The development of software to control a robot surgeon.

c) The development of software to operate a taxi meter.

d) The development of a secure battlefield communications system for the Ministry of Defence.

5   Complete the following table of characteristics of elicitation techniques (Table 3.1). (The first two columns and rows are already done.) If you have not already done so, you will probably need to study Chapter 9 first. Indeed, you may like to take a photocopy of the table and complete it as you read Chapter 9.

Table 3.1

Characteristic	Background reading	Interviewing	Questionnaires	Document inspection	Task observation	Discourse analysis	Use-cases	Brain storming	Requirements stripping
Possible limitations:									
Needs pre-existing system				✓		✓			
Needs paper-based pre-existing system				✓					
Needs customer requirements document									
Needs considerable expertise									
Mainly useful in initial stages	✓								
Mainly useful in later stages									
Relatively expensive		✓							
Inflexible									
Only gets information from inside heads		✓							
Only gets information that is outside heads	✓								
Possible strengths:									
Wide scope		✓							
Good for getting background information	✓	✓							
Good for getting problem domain information	✓	✓							
Good for getting requirements		✓							
Broad band communication		✓							
Easy to apply	✓	✓							
Relatively cheap	✓								
Flexibility		✓							
Can address a large target population									

Analysis

4

Let us start with a quick reminder of the definition of analysis used here:

through study of a problem domain, the achievement of understanding of and the documentation of the characteristics of that domain and the problems (requiring solution) that exist within that domain.

As an aid to achieving understanding, it is usual to develop abstractions of the problem domain that decompose it into its various elements and model the relationships between those elements. As discussed in 'analysis and design' (Section 2.7) such decomposition has much in common with internal design but there is a critical difference. Analysis seeks to unravel the structure of an *existing* system (the problem domain) whereas internal design *invents* a structure for an, as yet, non-existent system (the solution system).

Analysis is closely linked with the elicitation process (as described in the preceding chapter) and it will be assumed that the input to analysis is the relatively unprocessed information about the problem domain and the requirements that is contained within the elicitation notes and any associated documents gleaned from the problem domain. However, it is very much a two-way interaction and it is analysis that informs the elicitation process and provides many of the necessary prompts and questions. The two tasks proceed in parallel and are usually performed by the same staff.

The output from analysis is the analysis documentation, often referred to as the requirements document. This document should provide a complete description of all pertinent facets of the problem domain as well as a complete list of the client's requirements. Further detail will unfold in this chapter but, to set the scene, it is proposed that any approach to analysis should, wherever applicable, demand and facilitate description of:

- the structure of the problem domain (in terms of its sub-domains and their relationships);
- the problem domain data (both syntax and semantics);
- the innate properties and behaviour of the problem sub-domains;
- significant events and phenomena within the problem domain;
- the requirements (effects that the solution system should produce within the problem domain).

4.1   The trouble with analysis

As hinted at in the introduction[20], from the perspective that is presented here, analysis, as currently practised, is often flawed; sometimes deeply flawed. This creates a quandary; whether to describe analysis as you may find it, or whether to concentrate upon analysis as it should be. There seem to be good reasons to do both.

Common practice will be described but, since there are so many existing sources, fairly briefly. At the same time, the shortcomings and the difficulties that can arise will be highlighted.

But is it just me saying that all is not well with much current practice? Well no, and, once again, Michael Jackson puts it most elegantly:

> There's a big temptation to believe that you can describe the application domain and the machine all together, in one combined description. The justification for this belief is that some part of the machine is often a model of some part of the application domain. That means that there's some description that's true of both the machine and of the application domain. So why not just write that description and save some duplication of effort?
>
> Here's why. A description of a modelling relationship is always incomplete: there's more to say about the application domain, and more to say about the machine too. You need to say these things somewhere. You ought not to say them in the common description, because they're not common. In principle you really need three descriptions: the common description; the description that's true only of the machine and the description that's true only of the application domain. If you make all of those descriptions, and separate them carefully, you'll be all right.
>
> But if you only make one description, you'll surely be tempted to put things into it that describe only the machine, and to leave out things that describe only the application domain. After all, you have to describe the machine sooner or later, don't you?
>
> You can see the results clearly in many object-oriented modelling descriptions. Often they are accompanied by fine words about modelling the real world. But when you look closely you see that they are really descriptions of programming objects, pure and simple. Any similarity to real-world objects, living or dead, is purely coincidental.
>
> (Jackson, 1995, pp. 2–3)

Upon reflection, this is hardly surprising. Object orientation is based upon the notion of an object as a body of data encapsulated within the operations that access and amend that data; such objects interacting with each other only by the passing of messages. Software objects, in the solution system, can be

---

[20] If you have not already done so, it may be as well to read the introduction to analysis (Section 2.1) before this chapter.

constructed so that they fit this mould. But things of interest that happen to exist in the problem domain tend to be far more diverse.

As will be seen, similar criticism can be directed at the other widespread analysis approach, structured analysis. Not only are the descriptions of the problem domain and the solution system mixed, but the emphasis upon system modelling can be at the cost of ignoring the actual requirements.

It is suggested that, in large measure, these difficulties have arisen due to an over-concentration on the *means* of analysis rather than on the *ends*. The overall purpose may be seen as providing, in a readily understood form, all the information that is required in order to be able to perform the subsequent external design and specification of the required system. This entails distilling and refining the information that is collected in order to ensure that all relevant detail, but no irrelevant detail, is presented in a clear, logical and concise manner.

Highlighting the problems with conventional approaches may be seen as a good thing in itself but better still if there are ways of dealing with those problems. Happily, these are now emerging and an alternative approach will be described in some detail.

Perhaps the best way to compare these different approaches is to imagine yourself in the role of the person who will eventually have to idesign and build the system. Which requirements engineering approach will provide you with the information that you really need? I suggest that you reflect upon this question when you have finished this chapter.

4.2   Approaches to analysis

There are various ways in which analysis may be approached but those in widespread use are mainly distinguished upon the basis by which systems are decomposed. A brief, historical perspective provides an introduction.

The early days of analysis are shrouded in some mystery. As soon as non-trivial systems were being developed, analysis of a kind must have been performed. However, methods were *ad hoc* and there is little evidence as regards the techniques that were used. The few books that were written at the time contain little more than a general exhortation to 'study the problem domain' or, more often, to 'study the existing system'.

From these early, unstructured approaches, there emerged, in the 1970s, the first attempts at a standardised method. Under the general title of structured analysis (SA) various proprietary methods were developed and published. Strongly associated with such methods were people such as Tom DeMarco (1978) and many variations soon followed.

Some practitioners took the view that the relatively formal models adopted by such approaches could not accommodate either the social perspectives or the uncertainty that exists (at least in the early stages) in the understanding of the 'real world'. As a result, during the 1980s, various 'soft systems' approaches (probably the best known being Checkland's (1981)) were proposed to address such issues. These may well be viewed as a preliminary stage which complements rather than replaces the 'hard' approaches. As it happens, the soft systems approaches have not been widely adopted and so, whilst no criticism is implied, they will not be considered further here.

It was not until the 1990s that SA faced serious competition and that in the shape of object oriented analysis (OOA). Again, many variants soon appeared but, here also, the similarities outweigh the differences.

Recently, criticism of OOA has begun to emerge (for example, Alexander, 1999, and Kovitz, 1999) and arising from the work of Michael Jackson (1995), a third approach, as yet unnamed but based around problem frames, is taking shape. Here it will be referred to as problem domain oriented analysis (PDOA).

It is considered necessary for the budding software engineer to be introduced to all three approaches: the first two (SA and OOA) because they are widely used and are likely to be encountered in the commercial world in both new and old projects; the third (PDOA) because it appears to rest on a more secure foundation, helps identify weaknesses in the others and may well prove to be the way ahead.

Structured analysis and OOA are both very well documented and so a relatively brief overview is provided here. It is probably as well to point out that both these approaches support large commercial interests and an understandable enthusiasm verges on marketing hyperbole in some of the literature. Some balancing commentary is, therefore, also provided in conjunction with further references.

4.3   Structured analysis

There are two reasons why you might read this section. The first is for what might be termed academic purposes; the critical overview that is presented may assist in developing evaluative skills. The second is that you may well have to work on projects where such approaches have been or are being used. This brief view would then serve only as an introduction but full coverage is widely available (see, for example, Yourdon, 1989a, Brown, 1997, and Goldsmith, 1993). If neither reason applies, you may decide to skip the section.

With the benefit of hindsight, perhaps the greatest contribution of SA was simply to draw due attention to the early stages of the development process. Previously, this area had, as often as not, been seriously neglected and development was often viewed as just a matter of coding.

Methodologically, the great innovation was a move away from text-based analysis and specification documents towards the use of graphical modelling notations. This model-based approach set a trend that has continued to this day. Largely, this was a reaction to the previous practice of developing vast, unstructured documents (sometimes referred to as 'Victorian novels') which muddled together descriptions of the problem domain, pre-existing systems, assorted requirements, partial specifications for the new system and other, more or less relevant, matters.

From today's perspective, this may well have been an over-reaction. Certainly, there were some very poorly written requirements documents but to dismiss any approach because there are some poor practitioners[21] is dubious. Whilst 'officially' played-down, text continued to be used extensively within SA in the form of 'narrative descriptions', 'problem lists', etc. This was no doubt because text is an essential tool and there are often no reasonable alternatives. However, the dismissive approach to the use of text did nothing to improve the expertise that was applied in its use.

In line with much previous practice, SA generally centred upon modelling the pre-existing system[22]. This is not exactly the same as studying the problem domain but, particularly for information systems (see Section 1.5.1), it may come close enough. It is no coincidence that the bulk of software development at that time involved the 'computerisation' of fairly mundane, clerical, information systems. The pre-existing, document-based, manual systems could often provide a reasonable template for a computer-based solution.

The overall SA approach capitalises upon this by developing various 'models'[23]. Considerable flexibility is allowed, but, where appropriate, the starting point is a model of the 'enterprise' (which, for commercial systems at least, equates fairly well to the problem domain).

This would normally be followed by the development of a 'current physical' model of the pre-existing physical system (on the assumption that there was one). This model is then 'logicalised' by removing all references to physical data storage media, etc., and stripping it down to the logical essentials.

In the early days of SA, the 'models' consisted almost exclusively of data flow models[24] (recorded as data flow diagrams or DFDs). These, essentially procedural, models encouraged the development of a structural model of the problem domain or, more often, the pre-existing system. This was not an inventive or design process, it was a case of reflecting the inherent structure of a pre-existing system. With the caveat that the pre-existing system is not the same thing as the problem domain, this is, in part, consistent with the view of analysis that is presented here.

There is an omission however; there is no explicit mention of requirements. Rather, there is an implicit assumption that the pre-existing system already meets the requirements (apart, presumably, from the fact that it is not computer-based!). This assumption is carried through into the next stage where the model

---

[21] And, to be fair, because there were but primitive text-processing facilities available.

[22] In this context, a pre-existing system is an existing solution system (often, not a computer-based system) that operates within the problem domain and performs a similar function to the new system that is desired. There is, clearly, an assumption that there *will be* a pre-existing system.

[23] Structured analysis uses the word 'model' in a particular sense. The 'logical model', for example, actually consists of a set of models, in the usual sense.

[24] It is assumed that the reader is familiar with data flow modelling but if not, Section 13.1.1.1 contains an overview and references to further sources of enlightenment. The categorisation of models that is discussed in Chapter 10 may also be useful preparation if this is unfamiliar territory.

of the new, required system is, in its essence, derived from that of the pre-existing system.

The underlying, structural nature of the model is also inherited. In the subsequent 'structured design' process the logical model (of the pre-existing system) is modified as necessary to form the basic, logical design of a solution system. Often, the only significant modification is conversion from parallel to sequential processing.

From the viewpoint of requirements engineering, this is a questionable course. Development proceeds directly (and usually quite smoothly!) from developing a structural model of the operation of a pre-existing system (the 'analysis') to the modification of that model to provide the internal design for the new system (the structured design). But what we have lost, what has been squeezed out, is the production of a behavioural model of the new system; in other words, a proper, functional specification.

Within SA, there is no clear distinction between the analysis documentation and the specification. The logical model (consisting of, at least, a set of levelled DFDs and process specifications) may be referred to as the 'specification' but, as often as not, it differs little from the 'analysis' models of the pre-existing system. Such further detail as is added includes much that might better be deferred to the design phase. It follows that there is a heavy bias towards structural specification (see Section 5.3.4).

There have been efforts to persuade us that the DFD model can be considered a behavioural model because the processes really represent functions. In principle, this is possible and, provided that only *externally visible* functions are included, the DFD can be used to document a true functional decomposition (see Section 12.1.1). In practice, however, not only do internal functions tend to creep in (see the example on p. 67) but the functional decomposition also becomes the basis for the internal structure (which is now a widely discredited idea).

So, SA largely fails to distinguish between a requirement and the way in which it can be met. Requirements are, in effect, specified in terms of the design of a particular system that will meet those requirements. All but the lowest level internal design of the new system has been hi-jacked from the idesign phase and incorporated into the so-called specification.

4.3.1   Data modelling

Data flow models (typically recorded as DFDs) identify data but do little to define it. To address this point, the data flow models were, from the outset, supported by lists of descriptions of the nature and structure of the data flows themselves. Such lists are often called data dictionaries (DD) (see Section 14.5) and, despite some tendency to focus upon the syntax of the data they can (and should) also be used to explain what the data *mean* (i.e. the semantics of the data). They can, therefore, prove extremely useful; however, they do not always give a very clear picture of the overall structure of the system data.

In the late 1970s, largely thanks to the work of Chen (1976), this last point was addressed when SA was augmented with the addition of a data structure model, usually in the form of an entity relationship diagram (ERD – see Section 13.3.2). For information systems in particular, the data structure model can offer great insight into the problem domain[25].

However, the relationship between the data model (ERD) and the process model (DFD) is not a simple one and the integration of these two models within SA has proved problematical. Whilst the non-procedural nature of the data model may be viewed as a distinct advantage for requirements engineering purposes, the fact that it does not so readily convert to executable code has often been reflected in the data structure model being side-lined when it comes to the subsequent, structured design stage.

4.3.2   Evolution of SA

It is one of the later incarnations of SA, the structured systems analysis and design methodology[26] (SSADM) (see CCTA, 1995, or Ashworth and Slater, 1993) that has, perhaps, tackled this last problem most successfully. This version introduced entity life histories (ELHs – see Section 13.4.1). These link the changes of state of the various entities to the processes that are responsible for conducting those changes and, hence, provide a bridge between the procedural and the data models. In so doing they also define the valid sequences of events that can occur in the problem domain; an important consideration for certain types of problem.

The long standing omission of explicitly recorded requirements was also addressed by SSADM. Amongst other elaborations, it introduced the problem requirements list (PRL); a text-based, and essentially unstructured, list of problems (with the current system) and requirements (to be met by the new system).

In parallel, other variations, under the banner of real-time structured analysis (RTSA), developed elaborations that were directed at facilitating the modelling of real-time systems (see for example, Ward and Mellor, 1985). Data flow diagram notation was extended in order to accommodate control data (in this sense, data that trigger, enable or disable the execution of processes) and timing considerations. Entity life modelling (aka entity state modelling, and very similar to the ELH) was introduced to help model the changes of state of the system in question.

---

[25] It also points to the data model that may eventually need to be incorporated into the solution system but, unfortunately, this introduces another potential hazard. Care is needed in order to distinguish between a data abstraction of the problem domain and a model of the problem domain data that might be stored within the solution system. There is likely to be a good deal of overlap and they may even appear identical but this is really not the case (see Section 2.9).

[26] It is unfortunate that the term 'methodology' (originally meaning the study of methods) has been substituted for the perfectly serviceable term 'method'. One can only speculate as to the rationale but should also remember that, strictly speaking, the approach does not constitute a method anyway.

These extensions are of undoubted utility when it comes to modelling the internal processes of real-time systems and they could have proved useful in modelling real-time problem domains. However, following the precepts of SA, the system in question continued to be the pre-existing system or, latterly (see next section), the new, solution system. It may, therefore, be observed that their contribution has been largely confined to the sphere of internal design as opposed to requirements engineering.

4.3.3 Modern SA

Notwithstanding such developments, by the late 1980s, some of its chief proponents realised that SA was running into problems. Prominent amongst these was the phenomenon that became known as 'analysis paralysis'. The ever 'enhanced' method, coupled with the increasing size of the problems that were tackled, led to projects tending to become bogged-down in the modelling of the pre-existing system.

Ironically reflecting the 'Victorian novel' problem that it was introduced to combat, a morass of documentation was produced, much of it modelling the detailed process of the pre-existing system. It is highly questionable whether the *process* of a pre-existing solution system is a matter for detailed study anyway; the process of the *problem domain*, certainly, and maybe the *function* of a pre-existing system but that is not the same thing.

It might have been seen as a clue to the problem that sometimes much of this documentation was not used. After expending a great deal of effort and expense on its production it was simply side-lined.

Alongside the problems of modelling large, and possibly complex, systems there arose the problem of modelling non-existent systems. Software development was moving into new territory and it was no longer a sure bet that there would be some pre-existing system or, if there was, that it shed much light upon the requirements for, or design of, the new system. What system, for example, preceded the computer-based engine-management system? And how much could one learn about a word-processor application by studying someone using a typewriter?

Interestingly, for both problems (pre-existing system too large and pre-existing system non-existent) one solution emerged; do not bother modelling the pre-existing system at all (at least not in any detail), move right along to modelling the new system. As Ed Yourdon recommended:

> the systems analyst should *avoid* modelling the user's current system if at all possible. The modelling tools discussed in Part ll should be used to begin, *as quickly as possible*, to develop a model of the new system that the user wants.
>
> (Yourdon, 1989a, p. 323; my italic)

In a way, this was recognition of doing the wrong thing, but to stop doing the wrong thing is not the same as starting to do the right thing. To be sure, it was proposed that the model of the new system should be as abstract as possible without any implementation bias; however, in practice the model *does* usually form the basis of the internal design of the new system. Furthermore, it is a design that is, essentially, achieved through functional decomposition (see Section 12.1.1) and, whilst this may be an entirely appropriate mechanism for developing a functional specification, it is questionable whether it can produce satisfactory structural designs.

With the benefit of hindsight (!) a yet more fundamental flaw is apparent; the main objective of analysis, studying the problem domain, has been largely ignored. It has taken many of us a long time to appreciate this but the point is well made by Michael Jackson (1995).

4.3.4   Structured analysis; examples

These examples assume some familiarity with the various modelling techniques and references to the relevant sections of Part 2 of this book are provided in case they are required. Full requirements documentation for each case study may be found in Part 3 but there the analysis aspect is biased towards PDOA (see Section 4.5) rather than SA.

Fairly extensive examples of SA models are presented here, together with some commentary upon their derivation and utility. Utility will be adjudged within the context of the main objectives of analysis, those being acquiring understanding of the problem domain and, as mentioned in the introduction, providing 'a complete description of all pertinent facets of the problem domain as well as a complete list of the client's requirements'.

As also mentioned earlier, SA is far better suited to some types of application than others. It would be none too helpful to dwell upon examples for which it is poorly suited. A couple will be looked at briefly later in order to illustrate the point, but first, an information system.

4.3.4.1   Case 1, the yacht race results (YRR) program

The required system is a computer program that will assist in the calculation of results for sailing races. Further details, including elicitation notes can be found in Chapter 15. Note, however, that these documents are not an explicit part of SA although the existence of elicitation notes as the source of information is implied.

As we have seen, depending upon the version of SA that is applied, there are various possible starting points. An SSADM-like approach could be appropriate for a problem such as this and so I will start with a data flow model (see Section 13.1.1) of the pre-existing system. This is shown in Figure 4.1.

This is useful in itself but the meaning can be greatly enhanced by defining the various terms used, in particular, the names of the data flows, so there follows the corresponding DD. (A BNF-like style (see Section 14.3.4) is adopted and Section 14.5 gives more detail on DDs in general.)

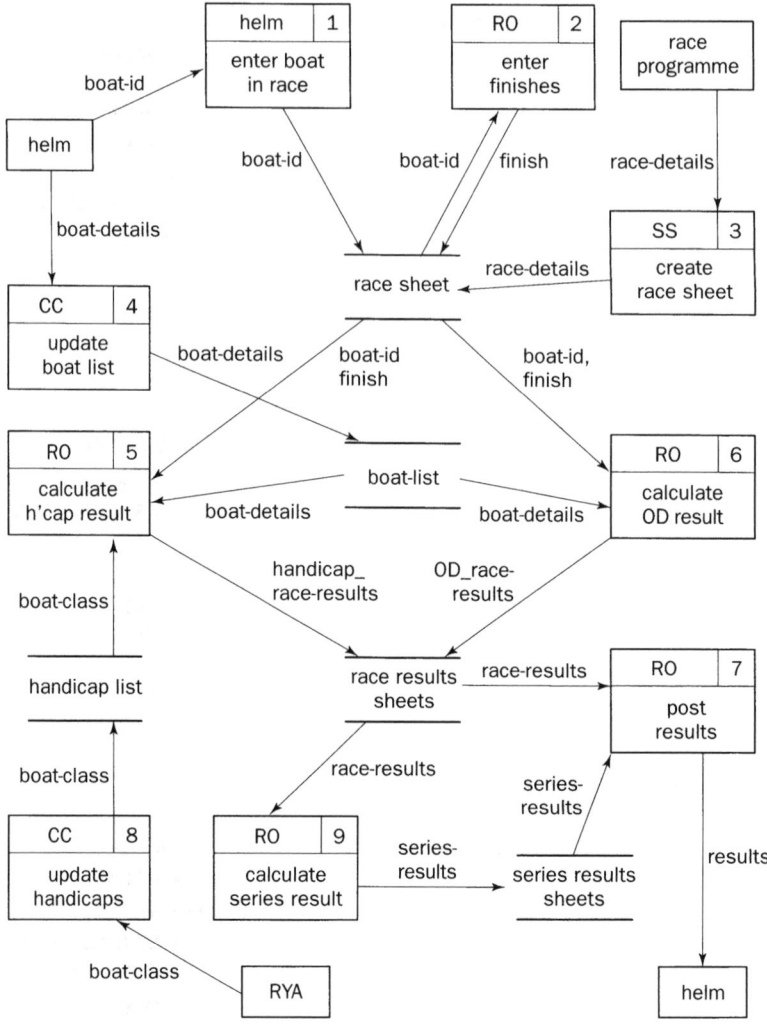

Figure 4.1

RO	::= (* race officer *);
CC	::= (* class captain *);
SS	::= (* sailing secretary *);
RYA	::= (* the Royal Yachting Association – the source of class handicaps *)

boat-details	::= boat-name, boat-id, helm-name;
boat-id	::= boat-class-name, sail-number,
boat-name	::= {alphanumeric}^{25};
boat-class-name	::= ^{1}{alphanumeric}^{10};
sail-number	::= ^{1}{digit}^{6};

helm-name	::= {alphanumeric}^{25};
	::= (* the person who sails the boat *)
boat-class	::= boat-class-name, handicap;
	::= (* a particular type of boat *)
handicap	::= handicap-type, handicap-value;
	::= (* a way of compensating for different inherent speed when different boat classes race against each other *)
handicap-type	::= "PY" | "TMF";
handicap-value	::= ^{3}{digit}^{4};
race-details	::= race-class-name, race-date, start-time, [race-name] [course];
race-class	::= race-class-name, race-class-type, [handicap-type, minimum-handicap, maximum handicap];
	::= (* an indication of the boat-classes) (that may enter a race *)
race-class-name	::= boat-class-name | ^{1}{alphanumeric}^{25};
race-class-type	::= "one-design" | "handicap";
race-date	::= day, ":", month, ":", year;
start-time	::= hour, ":", minute;
race-name	::= ^{1}{alphanumeric}^{25};
course	::= {alphanumeric}^{25};
minimum-handicap	::= handicap;
maximum-handicap	::= handicap;
race-results	::= handicap-race-results | OD-race-results;
handicap-race-results	::= race-details, {boat-name, sail-number, handicap, finish, [elapsed-time] [corrected-time]};
OD-race-results	::= race-details, {boat-name, sail-number, finish};
finish	::= "DNS" | "OCS" | "DNF" | " RTD" | "DSQ" | finish-time | race-position;
finish-time	::= hour, ":", minute, ":", second";
race-position	::= ^{1}{digit}^{3};
elapsed-time	::= ^{1}{digit}^{5}; (* in seconds*)
	::= (* the time a boat takes to complete a race (finish-time – start time) *)
corrected-time	::= ^{1}{digit}^{5}; (* in seconds*)
	::= (* the elapsed time adjusted in accordance with the handicap *)
series-results	::= series-name {race-number, race-date {boat-name, sail-number, points}, total-points, series-position};
series-name	::= ^{1}{alphanumeric}^{25};
race-number	::= "1" .. "99";
total-points	::= ^{1}{digit}^{3}; (* total points, after discards, in the series *)
series-position	::= ^{1}{digit}^{3};

race-sheet	::= race-details, {boat-id, [finish]};
boat-list	::= {boat-details};
handicap-list	::= {boat-class};
race-results-sheet	::= race-results;
series-results-sheet	::= series results;
day	::= "01" .. "31";
month	::= "01" .. "12";
year	::= "1900" .. "2999";
hour	::= "00" .. "23";
minute	::= "00" .. "59";
second	::= "00" .. "59";
alphanumeric	::= "a" .. "z" | "A" .. "Z" | "0" .. "9" | "-" | "'" | ".";

Note that all the data flows appearing on the DFD are defined and where these are composite data, that composition is fully elaborated.

As you may imagine, even for small problem domains, finalising such a model requires a fair bit of analysis and elicitation but it clearly makes much sense of the rather jumbled details in the elicitation notes. Were the problem more complex the DFD could be further decomposed into lower levels but caution must be exercised and we must not lose sight of the purpose. All we are trying to do is understand and describe the essential characteristics of the problem domain. Modelling the existing system is merely a means to an end and we do not need to explore the details of *how* it works any further than is necessary to understand *what it does*.

For an information system, such as this is, the problem data are of great significance and so we may profitably proceed by developing an ERD (Figure 4.2). (See also Section 13.3.2.) Whilst this is a model of the problem domain data, the data structure pertains to the solution system as well since the solution system is very likely to *contain* a data model of the problem domain.

Most, if not all, of the data attributes have already appeared on the DFD but entities do not necessarily map directly to data flows (or stores) and so we need a few additions to the DD and can also show the likely key attributes (underlined).

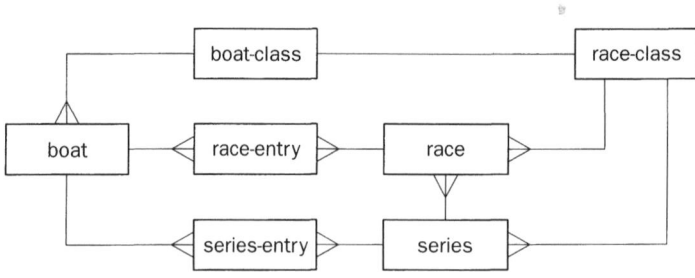

Figure 4.2

boat	::= boat-name, <u>boat-class-name</u>, <u>sail-number</u>, helm-name;
boat-class	::= <u>boat-class-name</u>, handicap;
race-class	::= <u>race-class-name</u>, race-class-type, [handicap-type, minimum-handicap, maximum handicap];
race	::= series-name | <u>race-class-name</u>, <u>race-date</u>, start-time, [race-name] [course];
race-entry	::= <u>race-class-name</u>, <u>race-date</u>, <u>boat-class-name</u>, <u>sail-number</u>, [finish], [elapsed-time], [corrected-time];
series	::= <u>series-name</u>, race-class-name, number-of-races, number of-races-to-count;
series-entry	::= <u>series-name</u>, <u>boat-class-name</u>, <u>sail-number</u>, [total-points, series-position];

We could also model the state changes of the problem domain entities using ELHs. These are all quite trivial in this case but an ELH for the boat entity is shown as an example in Section 13.4.1.2.

Alongside the development of the above models, we could well compile a PRL. This could be very similar to the requirements listed in Section 15.3.2.

The SSADM now proceeds by logicalising the DFD. In this case, we would remove all references to the agents (race officer, etc.) who perform the tasks and would replace the physical data stores with their logical equivalents derived from the data model. (For example, race-results-sheet would be replaced with the race and race-entry entities.)

One further step is the description of the (logicalised) processes in the DFD. These can shed further light upon the functionality of the required system. As an example consider process 5 on Figure 4.1, calculate-handicap-result. This would be described using some form of structured English or pseudo-code and could be along the following lines:

```
calculate-handicap-result
get race details
for each race entry
    case finish of
        finish-time
            if handicap-type = PY then
                corrected-time := elapsed-time × 1000 / handicap-value
            else (*TMF handicap*)
                corrected-time := elapsed-time × handicap-value
            insert into sorted list by corrected-time
    other (* DNS etc. *)
        add to end of sorted list
```

There are still some gaps in our problem domain description. In particular there is a lack of description of the various problem sub-domains (for example, what, exactly *is* a race-class?). These may well be covered by what SA vaguely refers to as 'supporting text'. This could well be along the lines of the descriptions

Figure 4.3

given in Section 15.3.1 (the PDOA document for this case study) but it is none too clear from the prescription of SA what is expected.

From this point on, SA advocates the elaboration of the logicalised DFD so that it can constitute a (procedural) 'specification' for the new system. Since this is tantamount to structural design which requirements engineering (as defined herein) excludes, I will leave it there, noting only that the documentation that has been produced so far could provide useful input for functional specification as described in Chapter 5.

Modern Structured Analysis (SA)

And now let us examine the way in which modern SA might tackle the same problem. (You will notice that I am using a different notation for the DFDs. This is of no great consequence but reflects the styles that are usually employed for each approach.) As previously discussed, modern SA largely ignores the problem domain and any pre-existing system and immediately homes in on the solution system.

The starting point may well be a context diagram (see Figure 4.3) for the new system. This is clearly a model of the solution system. The terminator (the user) is, in effect, a go-between for the solution system and the problem domain. It is the user that provides the updates to the presumed solution system model of the problem domain data and the user is also the recipient of the reports that are produced. In addition to the problem data (entry-data and reports) we can see the data (commands and messages) that pertain to a particular solution.

This does help establish the boundary of the system and tells us that the new system has only one external interface, that to the user. (Some practitioners would advocate substituting the various input and output (i/o) devices (keyboard, screen, printer, etc.) for the user. However, these 'standard' i/o devices are probably better considered as part of the system and any consideration of them can be deferred at least until the specification stage.)

In itself, the context diagram does not shed a great deal of light on the problem but it should be supported by a DD. This shares much with the version in the previous section but can start with the 'high-level' data flows from the context diagram:

entry data	::= boat | boat-class | race | series;
reports	::= race-results | series-results | boat-list | boat-class-list;
commands	::= add-boat-class | delete-boat-class | edit-boat-class | add-boat
	| delete-boat | edit boat | add-race | delete-race | . . . etc.

messages   ::= "The class name must be letters, digits, -, ' or . (max 25 characters)" |
"The class name must be unique" |
"The handicap type must be PY or TMF" |
"The handicap must be 3 or 4 digits (no decimal point required)" |
"This class cannot be deleted as it is in use" |
. . . etc.

which may then be decomposed into the various elements that we have met before:

boat   ::= boat-name, boat-class-name, sail-number, helm-name;

boat-name   ::= {alphanumeric}^{25};

boat-class-name   ::= {alphanumeric}^{10};

sail-number   ::= {digit}^{6};

helm-name   ::= {alphanumeric}^{25};

boat-class   ::= boat-class-name, handicap-type, handicap-value;

handicap-type   ::= "PY" | "TMF";

handicap-value   ::= ^{3}{digit}^{4};

race-class   ::= race-class-type, race-class-name, [handicap-type, minimum-handicap, maximum handicap];

. . . and so on . . .

By a rather different route (considering input to and outputs from the solution system) we have arrived at much the same data as before. And, as before, there is a great deal of useful information here although without supporting explanation it may be difficult to fully appreciate the meaning and significance of all of it. A further snag is that problem data (which are central to the problem domain, e.g. boat-details), are mixed up with data that the solution system generates (e.g., series-results) and with user messages and commands which pertain more to the requirements or external design (but we have to live with that). The next step could well be the development of a data model and (apart from details of notation) this would be identical to (and just as useful as) the one given in the previous section (Figure 4.2).

We now turn to modelling the functionality of the solution system. By the definitions given herein, this may well be considered more as specification than analysis but so the method goes. Figure 4.4 shows one possible design. Each of the bubbles in Figure 4.4 represents a function of the system and the functions may well reflect a, more or less, corresponding requirement. (But note that this is the closest we get to recording requirements.)

These functions may each be regarded as relatively high-level functions and we may choose to break them down further. For example, consider the calculate race result function. This could be decomposed as shown in Figure 4.5.

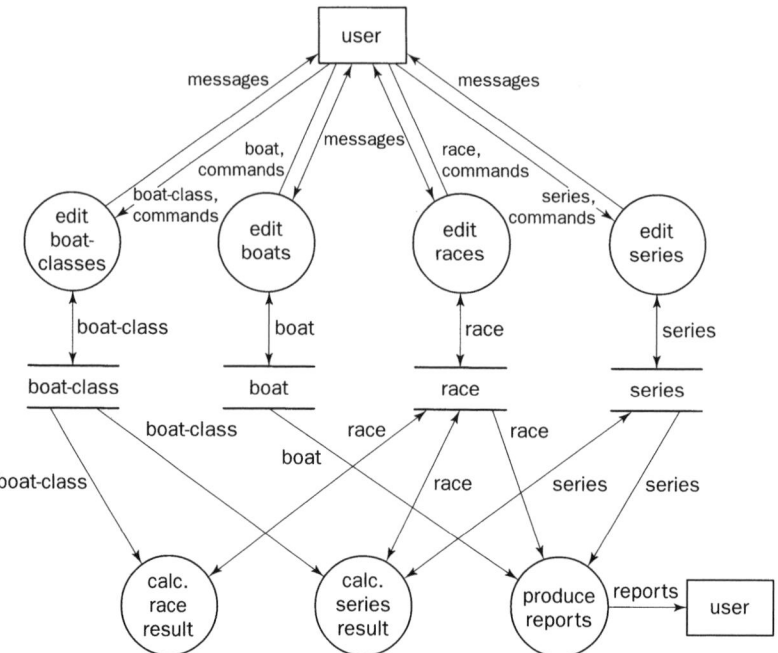

Figure 4.4

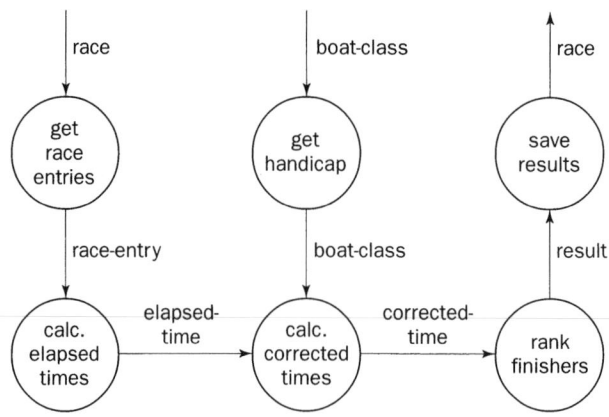

Figure 4.5

There could be several more of these second level DFDs and, for a larger system, the DFDs would extend to yet more levels. Dozens, if not hundreds of DFDs can, and have, been produced for some systems.

Finally, as far as modern SA is concerned, the operation of the lowest level processes is defined by way of process specifications (known as P-specs or mini-specs), usually using some form of pseudo-code (see Section 14.3.2). Here are a couple of examples:

calculate corrected times
get race details
for each race entry
      elapsed time = boat-finish-time – race-start-time

rank finishers
for each race entry
    case result of
        finish-time
           insert into sorted list by finish-time
        other (* DNS etc. *)
           add to end of sorted list

It is suggested that, provided the DFD and P-code model is kept reasonably abstract, it can be seen as modelling function rather than process. This is decidedly dubious. Even for the small example above, one can imagine various alternatives that would produce identical functionality. In the top-level DFD, there could be just one editing function for races and series, or the edit races function could be split into separate functions for editing general race details and for entering race finish times. Another variation would be separate data stores for general race details and race entries.

The second level DFD passes corrected times from calc-corrected-times to the rank-finishers process but these two processes could easily be combined into one and entries could be inserted into a sorted list as the corrected times are calculated. Another alternative would be for the sorting to be deferred until the reports are output.

All these alternatives reflect different design decisions. Some of them (such as the editing function options) affect the externally observable behaviour of the system and belong to the specification task. This illustrates the entanglement of analysis and specification within SA. Others (such as the result calculation mechanism) are truly structural design decisions that serve only to constrain the final implementation and (although some might still argue the case) they are regarded here as having no place in analysis (or specification) at all.

In any case, that is about as far as modern SA goes; it is now over to the system designers. Clearly, they would have some useful information here, notably the ERD and DD, but they may be left wondering about much else. Structured analysis does allude to 'supporting documentation' and this is presumably along the lines of the system description and requirements given in Section 15.1. Possibly, if you were the designer, you would rather settle for those instead.

4.3.4.2   Case 2, the lift controller

The required system is a software-based controller for lifts. As in the previous example, some form of elicitation notes (such as may be found in Chapter 16) will be assumed as the source of information. Note, however, that these documents are not an explicit part of SA although the existence of elicitation notes as the source of information is implied.

This is a different type of system from the last (a control system as opposed to an information system) but SA does not explicitly take any account of that and so perhaps the most significant difference is that, here, there is no pre-existing, manual system. There may have been some electro-mechanical pre-decessor system but I will assume that its workings are intractable and it is not considered a sound base from which to proceed. Our options are, therefore, to model the problem domain (as in 'traditional' SA) or to model the solution system (as in modern SA). I will attempt the former first.

Various sub-domains of interest may be identified within the problem domain, namely:

- users
- call-buttons
- send-buttons
- indicators
- motors
- sensors
- lifts
- door-controllers

and our prescribed task is to incorporate these into a DFD. In order to do this, they must be classified as terminators, processes, data stores or data flows. None of them seem to be data stores or flows so perhaps they should be represented as boxes of some sort which can be connected with data flows, along the lines of Figure 4.6. Even with some 'artistic licence' (the connection between the mo-tor and the lift is doubtless mechanical and scarcely constitutes a data flow), it is rather disconnected and there seems to be a distinct lack of processes.

In response to such difficulties, we may adopt the modern SA strategy, intro-duce the solution system and produce a context DFD as shown in Figure 4.7. This certainly looks more like progress but there are points to note. The user and the lift do not directly interface with the solution system (the lift control-ler) and so cannot be incorporated into the context diagram (important though they might be!). The other big problem is that we have said very little about the characteristics of any of the terminators (which, after, all, constitute much of

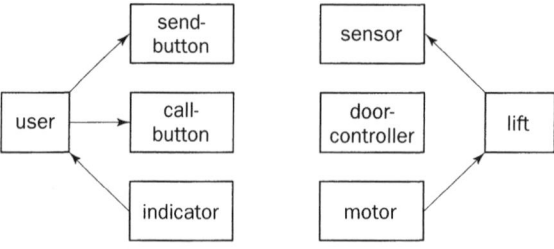

Figure 4.6

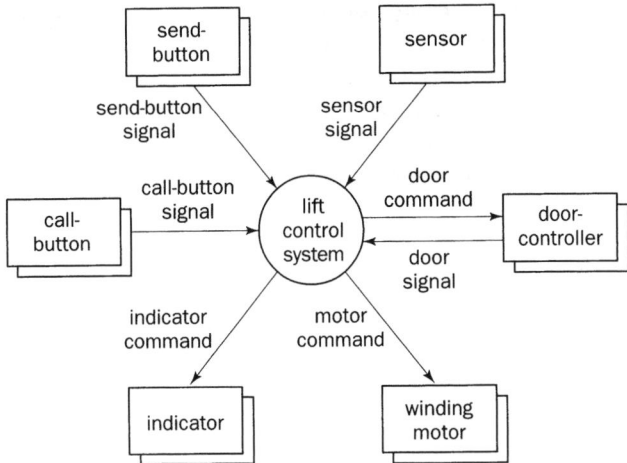

Figure 4.7

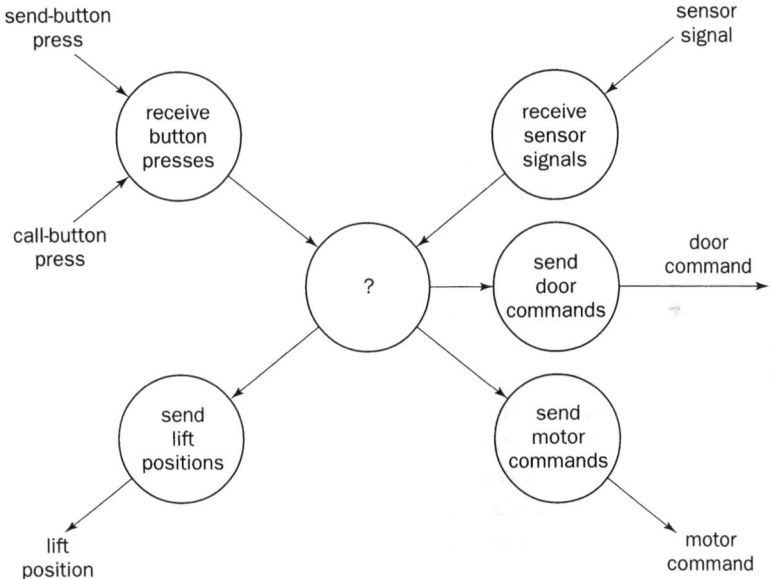

Figure 4.8

the problem domain). There is much that needs to be said (as is detailed in Sections 16.2.1.3 *et seq.*) but SA is not explicit about where and how this should be done.

The data flows that have been identified can (and should) be defined in a DD but, hopefully, the preceding case study has already adequately illustrated this aspect. We should now proceed by developing a lower level DFD for the solution system. Certain processes (functions) are implied by the external data flows and Figure 4.8 shows how these may be incorporated.

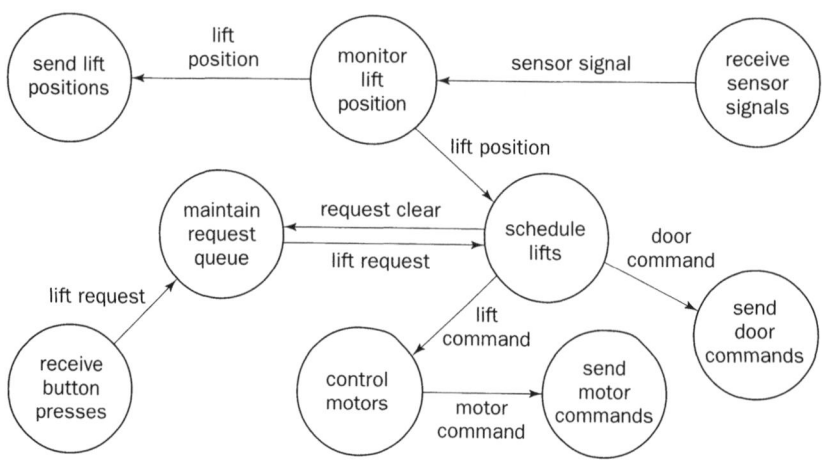

Figure 4.9

There is, however, still a distinct gap in the middle and it could be observed that we have added little of substance. If we wish to proceed with a description of the solution system behaviour we must introduce supposed processes as 'homes' for such description. Figure 4.9 shows one possible 'solution'.

Having taken this step (and probably decomposing some processes in more detail), it is now possible to describe the functionality of the system in terms of the operation of these sub-processes. For example, a Structured English description of the 'schedule lifts' process could well contain the following:

> **check lift position**
> **If** the lift is approaching a floor **then**
> **If** it is the top or bottom floor **or**
> there is a send-request for the floor **or**
> (there is a call-request **and**
> the lift is moving in the right direction) **then**
> send a lift-stop command

By a decidedly roundabout route we have managed to incorporate one of the requirements into our model!

The other strand to modern SA is the data analysis and this could well result in the ERD shown in Figure 4.10. As usual, the entities can be defined in terms of their attributes and this could result in the following additions to the DD:

building	::= number-of-floors, number-of-lifts;
floor	::= floor-id;
lift	::= lift-id, direction, position;
direction	::= "up", "down";
position	::= floor-id;

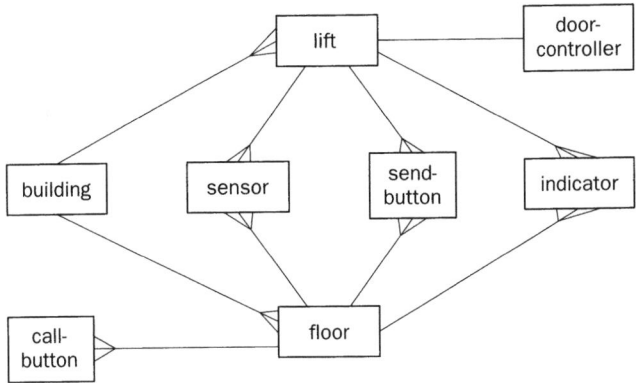

Figure 4.10

door-controller	::= lift-id, door-position;
door-position	::= "closed", "open", opening", "closing";
sensor	::= lift-id, floor-id, sensor-type;
sensor-type	::= "above", "below", "at";
call-button	::= floor-id, direction;
send-button	::= lift-id, floor-id;
indicator	::= lift-id, floor-id;
... etc	

This does provide some useful information about the problem domain. It could be further enhanced with some explanation of the semantics of the various terms although this is not a point that SA pursues (but see Section 14.4.1 for how it could be done).

Further development of the above models would concentrate upon elaboration and refinement of the DFDs. However, this becomes ever more clearly the internal design of the solution system and so I will leave it there and now reflect upon the contribution to problem analysis that has been achieved.

Description (and understanding!) of the problem domain seem sparse. Certain problem sub-domains (the terminators), together with some of their data attributes, have been identified but there is a lot more that the developers will need to know. A central problem is that it is possible to complete the prescribed models without being prompted to ask, or document the answers to, many critical questions about the problem domain. For example; where are the different types of sensor described? when a sensor is triggered, what does that indicate about the lift position? and so on.

Requirements are handled no better. The only place where they can be included is buried within the descriptions of various supposed internal processes. (Furthermore, any specification of the solution system behaviour is achieved only at the cost of introducing such putative solution system structure.)

The standard answer to such criticisms is that all this is covered in the 'accompanying narrative'. This fails to satisfy; partly because no useful guidance is given regarding the accompanying narrative, and partly because so much of import is deferred to this neglected catch-all.

So, for this control system, as regards the critical analysis matters of describing the problem domain and identifying the requirements, the method seems to have contributed little. It may provide a useful approach to structural design *once the problem domain analysis has been accomplished*, but that is another matter.

4.3.4.3 Case 3, the F2K drill file translator

The required system is a translator that will convert files in one format into another format. As in the previous example, some form of elicitation notes (such as may be found in Chapter 17) will be assumed as the source of information. Note, however, that these documents are *not* an explicit part of SA although the existence of elicitation notes as the source of information is implied.

The format of the input and output files is a given; it is part of the problem domain. Strictly, the terminators on a context diagram cannot be files, they should be systems, but the sources and sinks are, in this case, a little hard to pin down, so it is tempting to bend the rules a little and produce a context diagram along the lines shown in Figure 4.11.

The structure of the input and output files is crucial information and their definition can be contained within a DD along the following lines (this is an extract from the full version given in Section 17.1.2.1):

HEAD3-file	::= Hheader, ^{1}{Hcommand};
Hheader	::= Hboard-name, Hversion, Hdate, offset-x, offset-y, Hcomment;
Hboard-name	::= """, {character}^{32} , """;
Hversion	::= ^{3}{digit}^{3} ;
Hdate	::= dd, mm, yy;
offset_x	::= coord;
offset_y	::= coord;
Hcomment	::= """, {character}^{128} , """;
Hcommand	::= drill-number, x-coord, y_coord;
drill-number	::= ^{3}{digit}^{3} ;
... etc	

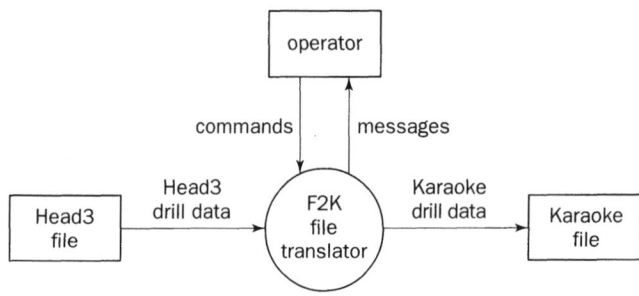

Figure 4.11

Figure 4.12

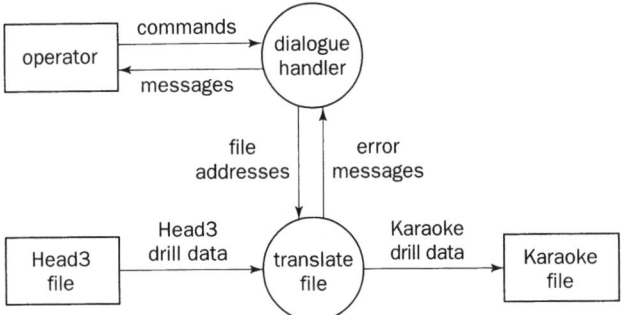

Figure 4.13

In addition to the file definitions, there could well be DD entries for the operator commands and messages:

messages   ::= "Enter input file path and name" | "File not found" |
                  "You do not have read permission for this file" | "Enter
                  output file path and name" | . . .

etc.

As previously, this solution data (which, strictly, belongs in the specification) is liable to be muddled with the problem domain data (the file formats) and that may be considered unsatisfactory.

The method requires the production of an ERD which, in this case, is easy but less than illuminating (see Figure 4.12). The DFD (see Figure 4.13) is similarly unchallenging but, likewise, sheds little light upon the nature of the problem.

The meat of this problem lies, of course, in the mapping between the input and output files. This can readily be defined non-procedurally (see, for example, Section 17.1.2.4); however, the only way that this can be handled within SA is in a procedural form within the P-spec of the 'translate file' process. This could be along these lines:

```
translate file
open input-file
open output-file
hole-count = 0
read input-file (Hboard-name, Hversion, Hdate, offset-x, offset-y, Hcomment)
marker = Hcomment
```

```
if century == 2000 then
        Kdate = "20" + Hdate
else
        Kdate = "19" + Hdate
Kversion = "0" + Hversion[1] + "." + Hversion[2] + Hversion[3]
Kboard_name = Hboard-name
write output-file (marker, Kdate, Kversion, Kboard_name, offset-x, offset-y)
for all Hcommands
        read input-file (drill-number, x-coord, y_coord)
        if first command or drill-number <> previous drill-number then
                write output-file ("drill ", drill-number)
        write output-file (x-coord, y_coord, "60")
        increment hole-count
write output-file (hole-count, "XXXXX")
```

It could well be argued that this is tantamount to designing a particular solution (rather than defining the problem). The interaction with the operator could be defined using a similar technique but this is clearly a specification matter and so will be deferred.

All the required models have now been produced and, by bending the rules a little, some useful information, notably the file formats, has been defined. Other aspects are less than satisfactory and you are invited to consider to what extent the objectives of analysis have been achieved.

4.3.4.4 Case 4, the Petri net diagram tool
The required system is a tool that will allow the user to produce diagrams of Petri nets and execute those nets. As in the previous example, some form of elicitation notes (such as may be found in Chapter 18) will be assumed as the source of information. Note, however, that these documents are *not* an explicit part of SA although the existence of elicitation notes as the source of information is implied.

Again, there is no pre-existing system to model, and so the starting point is a context diagram and a DD. The first, shown in Figure 4.14, poses little difficulty. Of itself, this provides little insight but the DD should make things clearer and so we move swiftly on.

But, the task is rather more problematical. At this stage, we probably do not know exactly what the editing commands or the user messages are; indeed,

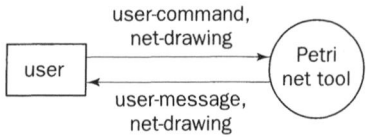

Figure 4.14

their precise nature amounts to solution data and is really a matter for specification. However, we do need at least to indicate what operations upon drawings are required and so we may decide to produce something along these lines:

editing commands	::= create-net | save-net | retrieve-net | copy-net | add-place | move-place | delete-place | add-transition | move-transition | delete-transition | add-arc | delete-arc | undo | etc . . . ;
create-net	::= /* Creates a new net drawing */;
add-place	::= /* Adds a place to the current net. */;
delete-place	::= /* Deletes a place from the current net. Any connecting arcs will also be deleted. */;
. . . etc	

The structure of a Petri net diagram is the problem data that is input to and output from the system and, not surprisingly, the definition of this is more straightforward:

net-drawing	::= [label], file-address, cycle-time, {place}, {transition}, {arc};
file-address	::= /* as determined by operating system */
cycle-time	::= "0.1" . . "5.0";
	::= /* the user defined time for one execution cycle */;
place	::= [label], initial-token-number, current-token-number, token-capacity, overflow;
transition	::= [label];
label	::= [1]{alphanumeric}[20];
alphanumeric	::= "a" . . "z" | "A" . . "Z" | "0" . . "9" | "-" | "''" | "." | "/";
initial-token-number	::= "0" . . "99";
current-token-number	::= "0" . . "99";
token-capacity	::= "0" . . "99";
	::= /* the user defined maximum number of tokens that a place can hold */;
overflow	::= boolean;
	::= /* whether or not a place, upon reaching its token capacity, will 'lose' additional tokens (or block further execution)*/;
boolean	::= /* true or false */

This is clearly useful information and we can also produce an ERD (Figure 4.15) to illustrate the structure of a net.

This just leaves the DFD and here it is difficult to know where to begin. There do not appear to be any data flows (other than those already identified) in the problem domain itself and there is no pre-existing system (other, perhaps, than someone sketching on a piece of paper). The only recourse is then, as per modern SA, to attempt to model the solution system. And the problem

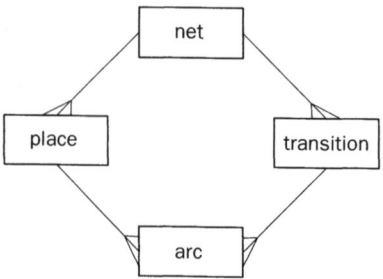

Figure 4.15

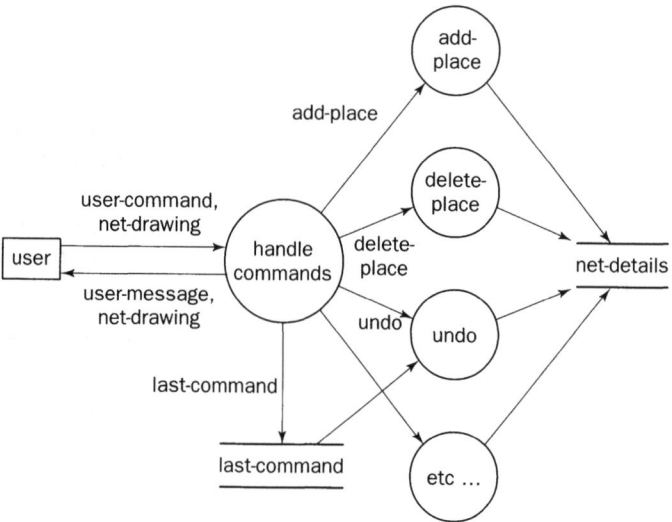

Figure 4.16

then is that the possibilities are legion. Do we, for example, have a process for each editing command, something like Figure 4.16? Or should we have had a process for editing each element of the drawing? Either way, does a DFD really shed much light upon the problem?

And note what has happened with the 'undo last operation' command. This has been handled by saving the last command (as indicated in the diagram). But that is not the only possibility. It could be done by keeping a copy of the entire drawing after each edit and then reverting to the copy. Such a decision would affect the diagram but not the functionality of the system. It is an idesign decision, not a requirements decision.

Furthermore, it is now obvious that we have not modelled the problem domain; the problem domain does not contain a process called 'handle commands' or a data store called 'last-command'. Nor is it a model of the pre-existing system – there isn't one. It is actually an outline internal design of the solution system.

What the designer of the system will really need to know is the way in which the editing commands are required to affect the net drawing. In other words, what is the mapping between each editing command and the content of the document. These are the real requirements and they *can* be defined (see Section 4.5.7.4) but it is difficult to place them in any of the SA models.

For workpiece problems, this approach is of dubious benefit; apart from the data model of the workpiece, there is little of value.

4.3.5   Structured analysis; summary

Structured analysis is an analysis approach with a relatively long tradition that has evolved in a subtle but fundamental way. It centres upon modelling the processing, data flows and stored data structures within a system but that system is not, generally, the problem domain. Originally, it was a presumed, pre-existing, solution system; latterly, it is the new, solution system.

The models employed appear to be reasonably intuitive and accessible to developers and clients alike. Where circumstances permit (i.e. when it is the right sort of application development), the original emphasis upon modelling the pre-existing system helps support the primary analysis goal of achieving understanding of the problem domain. However, various weaknesses can be identified, notably:

- SA down-plays the study of the problem domain (or, in the case of modern SA, any pre-existing system either).
- The lack of a sharp boundary between analysis and design can encourage premature idesign.
- A truly functional specification is absent.
- Requirements are, in effect, specified in terms of the idesign of a particular system that will meet the requirements.
- Idesign is developed using a questionable idesign technique, functional decomposition.
- SA is ill-suited to certain, by no means rare, types of application.

It may seem that a rather negative view of SA has been presented and it is only fair to point out that, for many enterprises, it was a large improvement upon the *ad hoc* methods that preceded it, and that for many years it was (and for many organisations still is) the workhorse method that has supported many a successful system development. To what extent this is thanks to the method and to what extent despite it is not easy to resolve.

4.4   Object oriented analysis

As with SA, there are two reasons why you might read this section. The first is for what might be termed academic purposes; the critical overview that is presented may assist in developing evaluative skills. The second is that you may well have to work on projects where such approaches have been or are being used. This brief view would then only serve as an introduction but full coverage is widely available (see, for example, Jacobson *et al.*, 1996, Yourdon, 1996, and Brown, 1997).

However, for OOA, there is a third reason. There is a very fine line (some would argue a non-existent one) between OOA and object oriented *design* (OOD) and it is the case that OOD provides a particularly fine basis for internal (structural) design; a task which you are likely to have to perform anyway.

As with SA, it is assumed that the reader is familiar with the basic modelling techniques and concepts but, if not, there is a brief introduction and references to further sources of enlightenment in Section 13.4.2.

The object oriented approach dates back to the late 1960s with the invention of the first object oriented programming language. From the outset, it was a way of modelling the *structure* of a system and it was not long before the paradigm was extended from programming into idesign where it has proved to be extremely helpful.

Extension into analysis is relatively recent and still evolving but the basic idea is that the underlying principles, models and notations of object orientation can be applied to analysis if only one concentrates upon modelling object classes from the problem domain (rather than, as in OOD, from the solution system). However, as highlighted by Jackson (1995) – see Section 4.1 – it does not always seem to work out that way. Given the commonality of the modelling techniques and the fact that some object classes superficially *appear* to be common to both domains (see Section 2.9), the line between analysis and idesign may become a vanishingly fine one[27]. As a result, within OOA, the sense of the term 'analysis' may not be consistent with the meaning that is ascribed in this book. There is usually some overlap in the general sense of 'investigating the problem domain', but it often seems to have more to do with high-level idesign (architectural design) of the solution system than analysis of the problem domain.

Jacobson, for example, is quite clear about this when he says that OOSE [object oriented software engineering] may be used from the time that the requirements specification exists' (Jacobson *et al.*, 1996, p. 110). The implied assumption is that analysis and specification (as described here) are precursors to object oriented 'analysis'. Apart from the confusion of terminology, this creates no great problem. However, others are more ambivalent and leave the suspicion that what is, to all intents and purposes, object oriented architectural design can somehow substitute for, what might be termed, 'true' analysis of the problem domain.

Interestingly, in this light, OOA shares several characteristics with SA:

---

[27] For example in Yourdon (1996), as part of an *analysis* case study (coincidentally, of a lift controller system), there is consideration of whether or not the floor object class should be made responsible for scheduling the lifts. Now this may be an important and valid idesign consideration but, clearly, the floors that exist in the *problem domain* are dumb objects that could not possibly undertake lift scheduling.

- The central model is a structural (as opposed to a behavioural) model.
- Despite some polemic to the contrary, in practice, the concentration is usually upon modelling the solution system (rather than the problem domain).
- Much of the literature tends to concentrate upon the minutiae of notations (rather than the fundamental principles).
- There is an implicit assumption that elicitation occurs, but most of the literature has little to say about it.
- There is often no clear distinction between analysis and specification (or, for that matter, idesign).
- All problem domains are assumed to be amenable to similar treatment.

From the viewpoint of requirements engineering, these characteristics might be regarded as serious weaknesses. Nevertheless, OOA has already displaced SA in many organisations and some significant developments have succeeded with it. This may be because the preceding stages are accomplished by other means or because other factors (such as pre-existing knowledge of the problem domain) allow 'shortcuts' (see Section 2.6.2).

As mentioned earlier, generally, little is said about elicitation within OOA and so it will be assumed to occur along the lines previously described. (But see also the reference to use-cases that follows below.)

The outline method for OOA is, then:

- Identify object classes within the problem domain.
- Define the attributes and methods of those classes.
- Define the behaviour of those classes.
- Model the relationships between those classes.

Subsequent steps then extend the model by adding classes that relate to the solution system behaviour and implementation. This gradual elaboration of the same model gave rise to the notion of 'seamless' development; maintaining the same conceptual models and notations throughout the phases of development. This notion is still promoted but it may be considered that there has never been any convincing justification for it (Jackson, 2001). Indeed, it could well be argued that it is quite proper for there to be 'seams' between structural models of the problem domain, behavioural models of the solution system and structural models of the solution systems.

In the light of the foregoing, it is not surprising that the distinction between the various versions of the class model is often glossed over. But there are those who recognise the significance. Fowler and Scott (2000), for example, highlight the three 'perspectives' of class models:

- conceptual (i.e. problem domain classes – pertaining to analysis);
- specification (i.e. interface classes);
- implementation (i.e. pertaining to internal design).

Clearly, it is the first that is of relevance here. (But we must still be cautious; even where a class is rooted in reality, there is still an important distinction between the problem domain object and any software parallel that might carry the same name.) The second will be revisited briefly in the specification chapter and the last are better regarded as object oriented *design* and so will not be further considered. Be aware, however, of the widespread lack of appreciation of the distinction.

Relatively recently, the method has been supplemented with a preceding step; the use of use-cases to help establish requirements. It is now quite widely advocated that, in the early stages, use-cases should be used to help elicit and record requirements. It may well be argued, however, that use-cases record functionality of the solution system (rather than requirements) and so their contribution is more in the area of specification than determining requirements. This approach, therefore, constitutes a shortcut that bypasses full consideration of the problem domain and its problems and proceeds directly to a definition of solution system behaviour. Better that though, than proceed directly to the architectural design of the solution system[28]! And if the problem domain is well known (as it often is) this is a shortcut that can work (see Section 2.6.2).

Although primarily promoted within the context of OOA, use-cases are actually quite independent and so are considered in more detail separately (in Section 12.3). Here it may be assumed that, if used, they could constitute, at least in part, a specification.

4.4.1 Object oriented analysis; examples

As for SA, examples, together with some commentary upon their derivation and utility, will be presented to help flesh out the picture.

As discussed earlier, object oriented analysis is not, despite claims to the contrary, always applied to analysis of the problem domain. However, within requirements engineering, that is the crucial issue and so, as for SA, utility will be adjudged within the context of the main objectives of analysis; acquiring understanding of the problem domain and providing a complete description of all pertinent facets of the problem domain as well as a complete list of the client's requirements. As before, we start with cases where progress is relatively straightforward.

4.4.1.1 Case 1, the yacht race results (YRR) program
The required system is a computer program that will assist in the calculation of results for sailing races. Object oriented analysis has little to say about the elicitation of information about the problem domain and so I will assume that this has already been accomplished and that some form of elicitation notes

---

[28] And far better to be fully aware that you *are* taking a shortcut and knowing what risks are attached.

Table 4.1

object class	attributes
boat	boat-name, boat-class-name, sail-number, helm-name
boat class	boat-class-name, handicap-type, handicap-value
race-class	race-class-type, race-class-name,
handicap-race-class	handicap-type, minimum-handicap, maximum-handicap
helm	helm-name
race	race-class-name, race-date, start-time, race-name, course
race-entry	boat-class-name, sail-number, race-class, race-date, race-time, result
race-officer	
series	series-name, race-class-name, number-of-races, number-of-races-to-count
series-entry	boat-class-name, sail-number, series-name

(along the lines of the examples that can be found in Chapter 15) already exist. We may therefore proceed with the principal analysis task of describing, or modelling, the problem domain and the associated requirements.

It is an inescapable feature of OOA that everything must be modelled in terms of object classes and so the identification of problem domain object classes is the obvious opening gambit. This can follow similar lines to the identification of entities; the essential entity question, 'what things in the problem domain have associated information that is of interest?' is supplemented with 'and what things in the problem domain require or can provide services?'

The candidate object classes shown in Table 4.1 might be identified without much difficulty. The principal attributes are also shown but the operations are omitted as these are mostly simple manipulations of the attributes (e.g. change-boatname( ), get-boat-name( ), change-boat-class-name( ), get-boat-class-name( ) etc.).

Race-officer has no relevant attributes but has been considered because race officers enter start and finish times and calculate results. But there is a snag in that these are operations upon the data of a race, a series or an entry (not a race officer). It might, therefore, be decided that operations such as calculate-results should be placed in the race class and series class. However, this is also problematical as it seems most unlikely that a *problem domain* race (as opposed to a solution system race) has the mathematical capability. And so we have an awkward choice: calculate result may be placed with a race officer class (which does not hold the relevant data) or with the race class which (in the problem domain) does not have the ability. With misgivings, I will opt for the latter and

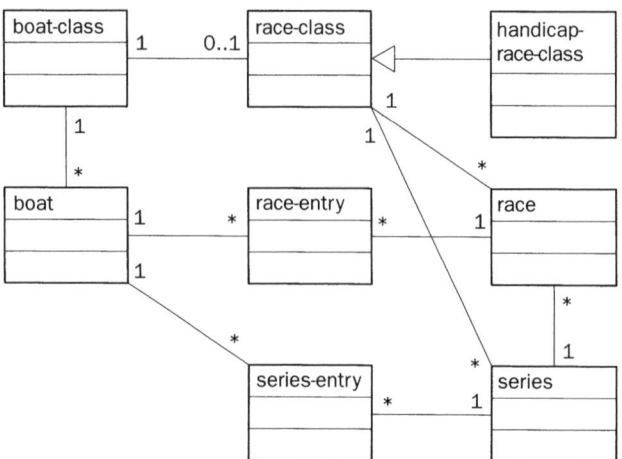

Figure 4.17

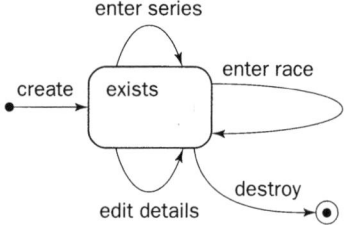

Figure 4.18

dispense with the race officer class (but note that the dilemma arose as a result of applying the object oriented paradigm to reality).

For information problems in general, and this problem in particular, the selected problem domain object classes correspond closely with the entities that could be identified during SA. The only significant difference here is the inheritance between race-class and handicap-race-class. A class diagram (Figure 4.17) can show this together with the associations.

The problem domain object classes do not exhibit a great deal of relevant behaviour but, such as it is, this could be captured with a state chart. Figure 4.18 gives an example for the boat class.

Another avenue that might be pursued is defining the effect of the operations. There is a standard UML (Unified Modelling Language) syntax for this:

visibility name (parameter-list): return-type-expression {property string}

but it is not of great relevance for problem domain modelling where it is better to concentrate upon the semantics of the operations (rather than the syntax). It is, perhaps, stretching the imagination to regard the following as an operation of a real boat but we could add some descriptions along these lines:

> **create-boat** (boat-name, boat-class-name, sail-number, helm-name)
> Creates a new boat with the given attribute values. Duplicate boat-class-name and sail-number are not accepted.

However, without straying further into specification or design of the solution system, that is about as far as we can go – and it may seem that it is not very far. There is a distinct lack of collaboration amongst the classes but that is explained by the fact that I have stuck to modelling the problem domain classes (which, being essentially data repositories, do not happen to collaborate much) rather than the solution system classes (with all their added functionality).

So, how much of the looked-for analysis output has been delivered? There is some useful information about the problem domain data but no more than a conventional data analysis would have delivered. Indeed, we are lacking a DD but, whilst they are seldom mentioned in the context of OOD, there is no reason why a DD (akin to that in Section 4.3.4.1) could not be added to define the various terms and data items.

And what else is lacking? As with SA, there is little description of the problem sub-domains (we still do not know, for example, what is really meant by a race-class), there are no clues as to how the solution system might access the data it requires, we do not know what queries must be supported or what reports are required. In other words, there is a complete absence of requirements. Object oriented analysis generally appears to assume that these are already known and documented in some form as it does not seem to contribute to this aspect. (It is sometimes suggested that requirements can be documented by way of use-cases (see Section 12.3) but use-cases actually describe the interaction between the solution system and its terminators which is really a matter of specification, not requirements.)

4.4.1.2 Case 2, the lift controller

The required system is a software-based controller for lifts. As for the previous example, I will assume that some form of elicitation has already been performed, and that elicitation notes (as per the examples that can be found in Chapter 16) already exist. We may therefore proceed with the principal analysis task of describing, or modelling, the problem domain and the associated requirements.

As per the previous case study, the identification of problem domain object classes is the opening gambit. The following candidate object classes (shown in Table 4.2) might be identified (some of the principal attributes and operations are also shown).

Having no obvious attributes or operations, user and lift-shaft look to be unlikely candidates. User may, however, be reprieved on the grounds that it uses a service (press) that is provided by other classes (the buttons). There is also some overlap with lift and motor; it seems that most of their shared operations really belong to motor. And it could well be that the two types of button could

Table 4.2

object class	attributes	operations
building	num-floors, num-lifts	
floor	floor-id, call	set-call, clear-call
lift-shaft		
lift	lift-id, direction, position	start, stop, get-direction, set-direction
send-button	lift-id, floor-id, pressed	press, unpress, check-press
call-button	floor-id, direction, pressed	press, unpress, check-press
sensor	floor-id, lift-id, type, status	get-status
indicator	lift-id, floor-id, on-off	set-on, set-off
user		
door	door-position	close, open, get-position
motor	lift-id	start, stop, set-direction

inherit from a super-class of button. We will return to such matters in a moment but first, a deeper look at what has been accomplished so far.

There is no question that these classes have some parallel in reality but it might be spotted that solution system bias is already creeping in. For example, a floor clearly exists in the physical world but, as modelled here, it has an attribute of whether or not is has an outstanding call. Few object orientation aficionados would question this; clearly the control system will need to know this information and the obvious place to store it is in the floor object. However, the *real* floor does not store any information; if you will excuse the anthropomorphism, it has no idea of whether or not it has an outstanding call. Similarly, the physical call-buttons do not know whether or not they have been pressed (as opposed to being pressed now), they have no memory; it is the solution system button objects that will handle this.

Anyway, continuing with the analysis, there is more to be said about the problem domain classes and, for a control system, a matter of prime concern is their behaviour. Object oriented analysis provides for such modelling with state charts and Figure 4.19 illustrates an example for the lift motor.

Whilst this succinctly captures important characteristics of the motor, there is more to say (about acceleration and deceleration for example) and some accompanying explanation (about which, object oriented analysis offers little guidance) is certainly required. It may also be observed that modelling the behaviour of problem sub-domains in this way owes nothing to object orientation *per se*. Any approach to analysis could have delivered such a model. It so

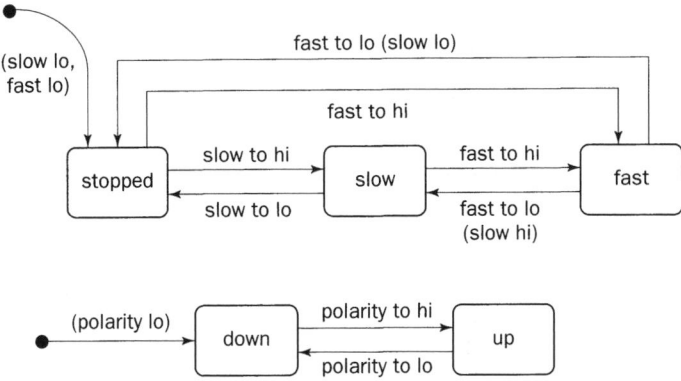

Figure 4.19

happens that the example requirements document in Section 16.2.1.4 opted for a decision table instead, and you may care to compare the two.

In passing, note that Figure 4.19 *does* relate to the physical motor. As can be seen, it is possible to reverse polarity (and hence, direction) independently of the motor's speed, even if it is running fast. This could have disastrous consequences but it is an inherent property of the motor that this can be done. Not surprisingly, there is a *requirement* that the lift controller must not let it happen and it may, therefore, be tempting to model the way in which the motor is *required to be made to behave*. This would result in the significantly different model shown in Figure 4.20. The version in Figure 4.20 might appear in the *specification* for the controller but it would be misleading (possibly, dangerously so) to include it as part of a model of the problem domain.

Having described the inherent behaviour of the classes, consideration must be given to the relationships between them. Figure 4.21 shows how the associations[29] might be depicted.

This class diagram may be compared to the ERD in Section 4.3.4.2 (Figure 4.10) and it can be seen that, apart from the inheritance of the buttons, it is, as one might expect, logically very similar.

However, we expect to get more from object orientation and we can, of course, also show the collaboration (aka 'uses' or service) links. To avoid too much clutter, I will show this on a separate collaboration diagram, see Figure 4.22. No, I have not forgotten to show the links. It so happens that the bulk of the problem domain object classes do not directly interact (at least, not by way of passing messages). It would be useful to show other forms of interaction that *do* exist in the problem domain (for example, the mechanical interaction between the motor and the lift and between the lift and the

---

[29] Regarding it as of little consequence for analysis, I will side-step the discussion about whether certain links are best represented in UML as associations, aggregations or compositions.

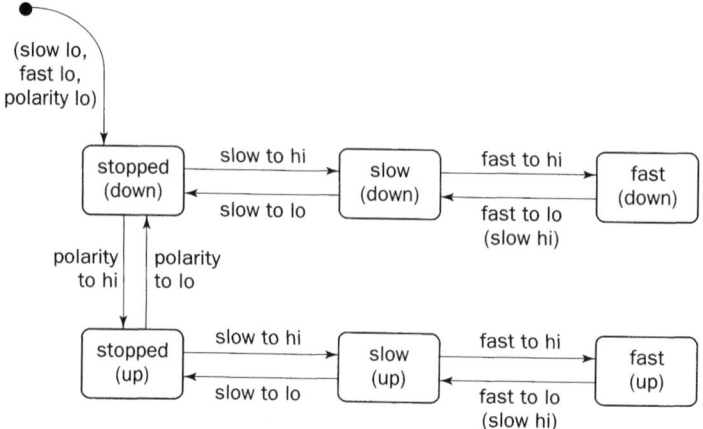

Figure 4.20

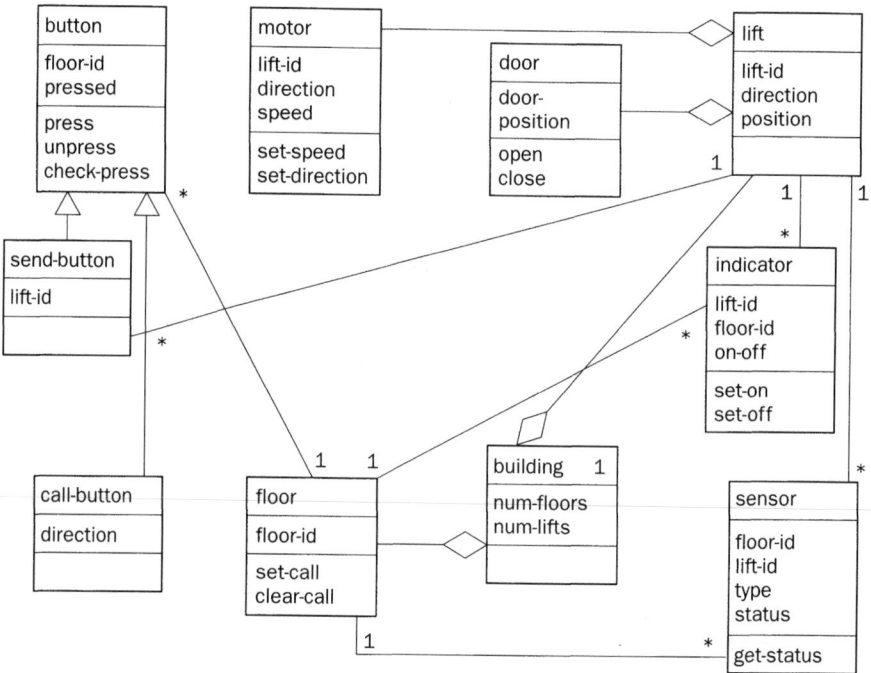

Figure 4.21

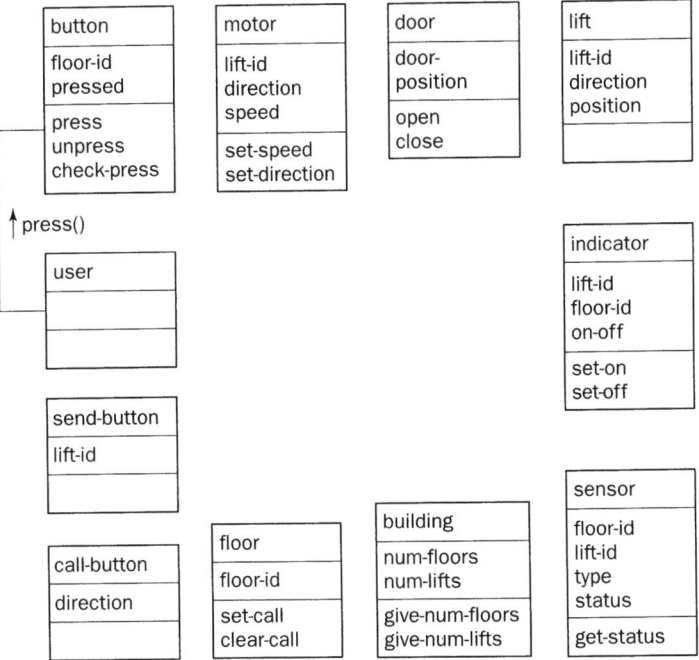

Figure 4.22

sensors), but surely it would really be forcing the issue to model this as message passing. Message passing is, of course, something that software objects do.

As with the SA, it is tempting to 'solve' the problem by introducing the controller object. Not only does this act as a mediator which links the other objects, the requirements for the system can also be reflected in its behaviour. The controller does not, of course, exist in the problem domain at all (that *is* the problem!), and whether or not the controller communicates with the outside world by message passing is also debatable. This further emphasises the common bias towards solution system design. However, for the record (and without going much further down the idesign path) Figure 4.23 shows a possible outcome from following this course. I will not pretend that great effort has been invested in this model and, as a design, it may leave something to be desired[30]. The point, however, is that it *is* a design; it describes the solution system rather than the problem domain.

Perhaps the main problem with all this is that a lot of what we will need to know about the problem domain is left unrecorded. What, for example, are the

---

[30] A far more thoroughly developed design for a similar system may be found in Yourdon (1996).

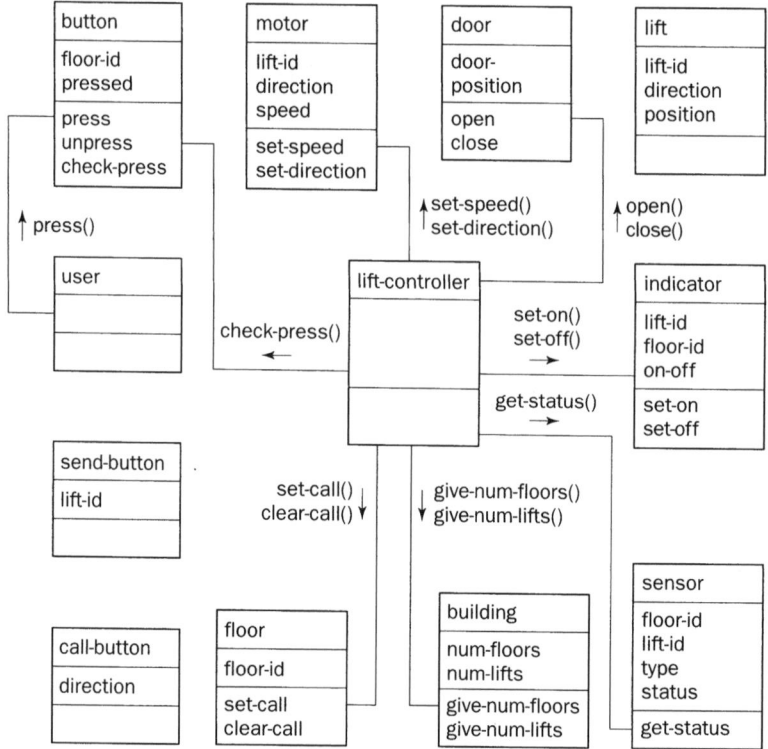

Figure 4.23

operating characteristics of the lift motor; how quickly, say, does it accelerate and decelerate? Notably, it is also difficult to find anywhere within the object models to record the actual requirements. Somehow this type of information must be communicated to the system builder but this appears to be largely beyond the scope of OOA.

4.4.1.3   Case 3, the F2K drill file translator

The required system is a translator that will convert files in one format into another format. As before, I will assume that the elicitation of information about the problem domain has already been accomplished by some unspecified means and that some form of elicitation notes (as per the examples that can be found in Chapter 17) already exist.

The only apparent object classes in the problem domain are the input and output files. A file is, by definition, inert; it is a repository for data but provides no services. It is, therefore, debatable as to whether these files are best represented as objects but we have no choice; OOA insists that everything is modelled as an object. A little force fitting may result in the objects shown in Figure 4.24. It would be possible to model the files' data structures using object class diagrams along the lines of Figure 4.25. This is OK, but

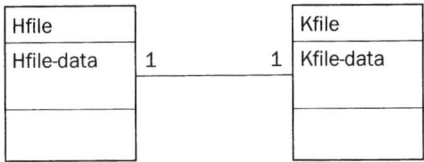

Figure 4.24

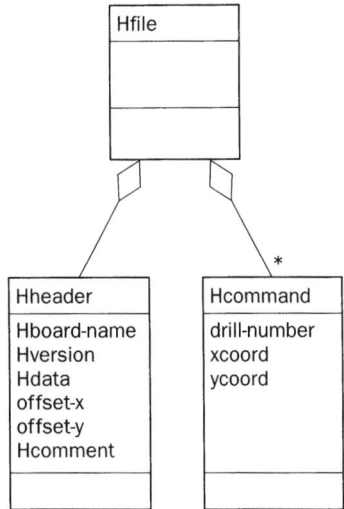

Figure 4.25

seems to offer no advantage over the more comprehensive and succinct BNF-style DD:

HEAD3-file	::= Hheader, $^1\{$Hcommand$\}$;
Hheader	::= Hboard-name, Hversion, Hdate, offset-x, offset-y, Hcomment;
Hboard-name	::= Hname;
Hversion	::= $^3\{$digit$\}^3$;
Hdate	::= dd, mm, yy;
offset_x	::= coord;
offset_y	::= coord;
Hcomment	::= Hname ;
Hname	::= """", $\{$character$\}^{32}$, """";
Hcommand	::= drill-number, x-coord, y_coord;
drill-number	::= $^3\{$digit$\}^3$;
x-coord	::= coord;
y-coord	::= coord;
coord	::= $^{16}\{$digit$\}^{16}$;
. . . etc	

It is rather difficult to know how to proceed from here. Various read/write operations could be added to the file objects but these really belong to the solution system file objects (that could well form part of a good solution system idesign). The problem domain objects have no behaviour or interaction that we can model.

As with SA, the crucial matter of the mapping from the input to the output data structure can be modelled only in a procedural way and then only if we invent a particular incarnation of a solution system 'translator' object. (A 'transformation rule set' object may, perhaps, be supposed but seems distinctly artificial.) So, I will leave it there and can only suggest that, without 'force fitting', the approach has contributed little, if anything, of value to the description of the problem domain or the definition of the requirements.

4.4.1.4   Case 4, the Petri net diagram tool

The required system is a tool that will allow the user to produce diagrams of Petri nets and execute those nets. As for the previous example, I will assume that some form of elicitation has already been performed, and that elicitation notes (as per the examples that can be found in Chapter 18) already exist. Note, however, that these documents are *not* an explicit part of OOA although the existence of elicitation notes as the source of information is implied.

The obvious problem domain object classes appear to be the Petri net diagrams and the various elements of those diagrams. (The user may be considered as a candidate object class but it is hard to think of any relevant attributes or operations.)

The object classes, their attributes, principal operations and associations may be depicted as in Figure 4.26. This is pertinent information but, as before, as regards the data, it says no more (indeed, rather less) than the ERD and DD that would be produced by other analysis approaches.

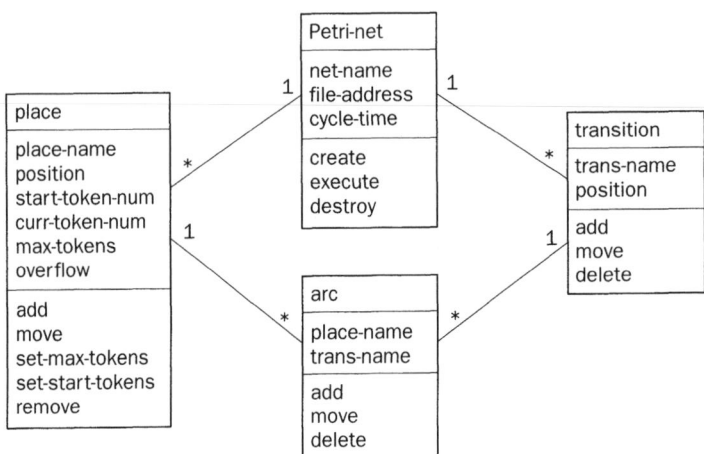

Figure 4.26

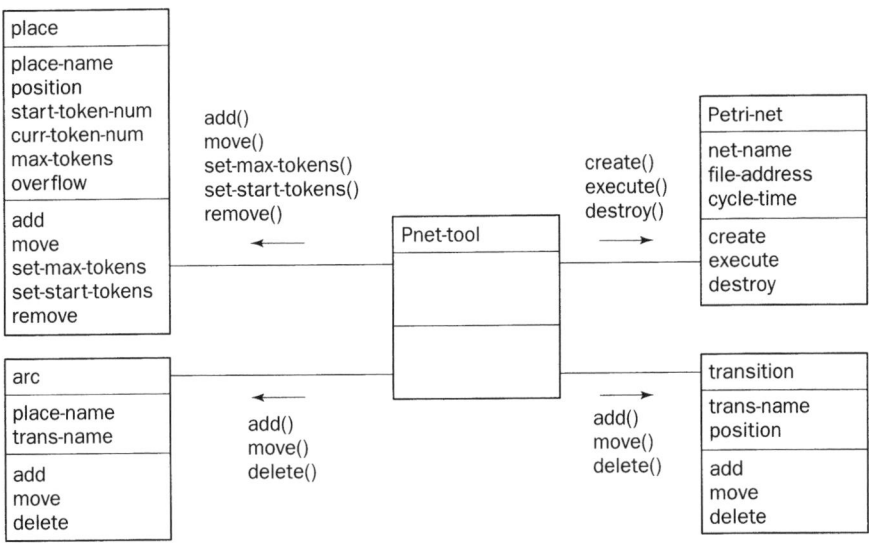

Figure 4.27

A collaboration diagram will show the 'uses' relationships but we run into the same problem as with the other case studies; the operations are used by an object class (in this case the tool itself) that does not exist within the problem domain. However, if we take the liberty of introducing such an object, Figure 4.27 might be the result.

This may be seen as of dubious value. From the requirements standpoint, what really matters are the effects that the various editing commands will have upon the Petri nets diagrams. At least some of this could be incorporated as commentary upon the operations, for example:

```
object class place
operations:
        set-max-tokens (max-tokens)
            /* sets the maximum number of tokens that a place can hold */
    etc.
```

However, it may be noted that this hardly depended upon the object oriented model. Strip away the headings, and the bulk of the text is a description of required behaviour that could stand by itself.

4.4.2   Object oriented analysis; summary

Like SA, OOA can be the subject of some fundamental criticism; the central point being that, as generally practised, OOA is not really analysis (in the sense that it is used here) at all. The starting point for OOA is a *pre-existing* requirements document (or even a behavioural specification) and so it is implicitly assumed that problem domain analysis (and possibly specification) has already been accomplished. Some proponents of the approach acknowledge this, others are less open but in neither case is much guidance given as to how the vital, preceding stage may be handled.

In fact, as illustrated in the foregoing examples, some of the object oriented modelling techniques *can* contribute to modelling the problem domain and its sub-domains but the object oriented aspect is pretty peripheral and little advantage seems to accrue.

The real subject matter of OOA is revealed as high-level, architectural, design of the solution system. The terminology is confusing but, provided we understand what is going on we can still make capital. As it happens, OOA is a very good approach to high-level design but, where necessary, it must be preceded by some other form of problem domain analysis and specification. However, where the problem domain is well known then we can certainly shortcut the problem domain analysis and this can largely explain how OOA has achieved many a successful development without any preceding stages.

4.5 Problem domain oriented analysis

Problem domain oriented analysis (PDOA) is so new that it has yet to be fully explored and documented. That said, it is only new in part; in equal, if not larger, measure, it is a return to what might be considered old-fashioned practice.

Relative to SA or OOA, PDOA places less emphasis on modelling and more on description. Where appropriate, that description incorporates some of the previously mentioned modelling techniques but, as often as not, it relies upon text.

There is an unambiguous separation of descriptions into those that concern the problem domain and those that concern the required behaviour of the solution system[31]. Two separate documents are recommended: the first contains a description of the relevant parts of the problem domain and a list of the problems requiring solution within that domain (i.e. the requirements); the second (the specification) contains a description of the behaviour that is required of the solution system in order to address the requirements. Only the first document is produced through analysis; the second is deferred to the subsequent specification task.

One new model, the problem frame, is introduced (see Jackson, 1995, Kovitz, 1999, and Jackson, 2001). This model not only helps separate the requirements from the problem domain's inherent properties, it also helps establish the *type* of problem domain. PDOA does not treat all problem domains in the same way. Dependent upon the type of problem domain, the analyst is guided to collect and record different information.

---

[31] Unlike SA or OOA, there is no description, even implied, of the *structure* of the solution system – that is left entirely to the design phase.

The PDOA approach is no more, indeed, probably less, prescriptive than any other. The general course of the procedure is, however, fairly well defined:

- Collect basic information and develop problem frame(s) in order to establish the type of the problem domain.
- Guided by the problem frame type(s), collect further detail and develop a description of the relevant characteristics of the problem domain.
- In conjunction with the foregoing, collect and document the requirements for the new system.

Critical for the second step are the guidelines, developed by Kovitz (1999), which, for each type of problem domain, list those elements of the problem domain which must be explored and documented.

4.5.1 Problem frames

Problem frames[32] model the problem domain as a set of inter-related sub-domains, where a sub-domain (often shortened to 'domain') is any part of the problem domain that may be usefully singled out.

Problem frames may be viewed as a development of context diagrams but with a different emphasis:

- Context diagrams model the *solution system* context.
- Problem frames model the *problem* context.

To this end, problem frames aim to capture significantly more information about the problem domain than a context diagram. A context diagram shows only those elements of the problem domain that are *external* to, and will *directly connect to*, the new, solution system. These elements are usually known as terminators since they terminate the input and output data flows to the new system. However, terminators are not necessarily the only sub-domains of relevance and vital sub-domains may, therefore, be ignored.

Context diagrams also ignore some relationships between sub-domains. For example, the rules that define the relationships between one problem sub-domain and another would not figure at all in a context diagram (by convention, no relationships between terminators are shown) but will actually correspond to the very requirements that must be satisfied.

It is, perhaps, surprising that the application of problem frames to software development problems is so recent but that is the case and so it should be emphasised that it is still in the early stages and, hence, evolving rapidly. Nonetheless, it already appears to offer significant advantages and the view is taken here that, as the technology matures, only further advantage can accrue.

---

[32] As described by Jackson (1995, 2001), based on the earlier work of Polya (1957) which is based, in turn, on the work of the ancient Greek, Pappus.

4.5.1.1   Problem frame types

One of the most significant differences between PDOA and any other approach to analysis is the way in which problem domains are categorised and, based upon that categorisation, handled differently. Knowing the *type* of problem helps guide the analysis (by indicating what questions to ask, what aspects to model, etc.) and the specification (and, ultimately, the idesign as well[33]).

As introduced in Section 1.5.1, Jackson (1995, 2001) proposes a categorisation that is far more objective than earlier attempts and is based upon the nature of the various problem sub-domains and the relationships that exist between them. A quick reminder:

- **Workpiece** system – where the system must perform directed operations upon objects that exist only within the system.

- **Control** system – where the system will control the behaviour of part of the problem domain. There are two variations here; the **required behaviour** frame (where the required behaviour is fully pre-determined by rules) and the **commanded behaviour** frame (where behaviour is controlled in accordance with commands issued by an operator).

- **Information** system – where the system will have to provide information about the problem domain. Here too there are two variations; where information is provided automatically (often continually) and where information is supplied only in response to specific requests.

- **Transformation** system – where the system must transform input data in a particular format into output data in a corresponding, particular format.

- **Connection** system – where the system must maintain correspondence between sub-domains that are not directly connected.

Each of these types of problem then has a characteristic problem frame but, before examining the various problem frames in detail, let us see how the method works for one particular example system, the Petri net diagram tool (see Chapter 18).

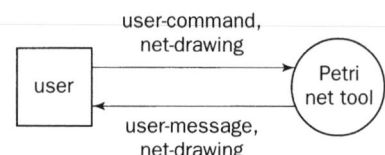

Figure 4.28

---

[33] As well as the requirements engineering related guidance that is presented here, Jackson (1995, 2001) talks about each problem frame having an associated 'solution method'. That is a way of tackling the subsequent *internal* design of that particular type of problem. Of the five frames so far identified (and within certain constraints), two have such a solution method and others are receiving attention. Whilst that might be considered a bonus, it is not of immediate relevance to the main consideration here, i.e. requirements engineering.

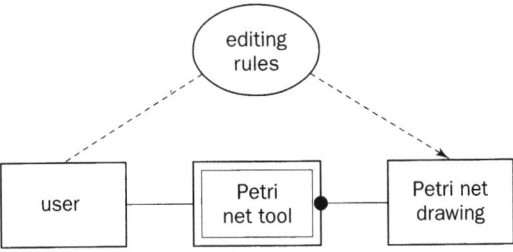

Figure 4.29

The context diagram (Figure 4.28) shows us little more than that there is a user. The Petri net diagram tool is fairly easily identified as being, essentially, a workpiece problem. The corresponding problem frame (Figure 4.29) not only accommodates the net document but also explicitly shows the rules that define the effect upon the net drawings of the operations that the user performs. The notation requires a little explanation:

- Domains of interest (which will be elements within the problem domain) are represented by rectangles.

- The solution system (or, as Jackson (1995) calls it, the 'machine') is shown as a double rectangle (or, alternatively, as a double side-barred rectangle.

  )

- Ellipses are used to show and name the significant logical relationships between domains. It should be noted that such domain relationships are tantamount to the *requirements*. In this example, the editing rules specify the effects that the user's editing commands should have upon the document being edited. It will naturally be a requirement that the tool brings about these effects.

- The plain lines joining domains indicate that there is some relationship between them. For software systems, this may well be by way of a data flow but any kind of interaction is accommodated. The critical test is whether or not the domains have any shared phenomena; whether there are any values or events that are shared between the domains.

- The dashed lines represent a requirement reference; that is there are requirements that refer to phenomena within the referenced sub-domain. An arrow head indicates that the requirement *constrains* phenomena within the sub-domain as opposed to simply referencing them. In the example above, requirements will reference editing commands from the user and stipulate the effect that these will have upon the document.

- Finally, the large dot is used to indicate that one domain is contained within another. In this case, the Petri net diagrams are contained within (and exist only within) the tool itself.

Table 4.3

Requirements document
The legitimate data structure[34] of the **workpiece**
The required **operations** and the effects that these should have upon the workpiece

Table 4.4

Specification
User interface and operating procedures

The most immediate advantage of this approach is that, having identified the type of problem, we are now guided as to the aspects of the problem that must be investigated and recorded. Table 4.3 and Table 4.4 (based upon Kovitz's content tables, Kovitz, 1999) indicate the content of the requirements document and of the specification for workpiece problems specifically. (It just so happens that, for the workpiece problem, these lists are relatively short, but that, in itself, is very useful to know!)

Note that these tables vary markedly for each type of problem and the indication of what can be omitted is just as useful as the indication of what must be included. For example, given a workpiece problem, there is no point in trying to identify the inherent behaviour of the workpiece sub-domain because, by definition, it does not exhibit any. Similarly, given a transformation problem, there is no point in trying to identify problem domain events because, by definition, there are none[35]; however, it *would* be crucial to define the input/output data set mapping.

4.5.1.2 Problem domains, requirements and mood

Unlike other approaches, PDOA clearly differentiates between the inherent characteristics of the problem domain and the changes that are required to be produced in the problem domain.

Jackson (1995) characterises this as a distinction of mood (in the grammatical sense). Statements about the inherent qualities of the problem domain are made in the *indicative* mood. Here are a couple of examples extracted from the case studies:

- When a lift is within 20 cm vertically (above or below) of the sensor's nominal position the sensor sends a hi signal; otherwise a lo signal.

---

[34] This is the structure *as evident to the outside world,* as opposed to the way in which it might actually be stored within the application; the latter is a matter for idesign (or, possibly, a design constraint).

[35] If there were, it would not be a transformation problem.

- For each boat, the elapsed time is defined as the difference, in seconds, between the race start time and the boat's finish time.

These are *facts* about the problem domain; they are entirely beyond the control or influence of the new, solution system that is to be built.

On the other hand, there are the things that the new system *can* influence; indeed, the effects that it is *required* to produce. Statements about these effects are made in the *optative* mood (they reflect the clients' chosen options). Here are some examples:

- The lift should not be stopped from fast mode but should always be switched to slow mode for at least one second before stopping.
- A lift will only reverse direction when stopped at a floor.

Given the inherent characteristics of the problem domain, it is within the capability of the new system to meet these requirements (or, if wrongly built, to fail to meet them!).

Some requirements standards have quite a lot to say about mood. You may find that words like 'shall', 'must' and 'will' are associated with differences in the 'importance' of requirements. This is a highly dubious practice. Far more important is a clear differentiation between *the way the world is* (problem domain description) and the *effects that the new system should produce* (the requirements). If there are requirements that are less urgent than others then the best way to handle this is to simply indicate which release of the new system should address them (see Kovitz, 1999).

4.5.1.3   Sub-domain interactions

As mentioned above, the lines connecting sub-domains represent relationships or interactions between them; these being in the form of shared or referenced phenomena. It is quite possible to describe these interactions more fully and this can provide considerable leverage when it comes to deriving a suitable logical behaviour for the solution system (i.e. when it comes to specification). Despite its significance, this topic is, unfortunately, too large to pursue in detail here and the interested reader must be referred to Jackson (2001). However, as will be seen, even without this enhancement, there is considerable mileage to be gained from the problem frame approach.

4.5.1.4   Sub-domain types and problem frame fitting

Spotting the correct type of problem frame to fit the problem is often straightforward but it can be tricky. A helpful strategy is to capitalise upon the constraints that the problem frames impose upon the characteristics of the sub-domains. For example, the workpiece frame demands that the workpiece itself be dynamic, inert and contained within the machine (i.e. it must be an intangible, software document). If the supposed workpiece sub-domain does not fit this pattern then you do not have a workpiece problem.

Certain domain characteristics have been mentioned in passing but it is now time to examine the full range. We may start by considering whether or not a domain changes over time. Most do, in which case they may be described as dynamic, but some are static. An example of the latter would be a CD-ROM based encyclopaedia; the application allows access to the data and queries can be answered; however, there is no provision for the content to be changed.

Dynamic domains may be further categorised into those that can change themselves (self-modifying) and those that are changed only by an outside agency. The latter may be called inert and, within software systems, are typified by files.

Self-modifying domains may be sub-divided yet further depending upon whether or not they require an external stimulus in order to change. An abstract data type (ADT), for example, might change its state only in response to an external stimulus or request and this type of domain will be referred to as reactive.

Other domains may change spontaneously and, for these, we must consider how controllable or predictable their behaviour is. If it is completely predictable (even if only stochastically predictable) then the domain may be described as programmable and this, of course, is the nature of most (but not all) software applications. If a domain's behaviour is partially predictable then it may be described as biddable and the human user typifies this type of domain. They may, for example, be asked to enter their password and they probably will, but there is no guarantee. Alternatively, a domain may be completely beyond control and these will be referred to as autonomous. An example of this would be a stock market index (or the weather!).

These considerations are summarised in Figure 4.30.

In parallel with the above considerations, domains may also be classified as tangible or intangible. Tangible domains are those that have a physical existence, such as human users and hardware; intangible would include software and other non-material objects such as sets of rules or the previously given example of an encyclopaedia.

Once domains are characterised, it is easy to check whether they comply with the requirements imposed by any chosen frame. There follows a basic description of the various frames including a characterisation of each of their sub-domains. Those seeking further detail, particularly on multi-frame problems, are referred to Kovitz (1999) and, of course, Jackson (1995, 2001).

Recall that Jackson (1995, 2001) identifies five basic problem frames:

- workpiece
- control
- information
- transformation
- connection

4.5.1.5   The workpiece frame
A specific example, the Petri net tool, was introduced earlier but the generic frame is as shown in Figure 4.31.

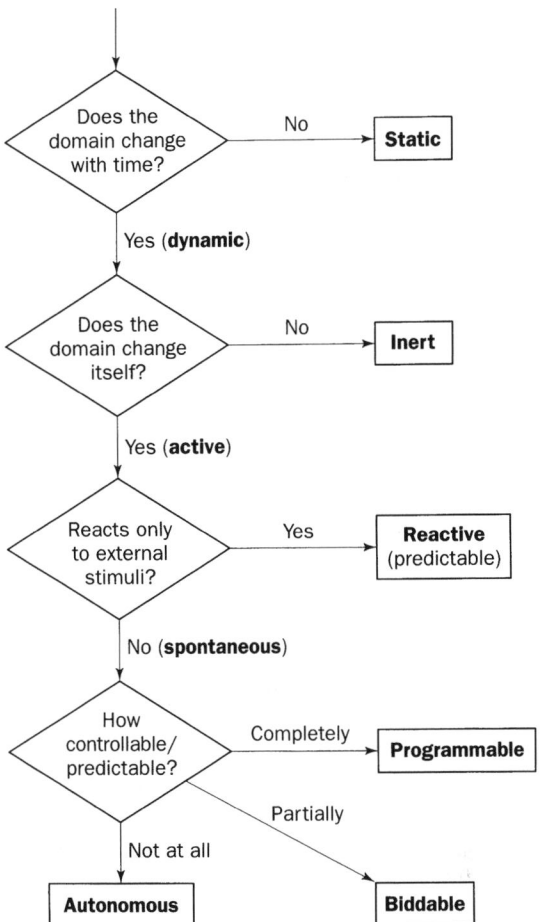

Figure 4.30

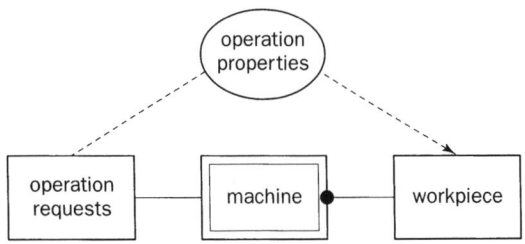

Figure 4.31

This shows that the workpiece (typically some form of document) is contained within the machine and, consequently, can be acted upon only by the machine. The machine (i.e. the software configured computer that is required to be built) performs various operations upon the workpiece in response to requests that are received. The source of the requests is likely to be a human user but it could be another machine. The effects that the operation requests should have upon the workpiece are defined by the operation properties.

It follows that the constituent domains have particular characteristics:

- The workpiece is dynamic but inert (it can change but it must *be* changed) and it is also intangible.
- The operation requests (usually tantamount to the user) are also dynamic but spontaneously active and biddable. The machine can offer certain options to the user and whilst they will often respond appropriately, they may not.
- The machine itself is dynamic, active and, of course, programmable.

The workpiece itself constitutes a *realised* domain; it is created within (and exists only within) the machine. Whereas an information system might contain a *model* of some external reality, the workpiece *is* the reality.

The workpiece problem is by no means rare and examples include:

- draughting tools;
- computer aided software engineering (CASE) tools;
- many office utilities such as word-processors and spreadsheets;
- desk-top publishing and web-site production tools.

Once a problem has been fitted to a particular frame, we can turn to Kovitz's tables content for guidance upon the information that must be elicited and recorded in the requirements document and the specification. I will return to the matter of specification in the next chapter but the requirements document content for the workpiece problem is shown in Table 4.5.

Table 4.5

Workpiece problem – requirements document	
content	**(some) relevant techniques**
The legitimate data structure[36] of the workpiece	BNF, File map, Structure chart
Operation properties (event responses) – i.e. the effects that the required operations should have upon the workpiece	Finite state machine (FSM), Text, Decision table, Use-case

---

[36] This is the structure *as evident to the outside world*, as opposed to the way in which it might actually be stored within the application; the latter is a matter for idesign (or, possibly, a design constraint).

Recall that the requirements document contains a description of the problem domain as well as the requirements themselves. When using problem frames, the requirements are identified with the ellipse on the diagram. In this case, it is, therefore, the operation properties (event responses) that form the requirements, the rest is the problem domain description.

Exactly how these aspects might be documented is another question. Textual description can always be used but certain modelling techniques often offer advantages and the table above also indicates some of the relevant modelling techniques. These are described in Part 2 of this book and the way in which they might be applied is illustrated in the examples that follow later in this chapter.

4.5.1.6 Control frame

The control frame applies where the system, or machine, will control the behaviour of some part of the problem domain in accordance with a prescribed set of behaviour rules. There are two variations upon this theme, the required behaviour frame and the, slightly more complex, commanded behaviour frame.

Required behaviour frame

In this variation, the required behaviour of the controlled system is fully defined by a set of pre-determined behaviour rules. The frame diagram is shown in Figure 4.32.

The controlled domain is not necessarily a single part and may consist of several sub-domains. It must also exhibit some behaviour (otherwise it would not need to be controlled) and it cannot be autonomous (because that would, by definition, be uncontrollable). The remaining possibilities are reactive, programmable or biddable.

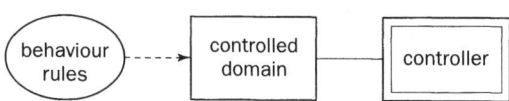

Figure 4.32

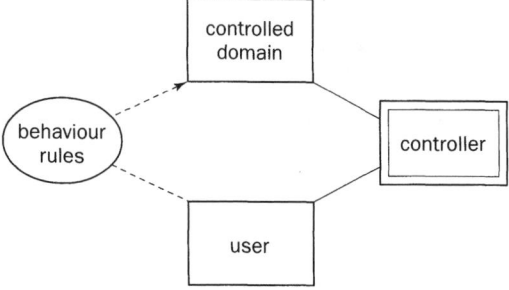

Figure 4.33

Commanded behaviour frame

In this variation, the required behaviour is commanded by a user rather than being fully determined by pre-defined rules. The user is assumed to be a spontaneous, autonomous domain that issues commands as they please. (They may, in fact, be responding to cues provided by the system (i.e. they are biddable) but that is ignored in this frame.) The frame diagram is shown in Figure 4.33. The behaviour rules (represented by the ellipse) constrain the commands that the operator can issue and define the resultant behaviour of the controlled system.

Control problems are also common and examples include:

- a lift (elevator) control system (as per the example in Chapter 16);
- the engine-management system as used in modern automobiles;
- a system for environmental control of a greenhouse;
- a security or fire alarm system.

The first two and, probably, the third of these are commanded behaviour systems; the last could (in the absence of further details) be a required behaviour system. The decision may not always be clear cut. Take, for example, an automatic dish washer. There is a user and they can select which programme to run but that is all; once that is done, the machine's operation is pre-determined. In such a case, the required behaviour frame may well be deemed more appropriate; it is, as usual, a case of deciding what is significant.

In either case, we can turn to Kovitz's tables for guidance upon the information that must be elicited and recorded in the requirements document (see Table 4.6). (And again, the way in which these aspects might be documented is examined in more detail later).

Here, it is the behaviour rules that constitute the requirements – the rest is the problem domain description.

Note also that whilst the controlled domain is often tangible, it need not be. It is quite possible to have a system controlling a virtual machine such as, for example, a computer or a telephone exchange.

4.5.1.7   Information system frame

Information systems exist in order to provide information about some part of the problem domain and are extremely common, but have nonetheless, in the past, been poorly understood. There are two variations upon the information system frame; the first, slightly simpler, version is where the system supplies information automatically (often continually). The problem frame is shown in Figure 4.34. This diagram shows that, according to some defined information function, the information system provides information (reports) about some part of the 'real world'.

In the second variation (Figure 4.35) information is supplied in response to specific requests. This diagram shows that the information system uses information about some part of the 'real world' to provide answers to information requests according to some defined information function.

Table 4.6

Control problem – requirements document	
content	**(some) relevant techniques**
Data model for relevant sub-domains in the controlled domain, if any (note, *optional*)	ERD and DD
The characteristics and *innate* behaviour of *each* sub-domain in the controlled domain, including the causal laws and the actions/events that the sub-domains can perform/undergo	Text, ELH, FSM, Decision table
Shared phenomena through which the solution system can monitor the controlled domain	Text (event list)
Actions in the controlled domain that the solution system will be capable of initiating	Text (action list)
Distortions and delays introduced by any connection domain (that is too trivial to document separately)	Text
Behaviour rules (i.e. how the controlled domain as a whole should be *made* to behave) and, for commanded behaviour, valid commands	Text, FSM, Decision table

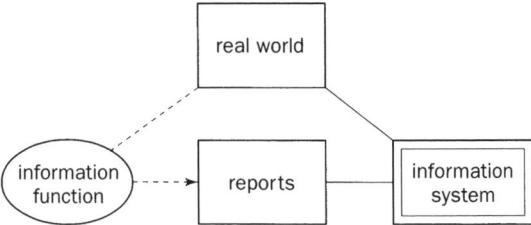

Figure 4.34

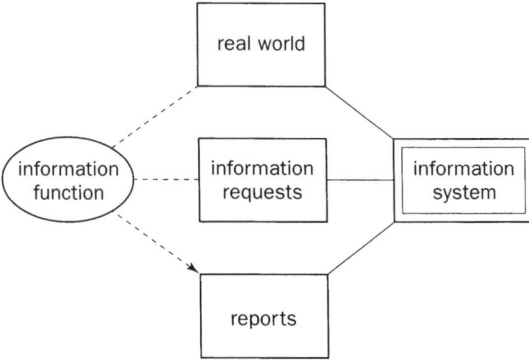

Figure 4.35

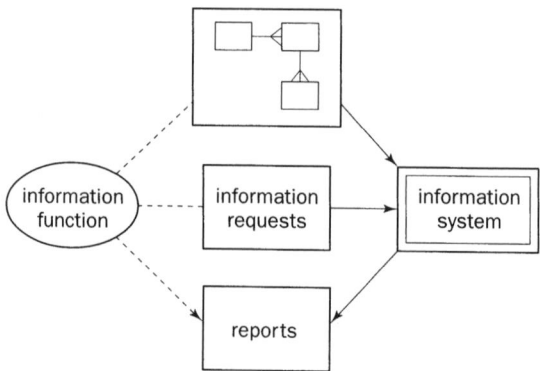

Figure 4.36

Since, by definition, an information system deals with data, in either case, the part of the 'real world' of interest consists of entities. These can be repres- ented by a data model (often in the form of an ERD) and may be shown within the 'real world' sub-domain box. Further, it can be deduced that the lines (showing the relationships) on the right of this problem domain are actually uni-directional data flows. (Whereas those on the left represent logical relation- ships.) Such considerations could be incorporated into the diagram as shown in Figure 4.36.

As has now been highlighted, for the request driven information system there are two, fundamentally distinct, types of input:

- updates about the state of the problem domain;

- requests for information about that problem domain.

Whilst these are shown as two separate lines in the problem frame diagram, this implies little about the *source* of these data. It may well be the case that both come from the *same* source[37] (as, for example, in the YRR case study where the user will enter details of boats, races, etc., and also request the output of race results).

It is possible for the 'real world' part of the problem domain to be a static domain and, again, the CD-ROM encyclopaedia provides an example. However, as previously indicated, the domain to be reported upon is more often dynamic and, importantly, always autonomous. Note that, as opposed to the control system, the information system exerts *no control over the problem domain* (only over any model of the problem domain that it contains).

Sometimes, the relevant part of the problem domain is intangible and exists within the same machine as the solution system. It is then possible for the

---

[37] And this is one of the problems with context diagrams; the two are easily muddled.

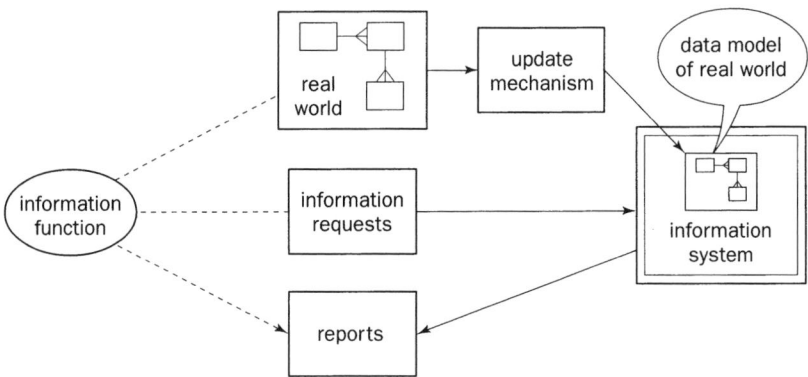

Figure 4.37

machine to access reality directly and report upon its state. This is the case with the CD-ROM encyclopaedia but it can also apply to dynamic domains and an example would be where a system is required to report upon the status of, say, workpieces or some intangible controlled domain such as the job queue controlled by a computer's operating system.

More often, the relevant part of the problem domain is not directly accessible to the information system and then it is usual for the information system to *contain a model* of the relevant part of the problem domain and use that model as the immediate source of information[38]. Clearly there must then be a mechanism to maintain correspondence between the problem domain and its model. A further elaboration of the information system problem frame (Figure 4.37) may help emphasise this important point.

Where the update mechanism is anything other than straightforward, it is probably best to model it explicitly as a connection domain (see Section 4.5.1.9).

Examples of information systems include:

- the YRR problem (as described in Chapter 15);
- a student records system in a university;
- many financial applications;
- an air traffic control support system (which, despite the name, does not control air traffic but simply reports upon it).

The requirements document content guidelines for the information system are shown in Table 4.7. In this case, it is the *information function* that represent the requirements, the rest is the problem domain description.

---

[38] Confusion between the problem domain and its model is, unfortunately, commonplace; see Section 2.9 for more on this.

Table 4.7

Information problem – requirements document	
content	**(some) relevant techniques**
The data model for the sub-domains (entities) in the problem domain that must be reported upon (includes their attributes and relationships)	ERD and DD
The characteristics of *each* problem sub-domain including all problem domain events that change the state of the problem domain (and hence the results of queries) and all possible sequences in which those events can occur	Text, Event list and ELH
How the system can access the state of the relevant sub-domains and events in the problem domain. (Or, for a static information system, how the software developers can access them.)	Text
Distortions and delays introduced by any connection domain (that is too trivial to document separately)	Text
Where initialisation data are to be extracted from pre-existing files, the relevant formats and access procedures (hopefully, by reference to pre-existing documentation)	File maps, Structure charts, BNF
The information function; i.e. the required reports and their relationship to the state of the real world and, where relevant, the queries to be supported	Drawings, Text, Tables

In addition to the above, it is common practice also to include a model of the data to be stored, about the problem domain, *within the solution system.* (As explained in Section 2.9, this may appear similar to, but is quite distinct from, the data of the problem domain itself.) Whilst common, this is somewhat controversial; development of the solution system data model could well be deferred to the specification stage or, even, idesign.

There is sometimes potential for confusion between information problems and workpiece problems. Take, for example, a machine-based telephone directory (as is commonly stored in a mobile phone). Are the data stored about people and their telephone numbers a model of some real-world domain (it does, after all, represent real people and real telephone numbers) or is it simply a workpiece document (a realised domain) that is stored within the machine and can be edited by the user?

The difference may appear subtle but it can be critical. Not perhaps in this example (where any mismatch between reality and the model will simply result in a wrong or unobtainable number) but it is now common to adopt realised

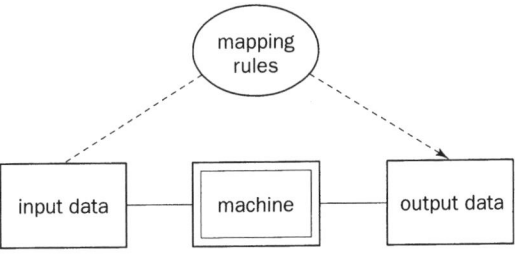

Figure 4.38

financial domains. Early, computerised, financial systems provided a convenient way of storing and manipulating data but they were only models of the relevant paper-based systems. It was the paper (such as invoices and cheques) that was the real, legally binding documentation. Often, that is no longer the case. Organisations have agreed that the 'oracle' is now the computerised records. What used to be an information problem has been replaced by a workpiece problem.

4.5.1.8   Transformation problem frame

This frame shown in Figure 4.38 models the problem where the system must transform input data in a particular format into output data in some corresponding, particular format. The machine does not, of course, change the input data; indeed, it is required that the input data domain is static. The output data domain is changed only by the machine and is, therefore, inert.

Direct access by the machine also implies that both input and output domains are intangible but, although this is the simplest case, tangible input domains may be accommodated if suitable connection domains are interposed. For example, a scanner (the connection domain) would allow hard copy documents to be read and then converted into a text file. This, an optical character recognition (OCR) machine, is just one example of this large class of problem which also includes:

- the drill file transformation program (as described in Chapter 17);
- an application to produce pictures from body scanner data;
- a program to calculate wages from time-sheets and pay-scales;
- a program to produce bank statements from lists of transactions.

The requirements document content guidelines for the transformation system are given in Table 4.8. Here the *mapping* between input and output represents the requirements – the rest is the problem domain description.

The transformation frame is also known as the JSP frame because there is a solution method (i.e. a method for tackling the idesign) for this type of problem and the method was invented by Michael Jackson (1975) and is called Jackson Structured Programming (JSP). You may well have heard of it but you may not have fully appreciated what type of problem it addressed.

Table 4.8

Transformation problem – requirements document	
content	**(some) relevant techniques**
Input and output data sets	DD (BNF), structure charts
Source and destination for data	Text
Mapping between input and output	Text, mapping table, structure charts

The solution method, JSP, places further tight conditions upon the nature of the input and output domains. Essentially, both must be sequential and must be definable by regular expressions. The mapping rules must also be relatively straightforward and these conditions may well preclude some problems (for example, the OCR problem mentioned above). However, it is only the solution method that is affected and that is not of immediate concern here; the elicitation and documentation guidelines still stand.

4.5.1.9 Connection frames

The connection frame applies where we must maintain correspondence between sub-domains that are not directly connected. Life would simpler if there could always be a direct connection (i.e. shared phenomena) between the two domains but, often, this is simply impossible.

Even so, we can sometimes choose to ignore the connection domain on the basis that we can live with the distortion that it introduces. But where we cannot (and we should always err on the side of caution) the connection domain should be explicitly explored. The nature of the shared phenomena and the achievable correspondence between the connected domains must be defined.

Generally, this arises as part of a larger problem, for example, where an information system needs to collect information about the problem domain or where a control system must be connected to the things that it controls. It is, therefore, often the case that one end of the connection machine connects to another machine that must also be built.

There are at least two versions of the connection problem and the first applies where you, the requirements engineer, have the option to edesign the connection domain. A typical example is where an information system relies upon human user input to maintain its view of the problem domain. The HMI is, then, the connecting machine that must be produced. Figure 4.39 illustrates this problem frame. The abbreviations RC and CM represent, respectively, the shared phenomena between Reality and the Connection domain and the Connection domain and the Machine. (These shared phenomena always exist between interacting domains but are not usually explicitly shown.)

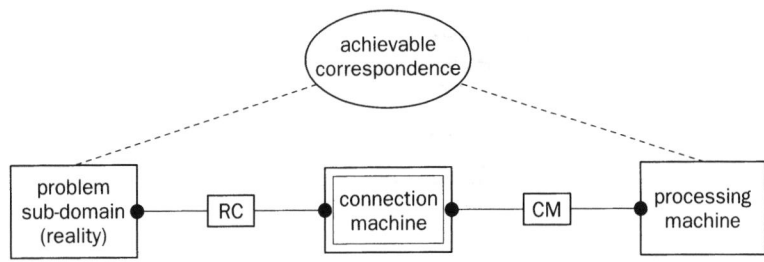

Figure 4.39

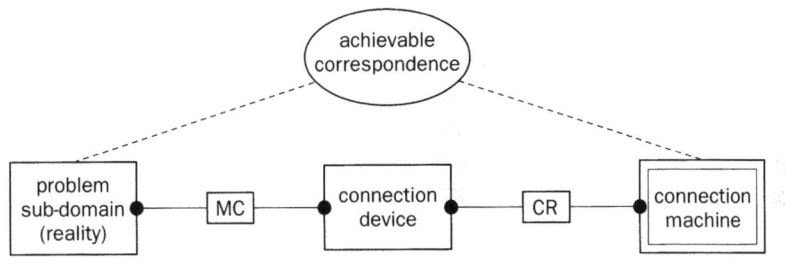

Figure 4.40

An alternative scenario is where the connecting domain is a given (e.g. sensors or actuators) that the machine must accommodate. This may be modelled as shown in Figure 4.40. An example of this kind would be a patient-monitoring system, which tracks a patient's temperature. The patient (and their temperature) composes the relevant part (sub-domain) of the problem domain and a thermocouple, say, is the connection device. The shared phenomenon (MC) between the patient and the thermocouple would be their (common) temperature; the shared phenomenon (CR) between the thermocouple and the monitoring machine would be, say, a voltage. Knowing the characteristics of the relevant part of the problem domain *and* the connection device, the connection machine can be designed to accommodate imperfections and detect, and even correct, errors that are introduced by the connection domain. For example, if the thermocouple were to indicate a temperature outside the possible human body temperature range or indicate an impossibly fast rate of change, the connection machine could flag a sensor failure. Note that if we had not identified the connection domain as such, but had treated the thermocouple as the reality, this would have been impossible.

In this scenario, the relevant part of the problem domain and the connection device are tangible, autonomous domains and the machine is, as usual, programmable. Connection problems are, however, somewhat variable and so the checklist (Table 4.9) must be regarded more flexibly. Here, it is the *desired mapping* that represents the requirements – the rest is the problem domain description.

Table 4.9

Connection problem – requirements document	
content	**(some) relevant techniques**
Relevant states and events in the problem domain	Event list, FSM
Redundancy (if any) in problem domain data (and, where there is redundancy, the rules for determining the most reliable data)	Text, Decision table
Information mapping introduced by any existing connection devices (including any distortion and delay)	Concurrent FSM, Text, Mapping table, Decision table
Desired mapping, to be effected between the connected domains	Concurrent FSM, Text, Mapping table, Decision table

Table 4.10

Frame	Sub-domain	Static	Inert	Reactive	Programmable	Biddable	Autonomous
Workpiece	Operation requests					✓	
	Workpiece		✓				
Control	Controlled domain			✓	✓	✓	
Information	Reality	✓					✓
	Requests					✓	
	Outputs		✓				
Transformation	Input	✓					
	Output		✓				
Connection	Connection device				✓		
	Reality				✓	✓	✓

4.5.2 Summary of required sub-domain properties

Table 4.10 summarises the properties that the key sub-domains must exhibit in order to fit properly the relevant problem frame. (More than one entry in a row indicates alternative options.)

4.5.3 Multi-frame problems

There is a snag with all this. Many real-life application domains pose complex problems; treating them as simple problems is unrealistic and likely to fail. The key to complex problems is to separate or decompose them into a number of simpler problems which, separately, are less challenging; what might be termed the 'divide and conquer' strategy.

One of the strengths of the problem frame approach is the rational basis (lacking in other approaches to analysis) that it provides for such problem decomposition. We proceed by recognising elements of the problem that fit simple problem frames. Some part of the problem will fit one frame but other parts will fit a different frame. Unless we are tackling two completely separate problems (which is possible and straightforward, just handle them independently) there will then be some overlap or commonality between the various frames. This is the multi-frame problem. (Note, in passing, that there is no guarantee that all useful, simple problem frames have, so far, been identified; you might discover a new one!)

The lift controller problem was previously presented as an example of a control problem. This covers the bulk of it but there is also an information system aspect in that the indicators report upon the positions of the lifts and at least one potential connection problem in that the button press signals take time to stabilise and may require 'de-bouncing'[39].

It is perhaps possible for a system to consist of two problem frames of the same type (maybe an information system could report upon two, separate realities) but, for analysis purposes, these may well be dealt with separately. So, if such combinations are ignored (and assuming for now that there *are* only five frames!) there are 10 possible dual-frame problems (see Table 4.11).

At the time of writing, it is unclear whether a multi-frame problem is best depicted using a single, composite frame diagram or whether the associated, simple frames should be depicted separately (with the common sub-domains being identified just by their matching labels). Kovitz (1999) takes the first

Table 4.11

	workpiece	information	control	transformation	connection
workpiece					
information	✓				
control	✓	✓			
transformation	✓	✓	✓		
connection	✓	✓	✓	✓	

---

[39] When an electrical switch closes, it takes time for the change in voltage to stabilise. Unless precautions are taken, a single closure may be interpreted as a multiple closure.

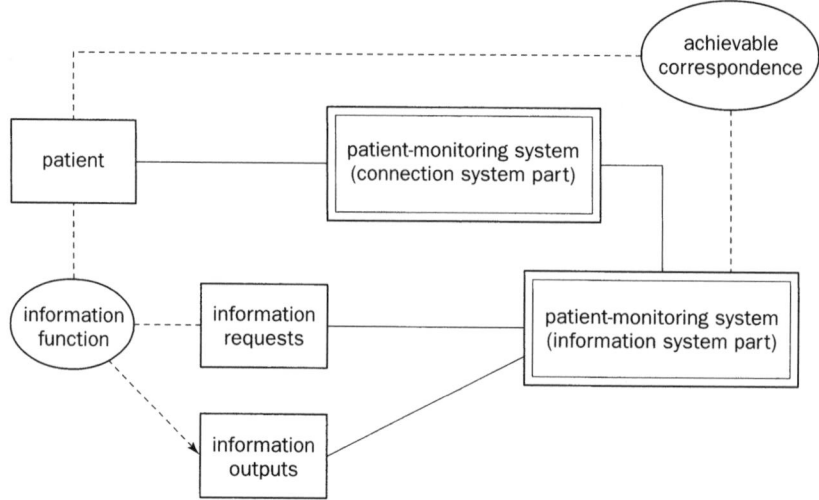

Figure 4.41

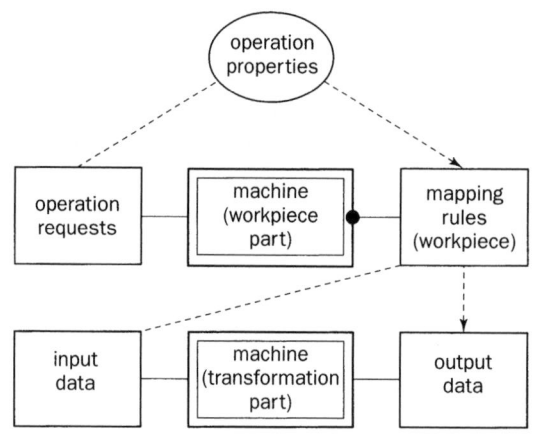

Figure 4.42

approach and Jackson (2001) the second. There follow examples of a few of the most likely combinations, for which I have opted to use composite frame diagrams. In each case, you may care to consider how these would appear if fully separated.

The first situation explicitly models the connection domain which updates an information system's model of reality. Figure 4.41 shows, as an example, the patient-monitoring system alluded to earlier.

Another combination that can be envisioned is where it is required that a transformation system has editable mapping rules. The mapping rules then become a workpiece and the combined problem frame could be pictured as in Figure 4.42.

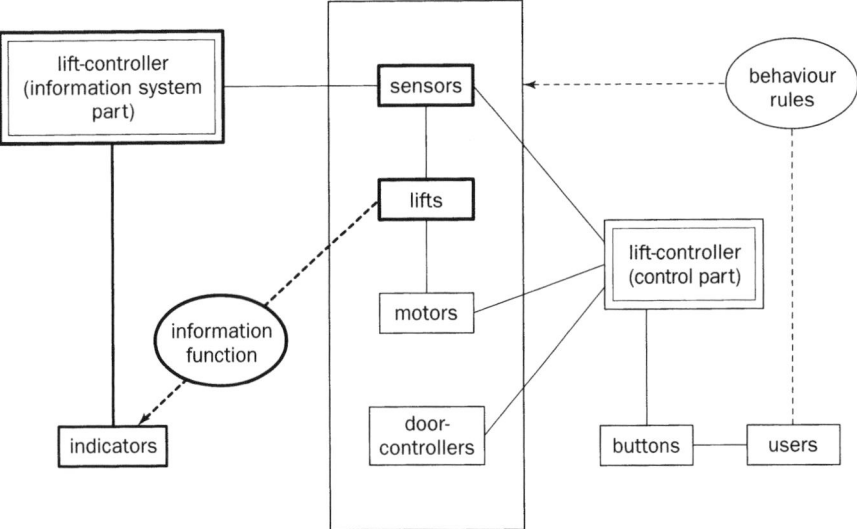

Figure 4.43

The lift control system can be revisited and the information system part (reporting upon the lift position) can be shown explicitly as in Figure 4.43.

The elements of the information system have been highlighted to aid identification but a little explanation may still be needed. The indicators correspond to the information outputs but the information requests are omitted as output is automatic and continuous. The information function, as usual, defines the required relationship between the problem domain and the output and finds expression in one of the requirements:

R15 **For each lift, one indicator at a time should be illuminated, that being the one for the floor that the lift is (approximately) nearest to.**

There is one other complication in that the information system does not (as is often the case) have direct access to the domain upon which it must report (i.e. the lifts). So, there is a connection domain via the sensors. This could be explicitly modelled and would make this a three-frame problem but, for fear of over-complicating the diagram, this has not been shown in this case.

The Petri net tool (see Chapter 18) provides the final example (see Figure 4.44); a workpiece frame (which provides for editing of nets) combined with a commanded behaviour control frame (which provides for execution of the nets).

Excluding combinations with replicated frame types, there are also 10 possible three-frame problems but only five four-frame problems and, of course, only one with all five frames. It seems likely that some of these are relatively rare and, in any case, their investigation will be left to others!

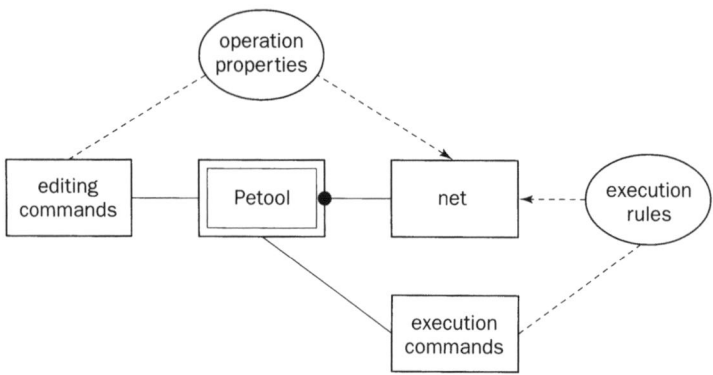

Figure 4.44

4.5.4   The application of problem frames

A straightforward strategy for applying the problem frame approach can be suggested:

- Abstract the problem domain:
  - identify the sub-domains;
  - identify sub-domain interactions (in terms of shared phenomena);
  - characterise each sub-domain;
  - generate a(n extended) context diagram.
- Recognise relevant, standard frame(s)[40].
- Fit frames to the problem (as best we can).
- Use Kovitz's table(s) (see Sections 4.5.1.5 *et seq*) for the relevant frame(s) to guide further analysis and documentation.

These steps are presented in the obvious order but there is likely to be considerable overlap and iteration.

The examples that follow in Sections 4.5.7.1 *et seq.* illustrate how this can work in practice.

4.5.5   Problem frames; summary

Problem frames model the problem domain as a set of inter-related sub-domains for the purpose of characterising the problem. They are a development of the context diagram that provides for a much tighter fit between the model and the particular problem.

As part of PDOA, problem frames offer certain advantages:

- They encourage an early focus upon the problem domain and the requirements (as opposed to any pre-existing system or the solution system).

---

[40] At least for single frame problems, there is evidence that, given only limited experience, this is not too difficult (Phalp and Cox, 2000).

- They help to identify the *type* of problem domain with which we are dealing. (A context diagram simply does not do this; the context diagram of *any* system will look much the same.)
- They accommodate those relationships between domains that actually constitute the requirements. (And identifying requirements is, after all, a primary concern of requirements engineering.)
- They allow specific guidance upon handling each type of problem.

4.5.6 Problem domain oriented analysis beyond problem framing

There is more to PDOA than problem frames although much of the remainder has already been, at the least, implied. Abstracting the problem domain as one or more problem frames identifies the pertinent sub-domains and, as indicated, provides (via Kovitz's tables) guidelines for those aspects of the sub-domains that require investigation and description.

There is no new technology required here; various, well established modelling techniques are suggested for the description of the indicated aspects. In addition, it is freely acknowledged that text provides the best (if not the only) means for documenting certain aspects of the problem domain and, generally, for the definition of the requirements.

A description of the relevant modelling techniques and guidance upon the usage of text are provided in Part 2 and Section 4.8.3 provides general guidance upon the content of a (heavily PDOA biased) requirements document. However, the latter is quite variable and so, as with the other approaches, further guidance on PDOA is probably best provided by examples; the application of PDOA to the various case studies will, therefore, now be presented.

4.5.7 Problem domain oriented analysis: examples

The full documentation for the case studies is presented in Chapters 15 to 18, each of which includes a PDOA type requirements document. This section presents some illustrative extracts together with commentary upon the analysis process.

Note that, whilst each element of the documentation is presented in turn, this does *not* represent any particular order in which they should be developed. Indeed, it is far more likely that the various elements will be developed concurrently. The elicitation notes, and other sources, provide information in a fairly haphazard order. If, whilst searching for entities (in order to construct a data model), one comes across, say, a requirement, it may be as well to insert that into an embryonic requirements list before continuing the entity search.

4.5.7.1 Case 1, the yacht race results (YRR) program

This problem is readily identified as an information problem; the main purpose of the required system is the production of reports upon the results of yacht races. A problem frame diagram can be produced but it is a perfectly standard one (and can be seen in Section 15.3.1.2) and so I will take that as read. (In passing, it can be noted that a context diagram (as on p. 64) could have been produced but it is really not of much use.)

Kovitz's (1999) requirements document content guidelines for the information system (Table 4.12) now points the way ahead. It is not necessary to address the items in this table in any particular order; indeed, there is likely to be some parallel development. Nonetheless, for the purposes of this section, the table provides a convenient sequence.

So we start by developing a model of the problem domain data (which are, of course, central to all information problems). The resultant ERD (Figure 4.45)

Table 4.12

Information problem – requirements document	
content	**(some) relevant techniques**
The data model for the sub-domains (entities) in the problem domain that must be reported upon (includes their attributes and relationships)	ERD and DD
The characteristics of *each* problem sub-domain including all problem domain events that change the state of the problem domain (and hence the results of queries) and all possible sequences in which those events can occur	Text, Event list and ELH
How the system can access the state of the relevant sub-domains and events in the problem domain. (Or, for a static information system, how the software developers can access them.)	Text
Distortions and delays introduced by any connection domain (that is too trivial to document separately)	Text
Where initialisation data are to be extracted from pre-existing files, the relevant formats and access procedures (hopefully, by reference to pre-existing documentation)	File maps, Structure charts, BNF
The queries to be supported and the relevant responses	Drawings, Text, Tables

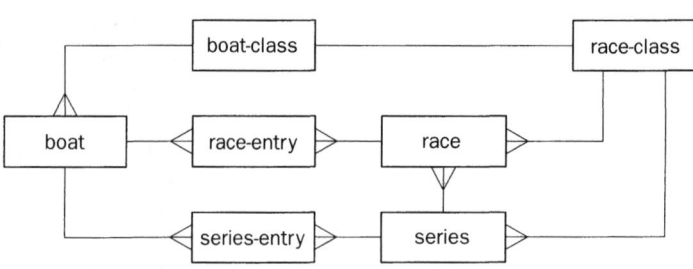

Figure 4.45

would be no different from that which could have been developed by 'traditional' approaches.

This ERD should be accompanied by a DD which defines the attributes of the entities. This also would be very similar to a conventional DD and here is a small extract:

boat-class	::= boat-class-name, handicap;
handicap	::= handicap-type, handicap-value;
handicap-type	::= "PY" | "TMF";
handicap-value	::= ^{3}{digit}^{4};

However, there were some complications that arose during this data analysis, particularly concerning the nature of boat and race classes. The ERD does not explain the semantics of these (or any other entities) and even the accompanying DD does fully address the problem. However, the second item in Kovitz's content table (Table 4.12) requires that each sub-domain be fully described and it is here that all can be made clear. There follow examples of possible entries for classes and handicaps.

Classes

Within yacht racing, the term 'class' is used loosely. There are actually two meanings:

A boat class is a type of boat (all boats of the same class are, within specified limits, the same). Each boat class will have a:

- boat class name
- handicap type
- handicap value

A race class indicates the types of boat that may enter a race. Races are either one-design or handicap. In one-design, all competing boats are of the same boat class and the race class name *will be* a boat class. In handicap races, different boat classes may enter and the race class name will not be the same as any boat class.

Each race class will have:

- a race class type ('one-design' or 'handicap')
- a race class name

and, for handicap race classes only, a:

- handicap type
- minimum handicap
- maximum handicap

Handicaps

Handicaps are used to adjust race times (see race result calculation, below). There are two handicap systems; PY and TMF. For each, any boat may have a handicap value.

▶

PY handicap values consist of a 4-digit integer and the corrected time is defined as:

corrected time ::= elapsed time x 1000 / PY handicap value

TMF handicap values consist of a 3-digit decimal (e.g. .977) and the corrected time is defined as:

corrected time ::= elapsed time x TMF handicap value

In either case, the corrected time is rounded to the nearest second (.5 is rounded up).

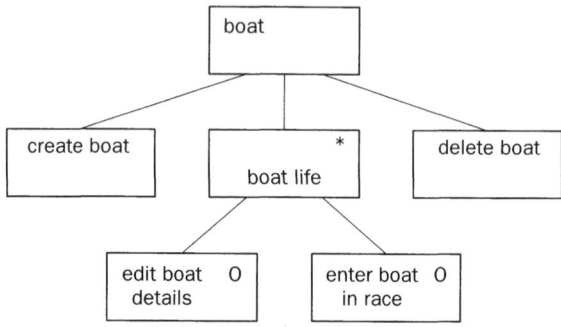

Figure 4.46

As indicated by Table 4.12, it is also possible to produce ELHs for the various entities. In this case, they are mostly trivial but Figure 4.46 gives an illustration for the boat entity.

The next point to address is the way in which the system can access the necessary information about the problem domain. In this case it is very simple; all information is entered by the user and a statement to that effect will suffice. It may also be adjudged that, for this system, there are no significant distortions or delays introduced by this update mechanism.

If it were the case that some pre-existing electronically stored data (for example, a database of boats and handicaps) were to be initially loaded into the system, then the way in which such data may be accessed would have to be detailed. However, I will assume that that does not apply here.

Finally, it is necessary to record the actual requirements. Section 4.6 has a little more to say about this (and the full set are given in Chapter 15) but, just to convey the flavour, here are a few examples for the YRR system:

R3 A boat may only be entered into a one design race (or series) if its boat class matches the race class.

R4 A boat may only be entered into a handicap race (or series) if its handicap type matches that of the race and its handicap value is within the (inclusive) range specified by the minimum and maximum handicap values.

R5 A boat that enters a series is automatically entered into every race in the series.

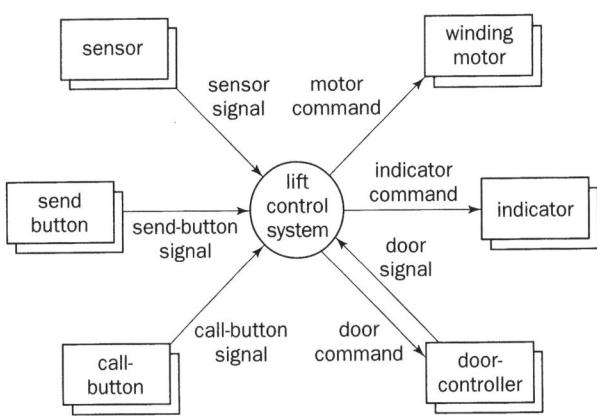

Figure 4.47

Clearly, this requirements document is rather different from that produced by the 'traditional' methods (as shown earlier). It gives far less, if any, indication of how the problem might be solved[41] but it gives far more information about the nature of the problem.

As per normal validation practice (see Chapter 6), there would have been a lot of checking back with the client (and any other information sources) during this stage and, before proceeding further, final approval of the requirements document should be sought.

The next step is the specification of the system behaviour that will produce the required effects in the problem domain (i.e. meet the requirements). A suitable system behaviour must be edesigned and documented but that is the subject of the next chapter.

4.5.7.2   Case 2, the lift controller

For PDOA, the problem domain is always the starting point. Let us assume that the new system is being commissioned by a lift manufacturer who wishes to acquire a new, software-based control system for a model of lift that is based upon pre-designed hardware.

Some initial insight might be gained with a context diagram as shown in Figure 4.47 (although, as noted earlier, this does omit certain problem sub-domains (such as the lift) which do not directly interface with the controller).

Working from the initial elicitation notes (which can be seen in Section 16.1) it should be possible to identify most, if not all, of the relevant problem sub-domains and, either via the context diagram or directly, develop a problem frame model as shown in Figure 4.48. (This is a little different from Figure 4.43

---

[41] Although for certain problem types there are known solution methods, see Section 4.5.1.1.

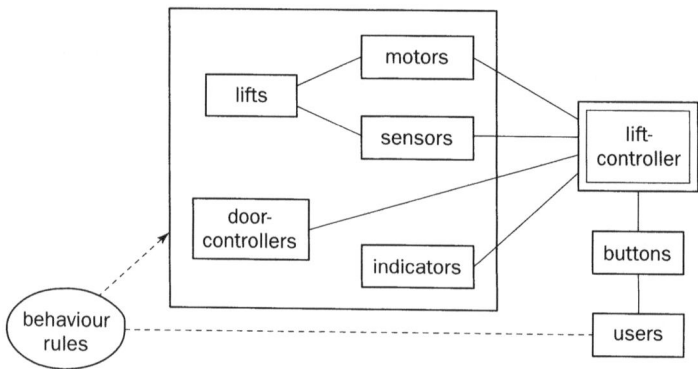

Figure 4.48

in Section 4.5.3 as the small information system aspect has not been modelled separately.)

Note how this model accurately reflects the elicited facts such as there being a connection between the lift controller (the machine) and the motors and the sensors but not, directly, with the lifts. It is also possible to check that the various problem sub-domains exhibit the correct properties (as per Section 4.5.2). In this case, the users are biddable and the other sub-domains are reactive or programmable which, for a controlled domain, is fine.

(In passing, also note that the problem (and the problem frame) would be very different if the lift hardware were not pre-defined and we were tackling the requirements engineering for a complete lift system. In that case, the problem is about moving people vertically within a building and even the fact that a lift must be used is really just a design constraint. The problem domain would include the potential users (and facts about them such as their size, weight, acceptable vertical acceleration, acceptable rate of air pressure change, speed of movement, etc.), the building (number of floors, etc.) and the anticipated traffic rates but not much else. It would still be a control problem but the things that would be controlled would be the users!)

Having identified this as a control problem[42] we can now turn to the relevant guideline (see Table 4.13) to see what aspects of the problem domain are relevant and, also, which modelling techniques, if any, are likely to prove useful. Using this table for guidance, further elicitation now proceeds. Note that the table need not be followed too rigidly; it is only for guidance, and it may well be appropriate to shuffle the order of items and, perhaps, combine some

---

[42] Arguably, there are some information system aspects to this problem. The indicators 'report upon' lift positions and the system indirectly 'reports upon' the number of lifts and the number of floors in the building. However, for present purposes, this will be regarded as insignificant as will any connection domains.

Table 4.13

Control problem – requirements document	
content	(some) relevant techniques
Data model for relevant sub-domains in the controlled domain, if any (note, *optional*)	ERD and DD
The characteristics and *innate* behaviour of *each* sub-domain in the controlled domain, including the causal laws and the actions/events that the sub-domains can perform/undergo	Text, ELH, FSM, Decision table
Shared phenomena through which the solution system can monitor the controlled domain	Text (event list)
Actions in the controlled domain that the solution system will be capable of initiating	Text (action list)
Distortions and delays introduced by any connection domain (that is too trivial to document separately)	Text
Behaviour rules (i.e. how the controlled domain as a whole should be *made* to behave)	Text, FSM, Decision table

elements. However, for illustrative purposes, an example of how each entry in the above table might be addressed follows (and the full document is given in Section 16.2).

The data model (which can be seen on p. 362) is a perfectly 'ordinary' one such as was produced using structured analysis and it can conveniently be recorded using an ERD. In addition to the elements of the controlled domain, it includes the entities building, floor and lift shaft since, although these cannot in any sense be controlled, the system will need to 'know' information about them (e.g. how many lift shafts there are).

Next, attention can focus upon the description of the problem sub-domains. Perhaps the trickiest question here is what information should be recorded and this is best answered by thinking about what the system developers will need to know. The lift winding motors prove to be amongst the most complex sub-domains and might be described thus:

Winding motors
Winding motors each have three control lines; slow, fast and polarity – which operate as per the decision table (Table 4.14).

In fast mode, the motor moves the lift at 1.2 m/sec (+/– 10%); in slow mode, at 0.3 m/sec (+/– 10%). The motor mechanism itself ensures a gradual acceleration and deceleration as per Table 4.15.

Table 4.14

	slow							
	hi				lo			
fast	hi		lo		hi		lo	
polarity	hi	lo	hi	lo	hi	lo	hi	lo
wind up fast	✓				✓			
wind down fast		✓				✓		
wind up slow			✓					
wind down slow				✓				
stop							✓	✓

Table 4.15

	time	distance
rest to fast	2 sec	1.2 m
fast to slow	1 sec	0.75 m
slow to rest	1 sec	0.15 m

(All figures are subject to a tolerance of +/– 20%.)

As can be seen, here, most of the necessary information is succinctly recorded using decision tables but suitable techniques must be selected in each case.

Probably alongside the development of the problem sub-domain descriptions, the shared phenomena (between the problem domain and the solution system) can be identified and documented. Such events include button-presses and sending signals to the motors and doors. These may be tabulated, for example, as shown in Tables 4.16 and 4.17.

Table 4.16

Events
call-button-press
send-button-press
at-floor(f)-sensor signal
etc.

Table 4.17

Actions
set-motor(l)-slow hi
set-motor(l)-fast hi
set-indicator(f) hi
etc.

The next matter for attention is any distortions and delays in the connection between the problem domain and the solution system. In this case, the stabilisation of signals is a matter of concern but a simple statement can be used:

> All input signals (i.e. from the terminators to the control system) may take up to 10 milliseconds to stabilise within the specified ranges.

Finally, it is necessary to record the actual requirements. Section 4.6 has a little more to say about this but, just to convey the flavour, here are a few examples for the lift system:

R1 The lift is never to be allowed to move above the top floor or below the bottom floor. (There is an emergency shut down system that will stop the motor if the lift goes above the top floor or below the bottom floor (by more than 10 cm) but this shut down system is beyond the scope of the control system.)

R2 The lift is not to be stopped from fast mode but should always be switched to slow mode for at least 1 second before stopping.

R3 The motor polarity is not to be changed whilst the lift is moving. (This could wreck the winding gear.)

R4 The lift is never to be moved with the doors open.

R5 With the stop delay correctly configured (as below) the lift will stop within +/– 1.5 cm of the floor being serviced.

As for the previous example, this requirements (analysis) document is different from that produced by the 'traditional' methods. It focuses entirely upon describing the problem domain and stating the requirements. Also as before, the analysis would be subject to validation before proceeding to the specification stage (described in the next chapter).

4.5.7.3 Case 3, the F2K drill file translator

From an initial appraisal, it is evident that this is a simple transformation problem. We may therefore proceed immediately to a problem frame diagram (Figure 4.49) and an assessment of the problem sub-domain types (as summarised in Section 4.5.2) can be used to confirm the fit of the problem frame.

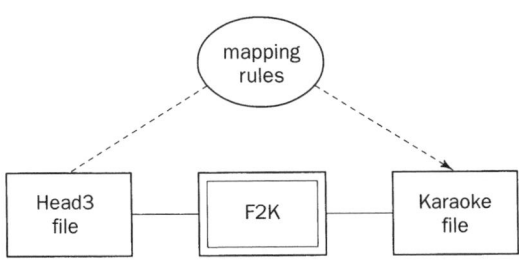

Figure 4.49

Table 4.18

Transformation problem – requirements document	
content	(some) relevant techniques
Input and output data sets	Data dictionary (BNF), (Jackson) structure charts
Source and destination for data	Text
Mapping between input and output	Text, mapping table, (Jackson) structure charts

The relevant content guidelines table (Table 4.18) can then be consulted.

This is (as it appears) relatively straightforward. The valid syntax of the input and output data sets must be defined and, using BNF, say, would be along these lines:

HEAD3-file   ::= Hheader, ^{1}{Hcommand};
Hheader   ::= Hboard-name, Hversion, Hdate, offset-x, offset-y,
                         Hcomment;
Hboard-name   ::= """", {character}^{32}, """";
Hversion   ::= ^{3}{digit}^{3};
Hdate   ::= dd, mm, yy;
offset_x   ::= coord;
. . . etc

The source and destination for the data sets may be simply stated:

The system is UNIX based, input and output being from/to UNIX files. Input and output files are both sequential text files consisting of a stream of ASCII characters. File terminators etc. are as specified in the UNIX manual (ref 1).

This only leaves the input/output mapping to be defined and, in this case, a table (Table 4.19) could be used. This mapping table constitutes the bulk of the requirements but there are a few others, mainly concerning the operator interface and performance. The full set are given in Section 17.1.3 but, just to convey the flavour, here is a small extract:

R2   Input file errors to be detected and as many errors as possible to be reported at the individual field level of detail.
R3   The program (F2K) to be invoked (from UNIX) by the operator.
R4   The operator to supply:
       the address of the input file
       the address of the output file
R5   A 50 Kb input file to be converted in less than 10 seconds.

And, for this particular problem that is about it; following validation, the requirements document can be fed into the specification task.

Table 4.19

Hfile	Kfile	Mapping rule (if not straight copy)
Hheader	Kheader	
Hboard-name	Kboard-name	
Hversion	Kversion	Insert "0" at front and "." before last 2 digits
Hdate	Kdate	Prefix H yy with "20", unless operator has indicated otherwise, in which case "19"
offset_x	offset_x	
. . . etc		

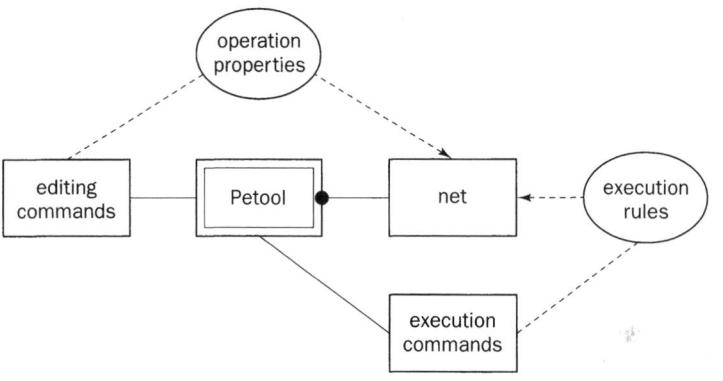

Figure 4.50

4.5.7.4   Case 4, the Petri net diagram tool

From an initial appraisal, it is evident that this is combination of a simple workpiece problem and a commanded behaviour control system (see Figure 4.50). The Petri net diagram meets the criteria for a workpiece in that it is created and exists only within the machine. Whilst the Petri net may be said to exhibit behaviour during execution, the net topology and initial marking are unaffected and thus the document meets the inertness requirement for a workpiece.

Kovitz's table for workpiece frames (p. 100) indicates that we must focus upon the legitimate data structure of the workpiece and the effects that the required operations should have upon the workpiece. For the control aspect, it is the required behaviour of Petri nets that is crucial together with the effects of the required behavioural commands (start execution, stop execution, etc.).

There is little point in launching into a full description of Petri nets; they are already well documented elsewhere and so we may proceed by referencing such

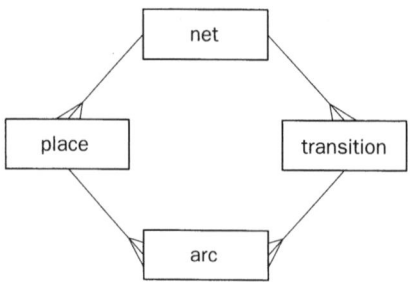

Figure 4.51

a source (for the purposes of this exercise, I will assume that the description given in Section 12.7 will suffice). We may then concentrate upon the specific variant that is required in this instance.

The required legitimate data structure of the workpiece may be described in the usual way with an ERD (Figure 4.51) and a DD.

net   ::= [net-name], file-address, cycle-time, {place}, {transition};
place   ::= [place-name], initial-token-number, current-token-number, token-capacity, overflow, {arc};
transition   ::= [trans-name], {arc};
net-name   ::= label;
. . . etc

The remaining task is the description of the required operations, commands and their effects; in other words, the requirements. For example:

R8 Places and transitions may be given attached labels.
R9 Arcs must connect a place to a transition, or vice versa (unconnected arcs are not allowed).
R10 An initial marking may be established by allocating tokens to places.
R18 It is possible to start, suspend, resume and end net execution.
R19 Execution will automatically stop when no transitions are enabled or when any place becomes full (in the latter case, all full places will be highlighted).

As can be seen, the operations (and their effects) are established at a relatively abstract level. Their detailed design (such as the precise mechanisms available to the user for attaching labels or allocating tokens) is deferred to the specification phase.

4.5.8   Problem domain oriented analysis; summary

Problem domain oriented analysis is a currently emerging approach to analysis that seeks to re-establish an early focus upon the problem domain. Via the

application of problem frames, different types of problem domains are identified and this characterisation is used to provide specific guidance as to the
aspects that require investigation and documentation and as to the modelling
and description techniques that might be applied.

There is a clear distinction between the description of the problem domain
and the requirements that must be met. The invention and definition of the
behaviour of the new solution system is kept separate and deferred to the
following, specification phase.

4.6 Writing requirements

Whatever approach is adopted for analysing and describing the problem
domain, it is also necessary to identify and record the actual requirements.
(If you need to refresh your memory, requirements and their categories are
described in some detail in Section 1.6.)

During elicitation, facts about the problem domain and requirements are
likely to be muddled together. However, they are quite distinct and their separation is one of the goals of analysis.

Most 'methods' and texts have little to say about this; indeed, elsewhere examples of requirements may be quite hard to find. There is often an implication
that requirements can somehow be embodied within models of the problem
domain or, more often, the solution system. But if we stick to the definition of
requirements as, 'the effects that the client wishes to be brought about in the
problem domain' it is hard to see how this might work.

In general, it is not possible to *model* requirements. A model might be *referenced* by a requirement, for example:

**It is required that the controlled domain behaves as per the state chart
shown below.**

but that is not quite the same thing. So, requirements must be stated and, for
this purpose, we use text.

As with the application of text in general, actually writing requirements is a
bit of an art and guidance is, perforce, quite general. Section 14.2 (use of natural
language) is highly pertinent and, beyond that, a few guidelines may be offered:

- Keep each requirement separate. Usually, each requirement can be stated in
  a single sentence. However, beware of artificially splitting a requirement;
  sometimes, it will take a paragraph or more to explain what is, essentially, a
  single requirement.

- Use modal verbs with discretion. Verbs such as 'shall', 'should' and 'must',
  generally contribute little to requirements statements. For example:

  The lift doors shall be cycled every time that a lift stops at a floor.

  seems to offer no advantage over:

  The lift doors are cycled every time that a lift stops at a floor.

- Use the present tense to state requirements. (Although, often, the future tense reads equally well. There seems little to choose between:

  All input to the system is entered by the user.
  All input to the system is to be entered by the user.

  and

  All input to the system will be entered by the user.)

- Factor out detail. For example:

  Upon command from the user, the system produces the following reports (content as defined in the data dictionary):

To the above list one might add, 'state requirements simply and clearly' but this is really stating the obvious.

So, guidelines are few and resort must, therefore, also be made to example. Numerous examples of requirements are provided in Sections 15.3.2, 16.2.2, 17.1.3 and 18.1.5. Logical ordering of requirements is also helpful and this is examined briefly in Section 4.8.3.

4.7 Summary of analysis

The following definition of analysis is proposed:

> **through study of a problem domain, the achievement of understanding of and the documentation of the characteristics of that domain and the problems (requiring solution) that exist within that domain.**

It follows that any approach to analysis should, wherever applicable, demand and facilitate description of:

- the structure of the problem domain (in terms of its sub-domains and their relationships);
- the problem domain data;
- the innate properties and behaviour of the problem sub-domains;
- significant events and phenomena within the problem domain;
- the requirements (effects that the solution system should produce within the problem domain).

Within this context, various approaches to analysis are considered.

Structured analysis, and its derivatives, have held sway for many years. Whilst the original versions were based around modelling the data flows and data structures of the problem domain (or, more often, a presumed, pre-existing solution system), modern structured analysis concentrates upon directly developing models of the solution system. The nature of the models is somewhat ambivalent, leading to a poor distinction between analysis, specification and, even, internal design.

Description of problem domain data can be quite good and, where this is significant (i.e. for information systems), a useful contribution may be made. However, other aspects are less well supported and so other types of problem are poorly addressed.

The requirements themselves are often given short shrift. The SSADM-like derivatives include a requirements list, but, generally, there is an early move to considering the way in which requirements may be *met* by the specification of a particular solution system behaviour. Such specification can be fairly implementation independent, but tends to be procedural (rather than functional).

Object oriented analysis is currently mainstream. It dictates that all systems be modelled in terms of objects but otherwise inherits much of its philosophy from structured analysis. There is usually no separation of the descriptions of the problem domain and the solution system and it delivers a high-level, design for the new, solution system. This may be accompanied by a behavioural specification in the form of use-cases.

Problem domain oriented analysis is presented as a preferred alternative which re-establishes emphasis upon the problem domain and requirements and, through problem domain classification, provides problem specific guidance to the analyst. It delivers a full description of the problem domain, a list of the requirements and, since specification is treated as a separate task (see next chapter), nothing else.

The view may be taken that PDOA is a complementary precursor to the established 'analysis' approaches.

4.8   The requirements document

The preceding examples illustrate much about the requirements document (also sometimes known as the analysis document). This section seeks to draw those examples together and add a few general observations.

Problem domain oriented analysis makes a clear distinction between documentation that relates to analysis and requirements and documentation that relates to the specification of any new, solution system. This section follows that presumption but attempts are made to indicate how the less separatist approaches (SA and OOA) can relate to this scheme.

4.8.1   Purpose of the requirements document

The primary role of the requirements document is to convey the necessary information about the problem domain and the client's requirements from the client (and associated stakeholders) to the designers[43] of the solution system. This role dictates both the style and the content of the document.

---

[43] Initially to the external designers but eventually to the internal designers as well.

4.8.2 Requirements document characteristics and style

In order to fulfil its role, the requirements document must be clearly understood by all relevant parties. To this end, it must be:

- of low ambiguity
- well organised
- complete
- consistent
- validatable
- modifiable

In part, these characteristics can be achieved through good style, which must take full account of the client and associated stakeholders. It is vital that they can check the accuracy of the information and the document must, therefore, be accessible and understandable to them.

This does not preclude the use of relatively formal descriptive and modelling techniques (as described in Chapter 8 and illustrated in some of the preceding examples). Some explanation or paraphrasing may be necessary at reviews but it is generally far easier to read and understand a well produced diagram, say, than it is to develop it in the first place. Also, it tends to be the case that where more formal techniques are useful (as, for example, in a safety critical, control system) the clients are more likely to be technically oriented.

Whatever other techniques may be used, text will play a major role and it must be well written. This book cannot address the matter of basic literacy but see Section 14.2 for some guidance.

A good, logical structure also helps a lot.

4.8.3 Requirements document content and architecture

There are, essentially, two things that the solution system designers need to know:

- what the problem domain is like – the nature of its various elements and their interactions;
- what are the requirements – what effects does the client want the new system to produce within the problem domain.

It will generally be appropriate to separate these two aspects in the document.

The problem domain is usually best introduced with a descriptive textual overview. Detail may be added with certain models, notably, a context diagram, a problem frame diagram and, where applicable, a problem domain data model.

Beyond this, we are best guided by Kovitz's content tables (see Section 4.5.1.5 *et. seq.*) which indicate, for each type of problem domain, the sub-domains and aspects of those sub-domains that are relevant. As indicated in those tables, various techniques (e.g. finite state machines) may be used to define the behaviour of sub-domains and the events that may be shared between the problem domain and any solution system.

It may also be noted that a common DD (see Section 14.5) is the best way of defining project related terminology including, of course, the various data that exist within the problem domain.

The various elements of the content help dictate the large scale architecture of the document, but it is important that a logical structure is maintained through to the detail. Tidiness is a highly desirable attribute for the requirements engineer (no groaning, please) with the relevant maxim being, a place for every thing and every thing in its place.

Requirements are normally recorded using text and, whilst there is little choice but to list them, it is generally possible to introduce some, more or less logical, ordering and, not least, to separate them by type. For multi-frame problems, it will often be appropriate to group functional requirements according to the various frames and, beyond this, there is usually some logical basis (such as time-ordering) for further organisation. Given the close relationship that often exists between requirements and the corresponding functions of the solution system (see Section 5.2), the structuring guidelines given in Section 5.4.4.2 may be of relevance here.

The requirements generally dictate (at least logically) the required output from the solution system and the detail of this is often best covered as additions to the DD. (For example, a requirement for the yacht racing results is that it produce a report upon the result of any selected race; the logical content of that report can be defined in the DD.)

In the light of the foregoing, a generic content for the requirements document may be put forward:

Document details (title, authority, revision history, etc.)
Problem domain description
> **Overview** (text + context diagram, problem frame(s), data model)
> **Sub-domains** – their characteristics, behaviour, etc. (generally the largest section but highly problem dependent – see Kovitz's tables (p. 96))

Requirements (generally, as text – see Section 4.6)
> **Functional requirements**
> **Performance requirements**
>> Speed
>> Capacity
>> Reliability
>> Usability
>> (etc.)
> **Design constraints**
> (plus any other relevant requirements categories, e.g. Preferences)

Data dictionary
References (to related documents – e.g. a specification for a problem sub-domain)

In addition to the above, it is sometimes appropriate to include the *reasons* for requirements (or, indeed, for the entire development). Often this is self-evident but, where it is not, the additional information may provide useful guidance to the designers when they are considering the various options and trade-offs that they face.

The content of the main sections of the document has already been described in detail but some of the other sections merit a little scrutiny.

4.8.3.1 Document details

As per any technical document, this section contains such information as:

- title
- authors
- documentation conventions/standards
- version
- change authority
- change history
- content
- etc.

To facilitate easy reference, there should be a fine sub-division of the document and it follows that the content list is often quite long but, given a good structure, it can be a real asset when navigating through the document.

4.8.3.2 Overview

This could equally well be called 'introduction' (or maybe, even, 'summary'). Its purpose is to introduce the subject matter and set the context for the new reader. It will usually include a brief overview of the problem domain and the essential problem but there should be no attempt to duplicate (or, far worse, substitute for) the full description given in the main body of the document.

4.8.3.3 References

The documents to reference are those that pertain to the project in particular (i.e. not, for example, to a general text such as this). Relevant documents could include:

- elicitation notes;
- specifications for interfacing systems (terminators);
- the project plan;
- the quality assurance plan;
- user manuals for any pre-existing system;
- development procedures that are imposed by design constraints;
- statutory requirements the system must meet;
- the specification for target hardware.

4.8.3.4 Glossary (DD)

All project specific terms should be defined. Bringing these definitions together into a glossary (or DD) is convenient for the reader and helps to insure against omissions and duplications. Definition mechanisms and naming guidelines are considered in the DD Section 14.5.

4.8.3.5   Index

An index is not essential but it is a useful navigational aid and, with modern tools, is relatively easy to implement and maintain.

A final note on requirements document content; just because some material has been produced during analysis, it does not have to be included in the document. Be ruthless in dumping anything that proves unhelpful; content earns its place by its usefulness to the target audience not by the effort (however great) that went into producing in it.

4.9   Exercises

1   Imagine yourself in the role of a system designer. What information would you want to be provided by the analysis documentation?

2   For each of the analysis approaches introduced (SA, modern SA, OOA and PDOA), decide which of the following statements is applicable:

   a)   It focuses upon the problem domain (rather than the solution system).

   b)   It allows seamless development.

   c)   It explicitly distinguishes between different types of problem.

   d)   It clearly separates problem domain description from requirements.

   e)   It gives clear guidance for requirements documentation.

   f)   It makes no contribution to internal design of the solution system.

   g)   It clearly dictates which modelling techniques to use.

3   From the system description given below, devise a suitable problem frame. (Remember, 'system descriptions' do not normally arise as part of the software development process, they are an educational expedient.)

   The turnstile consists of a rotating barrier and a coin slot and is fitted with an electrical interface. The mechanical apparatus has already been chosen and the development project is to provide the controlling software. To enter the stadium, a visitor must first insert the correct coin into the coin slot and then push the turnstile barrier for access. The turnstile is equipped with a locking device; when locked it prevents the barrier from rotating. The controlling software should only allow the barrier to rotate (once) when a valid coin has been inserted.

4   For the system described below, develop a requirements document using:

   a)   SA

   b)   OOA

   c)   PDOA

   Notes:

   •   This is a large exercise, each of the documents could take several hours to produce (although there will be considerable overlap).

- 'System descriptions' do not normally arise as part of the software development process, they are an educational expedient. In reality, you would be working from less organised elicitation documentation.

- The example requirements documents given in Part 3 should provide useful guidance. (An 'answer' for part (c) is to be found in the exercises for the next chapter; there is little point in looking at that first! In any event, remember that there is no single correct solution; good requirements documents for the same system can vary a great deal.)

- Your analysis will, doubtless, reveal various omissions and inconsistencies; that is part of the purpose of analysis. In reality you would raise and resolve queries; here you will have to make reasonable assumptions.

System description:

The system pumpmaster is required to assist in the operation of a petrol station forecourt. It will allow the sales assistant (the user) to monitor and control the operation of the petrol pumps. Via a small network pumpmaster can interrogate the petrol pumps to ascertain their status, the amount of petrol dispensed, etc., the commands given in Table 4.20 being available.

Table 4.20

Command	Response
unlock (pump_id);	ok (pump_id);
send_transfer_details (pump_id);	ok (pump_id, transfer_details);
set_price (pump_id, price);	ok (pump_id);
send_status (pump_id);	ok (pump_id, pump_status);

The petrol pumps are self-serve (i.e. operated by the customers) and each pump dispenses one particular grade of fuel. As fuel is dispensed, it measures and displays the volume and (using the set price) calculates and displays the cost. These transfer details (volume and cost) are available to pumpmaster upon request.

In normal operation, the customer will lift the nozzle and this triggers the resetting of the volume and cost display to zero. The customer replaces the nozzle when finished. The pump is then 'locked' and cannot be used again until it receives an unlock command (from pumpmaster).

Pumpmaster also controls a forecourt display which is in the form of a large electronic sign which shows the current fuel prices. It shows four prices and accepts the following sign command:

price_number, price;

There is also a cost display (a small electronic display at the pay desk) that, for the benefit of the customer, shows the current cost for the pump currently selected by the user.

Information regarding the state of the pumps, etc., is displayed to the user on a conventional graphical 14″ VDU and there will be a custom-built keyboard via which they can enter updates and control the system.

The user can set the price and name of up to six grades of fuel and the system will, upon request, produce a report listing the total volume sold for each grade.

Specification

5

5.1 Introduction

Specification may be regarded as a matter of converting requirements into behaviour or, more precisely, meeting requirements with designed functionality. Clearly, you must know what the problem domain is like and what the requirements *are*, and so the main input to specification is the requirements document. The output will be the specification document, of which more later.

Here is a reminder of the definition of the specification task given in the main introduction:

> **the invention and definition of a behaviour of a solution system such that it will produce the required effects in the problem domain.**

I say *a* behaviour because, generally, there will be more than one possible behaviour that will meet the requirements. (And note that it is mainly *functional* requirements (including performance requirements) that are of relevance here; with the exception of those that dictate a particular style or technology for the external interfaces, design constraints do not affect, at least directly, the behaviour of the solution system.)

As we will see, behaviour may be defined in terms of the interfaces between the solution system and those parts of the problem domain with which it will interact. A reflection of this fact is the view that specification concerns the *definition of the boundary of the solution system*. (A well conducted analysis will certainly have indicated the location and logical nature of those interfaces; it is now a case of pinning them down precisely.)

Inventing possible behaviours and choosing a particular behaviour is a matter of *external design* and this is the first strand of specification. Where the external design is complex (as is often the case with HMIs), it may well be passed over to specialists as a more or less separate task (see Section 2.4). All external design decisions will, of course, be apparent in the operation of the finished application and so are subject to the approval of the client[44].

---

[44] The situation with *internal* design decisions is quite the opposite. They will not normally be apparent to users of the final application and, other than decisions imposed as design constraints, are not normally subject to the approval of the client.

The term 'specification' is also used for the name of the document that is the end product of the specification process. It is the recording of the outcome of the external design decisions, the *documentation*, that is the other main strand of the specification task.

Constructing a good specification is a critical matter. This document is the primary output from the whole of requirements engineering, and it provides the link with the rest of the development process. The designers, programmers and testers must be given a clear and unambiguous picture of what they must deliver. At the same time, the document must be accessible to clients and potential users in order that they can validate the specification before construction proceeds.

Despite its importance, producing a good specification is a sadly neglected art. At best, the guidance given often amounts to no more than:

- a generic content list;
- an introduction to some, more or less useful, modelling techniques;
- and, maybe, a list of the desirable characteristics of the resultant document.

Helpful though these are, the situation may be compared to teaching someone how to make windows and staircases and install plumbing and then expecting them to be able to build a house given no more than a list of its desirable features. There are obvious holes in their expertise (and there are likely to be equally obvious holes in the resultant house!).

We can do rather better than that and the following topics will also be considered:

- application type *specific* content guidelines;
- the *architecture* of specification documents;
- the *selection* and *application* of modelling techniques;
- the use of *natural language* (NL) in specification.

This still leaves a couple of big gaps: the elements of good external design, and mastery of the available techniques. Some guidance on external design is given in Section 5.2 but, at least as far as interfaces to humans are concerned, the topic is covered in several courses and many books (and some references are provided). Most of the modelling techniques are introduced but, particularly in the case of formal methods (see Section 5.5.2) and NL, there is far more to know. References are given for the former and the foundations of good NL usage are, hopefully, laid in school; practice and following good example are the routes to further development.

Even given all this, specification does not become a routine activity. Systems have widely varying purposes and characteristics and this is reflected in specifications of many different 'flavours'. The task is truly in the domain of the expert and, to help generate that expertise, it is guidelines, suggestions and examples that must suffice. Even if it were possible, it would, therefore, be

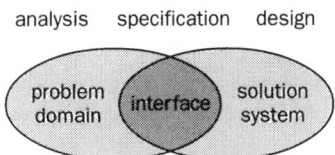

analysis   specification   design

problem domain | interface | solution system

Figure 5.1

inappropriate to present too prescriptive an approach, but this will not be used as an excuse to short-change this difficult but vital area.

Unlike analysis (which is a one off task for any given application), specification recurs repeatedly during the internal design phase. As the structure of the solution system is developed, the required behaviour of each of the various designed parts (sub-systems or modules) must be determined and documented. This process, of internal design and specification of the newly determined elements, is then repeated recursively for each of the modules (until such time as the modules are too small to require further decomposition). The input for specification therefore varies: for the 'whole system', the input is provided by the requirements document; for the various sub-systems, the input is the relevant idesign document. There are also some implications for the manner and style of the specification itself. The differences (mostly simplifications!) for lower level specifications will be considered in Section 5.5 after an examination of the highest, 'system' (or 'application') level specification.

5.1.1   External interfaces

Again harking back to the introduction, we may remind ourselves of the diagram above (Figure 5.1). This emphasises the fact that specification focuses upon the interface between the problem domain and the solution system; in other words, the external interfaces of the solution system. The context diagram is probably the most common way of illustrating the external interfaces and, as can be seen in the example in Figure 5.2, for every interface there is a terminator that receives data from and/or sends data to the solution system.

Since software systems interface with the outside world via the passing of data, it follows that they interface only with other data-processing systems. In practice, this restricts the possibilities to just three generic types of terminator:

- human beings[45]
- other software systems
- electronic hardware

---

[45] As yet, humans do not, of course, interface directly with software systems; there are always intervening devices. Nonetheless, particularly in the early stages, it is often appropriate to ignore such devices and operate at a higher level of abstraction.

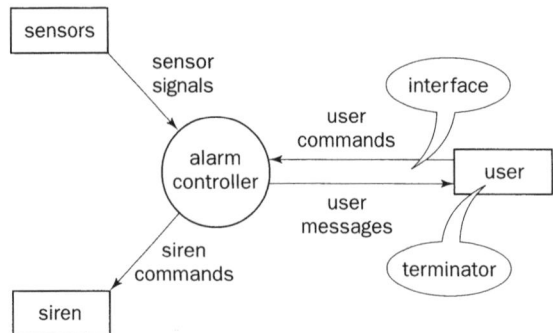

Figure 5.2

Identifying the individual terminators is an important pre-requisite to defining the interfaces. So much so, that (as is often the case with important concepts) various terms have arisen including **viewpoints** and **actors** (preferred by the use-case community (Jacobson *et al.*, 1996)).

(An aside: The notion of viewpoints has been exploited at some length within requirements engineering and certain approaches, notably controlled requirements expression (CORE) (Mullery, 1979), have been developed around the concept. CORE extends back to elicitation where the various viewpoints (in this context, virtually equivalent to stakeholders – see Section 2.2) are seen as the sources of requirements. The required functionality of the solution system is considered from the perspective of each terminator (known in this context as a *bounding* viewpoint) prior to a process of resolving conflicts and integrating the various views. Specification then proceeds by a process akin to functional decomposition (see Section 12.1) wherein separate functions of the solution system are known as *defining* viewpoints.)

It is likely that most of the terminators will have been identified during analysis but some may be added (or significantly elaborated) during specification, notably operator or administrator type interfaces.

Sometimes, the behaviour of the system can be cleanly partitioned along the lines of the external interfaces. For example, the lift controller system has an interface for the service technician (see Section 5.7.2) which is quite separate from that provided for the lift user. Where such partitioning occurs, it provides a very useful, high-level structuring mechanism for the specification; simply cover the functionality of each interface in a separate section.

Unfortunately, there are limits to how far this can be pursued. Often, functionality cuts across two or more interfaces; an input arising from one terminator causes a response to be output to other terminators. Taking the lift example again, an input from the buttons interface may cause responses at the motor interface and the indicator interface. In such cases, partitioning of behaviour by interface is not possible and, as will be seen, we must resort to other approaches.

5.1.2   Levels of abstraction of behaviour

The behaviour of a system may be determined at various levels of detail or abstraction. For example, one could specify that:

> When a valid sensor signal is received it is displayed on the screen.

As is required of a specification, this defines behaviour in terms of causal relationships between input and output. However, we could say more. We could, for example, define whereabouts upon the screen the signal is displayed, in what font and in what colour. For want of better terms, I will refer to the higher level, more abstract version as *logical* behaviour and the lower level, more detailed version as *physical* behaviour (although, these are really only the ends of a spectrum of detail). Ultimately (at the latest, when it is coded), the physical behaviour of a solution system will be determined in the minutest detail. There is, however, considerable latitude as to *when* this is done.

Within requirements engineering, as part of the specification task, we should, at the least, determine the logical behaviour. We then have a choice regarding the edesign of the physical detail (such as the appearance of screens, the wording of prompts, error messages, etc.). The main options regarding the detailed edesign are:

- include it within the specification task;
- factor it out as a separate external design task;
- leave it to the implementers.

The amount of low-level external design that is required varies greatly from one application to another (and even from one requirement to another). It transpires that there is a relationship between the type of problem domain and the type of external interfaces that are likely to be prevalent. This, in turn, indicates the external design effort that is likely to be required.

Transformation problems tend to fall at one extreme. The requirements document will detail the format of the input and output data as well as the required mapping between the two. The only matters likely to require further resolution (edesign) are the way in which the transformation is initiated (maybe by some command from an operator) and the way in which any problems such as a corrupt input file or an unavailable destination are reported.

Workpiece problems fall at the other end of the spectrum. Here, the detailed edesign of the user interaction constitutes a major element of the overall development effort.

Given the above, and the fact that there may actually be several levels of description, the considerations may be quite complex but, at the risk of over-simplifying, some common strategies are:

- include all detail within the specification;
- define the logical behaviour within the specification and have a separate detailed edesign task (and document);

- define the logical behaviour within the specification and leave the physical detail to be determined by the programmers at the implementation stage.

The first strategy is most commonly adopted where there are no complex interfaces (complex interfaces usually being those to humans (HMIs)) although it is always possible to produce a complete, fully detailed specification. The second strategy is more widespread where there *are* complex HMIs. Both the logical and physical versions of the behavioural specification are produced but they are kept separate[46]. The specification will, then, contain only a logical definition of the various inputs and outputs (and their relationships); the actual appearance of the interfaces will be defined elsewhere, probably in an HMI definition document. This does create potential consistency problems as there is an in-built redundancy (the logical version can be derived from the physical).

There also arises the question of whether or not the detailed version should be the subject of scrutiny by the clients and/or users. In my experience, this highly visible aspect of 'surface detail' is of great interest to them and can contribute greatly to the verification (and elicitation) of requirements. Seeing the way in which the system will actually be used can often reveal errors and misunderstanding concerning the original requirements.

The main hazards associated with the last strategy are the possible lack of edesign expertise on the part of the programmers and the fact that the details are not visible until after the system is built (and may then not meet with the client's approval). This strategy will not be considered further here. Nor will the second strategy be demonstrated as such, but some examples of (relatively simple) physical level HMI specification are included within the example specifications given.

The different levels of behavioural specification (logical vs physical) also have associated implications for the descriptive techniques employed. For example, formal methods (see Section 5.5.2) address only the logical level whereas representational models (see Chapter 11) address the physical level. This, and other matters, will be expanded upon in the following sections.

5.2   External design (edesign)

The starting point for devising functionality (i.e. useful behaviour) is, of course, the requirements, and the question may well be asked, 'what is the difference between a requirement and a function?' Quite often, it must be said, the answer is, 'not a lot'[47].

Consider this requirement from the lift controller case study:

A lift will only reverse direction when stopped at a floor.

---

[46] Heitmeyer (1985), for example, advocates this approach and it is implicit in much HMI work.
[47] As mentioned earlier, this is reflected in the fact that defined functions (in the specification) are often, loosely, referred to as 'requirements'.

Clearly there is a direct translation to a function of the lift controller:

> The lift controller will reverse the direction of a lift only when it is stopped at a floor.

However, it is not always quite that obvious. Here is another requirement for the same system:

Each lift should be used an approximately equal amount.

This requirement could be met by various behaviours of the solution system (i.e. the lift controller). It could always send the lift that has been idle for the longest time. Alternatively, it could send the one that has moved the least cumulative distance or even the one that has stopped at the least number of floors.

Even where requirements readily convert to functions, the result is usually at a high (logical) level of abstraction and, particularly for HMIs, there follows a process of reification. Consider this requirement from the YRR case study:

Subject to constraints detailed below, the user can enter, amend and delete details of: boat-class, boat, series, race, series-entry, race-entry.

Clearly, this can translate to a long list of functions such as add boat-class details, edit boat-class details, delete boat-class and so on.

As mentioned earlier, the level of abstraction of the functionality has implications for the specification techniques that are used. Commonly, the highest level functions (often mapping one for one to requirements and sometimes referred to as 'goals' or 'objectives') are, as above, specified using NL. At the next level down, graphical techniques (such as DFDs and state transition diagrams – STDs) often predominate and formal methods may be used, whilst at the lower, more detailed levels there is frequently reliance upon representational models and, more or less structured, text (as in use-case scripts or SA process specifications). Further comment upon and examples of the use of such techniques follow later.

And now, as examples of external design, consider a couple of individual requirements for what is essentially a control problem:

The lift must never be moved with the doors open.

There is not a great deal of choice as to how the new system behaviour will meet this requirement. It may well be reflected in the fragment from an FSM model shown in Figure 5.3.

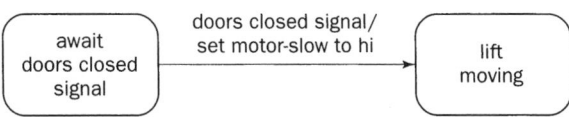

Figure 5.3

Figure 5.4

On the other hand, there might also be a requirement along these lines:

Via a simple interface, the service technician must be able to set:
- **number of lifts**
- **number of floors**
- **stop signal delay for each lift (in the range 0.10 to 0.40 seconds)**

It is usually the human interfaces that offer the greatest scope for invention and there are numerous ways in which the new system design might meet this requirement. With conventional i/o devices (screen, keyboard, mouse), one of the major decisions is whether to use a command driven interface or a direct manipulation interface. The latter can offer significant advantages in usability and has become by far the more common in recent years (but presents much greater challenges to the specifier!).

However, for the current example, custom built hardware seems appropriate. One possible design is shown in Figure 5.4.

The service technician can configure the controller though an interface (pictured above) consisting of a 30 character display and four buttons (left, right, up, down). There is also a key operated switch which must be switched to off in order to be able to change configuration.

The sequence of operation is depicted in the state chart (Figure 5.5).

In this case, via a series of edesign decisions, a simple, short requirement has been elaborated into a page or so of specification. (Specifications can be larger, sometimes much larger, than requirements documents.)

Precisely why these particular edesign decisions were taken is hard to explain. Like any design activity, it is a complex process with many considerations; however, HMIs tend to be the most complex, so much so that the extensive external design required has given rise to a separate literature and specialised courses upon this topic. For this reason, HMI design considerations will not be pursued much further but here are a few guidelines (all of such must be qualified by 'where appropriate' or similar) that are particularly recommended:

- never require the user to enter data that the system already knows;
- minimise the number of required user actions;
- do not allow the user to enter invalid data;

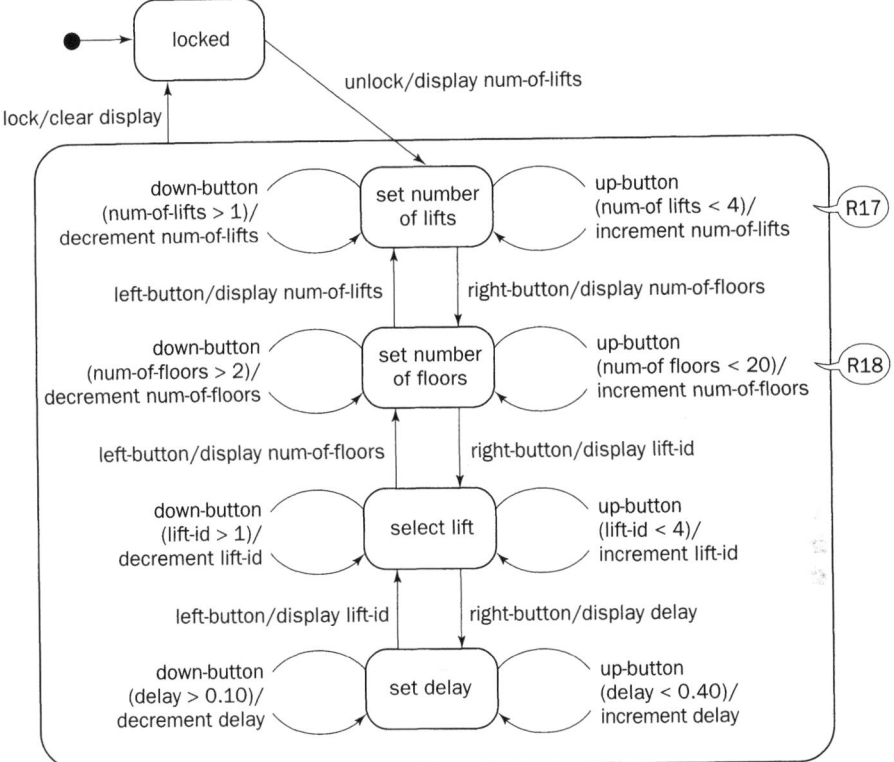

Figure 5.5

- give instant and precise feedback;
- always allow an escape route;
- maintain consistency.

The following may prove to be useful sources for pursuing the topic further: Faulkner (1998), Dix (1998) and Schneiderman (1997).

Before moving on, note also that, although the behaviour of the preceding example has been specified in considerable detail, it is still an external description of behaviour. It deals entirely with inputs to and outputs from the system and the relationships between them. There is no mention of any internal structure or component parts of the new system; that is deferred to the idesign phase.

5.2.1 Incorporating performance requirements

The external design must take account of the performance requirements and these tend to be woven into the designed functionality. Some typical examples arose in the last example where certain capacity requirements (maximum number of lifts, etc.) are reflected in the validation of input data and (in the full version of the specification, Section 16.3.3) the error messages that can arise (for example, 'MAX LIFTS = 4').

For many systems, speed or timing requirements are of no great consequence and general statements of response times (as would be found in the performance requirements – see Section 1.6.2) suffice. But for real-time systems, timing considerations are critical and more precise specification is required. There are relatively few techniques available to assist here, but extensions to some of the state-based models are useful and are described in Sections 12.6.8 (FSM) and 12.7.2 (Petri net).

Reliability requirements do not impinge much upon the external design; these are more a matter for the internal designers and implementers. On the other hand, usability requirements can have a wide ranging impact upon human interface designs and the sources referenced in the preceding section are of relevance.

There is little more general guidance to be given here, but once a design has been determined, it is always worth checking back against the requirements to ensure that all relevant performance requirements have been addressed.

5.2.2 Client and user involvement

The degree of client and/or user involvement in the external design task is highly variable. It is certainly the case that all matters of external design are eventually subject to client approval. However, the process by which the design is arrived at in the first place can span all levels of client/user involvement, from their fully dictating every detail, to their leaving the edesign entirely to the developer. Usually, there is an intermediate, participatory approach; the developer is likely to drive the process and supply most of the expertise and suggestions, but they will involve the client and potential users by eliciting their general preferences and getting them to review early designs, test out prototype interfaces and so on. Indeed, this is an area where throwaway prototypes (see Section 11.3) can be particularly useful and the development of use-cases (see Section 12.3) helps exploit their full potential.

Such exercises may initially be more time consuming but there is a pay-off:

- The users (and hence the client) are more likely to be pleased with the interface designs.

- The client/user involvement in the external design often reveals errors made in the original requirements (whilst they are still relatively easy to correct).

The last point helps illustrate the entanglement of elicitation, analysis and specification. During the specification task, whilst seeking client feedback upon a proposed interface design, the developer may well elicit information that requires further analysis!

5.3 Documenting behaviour

Having invented an appropriate behaviour for the solution system, the next task is to document that behaviour; in other words, to write the specification.

Actually, of course, the two tasks go hand in hand and so this is a rather artificial split. However, to keep things simple, this section will concentrate upon the documentation side and assume that the external design decisions have already been made.

Writing a specification may well be approached as a matter of definition; we need to define the designed behaviour of the solution system. So, we may progress by posing two questions:

- Exactly what must be defined?
- What mechanisms are available for producing the definitions?

Let us start with the first question.

5.3.1 What must be defined

Jackson (1995) speaks of the phenomena that are shared between the problem domain and the machine. For example, the lift controller system can tell where the lift is because, when the lift is at a floor, a sensor sends a signal to the controller. Or, in the case of the YRR program, when the solution system displays a message on the screen, this can be observed by (shared with) the user.

As mentioned earlier, in the case of software systems (since they are inherently intangible), these shared phenomena are always reduced to the form of data; input to and output from the required solution system. Frequently, we will be specifying a larger system only part of which will be realised with software. Nevertheless, here software is the focus and so it is data-based interfaces that are the prime concern. A most important 'specification principle' emerges:

> **If we fully determine the syntax and the semantics of its inputs and outputs and also the required relationships (both causal and timely) between those inputs and outputs, we can say all we need to say about the required behaviour of a solution system.**

For example, 'upon receiving a high signal on sensor line S3, the system must produce a high signal upon motor controller line M2 within 0.1 seconds' or, 'when the user selects "format" from the main menu, the format menu must be displayed within 0.5 seconds'. These are simple and fragmentary examples but hopefully they help convey the essence of this important notion[48].

These relationships between input and output are generally known as *event responses* (ERs) (the input is the event and the output is the response) and, clearly, they equate to the *functions* of the system. So, the first question has been answered; we must define functionality by way of the inputs and outputs and the relationships between them. The ways in which these may be defined (and a few other details!) constitute the rest of this chapter.

---

[48] There is always this connection between functions and data (or operators and operands). Indeed, a function cannot be defined without reference to some data (and, ultimately, data can only be defined in terms of functions). In passing, this can be helpful when designing objects – think of an attribute and an associated method will suggest itself – and vice versa!

5.3.2   Inputs and outputs

The problem domain determines the identity and the nature of the fundamental input and output (i.e. the problem data – see Section 2.8) to and from the solution system. For some types of system, there is little to add and, as indicated earlier, it is non-human interfaces that, generally, leave least to the imagination of the specifier. For example, the input and output file formats for a transformation problem will be fully determined by the problem domain itself and, more often than not, the nature of the signals from the sensors and to the actuators of a control problem will be fully determined.

However, particularly in the case of HMIs, the details of the interfaces are likely to be less constrained by the problem domain, and the requirements may give only a high-level indication. For example, 'all boat and race details are entered by the user'. Even if we assume (as should be the case) that boat and race details are fully defined, this still leaves open the details of the interaction between the user and the solution system.

In such cases, the specification will need to add considerably to the number of inputs and outputs. Prompts and other messages to the user will form additional outputs and the user commands that are required to navigate around the interface will form additional inputs. There is also the matter of handling invalid or unexpected input; the requirements may indicate only in general terms the way in which this should be done and the specification must add flesh to the bones. These additional data may be termed the solution data (see also Section 2.8).

5.3.2.1   The definition of inputs and outputs

The specification of the solution system may, then, be largely reduced to the definition of its external interfaces in terms of the inputs and outputs and the relationships between those inputs and outputs.

The first part of the task is the easier; indeed, in comparison to the second, it is almost trivial. The DD is the primary tool for data definition and the various techniques available are detailed in Chapter 14. Problem data should already be fully defined within the requirements document; it is necessary only to add the solution data (prompts, error messages, report formats, etc.) that the particular external design dictates.

The task may be aided further by considering the fact that there are but a limited number of mechanisms by which data can pass between systems, these being[49]:

- data stream
- data pool
- parameters

---

[49] The distinctions break down if examined too closely; nonetheless, they are useful abstractions.

For all these mechanisms, the syntax and semantics of the data must be defined but there are then further, specific considerations (in effect, guidelines) as to the characteristics requiring definition.

Data stream

At the application or system level, data stream interfaces are the most common. As the name implies, data may be viewed as flowing in a stream from sender to receiver. The defining characteristics of such communication are:

- first in first out (FIFO) – there is no overtaking in a data stream;
- buffering (usually) – the data wait in the stream until removed;
- read once – reading data effectively deletes them.

For any interface, there may be a multiplicity of data stream channels. Assuming digital communication, each channel is essentially uni-dimensional (data arrive one bit at a time) but, often, they are synchronised and it is more useful to operate at a higher level of abstraction. For example, eight parallel bit streams may be regarded as a byte or character stream.

Definition of a data stream requires:

- defining valid stream sequences (BNF or structure charts may well be used);
- (where multi-channel) assigning data to channels (a diagram or table may well be used);
- covering any timing/buffering considerations (given a finite buffer, if reading does not keep pace with writing, data will, eventually, be lost).

Very often (as, say, in the case of user input from a keyboard) only the first of these matters is of significance.

Data pool

A data pool[50] often takes the form of a file or an area of memory that is shared between the two domains in question. However, a single-wire connection may behave as a data pool. If, say, a terminator holds a wire at a particular voltage and it is up to the solution system to detect that voltage (whilst it lasts), this exhibits the characteristics of a data pool (rather than a data stream).

The defining characteristics of such communication are:

- often multi-dimensional data;
- data persist until overwritten (write once, read many times);
- data may be overwritten before they have been read;
- simultaneous access is possible (but may prove problematical!).

Definition of a data pool requires:

---

[50] Equivalent to what Jackson (1983) calls a state vector.

- for multi-dimensional pools, definition of a 'data map' (memory map or file map) showing the location of the data (drawings may well be used but other possibilities include BNF, etc.);
- definition of the read/write protocols. This can be a complex matter as it is usually necessary to ensure that the receiver 'knows' when new data are available and that data are not overwritten before being read. Semaphores are often used (see, for example, Silberschatz *et al.*, 2001 for more on semaphores).

Parameters

Parameter (argument) passing will be familiar to all software engineers as the usual way of passing data between the elements of software systems. In important respects, the safeguards provided by the language environment simplify the specification of such interfaces. Valid data typing and read/write protocols are, effectively, ensured 'for free' (provided only that choices between passing by address or value are correctly made). (Note, by the way, that global or common variables are, in effect, data pools!)

5.3.2.2   The definition of stored data

In principle, the *stored* data *within the solution system* does not have to be specified at all; it may always be deduced from the inputs and outputs. For example, the specification could show that the user enters some particular datum (say, the sail-number of a boat) into the solution system; it could also show that this datum subsequently appears upon one or more reports (outputs). Obviously the information must have been stored within ('remembered' by) the solution system but we could well choose to defer any indication of the data storage structure or mechanism to the subsequent idesign phase.

Nevertheless, it is common practice to include a logical data model (often in the form of an ERD – see Section 13.3.2) within the specification. This would often be based upon the data model of the problem domain that resulted from the analysis and was included in the requirements document. However, the two data models are distinct (see Section 2.9) and there may now be additions that explicitly show the storage of 'solution' data (typically, user options or preferences).

5.3.3   Input/output causal relationships (event responses)

Important though defining the inputs and outputs is, it is in itself inadequate. As we have seen, it is also necessary to define the causal and timing relationships between those inputs and outputs; in other words, the functions or event responses. These relationships may be described as *event responses* (ERs) since the inputs constitute events to which the solution system must respond in a particular way[51].

---

[51] For a system to exhibit useful behaviour (i.e. functionality) it must, at least stochastically, be predictable. It follows that its behaviour is, in principle (although see Section 5.3.5), definable.

There are a limited number of ways in which a system can respond to input[52]:

1. it can produce some output; or

2. it can change its internal state (so the input will affect some *future* response); or

3. it can do both 1 and 2; or

4. it can ignore it (which is, arguably, no response at all!).

The simplest systems are those that have no memory of past events and respond to just a single input. Such systems do exist and their i/o relationships are, generally, easy to specify. An example is that novice programmer's classic, the program that converts Fahrenheit temperatures to Celsius. The causal relationship between the input (F) and the output (C) may be defined as[53]:

$$C ::= (F - 32) \times 5 / 9$$

(It is assumed that the definition of the input and output has taken care of their form and range but specification of rounding rules would also be required, as would specification of the system's response to invalid input. Strictly, we should also define the permissible time interval between the arrival of the input and the production of the output.)

Rather more complex are systems that have no memory but take multiple inputs. A small elaboration of the previous example will serve. Suppose that the program is now required to perform the conversion in either direction; it will be necessary to input not only the temperature but also the direction of conversion. The output will then depend upon two inputs and the specification of the i/o relationship becomes slightly more complex.

Few real systems fall into either of the above, 'single-shot' categories. For most, their response at any time is determined not solely by the immediate input but also by previous 'remembered' input. Consider, for example, the lift controller; how does it respond to the sensor signal telling it that the lift is approaching a floor? Well, it depends. If the send-button for that floor has been pressed since the lift last visited the floor, then it should command the lift motor to stop; otherwise (dependent upon other previous input) maybe not.

It is theoretically possible to develop, for any system, an input tree, branching for all possibilities at every input. From such an input tree the response to

---

[52] It is not always obvious what constitutes 'an input'. Given the ubiquity of digital data-processing, there is an ultimate level of granularity imposed by the hardware (such as a bit or a character). However, it is often more meaningful to choose to operate at a higher level of abstraction (say, a number or a string or a command) and we are free to do so.

[53] This may look like a procedural specification (as is condemned in Section 5.3.4) but it is equally well regarded as a declarative (functional) specification and should be read as 'C is defined as . . .'. Just to make the point, there are at least three ways of implementing it; $C = ((F + 40) * 5/9) - 40$ or $C = F - 32 * 5/9$ or by using a look-up table and dispensing with calculations altogether.

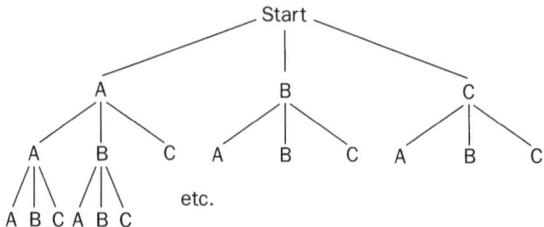

Figure 5.6

the next input can be determined. However, for most systems, this is unfeasible.

The example in Figure 5.6 models a system with just three possible different inputs (A, B or C). As can be seen, it would be awkward to show more than three successive inputs (and that is without showing any resultant output at all!).

Happily, this is usually unnecessary since only *some* of the previous input is relevant. We can, therefore, introduce the notion of *state* which is, in effect, a condensation of the input history which enables the response to the next input to be predicted. We can say that if the system is in a particular state then, no matter how it arrived at that state, it will respond to particular inputs in particular ways. Since this is so pertinent to specifying behaviour, there has been much development of state-based modelling techniques. Most of these are described in Part 2, Section 12.5, to which reference may be made as necessary, and examples of their application follow.

5.3.3.1 Categorising ERs

The view may well be taken that behaviour is behaviour and an ER is an ER. Nonetheless, regarding the pragmatics of specification, it can be useful to consider different types of ER, at least to some extent, separately[54].

As we have already seen (Section 5.1.1), the functionality of the system can sometimes be cleanly partitioned according to the various external interfaces (and their corresponding terminators). In effect, we can lump together all the ERs associated with each particular interface. This can provide a high-order structure. It also places some useful constraints upon the communication mechanisms (see Section 5.3.2.1) and, hence, the specification techniques, that are most relevant. The following categories may be identified:

- **hardware interfaces** – where the solution system connects with sensors, actuators, etc.;

- **user interfaces**;

- **operator interfaces** (the operator being a 'super-user' or administrator with additional powers for system configuration, archiving, etc.);

---

[54] The following categorisation is derived partly from the work of Kovitz (1999).

- **APIs** (application programmer's interface) or **software interfaces** – it is not uncommon for certain applications (in particular, transformation and connection applications) to form part of a software 'tool set' that can be used by other software.

Orthogonally to the above, we may categorise upon the basis of ERs relating to:

- valid problem data[55] and where an output is produced; what might be termed the 'ordinary' **output ERs**;
- valid problem data and where a change of state (of the solution system) results – these will be referred to as **state ERs**;
- invalid problem data – often defined in terms of **validation rules**; the requirements document will largely determine what constitutes valid problem data but there may be some elaboration and it is also necessary to specify how the solution system *responds* to invalid input (by producing error messages, etc.).

So, for example, within a specification, we might choose to have separate sections defining, say, the user and the operator interfaces and, within each of those sections, further divide upon the basis of output ERs, state ERs and validation rules.

Further structuring of ERs (or, if you prefer, behaviour) is generally desirable and is frequently along the lines of likely time sequencing. However, this must be approached flexibly on a case-specific basis.

A few notes and examples for each type of interface and ER will now be given and, after considering some other general matters, assorted specification examples taken from the case studies will follow.

Hardware interfaces

Hardware interfaces are usually associated with control systems, such as the lift controller example, where the solution system will sense events in the problem domain via various transducers and initiate actions via actuators. The sensing aspect (but only the sensing aspect) may also be associated with certain information systems, which might be generally referred to as monitoring systems. Hardware interfaces are also commonly associated with connection systems, but are unlikely to be a significant feature of workpiece or transformation systems.

Applications may communicate with hardware via data streams or data pools (as described in Section 5.3.2.1). Although users actually interface with applications via various hardware devices, these devices are generally considered as part of the application. In other words, the system boundary is set outside the interface devices, and we simply consider the interface between the human and the solution system.

---

[55] i.e. data emanating from the problem domain – see Section 2.8.

User interfaces

User interfaces are, generally, of most significance for workpiece systems, closely followed by information systems. They may also figure fairly large in control and communication systems, but are often relatively trivial in transformation systems.

Certain interface devices (keyboard, screen and mouse) predominate and tend to constrain the external design. However, there are other possibilities and custom-built devices can always be invented.

Data streams are the usual input mechanism but it may be more useful to regard the form filling style of input as a data pool. There are many other possibilities but output to users is more often by way of screens which are also a kind of data pool.

Whilst it is by no means always the case, user interfaces, in particular, may be very sophisticated and complex. This is particularly true of the modern style of direct manipulation interface. The older style, text-based, command line interfaces placed greater demands upon the expertise of the user but were relatively simple to define. The modern, graphically-based, direct manipulation interface makes life simpler for the user but much more difficult for the specifier. It is not possible to do full justice to the edesign considerations here, but most of the useful documentation techniques are introduced.

Operator interfaces

Whereas it might be said that a solution system should be designed to meet the needs of the users, there is a sense in which operators (system administrators, etc.) are required to meet the needs of the system. In the way that they are referred to here, operator interfaces are seldom dictated by the requirements; rather they are introduced during specification as an invented part of the solution to the original problem.

That said, operators are humans and many of the same considerations apply to the design and specification of their interfaces. Perhaps the main differences are that it is often possible to assume greater expertise on the part of an operator and, given their relatively infrequent interaction with the system, lower efficiency of the interface may be acceptable.

Application programmer interfaces

Application programmer interfaces is, perhaps, a misnomer since, whilst the specification must be understood by a programmer, the interface is actually to another software system. Application programmer interfaces may arise at the application level (particularly for financial systems) but are far more common when specifying lower level, sub-systems. They may employ data streams and pools but usually pass data by way of parameters (see page 148). Section 5.5.3.1 provides an example of the definition of this type of interface.

Output ERs

These occur where the solution system responds to an event by producing some output. The ER will be designed such that it meets some requirement; here is an example taken from the lift controller problem:

With the stop delay correctly configured (as below) the lift should stop within +/– 1.5 cm of the floor being serviced.

In order to specify a behaviour that will meet this requirement, we need to know more about the relevant shared phenomena (inputs and outputs). A good requirements document will give us this information in the description of the problem domain and the relevant extracts are:

- 'All signals to and from the lift system components are via electric cables. All signals operate upon a hi/lo basis.'

- 'Winding motors each have three control lines; slow, fast and polarity – which operate as per the decision table[56] (Table 5.1). In fast mode, the motor moves the lift at 1.2 m/sec (+/– 10%). In slow mode, at 0.3 m/sec (+/– 10%). The motor mechanism itself ensures a gradual acceleration and deceleration as per Table 5.2. (All figures are subject to a tolerance of +/– 20%.)'

Table 5.1

slow	hi				lo			
fast	hi		lo		hi		lo	
polarity	hi	lo	hi	lo	hi	lo	hi	lo
wind up fast	✓				✓			
wind down fast		✓				✓		
wind up slow			✓					
wind down slow				✓				
stop							✓	✓

Table 5.2

	time	distance
rest to fast	2 sec	1.2 m
fast to slow	1 sec	0.75 m
slow to rest	1 sec	0.15 m

---

[56] If you are unfamiliar with decision tables, see Section 12.4.

- 'Sensors detect the presence of a lift. When a lift is within 20 cm vertically (either side) of the sensor's nominal position it sends a hi signal; otherwise a lo signal. Each lift shaft has a set of sensors for each floor. For each floor (except top and bottom), there is a proximity-sensor (aka the "at-sensor") at the nominal floor position, an above-sensor 1.5 m above (the nominal floor position) and a below-sensor 1.5 m below. The top floor has proximity- and below-sensors only and the bottom floor proximity- and above-sensors only.'

If we concentrate just upon the stopping requirement quoted above (and presume the preconditions that the decision to stop has already been made, the lift is approaching the floor and the lift is moving slowly), we can extract the precise information that we need:

- the lift will be moving at 0.3 m/sec (+/− 10%);
- the proximity-sensor signal will go hi when the lift becomes within 20 cm of the floor;
- the lift motor is stopped by setting the slow and fast lines to lo;
- the lift will move 0.15 m (+/− 20%) before it actually stops.

We can therefore calculate that in the 'worst' case the lift will be travelling at 0.33 m/sec and will travel 18 cm before it stops. This allows just 2 cm movement, which would take 0.06 seconds, before the stop signal must be sent. At the other extreme, the stop delay would have to be 0.3 seconds. This looks feasible and the requirements document also tells us that the stop delay is configurable by the technician. So we could frame a specification fragment for the relevant ER:

> When the lift is stopping at a floor, upon receipt of the floor proximity-sensor hi signal, the controller will set the motor fast and slow lines to lo after a delay of stop-delay.[57]

This fragment of controller behaviour could equally well be documented using a more formal technique such as an FSM model depicted using an STD (see Figure 5.7). Indeed, this approach would probably make it easier to integrate this particular element of the behaviour with the rest.

State ERs
These occur where the solution system responds to an event by changing the data that it stores within itself, in other words, its state.

---

[57] Probably elsewhere in the specification, we would say that the stop-delay is configurable by the service technician at between 0.03 and 0.6 seconds.

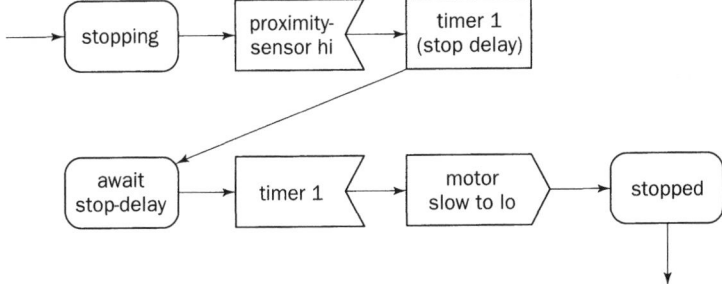

Figure 5.7

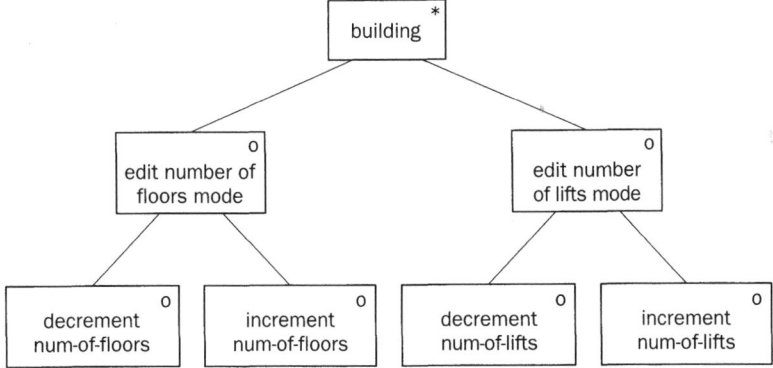

Figure 5.8

Let us revisit another requirement for the lift system:

R15   Via a simple interface, the service technician must be able to set:

- **number of lifts**
- **number of floors**
- **stop signal delay for each lift (in the range 0.10 to 0.40 seconds)**

Section 5.2 indicated the behaviour that was designed to meet this requirement. As well as the output responses, there was some indication of the relevant state changes; however, it is often considered desirable to define these more explicitly and in terms of the affected elements of the data model. Consider, for example, the relevant events and state responses concerning the number of lifts and the number of floors. These attributes should have been identified during the analysis phase (as they form part of the problem domain data) and should have been associated with the entity 'building'. The events causing changes in that entity could be summarised in an ELH (see Section 13.4.1) as shown in Figure 5.8.

Table 5.3

current number of lifts (n)	1		2 .. 3		4	
button pressed	↑	↓	↑	↓	↑	↓
'NUMBER OF LIFTS = ', n	✓		✓	✓		✓
'MAX LIFTS = 4'					✓	
'MIN LIFTS = 1'		✓				

Error responses (validation rules)
Here are a couple more requirements for the lift controller system (as used in Section 5.2):

R16   The maximum number of lifts is 4, the minimum 1.
R17   The maximum number of floors is 20, the minimum 2.

The behaviour of the system must be defined in such a way that these require-ments are respected. At its simplest, the system might simply ignore any input which attempts to set numbers outside these limits. More helpfully, it could be decided that the system would produce suitable error responses. These might be presented as a text list, incorporated into an STD (as is illustrated in the next section) or a decision table (see Section 12.4) such as Table 5.3 might be used.

5.3.3.2   Integration of ERs
It is not possible to generalise but sometimes it may be adjudged that max-imum clarity is achieved by integrating the specification of the foregoing types of ER. Figure 5.9 shows an example of an STD (see Section 12.6 for details of the notation) which integrates ERs for (part of) the preceding examples.

5.3.4   Procedural vs functional specification

Specification is essentially about defining the chosen behaviour of the solution system. However, it is equally possible to apply the name 'specification' to the document that defines the chosen *structure* for the solution system. This is, clearly, rather confusing and so I shall reserve 'specification' for definitions of behaviour and use the term 'design document' for definitions of internal design or structure. Unfortunately, the potential confusion does not end here!

As we have seen, defining behaviour is (mostly) a matter of defining inputs, outputs and the relationships between those inputs and outputs. A very simple example is, 'when the operator presses this button the bell rings'. The input is the button press, the output is the bell ringing and the causal relationship between the two is, at least, implied by the conditional conjunction 'when'.

There is little choice about the way in which inputs and outputs are defined but when it comes to defining the relationships *between* inputs and outputs (i/o relationships) there is a fundamental choice to be made; i/o relationships may

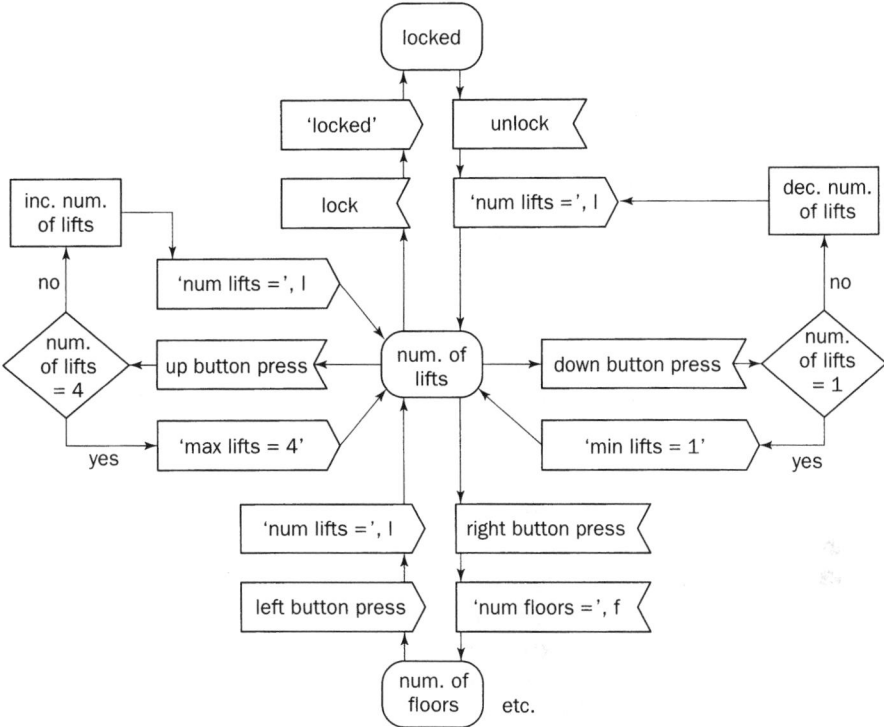

Figure 5.9

be defined *functionally* or *procedurally*. The following sample fragments of speci-fications illustrate this point:

Functional[58]**:**
results_list ::= race_name, race_date, race_start_time, {boat_id,
                 boat_finish_time, elapsed_time, position};
                 (*boats are sorted in order of elapsed times; shortest time first *)
elapsed_time   ::= (* boat_finish_time – race_start_time *);

Procedural (1):
for all boats
        elapsed_time = boat_finish_time – race_start_time;
end (for all)
sort boats by elapsed times (*shortest time first*)
output (race_name, race_date, race_start_time)
for all boats in sorted list
        output (boat_id, boat_finish_time, elapsed_time, position)
end (for all)

---

[58] Use is made here of extended Backus Naur Form (BNF). See Section 14.3.4 if this is unfamiliar.

The difference may appear subtle but it is not insignificant. The functional specification defines the end results; the procedural specification defines a possible *means* as well.

Here is another procedural specification for the same function:

Procedural (2):
output (race_name, race_date, race_start_time)
for all boats
      boat_elapsed_time = boat_finish_time – race_start_time;
      insert boat into sorted list (*shortest time first*)
end (for all)
for all boats in sorted list
      output (boat_id, boat_finish_time, elapsed_time, position)
end (for all)

Notice how, in addition to defining *what* is required to happen, each of the procedural specifications strongly implies the *way* in which it should be done. The functional specification allows either of these (and other) ways.

Now, procedural specifications (of behaviour) *do* work, because form (or structure) determines function. In other words, the structure of a machine, a device or any system, determines what it does (or how it behaves). The structure of a bicycle, say, determines that, when properly ridden, it will travel along the ground. It would not prove a lot of use for, say, opening tin cans. For that you would need a different structure; that of a can opener. There are, of course, several different designs (structures) of can opener but they all perform the same function. And this is a general rule: as illustrated in Figure 5.10, for given functionality there are many possible structures; but for any given structure, just one behaviour is determined. This fully applies to software, and the boat finishing order example given above illustrates the point as well as any.

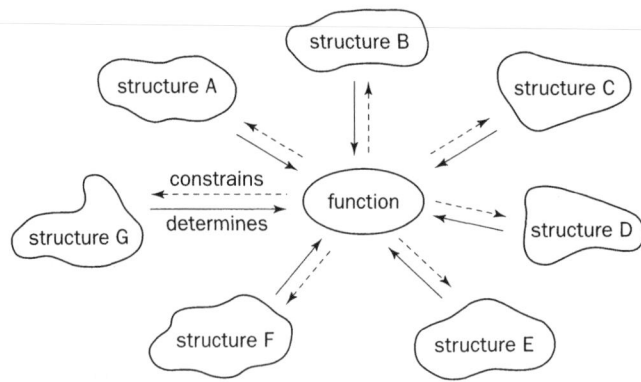

Figure 5.10

So, we have a choice; we can write functional specifications or we can write procedural (i.e. structural) specifications. It is the former that is the right choice. Procedural specifications are a *bad idea*, for two reasons.

Firstly, in order to validate the specification, the client has to *work out* the functionality from the structure. Given relevant expertise, it is always possible to do this but it might prove tricky. To return to the example of can openers, if you were presented with a mystery gadget (that happened to be a new type of can opener) you might be able to work out its purpose, but you might not. Given the structure of a new piece of software, a client might be able to work out how it behaves but, again, they might not. At best, it requires additional expertise and, at worst, it introduces the possibility of errors.

Secondly, the idesigner may be unnecessarily influenced. The challenge for the idesigner is to invent a structure for the system such that it does what it should (has the correct functionality) and is well structured and, hence, maintainable[59].

Inherently, there is *no difference* between a procedural (structural) specification and an internal (structural) design document; it is simply a matter of *intent*. The procedural specification is saying 'I want the system to behave *as if* it were built in this way'. The design document is saying 'I want you actually to build the system this way'. With the best will in the world, given a procedural specification, it may be difficult for the idesigner to remember that the former intent applies. Rather than 'start from scratch' and develop an idesign to the best of their ability, they may incorporate idesign decisions that were taken, without due care and attention, when the specification was being written.

In fact, there is a third (although minor) reason not to use procedural specifications. It is generally *less work* to produce functional specifications. Not surprisingly, functional specification will provide the focus for this chapter.

(It may seem that this section has laboured an obvious point. If you think so, just take a close look at the example 'specifications' published in many books. Not only is it often hard to differentiate between the analysis and specification documentation, but there is also a tendency to rely heavily upon procedural specification.)

5.3.5   Specification by rule vs example

Event responses may be complex and a system's response may be determined by a long history of past input. The techniques listed above help handle this but, to be frank, it may not always possible to specify causal i/o relationships fully; the rules are just too complicated. Resort must then be made to specification by example, in the hope that the implementers will make sensible decisions based upon the examples. However, that should be the last resort; usually, behaviour can and should be fully specified in terms of the rules governing the relationships between the inputs and outputs.

---

[59] The world changes – the correct functionality today may well not be the correct functionality tomorrow – if it cannot be changed, sooner, rather than later, the product becomes useless.

Note that it is always possible to provide an illustrative example *as well* as the rules and this can make a specification easier to understand.

5.3.6   Input/output timing relationships

In comparison to the development of techniques for defining causal i/o relationships, relatively little has been done about defining timing relationships. Where this is important (notably for real-time systems) extensions to some of the state-based models are useful and are described in Sections 12.6.8 (FSM) and 12.7.2 (Petri net).

5.4   The specification document

Several fragments of specification documentation have been presented in the preceding sections. Part 2 introduces all the relevant modelling and documentation techniques and Part 3 provides examples of complete specifications. However, as the principal deliverable, or end product, of requirements engineering, the specification is a critical document and merits a little more examination.

5.4.1   Purpose of the specification

To many of us it seems self-evident that the required behaviour of the new system should be documented. But there are others (and I have worked with them!) who appear to think that, provided 'everyone knows' what is required, there is no point in expending the effort to document it. So, just in case you find yourself in the position of having to convince someone (your boss?) that it is worth writing a specification, here is a handy list of reasons:

- to give full visibility to the required behaviour so that it can be reviewed and formally agreed (prior to implementation), hence minimising re-work;

- to provide a secure record of required behaviour and thereby insure against the loss of key personnel[60];

- to ensure that the correct information is accurately and economically communicated to the implementers, minimising errors in communication across the team;

- to provide the baseline against which functionality can ultimately be tested, allowing efficient and complete testing (by third parties, if desired);

- to provide the necessary information for production of user manuals, etc. (if desired, in parallel with idesign and implementation[61]);

---

[60] This is, of course, an advantage for the organisation, not for the individual who knows. The unscrupulous requirements engineer may prefer not to produce documentation so that they can apply pressure along the lines 'give me a big pay rise or I will leave and take the vital knowledge with me'.

[61] This can achieve very significant savings in overall development times.

- to eliminate (or, at least, minimise) post-delivery arguments between client and developer as to the 'correct' functionality;
- to facilitate future maintenance, including the handover from development to maintenance staff;
- to facilitate the future development of new systems with similar functionality[62];
- to provide an unambiguous milestone (i.e. specification sign-off) for monitoring progress;
- to allow more accurate estimates of future development effort[63].

5.4.2 Characteristics and style of the specification

In order to fulfil these roles, the specification must exhibit certain characteristics (many of which are in common with the requirements document). There is widespread agreement on this point and the following list, drawn from several sources[64], reflects this consensus:

- understandable to all relevant parties;
- low ambiguity;
- well organised;
- functional view, not structural view (design constraints excepted);
- completeness;
- consistency;
- enable automated:
  - checking;
  - test generation;
  - prototype generation (animation);
- validatable;
- modifiable;
- traceable.

Unfortunately, simply agreeing upon desirable characteristics does little to assist in achieving those characteristics. For a start, the relationships between the characteristics are complex and not always synergistic. For example:

- maintainability (readily modifying the specification without compromising other properties) depends critically upon human understanding;

---

[62] The partial re-use of old specifications can also achieve very significant savings.
[63] Provided that similar specification and development techniques are used, the size of the specification can help refine estimates of workload for the later stages of development.
[64] Abbot and Moorhead (1981), Alford *et al.* (1976), Balzer and Goldman (1981), Davis (1988a), IEEE (1984), Kaposi and Myers (1990), Levene and Mullery (1982), Sklaroff and Smith (1988), Wasserman and Stinson (1979) and Yeh and Zave (1980).

- understanding depends principally upon low ambiguity, accessibility and good organisation of the specification;
- low ambiguity may be achieved through greater formality but this can compromise understandability;

and so on.

The implications for the specification techniques used, the architecture of the document, etc., are examined in the following sections.

5.4.3   Specification content and architecture

The organisation of the specification is a major factor in determining its usefulness; particularly its understandability and modifiability. But what is it that must be organised; what should be in the specification in the first place?

In essence, specification content precisely matches the previously given definition of the specification activity:

definition of behaviour of the new system

Before considering this in more detail, it is perhaps useful to have an appreciation of what should *not* be in the specification. The *IEEE Guide to Software Requirements Specifications* (ANSI/IEEE Std. 830 1984), is quite explicit:

> The SRS [specification] should not normally specify design items such as:
>> partitioning the software into modules,
>> allocating functions to modules,
>> describing flow of information or control between modules,
>> choosing data structures
>
> (IEEE, 1984, p. 31)

Note that this entirely supports the earlier point (Section 5.3.4) that specifications should be functional rather than structural or procedural[65].

In other words, any information relating to the internal structure of the system should be excluded. (The exception to this is any design constraint, as already detailed in the requirements document, that the client wishes to impose.) It may well be that by the time the specification is completed, some idesign decisions have been made and documented, but this does not mean that such design documentation has to be included in the specification; it can readily be recorded separately.

Other topics normally excluded from the specification are:

- project plans:
  - schedules;
  - staffing;

---

[65] Although, if the exemplars in the IEEE text are examined closely, one may be led to question whether this is a case of 'do as I say, not as I do'.

- costings;
- procedures, etc;
- product assurance plans:
  - quality assurance plans;
  - configuration management procedures;
  - test plans, etc;
- commercial constraints (i.e. delivery time and cost constraints, which are preferably embodied in the contract and/or the project plans);
- the reasons or justification for specified behaviour[66].

So much for what should *not* be included, but what does this leave? Unfortunately, the picture now becomes a little more confused. This is largely due to the fact that many sources do not separate requirements engineering documentation (as recommended here) into the requirements (analysis) document and the specification. A quick reminder – a requirements document contains:

a description of the problem domain +
a list of requirements to be met (problems to be solved)

and a specification document contains:

a definition of a behaviour of the solution system that will meet the requirements (solve the problems).

The content suggested by other sources often reflects a combination of these two documents. A typical example can be found in the *STARTS Guide* (DTI/NCC 1986)[67]:

Level 1 – *Introduction*
      background
      outline system requirement
      outline system environment
      structure of the document
      definitions
      references

Level 2 – *User Description*
      the environment
      the users of the system

---

[66] This last point is somewhat contentious. The justification for specified behaviour is important, it is just that most users of the specification do not need to know and the inclusion of such material can clutter the specification. Where necessary (e.g. for preferences – see Section 1.6.5) it can be included and, in any case, backwards traceability through the analysis document and elicitation notes to the original source should be possible if you *do* need to know. There has not been a great deal of work on backwards traceability but see, for example, Finkelstein and Potts (1986).
[67] See also MIL-STD-498 (1985).

function
operation
life-cycle aspects
performance
constraints
assumptions

As implied by the section names, this document would include a description of the problem domain ('the environment'), a list (at least in outline) of the requirements and a description of the required behaviour of the new system ('function' / 'operation'). Having separated the first two topics out into a separate requirements document, we can concentrate only upon the last and so simplify things somewhat.

Certain document sections (contents list, overview, glossary, references, index) arise simply as standard parts of any technical document. They are there to facilitate use of the document.

Although not strictly necessary, it is often convenient to replicate the requirements (functional, performance and design constraints) from the requirements document and this will be assumed. (The requirements are often, in fact, quite short compared to the problem domain description or to the specification of new system behaviour and so this does not lead to a great increase in document size.)

The core of the specification is the behavioural description of the new, solution system. Hence, we arrive at the following suggested specification content:

Document details (title, authority, revision history, etc.)
Overview (of problem domain and solution system)
Requirements (replicated from requirements document)
    Functional requirements
    Performance requirements
    Design constraints
System behaviour (generally, by far the largest section)
References
Glossary (DD)
Index

Optional extras are:

- assumptions – better to resolve any unknowns and thus eliminate assumptions but, if this is not possible, then it is best to make them obvious,

- non-implemented functions – occasionally, it will not be possible to meet all requirements and, again, it is usually best to make this obvious.

The various types of requirements were described in Section 1.6. System behaviour (the major part of the document) is the main topic of this chapter. The other parts warrant brief consideration first. (Some of the following overlaps with the requirements document but is repeated here for convenience.)

5.4.3.1   Document details

This is as for any technical document:

- title
- authors
- documentation conventions/standards
- version
- change authority
- change history
- content
- etc.

It is normal for the specification to be hierarchically structured (see Section 5.4.4.1) and, to facilitate easy reference, there should be a fine sub-division. It follows that the contents list is often quite long but, given a good structure, it can be a real asset when navigating through the document.

5.4.3.2   Overview

This could equally well be called 'introduction' (or maybe, even, 'summary'). Its purpose is to introduce the subject matter and set the context for the new reader. It will often start with an overview of the system that is being specified, usually in terms of its overall purpose. It is likely that this will include a *brief* overview of the problem domain but there should be no attempt to duplicate (or, far worse, substitute for) the full description given in the requirements document.

It is possible also to provide a summary, or synopsis, of the remainder of the specification document, but this should be approached with some caution. The contents list should already give a good guide; further duplication entails the danger of inconsistency between the two versions. This becomes increasingly likely as the document evolves; changes may be made to the body of the document that are not reflected in the summary (or vice versa).

There is also a temptation to view a summary as a substitute (if only temporary) for the full, detailed specification. I have witnessed a project where the summary was the only part of the specification that was ever written. This is tantamount to proceeding with a very inadequate specification (and, in that case, as in most cases, the price was paid).

5.4.3.3   References

The documents to reference are those that pertain to the project in particular (i.e. not, for example, to a general text on writing specifications). Relevant documents could include:

- elicitation notes;
- the requirements/analysis document;
- specifications for interfacing systems (terminators);

- the project plan;
- the quality assurance plan;
- user manuals for any pre-existing system;
- development procedures that are imposed by design constraints;
- statutory requirements the system must meet;
- the specification for target hardware;
- and so on.

5.4.3.4   Glossary (DD)

All project specific terms should be defined. The specification will inherit the terms that are employed in the requirements document, but is likely to extend the number by adding the solution data (see Section 2.8).

Bringing these definitions together into a glossary or DD is convenient for the reader and helps insure against omissions and duplications. Definition mechanisms and naming guidelines are considered in the section on DD (Section 14.5).

5.4.3.5   Index

An index is not essential, but it is a useful navigational aid and, with modern tools, is relatively easy to implement and maintain.

5.4.4   Organisation

Common sense indicates that organisation and layout would have a great effect upon on the usability and comprehension of specifications. Curiously, the matter has received scant attention and is certainly not an aspect of specification that is well addressed by most authors. Turski's observation, 'Requirement specifications being usually a huge collection of heterogeneous details structured according to some irrelevant principle' (Turski and Maibaum, 1987, p. 27) is still highly pertinent.

The outline content given in the previous section provides guidance as to the high-level structure. However, for specifications of any size, we need to go further and consider the finer organisation, particularly of the description of system behaviour (which, generally, constitutes the bulk of the document).

5.4.4.1   Hierarchy

It is suggested here that, as is so often the case, a hierarchical approach usually provides the best basis for document structuring[68]. Before offering guidance as to how the necessary specification content can be massaged into such a hierarchical structure, it is perhaps worth considering briefly how such a structure is best represented within the document.

---

[68] As Wirth (1974) says, a hierarchical structure may not be the way we design things, but it is a good way of explaining the result to somebody else.

The physical world provides only the dimensions of space and time by which we can separate things[69]. Only dynamic models (prototypes – see Section 11.3) can make use of the time dimension and so it is the space dimensions that must be used to separate and order things in documents.

Text is, essentially, one-dimensional, consisting of a string of characters, whereas diagrams (and tables) are essentially two-dimensional[70]. *Structured* text, as in pseudo-code can, however, with the use of indentation, also model in two dimensions; it is this sort of approach which we usually adopt when giving documents a hierarchical structure.

It is also possible to model the time dimension within static models by using one of the space dimensions to represent time. This can be in the form of a vertical or horizontal 'time-line'; in its simplest form, just listing things down the page in the order in which they occur. (Of course, representational prototypes (which operate in 'real' time) have significant advantages if circumstances permit their use.)

Systems are often best regarded as multi-dimensional, and this can be reflected in their definitions by using the various partitions and levels of the hierarchical structure[71]. Below is an extract from an actual specification contents list which was structured in such a way. At different levels, the structure models, by their separation in space, the different external interfaces, the concurrent availability of various options, the sequential ordering of certain actions and so on.

1. SYSTEM OBJECTIVES
2. EXTERNAL INTERFACES
   2.1. Human Interface (see section 3)
   2.2. Software Interface to CAMEO PCB Layout
      2.2.1. Placed Part to Device Allocation
      2.2.2. Netlist
      2.2.3. Supplementary Parts List
   2.3. Software Interface to MicroQUAD
      2.3.1. Placed Part to Device Allocation
      2.3.2. Netlist
   2.4. Back Annotation From PCB Layout Systems
   2.5. Software Interface to Logic Simulators
   2.6. Plotter Interface
   2.7. Printer Interface
      2.7.1. Graphical Format
      2.7.2. Text Format ▶

---

[69] Slightly frivolous, but nonetheless accurate and useful, definitions are:
- space – what stops everything being in the same place;
- time – what stops everything happening at once.

[70] The use of a 'whole new dimension' to separate and structure elements is probably *the* most significant advantage of graphical techniques.

[71] Programmers may appreciate the analogy with the way in which compilers instantiate multi-dimensional arrays in the essentially uni-dimensional computer memory.

3. THE OPERATOR INTERFACE
   3.1. Hardware
      3.1.1. Screen
         3.1.1.1. Cursor
         3.1.1.2. Windows
            3.1.1.2.1. Graphics Windows
            3.1.1.2.2. Text Windows
            3.1.1.2.3. Menu Windows
      3.1.2. Mouse
      3.1.3. Keyboard
   3.2. Units and Co-ordinates
   3.3. Data Entry
      3.3.1. Notation
      3.3.2. General Characteristics
      3.3.3. Journaling
      3.3.4. Start Up
      3.3.5. List drawings
      3.3.6. List libraries
      3.3.7. Edit drawing/library
         3.3.7.1. Control menu
            3.3.7.1.1. Window
               3.3.7.1.1.1. Enter Window Name
               3.3.7.1.1.2. Digitise Within Existing Window
               3.3.7.1.1.3. Select From Window Menu
            3.3.7.1.2. Pan
            3.3.7.1.3. Graphics menu
            3.3.7.1.4. Status menu
            3.3.7.1.5. Plot
4. PERFORMANCE
   4.1. Speed
   4.2. Capacity
5. CONSTRAINTS
   5.1. Commercial
      5.1.1. Cost limits
      5.1.2. Timescales
   5.2. Technical
      5.2.1. Hardware
      5.2.2. Software
      5.2.3. Other
   5.3. Anticipated enhancements

There are, then, adequate possibilities for the accommodation of the required structure within the specification and it is now time to consider how, in general, these might be used.

5.4.4.2 Structure

The highest hierarchical division of the document reflects the divisions of a 'standard' technical document and has already been suggested through the contents list (Section 5.4.3):

- document details;
- overview (of problem domain and solution system);
- functional requirements (replicated from requirements document);
- performance requirements (replicated from requirements document);
- design constraints (replicated from requirements document);
- system behaviour;
- references;
- glossary (DD);
- index.

Requirements and design constraints have been covered in Section 1.6. This leaves the 'system behaviour' section requiring further organisation. This may well comprise 80% of the whole specification and it is here that the trickiest structuring problem resides.

The aspects of system behaviour that require specification vary somewhat across the types of application domain but, as we have seen, this is largely a matter of emphasis. Every system's behaviour can be viewed in terms of inputs and outputs and the relationships between them. Partitioning this behaviour can be difficult but there are a few useful guidelines.

As mentioned in Section 5.1.1, where the system has external interfaces to several problem domain sub-systems (terminators), it may be possible to treat these more or less independently. If so, this gives a useful high-level structure to this section. For example, with the lift controller, the interface to the service technician could be treated separately from the interfaces to the other terminators.

Beyond (or in the absence of) this, the usual resort is to some form of functional decomposition. Functional decomposition, as a specification technique, is described in detail in Section 12.1, but it also provides a very useful basis for specification document structuring. At the highest level, the external design is likely to create a fairly tight mapping between (functional) requirements and functions of the new system. For example, the YRR program has the following requirement:

R4 Upon command from the user, the system will produce the following reports (content as defined in the data dictionary):
- **boat-class-list**
- **boat-list**
- **series-list**
- **series-details**

- series-results
- race-results

It is possible (although not inevitable) that the solution system edesign will provide a reports function with sub-functions for the various reports. This functional structure could well be reflected in a relevant section and sub-sections of the specification document.

There are few alternatives to such function-based structuring, but one is temporal structuring. Again, consider the lift controller system. One of its functions is call servicing (a lift must stop at a requested floor); another is establishing a call (by pressing a call-button). It would seem to be more logical to describe the means for establishing a call before describing the way in which it is serviced.

Similarly, it may sometimes be appropriate to deal with the handling of erroneous input (error conditions) separately from (and after) 'normal' operation.

Another (not necessarily very different) approach is 'user manual' structuring. It has been suggested (Howes, 1987) that a good user manual is tantamount to a specification in itself. This is debatable since the purpose and, hence, the style of the documents is (or should be!) significantly different and, of course, systems may well have external interfaces to terminators other than users. Nonetheless, where there is a user interface, even though the style may be very different, the *ordering* of the description of the functionality could be very similar.

These structuring mechanisms are not mutually exclusive. It would be quite possible to have a high-level division based upon separate external interfaces, and then to have a functional breakdown for one external interface and a temporal one for another. (The case study specifications in Part 3 provide examples of some possibilities.)

Whatever basis the structure is built upon, it will not spring into existence fully formed. As external design and documentation proceed, fragments of the specification are most unlikely to be developed in the order in which they will eventually appear in the document. However, by giving the overall structure some consideration from time to time, it is possible to start fitting pieces into the correct 'slots'. In the early stages, the structure itself is liable to be evolving fairly rapidly and this obviously complicates the issue; however, with experience, it becomes easier to anticipate the final shape[72].

Figure 5.11 represents a hierarchical structure of a document with the dark circles representing the first parts to be written occupying their appropriate slots. This may be regarded as rather like fitting a jigsaw puzzle together; the big difference being that there is no pre-defined solution!

In practice such a structure is represented textually and, below, is shown (in part) the exact equivalent of Figure 5.11 using indentation and hierarchical

---

[72] Younger readers may find it hard to appreciate how much easier this has become with the advent of electronic document editing. Sections may be inserted and moved around with consummate ease. Pity the specifiers of yore who had to work with typed or hand-written copy!

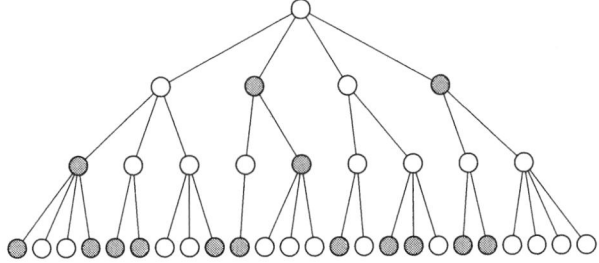

Figure 5.11

section numbering. (The bold text corresponds to the shaded circles above but note that the top level circle does not figure as that represents the whole document.)

1
    1.1
        1.1.1
        1.1.2
        1.1.3
        1.1.4
    1.2
        1.2.1
        1.2.2
    1.3
        1.3.1
        1.3.2
        1.3.3
2
    2.1
        2.1.1
    2.2
        etc.

5.5 Approaches to specification

As previously indicated, recognised methods tend to blur the distinction between analysis and specification. It is, therefore, difficult to identify many well defined and different ways in which specification may be addressed. In a sense, this may be a relief; specification is specification and that is that. However, there are a few points to note and one particular approach, the formal methods, is worthy of considerable attention.

This is also a convenient point at which briefly to consider the specification of sub-systems (lower level specification). Whilst it is not really a different approach, there are some particular considerations.

5.5.1   Object oriented specification (OOS)

Since the publication of Jacobson *et al.*'s work (1992) on use-cases (see Section 12.3) these have rapidly gained popularity as a specification technique. This may well be because they plugged a gap in the object oriented method which, hitherto, had largely assumed that specification had already been accomplished by some other, unspecified, means.

(In passing, it is interesting to note that, within the context of OOA, specification (with use-cases) is seen as *preceding* analysis; a further indication that object oriented 'analysis' actually addresses the high-level idesign of the solution system rather than, as advocated here, investigation of the problem domain (see Section 4.4).)

Whilst use-cases are closely associated with OOA, they are not inherently object oriented, and so simply employing use-cases can hardly be said to justify the label OOS. We may, therefore, ask whether there *is* such a thing as truly object oriented specification.

Where OOD is used for the internal design of the system, it will, of course, be object classes that are being specified at the *lower* structural levels. Since this is clearly the specification of object classes, it is perhaps here that the label OOS may reasonably be applied. That said, the way in which an object class may be behaviourally specified differs little, if any, from that by which the behaviour of any system (or sub-system) may be specified!

It may also be possible to regard the whole solution system as a single object (in the software object sense), but this seems to offer no advantage. Indeed, it may be argued that whole systems are more heterogeneous and have more varied and complex interfaces than (software) objects.

The term OOS may also be associated with the practice of 'specifying' a whole system as a *set of interacting objects*. This, however, is tantamount to internal design specification or, at best, procedural specification (see Section 5.3.4) and is no substitute for proper, system-level *behavioural* specification. The only valid role for OOS that is accepted here is, therefore, the specification of system components as part of internal design.

The above points perhaps explain the relative scarcity of texts upon the subject of OOS. A notable exception is Lano and Haughton (1994) but, whilst this is a fine text upon the topic of (mainly) formal specification (see Section 5.5.2), study reveals that it is actually about the specification of systems. Whether or not some of those systems happen to be objects is pretty much irrelevant.

5.5.2   Formal specification

Formal specification is used here in the restricted sense of specification using formal methods; formal methods being the collective name for a group of specification techniques that share the characteristic of an underlying, mathematical notation.

'Formal methods' may be considered something of a misnomer since most are more akin to techniques than methods and they have not, in any case, cornered the market in formality; other techniques (for example, FSMs) can achieve a high degree of formality. 'Mathematically-based techniques' might be a more descriptive label but, nevertheless, it is the term 'formal methods' that is widely accepted.

During the late 1980s and early 1990s there was enormous investment in research in this area (for a few years, it accounted for around half of all published requirements engineering research). Not for the first time (or, doubtless, the last) a new approach was hailed as the grand solution to all software development difficulties.

Such applause rested upon the big idea that, if a system could be specified using a formal, mathematical notation then, not only would the specification be amenable to various proofs of logical consistency, but it would also be possible to derive implementations that could be shown to produce the specified behaviour. In other words, it could be proved that, provided only that the specification were correct, there were no bugs in the final programs.

Unfortunately, although possible in principle, such proof has, despite all the effort, proved, as yet, impracticable. It is also the case that the expertise in predicate calculus required of the formal methods practitioner has remained relatively rare, and the approach has not proved particularly accessible for clients or potential users. Furthermore, whilst this varies from one formal method to another, there are limitations as to what *can* be specified using formal methods. This largely corresponds to what is loosely referred to here as specification at the logical level (see Section 5.1.2); the physical detail of interfaces is difficult, if not impossible, to address. All this contributes to the fact that the adoption of formal methods has been quite limited.

Nevertheless, it is now widely accepted that formal methods do have a role (not as large a role as that originally promoted but larger than that currently practised) within specification. The precision that they provide can help eliminate ambiguity and misunderstanding in this area.

Formal methods constitute a large subject and, by way of introduction, only an overview of one common incarnation is presented. (And then only in so far as the development of specifications is concerned; any contribution to the subsequent derivation of an implementation will be ignored.)

This is certainly insufficient information to enable use of the approach, but we can hope that it will convey the flavour and, perhaps, whet the appetite for further study.

5.5.2.1 The Vienna development method (VDM)

The Vienna development method is probably the most widely used of the formal methods. It is a state-based approach. The data that must be stored within the solution system are defined together with the effects of the various operations or functions upon that data. At first sight this might look like a procedural approach to specification (see Section 5.3.4), but this is hardly the case; stored data and functionality are defined in an abstract manner that places little constraint upon the subsequent idesign.

We start by defining the system's stored data which, in VDM parlance, constitutes the *state* of the system. The state declaration consists of various sections, identified by certain keywords (shown below in bold):

types

list of type declarations

state

list of variable declarations

inv

state invariants (i.e. rules that constrain the possible values of the variables)

init

declarations of initial variable values

end   (of the state declaration)

There are just four constructs available for the definition of the data:

- sets;
- sequences;
- composites (similar to records);
- maps (which are used to represent associations).

These can however be combined to make arbitrarily complex data types.

As mentioned earlier, a mathematical notation is adopted and, for VDM (as with many formal methods), this is based upon predicate calculus. This may well be familiar to you, but Section 14.3.5 provides a very brief introduction and, for convenience, here is a list of the more common special symbols that are used.

separators

{ }	delimits a set
[ ]	delimits a sequence (but also used to index a set)
,	separates elements in a set or sequence (or parameters in a list)
=	separates a type from its type definition
::	separates a composite object from its component list
:	separates a component of a composite object from its type definition (or a parameter from its type definition)
|	within data declarations, separates the name from any list of properties; can be read as 'such that' or 'where' (and also used to mean 'or')
•	separates bound variable declarations from the body of a predicate; can be read as 'it is the case that'

$\underline{\Delta}$ within the definition of invariants and initialisations, separates the name from the conditions; can be read as 'is defined thus' (and is used in a similar way within explicit function definitions)

quantifiers

$\forall$ the universal quantifier; 'for all'

$\exists$ the existential quantifier; 'there exists'

$\exists!$ the unique existential quantifier; 'there exists just one'

logical operators

$\wedge$ and

$\vee$ or

$\neg$ not

$\Rightarrow$ implies; 'it follows that'

$\Leftrightarrow$ equivalence; 'is equivalent to'

$\mapsto$ the map operator; indicates the mapping between an ordered pair, e.g. 'a $\mapsto$ b' should be read as 'a maps to b'

$\backsim$ the 'hook'; placed over a variable, is used to refer to an old value that is being overwritten

set operators

-set   the set constructor

$\in$ membership; e.g. a $\in$ A (a is an element of the set A)

$\notin$ non-membership; e.g. a $\notin$ A (a is not an element of the set A)

$\subseteq$ subset; e.g. A $\subseteq$ B (A is a subset of the set B)

$\subset$ strict subset; (i.e. a subset that is not equal to the superset)

$\cup$ union; e.g. A $\cup$ B (gives the set that contains all the (non-duplicate) elements of A and B)

$\cap$ intersection; eg. A $\cap$ B (gives the set that contains all the elements that are common to A and B)

pre-defined sets

$\mathbf{Z}$ integers

$\mathbf{N}$ natural numbers (i.e. positive integers)

$\mathbf{N}_1$ natural numbers excluding 0

$\mathbf{R}$ real numbers

$\mathbf{B}$ booleans (true, false)

Char   all the printing characters

map operators and functions

$\xrightarrow{m}$	the map constructor
†	the map overwrite operator; allows the designated elements of a mapping to be added or overwritten without changing the rest
dom	the domain function; if m is a map of a to b, then dom m returns those elements of a which are mapped to b

Sequence operators and functions

*	the sequence constructor
len	gives the length of a sequence
⌢	concatenates sequences, e.g a ⌢ b adds sequence b to the end of a
hd	head – evaluates to the first (head) element of a non-empty sequence
tl	tail – evaluates to the sequence less the head element
cons	adds an element to the start of a sequence
†	over-writes a specific element of a sequence, e.g. [1, 2, 3](2)† 4 evaluates to [1, 4, 3]

No doubt, examples will help illustrate the approach (and the use of the symbols). These will be based upon a somewhat modified version of the YRR case study (see Chapter 15).

Clearly, details of boats must be stored within the system (otherwise it could not produce reports containing those details) and it may well be decided that each boat should be stored as a composite consisting of boat_class, sail_number, boat_name and helm_name. However, an individual boat is identified only by its sail_number and boat_class and so it is better to declare this first and then map the set of boat_ids to the set of other, associated details. (Note that in the following, by convention, variable names start with a lower case letter and types with upper case.)

$$
\begin{array}{ll}
\underline{\text{Boat\_id}} \qquad :: & \\
\quad \text{boat\_class} & : \text{Class-name} \\
\quad \text{sail\_number} & : \text{Sail-number} \\
\quad \text{inv- Boat\_id (bi)} \; \underline{\Delta} & \forall\, a,b \in bi \bullet a = b \vee a.boat\_class = b.boat\_class \Rightarrow \\
& a.sail\_number \neq b.sail\_number
\end{array}
$$

This invariant ensures uniqueness and is to be read as: for the set bi of type Boat_id, it is the case that, for all a and b that are members of the set bi, it is the case that a is the same as b or, if their boat_class is the same then it follows that their sail_numbers are different.

$$
\text{Boat} \;=\; \text{Boat\_id} \xrightarrow{m} \text{Boat\_details}
$$

A boat type consists of a boat_id (as defined above) mapped to a corresponding set of boat_details:

    Boat_details   ::
            boat_name   : Name
            helm_name   : Name

Since order is unimportant and uniqueness is required, the boats within the system could well be represented as a set. The set of boats would be a set of type Boatset and could be defined thus:

    Boatset = Boat-set

where '-set' at the end of the expression is a special constructor for creating a set type.

We can now create sets of boats of the defined type Boatset, for example:

    boats = Boatset

(Or we could have done it 'all in one', without the explicitly named type, thus:

    boats = Boat-set)

There is still the matter of defining Sail-number and Boat-class. For illustrative purposes let us assume that Sail-number is a positive natural number in the range 1 . . . 99999. Positive natural numbers (along with integers, reals, etc.) are a pre-defined type represented by N and we may specify the required sub-range thus:

    Sail-number   =   {sn $\in$ N | sn $\leq$ 999999}

which is read as 'Sail-number is one of sn where sn is a member of the set of positive natural numbers such that sn is never more than 999999'.

Assuming that Boat-class is a character string, it may be defined as:

    Boat_class = Char*

You may have noticed that, in effect, we are defining the syntax of the data. As has been mentioned before, it is also a good idea to designate the meaning (semantics) of the base terms. This is illustrated in Section 14.4.1 and so will not be pursued further here.

Putting the preceding bits together and adding a few more representative items could result in a state declaration along these lines:

values

MINPY	:	700	/* the minimum value of a PY handicap */
MAXPY	:	1400	/* the maximum value of a PY handicap */

types

Class_name	=	Name
Class	=	Class_name $\xrightarrow{m}$ Handicap
Handicap	=	$\{h \in \mathbb{N} \mid (h \geq \text{MINPY}) \land (h \leq \text{MAXPY})\}$

The type Class (of boats) is declared as consisting of a name and a handicap. Uniqueness of class names is assured by their being members of the set Class_Name.

Boat_id	::	
boat_class		: Class-name
sail_number		: Sail-number
inv- Boat_id (bi)$\underline{\Delta}$		$\forall$ a,b $\in$ bi $\bullet$ a = b $\lor$ a.boat_class = b.boat_class $\Rightarrow$
		a.sail_number $\neq$ b.sail_number
Boat	=	Boat_id $\xrightarrow{m}$ Boat_details
Boat_details	::	
boat_name		: Name
helm_name		: Name
Sail-number	=	$\{sn \in \mathbb{N} \mid sn \leq 99999\}$
Race	=	Race_id $\xrightarrow{m}$ Race_details
Race_id	=	token

'Token' is a special VDM term for an (as yet) unspecified, unique identifier (in other words, a key).

Race_details	::	
date	:	Date
time	:	Time
race_class	:	Race_class
race_name	:	Name
course	:	Course

A boat may enter more than one (indeed, a set) of races and this might be termed the race programme for the boat. So, each boat_id can be mapped to a set of entries and the programmes for all the boats could be defined thus:

Boat_programmes   =   Boat_id $\xrightarrow{m}$ Entry_details-set

The details for each entry include the race_id and can be defined as:

Entry_details ::

    race_id   : Race_id

    finish_time   : Time

    elapsed_time : $\{et \in N_1 \mid et \leq 99999\}$ /*elapsed time in seconds */

    corrected_time : $\{ct \in N_1 \mid ct \leq 99999\}$ /*corrected time in seconds */

    position   : $\{p \in N_1 \mid p \leq 99\}$

And to round off, here are the details of the remaining types:

Race_class   = Name

Name   = Char*

inv-Name(n) $\triangle$ $len(n) \leq 20$

Time   ::

    hour   : $\{h \in N_1 \mid h \leq 59\}$

    min   : $\{m \in N_1 \mid m \leq 59\}$

    sec   : $\{s \in N_1 \mid s \leq 59\}$

Date   ::

    day   : $\{d \in N_1 \mid d \leq 31\}$

    mon   : $\{m \in N_1 \mid m \leq 12\}$

    year   : $\{y \in N_1 \mid y \geq 2000\}$

state   race_programme **of**

    classes   : Class-set

    boats   : Boat-set

    races   : Race-set

    entries   :   Boat_programmes

inv

    /* there are no invariants on the state */

init

    classes   = { }

    boats   = { }

    races   = { }

    entries   = { }

end

So far, so good; we are now in a position to specify the required behaviour of the system. The next step is to define the necessary operations and/or functions in terms of their inputs and outputs and the effect, if any, that they have upon the state.

A VDM operation is defined in terms of the relationship between its input and output. It is permissible to resort to an algorithmic (procedural) definition which, in a similar way to a conventional programming language, defines the effect of the function in terms of the way in which it might be computed. Sometimes this produces a significantly simpler definition but, otherwise, we can (and should) avoid introducing any possible design constraints by sticking to a non-procedural definition. This is accomplished by just stating the conditions that pertain prior to the invocation of the operation (the pre-conditions) and the conditions that will pertain after the invocation of the operation (the post-conditions).

This is known as an implicit definition and takes the general form:

operation_name (input parameter list) output parameter list
pre
      any pre-condition(s) (if there are none, then simply the boolean, "true")
post
      post-condition(s)

Each parameter list is a list of paired parameter names and types (param1: type1, param2: type2, etc.), pre and post are reserved keywords that introduce the pre-conditions and post-conditions.

Pre-conditions impose any necessary constraints upon the permissible values of the parameters (in effect, their validity). Post-conditions define the effect of the operation in terms of the relationship between the parameters and the result and any effect upon the state (i.e. the stored data). Where an operation accesses the state it is necessary also to declare this using the reserved words ext (short for external) and rd (read) or wr (read/write) as appropriate.

This is illustrated in the following example which concerns the operation that adds a (pre-defined) boat into the set of boats (by convention, operation names are shown in upper case):

ADD-BOAT (boat_id: Boat_id, boat_details: Boat_details)
ext wr boats   :   Boat-set
pre
      boat_id $\notin$ dom boats
post
      boats   = $\overleftarrow{\text{boats}}$ † {boat_id $\mapsto$ boat-details}

The pre-condition simply states that the boat_id is not already in the boats domain. The post-condition states that boats is overwritten with a new version that is the same as the old, with the exception that the new boat_id (mapped to its relevant details) has been added.

The next example concerns the operation that enters a boat into a race (in this case, comments are shown using the common VDM convention):

ADD_ENTRY (boat_id: Boat_id, race_id: Race_id)
ext rd boats   :   Boat-set
             races   :   Race-set
      wr entries :   Boat_programmes
pre
      boat_id $\in$ dom boats P
      race_id $\in$ dom races P

$\forall$ e $\in$ entries (boat_id) • e.race_id $\neq$ race_id
/* for any existing entry for the given boat, it is the case that the race_id is different from the that given */

post

entries = entries $\dagger$ {boat_id $\mapsto$ entries (boat_id) $\cup$ {mk_Entry_details (race_id, –, –, –, –)}}
/* entries is the same as the old version with the exception that the entry for the relevant boat_id is now mapped to the new entry (in addition to any pre-existing entries). The new entry has been created with the appropriate race_id (other details are, as yet, undetermined). */

Many more operations would have to be defined in order to complete the specification but, since the intention here is just to give an idea of the form of formal specifications, I will leave it at that.

It is perhaps worth mentioning that, as well as operations, VDM supports the definition of functions. In a very similar way to many programming languages, functions differ from operations in that they return a single value. It is also the case that, within VDM, functions cannot access the system state and so the result of a function depends only upon the values of its parameters. The general form of a VDM function is:

function-name (parameter-list) result-name: result-type
pre
        any pre-condition(s)
post
        the post-condition(s)

As previously indicated, writing VDM (or predicate calculus in general) requires some expertise and significantly more study would be required to achieve competence. It is to be hoped, however, this has been enough to indicate its nature and the contribution that can be made.

So, in summary, VDM (in common with other formal methods) provides a means for the rigorous specification of system behaviour. This helps identify errors and has clear potential benefits for critical systems. Considerable expertise is required in order to develop such formal specifications, and this is one reason why they have not been widely adopted. However, their interpretation is relatively easy and, with some accompanying narrative, they are accessible to non-experts. They operate at a relatively abstract, 'logical' level and, whilst this helps avoid the introduction of design constraints, we usually resort to other techniques when specifying details of human interfaces, etc.

5.5.3   Lower level specification

The bulk of this chapter concerns the specification of applications or 'whole systems' as occurs during the requirements phase of a project. But, as development proceeds, the internal design will decompose the system into its constituent sub-systems (modules, classes or whatever) and sub-sub-systems (etc.) each of which requires specification in turn. This may be viewed as a recursive specification, idesign, specification, idesign (and so on) cycle which eventually terminates with the lowest level modules. (The nature of these modules will vary depending upon the implementation technology but procedures, functions, operations and methods are common.)

The specification of the behaviour of these sub-systems is just as important as the specification of the whole system. However, the considerations are rather different and, generally, the task is simpler.

For a start, *within* software systems, all interfaces are, of course, with other software. This places considerable constraints upon the nature of those interfaces and, together with the fact that sub-systems are necessarily smaller, contributes to the relative simplicity and ease of specification as we move to the lower levels.

Another difference is that, instead of working from a requirements document, the specifier is working from the relevant internal design document. Indeed, it may be argued that the design document is little more than the sum of the specifications of the components that it dictates.

There is also the matter of target audience; low-level specifications are not, generally, for consumption outside the developer's organisation. They are written by technical staff to be read by other technical staff.

So, low-level specification may be regarded as requiring only a sub-set of the skills needed for high-level specification; in particular those needed for the specification of software interfaces (or APIs). What more needs to be said is perhaps best conveyed by an example.

5.5.3.1 Low-level specification example

Suppose that as part of the internal design for the lift controller system it has been decided that there should be a floor request queue (FRQ) to be instantiated as an abstract data type (ADT). The design of the system (in effect, the requirements for the FRQ) dictates that the following operations are required[73]: add_floor_request, more_requests, next_request, floor_request, clear_floor_request.

The basic approach to specifying the behaviour of this ADT is the same as for a whole system; it is necessary to define the acceptable inputs and outputs and then define the causal relationships between them, not forgetting any exceptional or error conditions[74]. This may be viewed as specifying the *syntax* and the *semantics* of the operations to be provided by the ADT.

---

[73] A particular implementation language may have been selected by this stage. If so, it may as well be utilised; otherwise (as here) some form of pseudo-code can be used.

[74] Note that, thanks to the parameter typing that may be enforced by the run-time environment, software interfaces are, generally, subject to far fewer problems arising from invalid input.

In this case, I will assume that, as usual, data are passed by way of parameters and, as is also likely, that strict type definitions have already been produced as part of the idesign. (For example, floor is an enumerated type that is constrained within the range ground_floor to top_floor.) It is then only necessary to indicate which parameters are passed and in which direction:

```
add_floor_request (IN – floor: floor_type; direction: direction_type);
more_requests (): boolean;
next_request (IN/OUT – floor: floor_type; direction: direction_type);
floor_request (IN – floor: floor_type; direction: direction_type): boolean;
clear_floor_request (IN – floor: floor_type; direction: direction_type);
```

This completes the definition of the syntax but we must still define the semantics; what, precisely, are the *effects* of these operations[75]? It is also helpful to provide an overall view of the purpose or function of the ADT. (Text is often used for this but there are various options regarding specification technique and, bearing in mind the target audience of low-level specifications, formal specification (see section 5.5.2) of the semantics is a realistic alternative to text.) So, adding these elements gives the complete specification:

floor_request_queue
/* This ADT provides for the storage of requests from call_buttons. Call_buttons are the buttons outside the lift on each floor that are used to call lifts. Note that most floors have an UP button and a DOWN button but the top_floor has no UP button and the ground_floor has no DOWN button. Floor requests may be serviced by any lift that is travelling in the correct direction. */

add_floor_request (IN – floor: floor_type; direction: direction_type);
/* Adds a call-button request to the queue. If the particular floor and direction are already requested, there will be no effect. As the top_floor and the ground_floor have only one button, in those cases, direction is ignored. */

more_requests (): boolean;
/* a function which returns true if there are any more floor requests */

next_request (IN/OUT – floor: floor_type; direction: direction_type);
/* finds the next request in the given direction from the given floor. For example, if the given floor is 3 and the direction is UP it will check from floor 4

▶

---

[75] This step is sometimes omitted and the results can be costly. I well remember an operation of a graphics sub-system that was defined thus:

draw_arc (arc_centre, arc_start, arc_end: coord_type);

It was not until system integration that it was discovered that the implementers of the graphics package had decided to draw the arcs anti-clockwise whereas the implementers of the application, of which it was a part, had assumed that arcs would be drawn clockwise. It would have been less expensive to fix if many copies of the graphics software had not, by this time, been burnt into PROMS.

to the top floor (in that order) and return the floor and direction of the first floor_request found. Note that the parameters serve two purposes; as IN parameters they define where to search, as OUT parameters they define the request that was found. If no request is found, floor and direction are returned unchanged[76].*/

floor_request (IN – floor: floor_type; direction: direction_type): boolean;
/* a function which returns true if there is a request for the particular floor and the particular direction. As the top_floor and the ground_floor have only one button, in those cases, direction is ignored. */

clear_floor_request (IN – floor: floor_type; direction: direction_type);
/* removes the specified request from the queue. As the top_floor and the ground_floor have only one button, in those cases, direction is ignored. */

5.6 Specification techniques and mechanisms

We have seen that specification is, essentially, a matter of defining the behaviour of the solution system. It is suggested that this is best done in terms of the inputs to and outputs from the solution system and the relationships, both causal and timely, between those inputs and outputs. Various means of definition have been introduced in passing but, before proceeding to more extensive examples, it is probably as well to take a more comprehensive view of the available technology and its application.

Whilst there may be varying degrees of formality, definitions are usually thought of as being text-based. Natural language is a uniquely powerful tool and has a critical role to play; however, some of the required definitions may best be provided by the various modelling techniques. At least in theory, in recent years the emphasis has tended towards system modelling rather than definition but it transpires that the dividing line may be a thin one. Section 13.3.2 demonstrates that sets of definitions can constitute a model.

Input/output data definition is the relatively simple part. The DD produced during analysis can be extended to include the solution data using the same techniques (such as BNF). However, when it comes to specifying the appearance of screen-based output it is often helpful to employ representational models (drawings) as well.

Input/output relationships are relatively difficult to pin down, but there is a much wider choice of technology. This is summarised in Table 5.4. (Note that only the most common and apposite usage of techniques is shown; there are some other possibilities.)

---

[76] It is not really a specification matter, but you may care to debate whether or not this is a *good* design!

Table 5.4

Defined aspect: \ Technique	Representational drawing	Throwaway prototype	Decision table	Functional decomposition	Use-case	Task action grammar	FSM	Petri net	ELH	DD (BNF)	Formal methods
I/O solution data										✓	✓
SS appearance	✓	✓									
SS behaviour (ER actions)		✓	✓	✓	✓	✓	✓	✓			✓
SS state (ER states)							✓	✓	✓		✓
Timing							✓	✓			

Descriptions of the various techniques may be found in Part 3.

In addition to the aspects tabulated above, it is common practice to include a definition of the solution system's *stored* data (using, say, an ERD). This is not, however, essential, nor is it recommended.

5.7 Specification examples

Having examined the 'theory', it is now time to look at the practice of developing specifications from requirements. Remember that the objective is to devise and document a behaviour of the solution system that will meet the requirements. As with so much of requirements engineering, there is no simple, formulaic procedure to follow and so, again, resort is made to a series of examples with accompanying commentary.

There are many options regarding the style and the level (see Section 5.1.2) of specification. If the full, physical detail of the interaction is specified, then the appearance of the system (as well as its behaviour) will require description.

Of the four examples that follow, the first three illustrate specification at the physical level, the fourth at the logical level, but with indications of the 'extras' that would be required to fully specify the interface.

Variation in style and technology is also illustrated. Notably, the first example relies largely upon text (and representative drawings) the fourth relies largely upon state charts.

For reference, the complete, un-annotated specifications can be seen in Sections 15.4, 16.3, 17.2 and 18.2.

5.7.1 Case 1, the yacht race results (YRR) program

When developing a specification, the main point of reference is the requirements document. For the YRR program this is given in Section 15.3 but, for convenience, the requirements are reproduced here:

R1   Subject to the constraints detailed below, the user can enter, amend and delete details of: boat-class, boat, race, series, race-entry, series-entry.

R2   A boat cannot be entered into the system unless it has a boat class and sail number.

R3   A boat may only be entered into a one design race (or series) if its boat class matches the race class.

R4   A boat may only be entered into a handicap race (or series) if its handicap type matches that of the race and its handicap is within the (inclusive) range specified by the minimum and maximum handicaps.

R5   A boat that enters a series is automatically entered into every race in the series.

R6   If a boat's details are amended, this will not automatically affect the outcome of any races where the boat's result has already been entered but the user may opt for the race (or series) outcome to be recalculated.

R7   The outcome for races and series should be available (for reports) as soon as the relevant data are entered but for incomplete series, the outcome will be shown without any discards being made.

R8   Upon command from the user, the system will produce the following reports (content as defined in the data dictionary):

R8.1   boat-class-list

R8.2   boat-list

R8.3   series-list

R8.4   series-details

R8.5   series-outcome

R8.6   race-outcome

R9   All reports will be output to screen and may also be printed upon user request.

R10   The system should respond to all user input within 1 second and, subject to printer speed, should produce a series outcome report for a series with 10 races and 50 boats entered within 5 seconds.

R11   The system should handle at least the following capacities:

R11.1   99 boat classes

R11.2   999 boats

R11.3   999 races

R11.4   999 series

R12 This is not a critical system but it should be available at least 20 hours per week and, subject to usual back-up practice, should not lose data.

R13 To save user effort, wherever possible, the most likely values for data should be presented during data entry, for example:

- where boat details are being entered, it is likely that a boat will have the same class as the last one entered

- where races are being added to a series, it is likely that all races in the series will have the same start time

R14 All data should be validated as soon as practicable after entry and the user should be advised of any errors.

R15 A WIMP type interface is required.

R16 The system should operate upon a JCN compatible PC under the Fenestra 99 operating system.

R1, R8 and R15 are clearly central to the required functionality of the system and it may be noted that a direct manipulation ('WIMP type') interface is dictated (so no choice about that). Some resultant, early edesign decisions are:

- There should be a set of overlaying windows, one for each of the main editing functions (boat-class, boat, race, series, race-entry and series-entry).

- Reports should be available from the relevant editing screens.

The high-level navigation will have to be designed, but this is often easier when there is a better sense of the lower level interaction. It may, therefore, be best to work on one of the editing screens first. The boat-classes editing is not only logically first (there must be a class before a boat can be entered and there must be a boat (and a race) before a boat may be entered in a race), but also appears to be a relatively straightforward starting point. In this example, behaviour will be documented at the 'physical' level and, in such cases, it is often easier to start with the appearance. A possible window appearance, based upon the given attributes of boat-class, is shown in Figure 5.12.

A simple representational drawing has been chosen and, as can be seen, some realistic, sample data have been included. This makes it far easier for clients and users (and, even, the designers) to appreciate the operation and, hence, validate the specification.

It is now necessary to explain the way in which the window operates (the behaviour). There is considerably more choice regarding documentation technique here but, for this example, I will illustrate how plain text might be used. There follows the sort of explanation that might accompany the drawing. (As well as addressing part of R1, much of this reflects the wide ranging usability requirements (R13 and 14), but where other requirements are explicitly addressed this has been flagged):

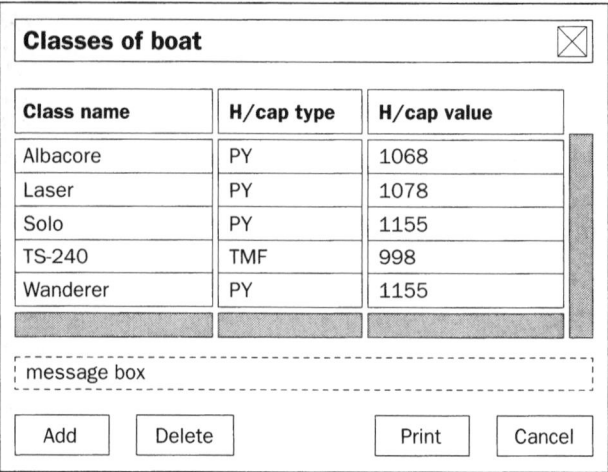

Figure 5.12

- This drawing is to scale (within an acceptable tolerance of +/– 10%).
- 6 lines for classes are always displayed: unused lines are 'greyed out'.
- The last line is kept blank (greyed out) to allow for additions (see below).
- If more than 5 classes are entered, the scroll bar (on the right) becomes active.
- Column width may be adjusted by picking and dragging the column separators.
- There is a minimum column width of one character.
- Entries may be sorted by any column. The required sorting column is selected by clicking on its heading (e.g. 'Class name').
- The message box is only visible when a message is on display.

Class editing

- The usual WIMP-type editing mechanisms may be used (e.g. highlight and delete, paste, overtype, etc.).
- A field entry is invalid if it does not comply with the type definition (given in the Data Dictionary) or, in the case of the class name, if it is not unique.
- Editing of a field (i.e. one column of one row), is terminated by:
  - pressing the return or enter key (which also moves the cursor down one row)
  - pressing the tab or shift/tab keys (which also moves the cursor forward or back one field)
  - clicking the mouse button to move the cursor out of the field
- An attempt to terminate entry of invalid field data or a complete entry (row) will result in an error message and the cursor will be placed in the relevant, invalid field.

Possible error messages for class editing:

R11
(part)

- No more classes may be added (maximum 99).
- The class name must be letters, digits, -, ' or . (max 25 characters).
- The class name must be unique.
- The handicap type must be PY or TMF.
- The handicap must be three or four digits (no decimal point required).
- This class cannot be deleted as it is in use.

Messages are displayed until a valid entry is completed or another message overwrites or 'Cancel' is selected.

The 'Cancel' button may be selected to 'undo' editing of the current entry. If it is a new entry then no entry will be added. If an existing entry were being edited then it will revert to the previous values.

To add a class entry, the last (greyed out) line is overwritten (and, upon completion, a new, blank (greyed out) line will be created). The user may either move the cursor to this line or click the 'Add' button which will automatically scroll to this last (blank) line and place the cursor in the first field.

To delete a class entry the user must highlight the whole line (either by click and drag or by clicking just to the left of the class name) and then click the 'Delete' button (or type cntrl x).

If the handicap type or value for a particular class are changed and there are one or more boats assigned to that class, any of which have one or more race entries, then a pop up window appears (Figure 5.13).

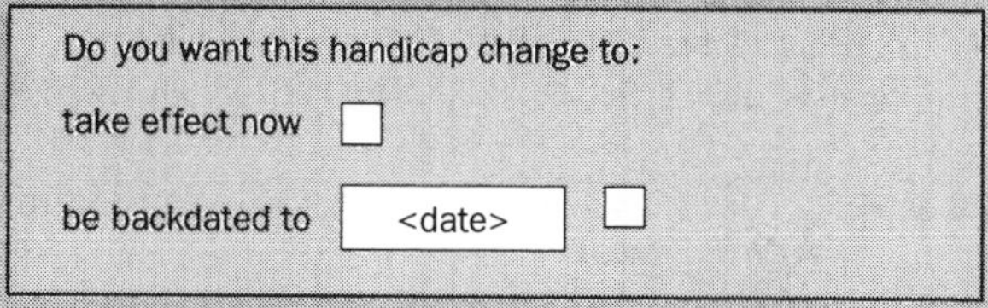

Do you want this handicap change to:

take effect now ☐

be backdated to <date> ☐

R6

Figure 5.13

The user may, optionally, overwrite the default date (today) and then click the 'now' box or the 'backdate' box. All races on or after the chosen date will then have their results (re)calculated according to the new handicap.

R8,
R9

To print the class listing, the user clicks on the 'Print' button. The report is headed:

Classes of boats <date>

(Where <date> is the current system date.) Below this, the column (field) headings are printed (and, if the report extends over more than one page, are repeated at the top of subsequent pages) followed by the classes, listed as displayed.

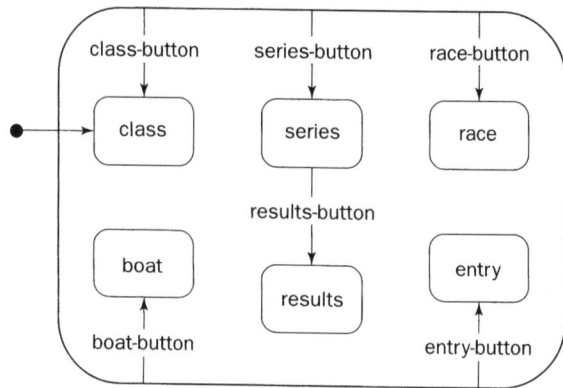

Figure 5.14

There are numerous other possibilities regarding the edesign of this interaction but we can hope that this example serves the purpose of illustrating the kind of information that is pertinent.

There are also several possibilities regarding the documentation techniques. A prototype could be built that would define both the appearance and behaviour (but, by its very nature, that cannot, of course, be illustrated in a book). Some form of FSM is another possibility for defining the behaviour. Returning, for example, to the high-level navigation of the system, Figure 5.14 is a state chart showing how the user can move from screen to screen.

As for the rest of the specification, it is very much a matter of more of the same. The trick, however, is not to be repetitive. When it comes to the next window, make it as alike as possible and, in the specification, write 'this screen operates in a similar manner to the last one, the differences being . . .', or words to that effect.

For reference purposes, a complete specification for this system can be found in Section 15.4.

5.7.2   Case 2, the lift controller

When developing a specification, the main point of reference is the requirements document. For the lift controller this is given in Section 16.2 but fragments will be reproduced here as necessary including, for starters, the requirements (which are often copied into the specification anyway):

R1   The lift should never be allowed to move above the top floor or below the bottom floor. (There is an emergency shut down system that will stop the motor if the lift goes above the top floor or below the bottom floor (by more than 10 cm) but this shut down system is beyond the scope of the control system.)

R2   The lift should not be stopped from fast mode but should always be switched to slow mode for at least 1 second before stopping.

R3   The motor polarity must not be changed whilst the lift is moving. (This could wreck the winding gear.)

R4   The lift must never be moved with the doors open.

R5   With the stop delay correctly configured (as below) the lift should stop within +/– 1.5 cm of the floor being serviced.

R6   A call is established by pressing a send-button (inside the lift) or a call-button (outside the lift) for the relevant floor and, in the case of call-buttons, for the relevant direction. (Duplicate calls are ignored.)

R7   Calls are cancelled only when serviced by a lift.

R8   To service a send-button call, the relevant lift must stop at that floor. A call-button call may be serviced by any lift that is travelling in the correct direction stopping at that floor.

R9   A lift will stop at a floor if:

R9.1   there is a send-button call for that floor or

R9.2   a call-button call and the lift is moving in the right direction or

R9.3   it is the top or bottom floor

Where there is more than one lift:

R10   Send-button calls must be serviced by the relevant lift.

R11   Call-button calls should be serviced by the lift that is likely to arrive there soonest. (It is appreciated that this cannot be guaranteed because the selected lift might be requested to service a new call whilst en route.)

R12   Each lift should be used an approximately equal amount.

R13   A lift will only reverse direction when stopped at a floor.

R14   A lift will only reverse direction if it has no outstanding calls in its current direction of travel.

R15   For each lift, one indicator at a time should be illuminated, that being the one for the floor that the lift is (approximately) nearest to.

R16   The service technician must be able to set:

R16.1   number of lifts

R16.2   number of floors

R16.3   stop signal delay, for each lift (in the range 0.10 to 0.40 seconds)

R17   The maximum number of lifts is 4, the minimum 1.

R18   The maximum number of floors is 20, the minimum 2.

R19   The control system should not violate any safety requirements. Non-safety-critical control errors (e.g. lift sent to wrong floor) should not occur more than once per week of operation.

R20   The control system must fit within a volume of 1 x 0.5 x 0.5 m.

R21 The control system must operate over a temperature range of 0–40°C.

R22 RF emissions must comply with BS50081-2.

A reasonable starting point is to consider what interfaces will exist between the new, solution system (the lift controller) and its operating environment. The problem frame diagram and (to a slightly lesser extent) the context diagram are of great help here; it may be determined from these that the controller interfaces directly with various pieces of hardware (buttons, sensors, motors, etc.) and indirectly with the lifts and users.

Although not directly imposed by the problem, the requirements (R16) make it clear that there must also be an interface to a service technician. This last stands apart from the rest and so can be defined in a separate section. In fact, this has largely already been done as an example of external design in Section 5.2. There is, however, some interaction with the rest of the system, and it may well be necessary to introduce a statement (indeed, a warning!) to the effect that when the service technician key is turned, all lifts will stop. In passing, it is worth noting how some of the performance requirements (R17 and R18) find expression in the technician interface where any attempt to exceed the defined limits results in an appropriate error response.

For this system, the *appearance* of the user interface is virtually pre-determined by the given hardware (buttons and indicators). However, the *behaviour* of the system, as apparent to the user, remains to be defined. To a large extent, what the user experiences is the emergent (i.e. controlled) behaviour of the lift(s) and associated hardware. It, therefore, makes sense to define that first.

The 'appearance' of the hardware interface boils down to the connections between the controller and the hardware. Inventing the detail of those connections is an element of the external design. The only real guidance that can be given for such cases is to apply some logic (common sense?) but, once devised, the allocation of ports and pins can be specified with suitable tables. A small sample is given in Table 5.5 (the full table is in Section 16.3.1.1).

The behaviour of the lifts must be described in terms of 'cross-interface' functions which involve all the remaining interfaces (buttons, motors, etc.). For example, the motors must be started and stopped in response to button presses and sensor signals.

Table 5.5

Port	Purpose	Pin 0	Pin 1	Pin 2	Pin 3	...	Pin 29	Pin 30	Pin 31
1	spare								
2	up call buttons	floor 0	floor 1	floor 2	floor 3	etc. (to 20)	unused	unused	unused
3	down call buttons	unused	floor 1	floor 2	floor 3	etc. (to 20)	unused	unused	unused

Experience suggests that, for such cross-interface functionality of event driven systems, FSMs often prove the most effective definition technique. An STD or state chart may therefore be attempted.

For the novice, the starting point for such a model is often a sticking point. One useful approach is to start by listing the events (extracted from the description of the problem sub-domains in the requirements document) that the solution system may detect. In this case we have:

- above-floor-sensor goes hi
- above-floor-sensor goes lo
- below-floor-sensor goes hi
- below-floor-sensor goes lo
- at-floor-sensor goes hi
- at-floor-sensor goes lo
- call-button goes hi
- call-button goes lo
- send-button goes hi
- send-button goes lo
- doors-closed-sensor goes hi
- doors-closed-sensor goes lo

It transpires that these are not all relevant (the controller needs to know when a floor-sensor signal goes hi but not when it goes lo) but this is still a good starting point.

Next, it is usually helpful to consider the states that the system in question (in this case a lift) might occupy. It is not necessary to start with a comprehensive list; if a few states can be identified, drawing can commence. Do not postpone drawing until you know the 'answer' (because, that way you will never start) and do not expect to get it right first time! There is really nothing to beat pencil and paper for the first drafts and I would reckon on at least the first two or three being filed in the bin pretty promptly.

Some obvious states to start with here are 'lift stopped', 'lift moving fast' and 'lift moving slowly'. One can then consider the events that trigger the relevant transitions and an embryonic state chart can be drawn. It is then a case of developing the model, the main considerations being how accurately and comprehensively it addresses the relevant requirements and how easy it is to understand. As an example of such considerations, I experimented with concurrent FSMs for speed and direction but, because too many ERs depend upon speed *and* direction, eventually, decided that a non-concurrent model was clearer. Figure 5.15 illustrates the final (at least for now) model that emerged (but bear in mind that this is only one of a number of possible edesign solutions).

Exceptionally, this state chart has been annotated to show whereabouts the various requirements are addressed. As can be seen, in this case, the mapping

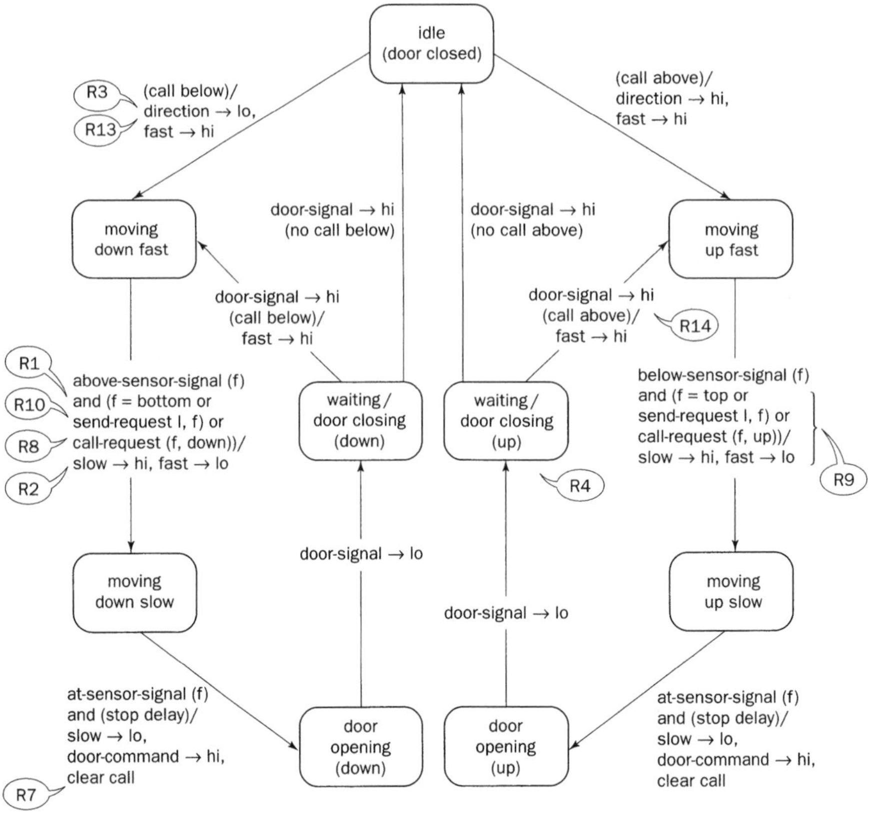

idle
(door closed)

R3 (call below)/
direction → lo,
R13 fast → hi

(call above)/
direction → hi,
fast → hi

moving
down fast

door-signal → hi
(no call below)

door-signal → hi
(no call above)

moving
up fast

door-signal → hi
(call below)/
fast → hi

door-signal → hi
(call above)/
fast → hi

R14

R1
R10
R8
R2

above-sensor-signal (f)
and (f = bottom or
send-request l, f) or
call-request (f, down))/
slow → hi, fast → lo

waiting /
door closing
(down)

waiting /
door closing
(up)

R4

below-sensor-signal (f)
and (f = top or
send-request l, f) or
call-request (f, up))/
slow → hi, fast → lo

R9

moving
down slow

door-signal → lo

moving
up slow

door-signal → lo

at-sensor-signal (f)
and (stop delay)/
slow → lo,
door-command → hi,
clear call

R7

door
opening
(down)

door
opening
(up)

at-sensor-signal (f)
and (stop delay)/
slow → lo,
door-command → hi,
clear call

Figure 5.15

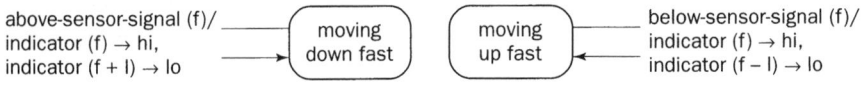

above-sensor-signal (f)/
indicator (f) → hi,
indicator (f + l) → lo

moving
down fast

moving
up fast

below-sensor-signal (f)/
indicator (f) → hi,
indicator (f – l) → lo

Figure 5.16

from requirements to solution system behaviour is not a simple one. This model goes a long way towards achieving the major objective of defining the solution system behaviour but there is a bit more yet to do.

The operation of the indicators (R15) could have been incorporated into the above state chart but at the risk of over-crowding and it is conveniently handled separately as shown in Figure 5.16.

Requirements R8, R11 and R12 (covering the allocation of lifts to calls) are difficult to reflect in a model but suitable behaviour to meet them is readily described textually:

Where there is more than one lift, call-button-signals are handled thus:

- Allocate the call to the lift with the shortest response time.
- If lifts have equal response times, then select one of those lifts randomly.

Response time for each lift is calculated as:

(1.2 * floor-height (metres) * number-of-floors-to-travel) +
number-of-stops-en-route * waiting-time (seconds) + 8)

R5 (accuracy of stop position) is an interesting one. Using the given facts about the problem domain some calculations can determine the feasibility of meeting it. This is detailed on p. 153 from which the conclusions are:

- The lift will be moving at 0.3 m/sec (+/– 10%).

- The proximity-sensor signal will go hi when the lift becomes within 20 cm of the floor.

- The lift motor is stopped by setting the slow and fast lines to lo.

- The lift will move 0.15 m (+/– 20%) before it actually stops.

We can therefore calculate that in the 'worst' case the lift will be travelling at 0.33 m/sec and will travel 18 cm before it stops. This allows just 2 cm movement, which would take 0.06 seconds, before the stop signal must be sent. At the other extreme, the stop-delay would have to be 0.3 seconds. This looks feasible and the requirements document also tells us that the stop-delay is configurable by the technician. We now know the range and granularity (0.01 seconds) that must be allowed and can design the technician interface accordingly.

Since the stop accuracy is required to be within 1.5 cm, the tolerance of +/– 3 cm (20% of 0.15 m) on the stopping position could cause a problem. The crucial question (not clear from the requirements document) is whether this varies for every stop or varies between lifts (but is, more or less, constant for any given lift). We may well have to check back with the client; if the former supposition is true, we cannot meet the requirement (without changes to the hardware); if the latter is true, we can but it means that the stop-delay must be set individually for each lift (and again, the technician interface can be specified accordingly).

The performance requirements (R17 and R18) concerning the numbers of lifts and floors also find expression in the technician interface. A possible edesign for this is included in the complete specification (Section 16.3.3).

Despite having fully specified the behaviour of the system, in order to aid understanding and validation, it may still be as well to model the user perspective of the emergent behaviour explicitly. Use-cases constitute a suitable technique and here is an example:

NORMAL JOURNEY
User calls lift and travels to required destination floor.
Actors
　　User
Pre-conditions:
　　None
Post-condition:
　　The user will be at their required destination floor
Interaction

1　The user arrives outside a lift door and presses the relevant call-button

2　A lift arrives and the door opens

3　The user enters the lift

4　The user presses the send-button for the required destination floor

5　The door closes, the lift travels to the destination floor (possibly stopping at other floors en route) and the door opens

6　The user exits the lift

The number of use-cases that may be produced is arbitrary, a couple of other possibilities being:

Lift already at start floor, door open
Lift already at start floor, door closing

These could be written as separate use-cases or as extensions or alternates (see Section 12.3.6.2). A further option is to introduce some selection logic and combine the various cases in a style akin to functional decomposition (see Section 12.1.1):

The user arrives outside the lift entrance.
Case of lift:
　　present, doors open
　　　　The user enters the lift;
　　present, doors closed or closing
　　　　The user presses the call-button for the desired direction of travel
　　　　The doors open
　　　　The user enters the lift;
　　not present
　　　　The user presses the call-button for the desired direction of travel
　　　　When the lift arrives
　　　　　　The doors open
　　　　　　The user enters the lift;

> The user presses the desired send-button
> The lift travels to the requested floor (possibly stopping at other floors en
> route)
> The lift stops at the requested floor
> The lift doors open
> The user leaves the lift

The remaining requirements are the reliability requirement (R19) and the design constraints (R20 to R22). These cannot be reflected in the specification; they simply remain as requirements.

So, that completes the specification task; a full version of the document can be found in Section 16.3.

5.7.3   Case 3, the drill file conversion system

When developing a specification, the main point of reference is the requirements document. For the drill file conversion problem this is given in Section 17.1 but fragments will be reproduced here as necessary including, for starters, the requirements (which are often copied into the specification anyway):

R1   The input file, in Head2 format, is to be converted to produce an output file, in Karaoke3 format, according to the given mapping.

R2   Input file errors to be detected and as many errors as possible to be reported at the individual field level of detail.

R3   The program (F2K) to be invoked (from UNIX) by the operator.

R4   The operator to supply:

R4.1   the address of the input file

R4.2   the address of the output file

R4.3   the century

R5   A 50 Kb input file to be converted in less than 10 seconds.

R6   The only limit on file size to be machine capacity.

The external interfaces to this system are few and simple (which is not atypical of transformation problems). Indeed, there are only two significant matters to address; the invocation of the program by the user and the reporting of errors in the input file.

The principal edesign decisions are to have a command line interface to the user (a form-filling interface would be a perfectly reasonable alternative) and to report errors to stderr (which seems entirely reasonable for a UNIX-based system). Command line interfaces are readily documented using some form of structured text and the proposed functionality might be documented along these lines (where > indicates an output, < indicates an input, ' ' enclose literals and < . . > enclose variables):

```
1     >     'Enter name and path of input file'
      <     <input-file-path>
      possible errors:
            >     'File not found' – goto 1
            >     'You do not have read permission for this file' – goto 1
2     >     'Enter name and path of output file'
      <     <output-file-path>
etc . . .
```

Error reporting can be handled is a similarly straightforward manner:

When encountering an error, F2K will attempt to check the remainder of the
input file and report any further errors up to a maximum of 20.
    The following error messages may be produced:

- 'Header <field-name> invalid'

- 'Command number <n>, <field name> invalid'

Where n is the number of the command (counted sequentially from the start)
and field-name is one of:

- board-name

- version

- date

    etc . . .

And that is really about all there is to it. A full version of the document (which
is not a lot larger) can found in Section 17.2.

5.7.4   Case 4, the Petri net diagram tool

When developing a specification, the main point of reference is the requirements document. For the Petri net diagram tool this is given in Section 18.1,
but the requirements (which are often copied into the specification anyway) are
reproduced here for convenience:

R1   Petool provides for the creation, editing, saving, copying, execution
and deletion of (diagrams of) Petri nets.

R2   Each net drawing is to be saved to (retrieved from) a user designated
file.

R3   Drawings are created interactively, on screen, using mouse, menus
and keyboard.

R4   Subject to the constraints given below, individual drawing elements
may be added (at a fixed size), moved and deleted.

R5 The following drawing elements are accommodated:

  R5.1 places

  R5.2 transitions

  R5.3 arcs

  R5.4 tokens

R6 Conventional representation is to be supported, along these lines:

Place: ◯   Transition: ▨   Arc: ⟶

R7 Tokens may be represented as dots (within places) or just their number may be indicated.

R8 Places and transitions may have attached labels.

R9 Arcs must connect a place to a transition, or vice versa (unconnected arcs are not allowed).

R10 An initial marking may be established by allocating tokens to places.

R11 Places have a minimum of 0 tokens and a maximum token capacity may be set by the user (the default being the given capacity limit).

R12 The user can choose whether a place, upon reaching its maximum token capacity, will 'overflow' (and lose additional tokens) or if it will become 'full'.

R13 The current number of tokens at a place is always visible.

R14 Places and transitions may be moved (probably by 'click and drag'). Any associated labels and tokens are automatically moved and the connectivity of any attached arcs is maintained.

R15 The deletion of a place or a transition results in the deletion of all connected arcs.

R16 Only synchronous execution is supported.

R17 Execution speed is determined by the user and may be changed during execution.

R18 It is possible to start, suspend, resume and end net execution.

R19 Execution will automatically stop when no transitions are enabled or when any place becomes full (in the latter case, all full places will be highlighted).

R20 Currently enabled transitions (i.e. where all incoming arcs connect to places with at least one token) are differentiated (probably by colour).

R21 Petool should respond to net editing commands within 0.5 seconds.

R22 Petool should complete save, copy and retrieve commands within 5 seconds.

R23 Execution speed can be varied between 0.1 and 5 seconds per firing cycle.

R24 Petool will accommodate at least:

    R24.1 10 nets

    R24.2 30 places per net

    R24.3 50 transitions per net

    R24.4 99 arcs per net

    R24.5 99 tokens per place

R25 **File handling and drawing operations should, wherever reasonable, follow the conventions adopted by established drawing utilities. (It may be assumed that users are familiar with the concepts and notation of Petri nets.)**

As mentioned earlier, this specification will be at the 'logical' level and will mainly make use of state charts (see Section 12.6.11). The results are presented in a, hopefully, logical order but I will not pretend that the design was developed in such an orderly fashion. As is usual, there was much iteration and revision.

A good starting point may be the consideration that most of the functionality of the system is only available when a drawing is loaded. This leads to a high-level distinction between what might be termed the 'drawing-loaded' and 'drawing-not-loaded' states. Further consideration of the possible transitions between these states gave rise to the model shown in Figure 5.17.

Whilst the meaning of most of the labels is fairly obvious, some need a little explanation and it does no harm to list all triggers (events) and actions (responses).

Triggers (events):

new	::= /* user command to create a new drawing file */;
open	::= /* user command to open an existing drawing file */;
close	::= /* user command to close currently open drawing file */;
save	::= /* user command to save currently open drawing file */;
save-as	::= /* user command to save current drawing to a new file. (This is the (only) way in which copying of drawings is realised) */;
quit	::= /* user command to terminate execution of the application */;
cancel	::= /* user command to cancel current action */;
no	::= /* user command to reject offered option */;
yes	::= /* user command to accept offered option */;
edit	::= /* represents any editing command (detailed later) */
new-file-name	::= /* user entered name for a new file. To be valid it must comply with operating system constraints upon file names and must not already exist */;
old-file-name	::= /* user entered name for an existing file. To be valid it must already exist */;

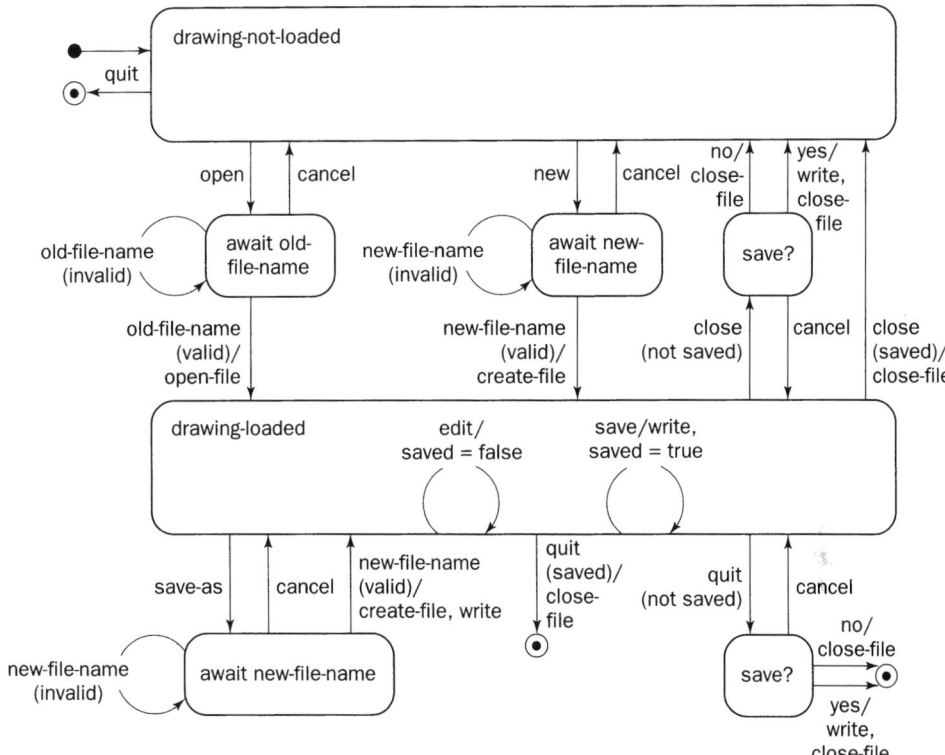

Figure 5.17

Actions (responses):

create file   ::= /* create and open a new drawing file with the given
               name */;
open-file   ::= /* open an existing drawing file with the given name */;
close-file   ::= /* close currently open drawing file */;
write   ::= /* overwrite currently open drawing file to reflect edits
               since last save */;

So far, nothing has been said about the way in which the user effects the commands and it is not the intention to pursue this here. However, it may be observed that this would not be too onerous to add, and it might be supposed that the first six commands (triggers) would be accessible as drop down menu options, the next three as dialogue box options and so on. Accompanying representative drawings of screens would pretty much complete the picture.

But to continue with the logical specification, there is no more to say about the drawing-not-loaded state and so we may now focus upon what can happen when a drawing is loaded. Again, there are two principal (sub-)states; editing the drawing and executing the Petri net. Executing the Petri net is, perhaps, the simpler of the two and its operation, together with the transitions to and from the editing state, is modelled in Figure 5.18.

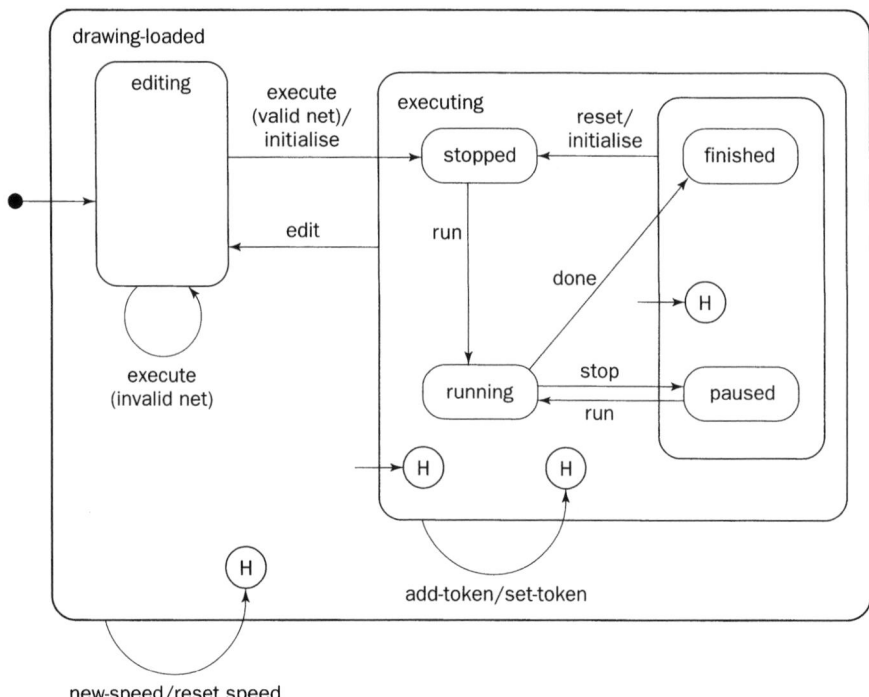

Figure 5.18

As before, events and responses can be listed and any necessary explanation may be added. Here are a few of the less obvious ones:

done   ::= /* occurs when the net cannot execute further, because there are no more enabled transitions or a place has reached its token limit and is not set to overflow */;

initialise   ::= /* resets the net to its initial marking */;

add-token   ::= /* user command to add another token to a specific place */;

new-speed   ::= /* user command to adjust the execution speed (period) of the net */;

It is probably also worth explaining that, in this context, a valid net is an executable net, i.e. there must be at least one connected and enabled transition.

The above model realises several more key requirements (notably R17, R18 and, in part, R19). As is normal, it also incorporates several somewhat arbitrary external design decisions. For example, the ability to reset from the paused state is not explicitly required nor is the option to add tokens during execution, but both seem desirable and easy to accommodate.

The 'running' state is probably the only executing sub-state that need be defined in greater detail. In order to be able to show the highlighting of enabled

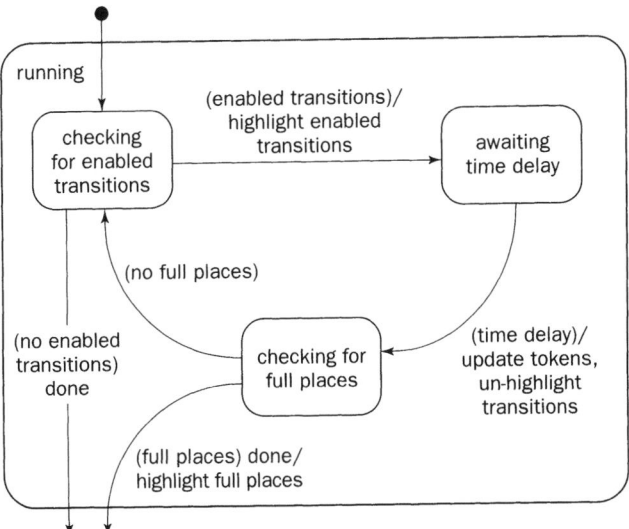

Figure 5.19

transitions and full places (as required by R19 and R20) it is necessary to introduce some transient sub-states as shown in Figure 5.19.

There is more yet to do regarding the detail of the editing state but, since
this is essentially 'more of the same', I will leave it there. As has hopefully been
illustrated, this approach provides a realistic and more rigorous alternative to
text-based specifications. The full specification may be found in Section 18.2.

5.8   Exercises

1   Explain why, during specification, it is important to identify the various external interfaces of the solution system.

2   The behaviour of the solution system may be specified at the 'logical' and at the
'physical' level. Explain the difference and discuss the alternative options as to when
each level is fully determined.

3   Explain the relative advantages and disadvantages of functional and procedural
specification.

4   Develop a specification for the pedometer, the requirements document for which is
given in Section 5.8.1. Notes:

- A style similar to that used in the example in Section 5.2 may be adopted and the
resultant documentation could well be of a similar size (a page or two).

- There are many possible 'solutions' as the outcome depends upon the edesign
decisions taken and the specification techniques selected.

- You may discover omissions and ambiguity in the given requirements document. In
reality you would raise and resolve queries; here you will have to make reasonable
assumptions.

5 Identify which of the following should be in a specification document, which may be and which should not be:

a) the reasons for the external design decisions;

b) project deadlines;

c) performance requirements;

d) the solution system data model;

e) definitions of solution system inputs and outputs;

f) description of solution system sub-systems (modules);

g) project staff task allocations;

h) test plans;

i) definition of the relationships between solution system input and output;

j) description of the flow of data between solution system modules;

k) quality assurance plans;

l) an overview of the problem domain.

6 Develop a specification for the petrol forecourt system, the requirements document for which is given in Section 5.8.2. Notes:

• This is a large exercise and could take several hours.

• The example specifications given in Part 3 should provide useful guidance.

• Since the outcome depends upon the edesign decisions taken and the specification techniques selected, there are many possible 'solutions'.

• You may discover omissions and ambiguity in the given requirements document. In reality you would raise and resolve queries; here you will have to make reasonable assumptions.

5.8.1 Pedometer requirements document

5.8.1.1 Problem domain

The pedometer is small electronic device worn on the person which calculates how far they have walked (or run). It counts the number of steps they have taken by detecting the jolting movements and converts this to a distance thus:

Distance ::= number-of-steps × step-length / 100 000

5.8.1.2 Data dictionary

step	::= /* distance moved in one pace (i.e. from one footprint to the next) */;
distance	::= /* distance walked in kilometres to two decimal places */;
	::= "00.00" .. "99.99";
step-length	::= /* length of step in centimetres */;
	::= "50" .. "150";
HH	::= "00" .. "23";
MM	::= "00" .. "59";

5.8.1.3 Requirements

R1 The device must be small (max. $60 \times 60 \times 20$ mm) and light (max. 75 grams).

R2 The device will have a five-digit display.

R3 It should be operated by push buttons and (to keep costs down) the number of buttons should be as low as possible, consistent with R8.

R4 When not being used as a pedometer, it will display the time in the form 'HH MM'.

R5 The user must be able to set the time.

R6 The user must be able to set the step length.

R7 The user must be able to reset the distance to zero.

R8 The device must be easy to operate.

5.8.2 Pumpmaster requirements document

5.8.2.1 Problem domain description

Overview
The system pumpmaster is required to assist in the operation of a petrol station forecourt. It will allow the sales assistant (the user) to monitor and control the operation of the petrol pumps.

Figure 5.20 Context diagram

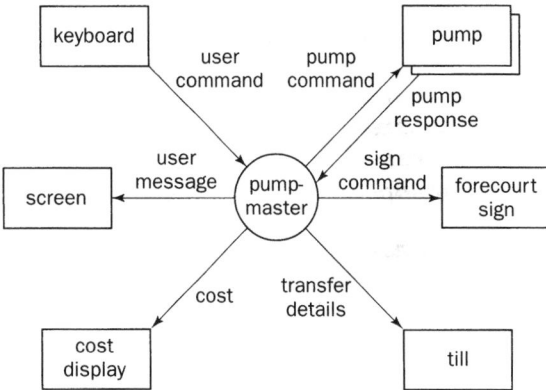

Figure 5.20

Figure 5.21 Problem frame
This is, essentially, a control system but with a small information system aspect regarding the prices of fuel and the volume of sales.

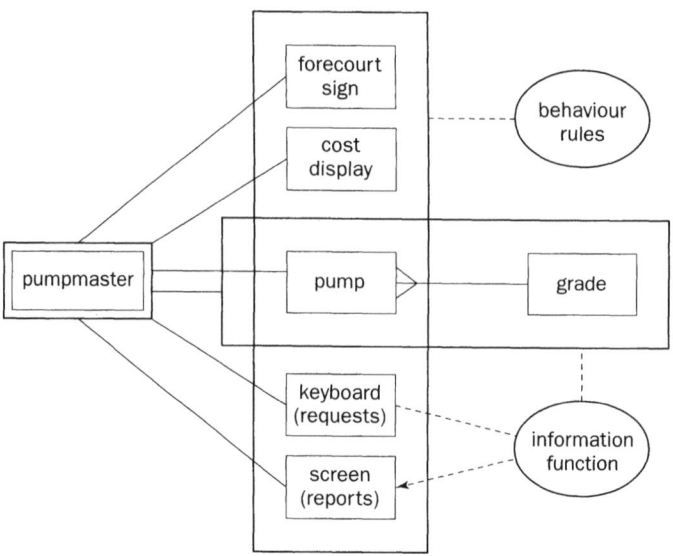

Figure 5.21

5.8.2.2 Sub-domains

Pump

The petrol pumps are self-serve (i.e. operated by the customers). Each pump dispenses one particular grade of fuel and, as fuel is dispensed, it measures and displays the volume and (using the set price) calculates and displays the cost. These transfer details (volume and cost) are available to pumpmaster upon request.

In normal operation, the customer will lift the nozzle and this triggers the resetting of the volume and cost display to zero. The customer replaces the nozzle when finished. The pump is then 'locked' and cannot be used again until it receives an unlock command (from pumpmaster). The STD in Figure 5.22 shows the relevant pump behaviour. The pumps are connected to pumpmaster via a communication network and the commands/responses shown in Table 5.6 are available. A response (to a valid command) is made within 0.1 seconds.

Forecourt sign

The forecourt display is a large electronic sign which shows the current fuel prices. It shows four prices and accepts the following sign command.

  price_number, price;

The only response is that the display changes appropriately.

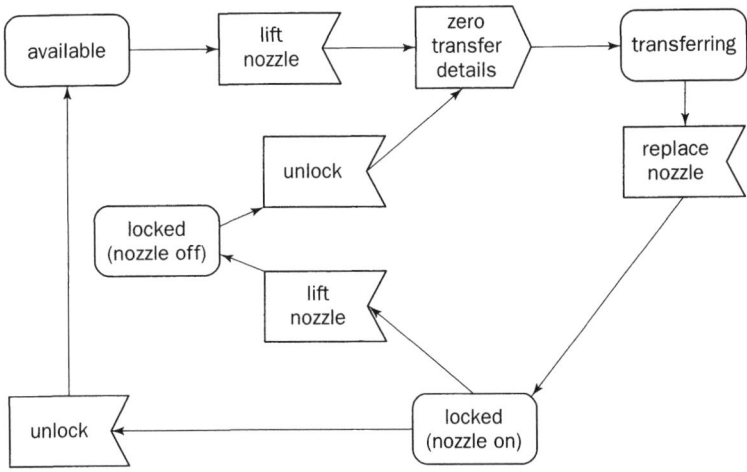

Figure 5.22

Table 5.6

Command	Response
unlock (pump_id);	ok (pump_id);
send_transfer_details (pump_id);	ok (pump_id, transfer_details);
set_price (pump_id, price);	ok (pump_id);
send_status (pump_id);	ok (pump_id, pump_status);

Cost display

The cost display is a small electronic display at the pay desk that, for the benefit of the customer, shows the current cost for the pump currently selected by the user.

Screen

The screen is a conventional graphical 14″ VDU that displays information to the user.

Keyboard

The keyboard will be custom-built to accommodate the specified operation of the system.

Figure 5.23 Data model

Figure 5.23

Data dictionary

grade	::= /* the type of a fuel (e.g. un-leaded, diesel etc.) */;
	::= grade_name + price + volume_sold;
grade_name	::= ^{1}{char}^{10};
pump	::= pump_id + pump_status + grade_name + transfer_details;
pump_id	::= ^{2}{digit}^{2};
pump_status	::= "available"	"delivering"	"locked_on"	"locked_off";
transfer_details	::= volume + cost;
volume	::= /* the volume, in litres, of fuel for a particular transfer */;
	::= ^{1}{digit}^{3} + "." + ^{2}{digit}^{2};
volume_sold	::= /* total volume, in litres, of a particular grade of fuel sold (since it was last reset) */;
	::= ^{1}{digit}^{5} + "." + ^{2}{digit}^{2};
price	::= /* the price (in pence) for a litre of fuel */;
	::= ^{1}{digit}^{3} + "." + digit;
cost	::= /* cost (in pounds and pence) for a particular transfer */;
	::= ^{1}{digit}^{3} + "." + ^{2}{digit}^{2};
pump_command	::= unlock	send_transfer_details	set_price	send_status;
unlock	::= "unlock (" + pump_id + ")";
send_transfer_details	::= "send_transfer_details (" + pump_id + ")";
set_price	::= "set_price (" + pump_id + ", " + price + ")";
send_status	::= "send_status (" + pump_id + ")";
pump_response	::= "ok (" + pump_id + [", " + (transfer_details | pump_status)] + ")";
sign_command	::= price_number, price;
price_number	::= "1" .. "4";
user_commands	::= /* see requirements */;
user_messages	::= /* see requirements */;

5.8.2.3 Requirements

Functional

R1 As selected by the user, pumpmaster can operate in transfer mode or set-up mode.

R2 Whilst in set-up mode all pumps are locked.

Whilst in set-up mode the user can:

R3 reset the forecourt sign display,

R4 add or remove a grade,

R5   add or remove a pump,

R6   reset the grade for any pump,

R7   reset the price and volume total for any grade,

R8   request the system to display (on the screen) a sales summary showing the total volume sold for each grade of fuel.

Whilst in transfer mode:

R9   the transfer details for all pumps are displayed upon the screen,

R10   the user can select a particular pump as the current pump,

R11   the cost for the current pump is displayed upon the cost display.

R12   When a transfer is complete (i.e. the nozzle is on and the transfer details are not zero) the user can command pumpmaster to send transfer details (for the current pump) to the till.

R13   When (and only when) transfer details have been sent to the till, the user can unlock the relevant pump.

Performance

Speed

R14   The system should respond to all user commands within 0.5 seconds.

R15   The screen should be updated to reflect pump transfer details within one second.

Capacity

R16   The system must handle at least 16 pumps.

R17   The system must handle at least six grades.

Reliability

R18   The system should be fully operational for at least 160 hours per week.

Usability

R19   The user should be given adequate prompting and feedback such that a novice can learn to operate the system efficiently with 10 minutes training and 30 minutes practice. As a measure of efficiency, they should be able to:

- select a pump, send transfer details to the till and reset the pump within six seconds;

- starting from transfer mode, reset a sign price, a grade price and a pump grade within two minutes.

R20   Wherever it makes sense to allow it, the user should be able to 'undo' the last command.

Validation

6

As noted in Section 2.5, requirements validation seeks to discover (and correct) any errors that occur during the requirements engineering phase. Ideally, we wish to ensure that problem domain characteristics and system requirements are fully and precisely determined; and that the specification unambiguously defines a system behaviour such that, given the problem domain characteristics, it will satisfactorily meet the various requirements.

It is pertinent to note that the requirements document describes the characteristics of something that exists (the problem domain); it can thus be wrong in the sense that it is not a true description. The specification, on the other hand, describes something that does not, as yet, exist (the solution system); it cannot thus be wrong in the same sense (although it may be ambiguous or describe a behaviour that is inappropriate).

There is certainly some overlap between the mechanisms and techniques used for the original performance of the requirements tasks and those used for validation, but it may be useful to summarise the latter thus:

- simple **checks**;
- **review** of documents;
- **logical analysis** (particularly when using formal techniques);
- use of **prototypes**, **use-cases** and similar checking mechanisms;
- **functional test planning**;
- development of the **user manual**.

6.1   Simple checks

Almost too obvious to mention (but easily overlooked!) are simple checks for conformity. These are particularly relevant at two points:

- Upon completion of the requirements document, check through the elicitation notes to ensure that every single entry has been reflected within it (or has been deliberately ignored).
- Upon completion of the specification, check through the requirements document to ensure that every single requirement has been reflected within it (or has been deliberately omitted).

6.2   Review

In this sense, a review is a detailed examination of a document for the purpose of obtaining constructive criticism; particularly, the detection of errors. Where the document is a design document, the activity is often called a design review, but the review of requirements related documentation follows very similar lines.

Whilst the objective remains the same, there are several variations upon the review theme; where just one person examines a document it may be termed an inspection, where a group of peers are led through a document it may be termed a 'walk-through'. Only an outline of the review process is presented here and further information may be found in Fagan (1999), Parnas *et al.* (1990) and Yourdon (1989b).

Reviews usually involve a small group and certain roles may be identified:

- the **presenter** (often the author) leads the group through the document;
- the **scribe** keeps a note of all the points that are raised;
- the **referee** prevents digression and resolves disputes.

In addition, there will attend the various experts. In the case of requirements phase reviews, these will include experts in the problem domain and the requirements (quite possibly users of pre-existing systems or potential users of the new system) and maybe experts in external design, documentation standards and so on. Formal reviews, prior to document sign-off, will also include client representatives.

Further points to note are:

- If it is not documented, it cannot be reviewed.
- The review should concentrate upon *finding* faults, not resolving them.
- All participants must prepare for the review and documents should be circulated in good time for them to be studied in detail.
- There must be mechanisms to ensure that points raised at the review are not forgotten.
- Group review is relatively expensive in working time and document examination by one or two people (other than the author(s)) is a cheaper alternative for work in progress.
- If review is not fairly prompt, documents tend to 'set'; changes are harder to effect (whilst other work, based upon the possibly erroneous documents, continues).

6.3   Logical analysis

Where system behaviour is defined using a notation with clear syntactic and semantic rules it is, in principle, amenable to a degree of logical analysis for internal consistency. This notion has mainly been promoted within the context of the formal methods (see Section 5.5.2). However, any reasonably formal modelling technique may be subject to logical analysis. For example the common FSM model may be checked to ensure that:

- every trigger (event) is recognised in at least one state;
- every transition has one and only one trigger;
- every state (except the start state) is reachable by at least one transition;
- etc.

A problem with formal methods is that they are often inaccessible to clients and users. Nevertheless, for critical systems, it may well be considered worthwhile to duplicate, at least in part, a less formal, client oriented specification using formal methods purely to allow a more rigorous logical analysis.

6.4 Prototypes, use-cases, etc.

One of the best ways to check that information has been correctly elicited and recorded is to present it in a different (derived) form. A particularly effective means is the development of a prototype that explicitly demonstrates the behaviour (as defined in a specification). Such prototypes make it very obvious to users and clients (or their representatives) whether their ideas and wishes have been correctly interpreted (and equally obvious if their original thoughts need revision).

Ideally, such prototypes are automatically generated from specifications, since this eliminates the possibility of any inconsistency between the prototype and the specification (from which the final system will be derived). If relatively formal specification techniques and appropriate software tools are used, automatic derivation is possible. (For example, state charts (see Section 12.6.11) can be produced and executable versions derived using the tool Statemate (Harel *et al.*, 1990).)

In the absence of dynamic prototypes, 'paper-prototypes' (see Section 11.2.1) confer many of the advantages (and often at less cost). In either case, prototypes may be combined with the use of illustrative use-cases which 'walk' clients and/or users through the operation of the hypothetical new system.

6.5 Functional test design

One of the most desirable characteristics of specified system behaviour is that it should be testable. The best way of ensuring that it *is* testable is to try and design suitable tests.

Here is not the place to describe functional test design[77], suffice it to say that system level, functional tests can be designed as soon as the specification is

---

[77] Several texts are available, for example, Beizer (1990) or Kaner *et al.* (1993).

produced. The tests cannot, of course, be *executed* until the system has actually been constructed and this may not be for some time. However, the author has observed that *designing* functional tests reveals as many errors in the specification as executing the tests discovers in the final product. To an extent this may simply be due to the close examination of the specification that test design imposes but, additionally, it may be that the specification must be examined from a rather different viewpoint; that of testability.

Early functional test design is, therefore, highly recommended as an effective method of specification validation. Furthermore, since system level, functional tests need to be designed sooner or later anyway, it is, effectively, 'for free'.

6.6   User manual development

A good specification (together with HMI documentation, if that is separate) will provide all the information that is required to write the user manual. As with functional test design (above) this task is often left until after the system has been implemented. However, there may be great savings in overall development time if user manual production (and functional test design) proceed in parallel with system implementation.

As with functional test design, user manual production enforces a close examination of the specification and any omissions or inconsistencies tend to become apparent. Clearly, the sooner such defects are discovered, the sooner they can be fixed and the less time will be wasted on re-visiting subsequent work. Early user manual production is, therefore, also highly recommended.

Where next?

7

This book is 'only' an introduction to a large subject. It aims to establish a firm grounding and it is hoped that the reader will now be in little doubt as to what *is* a requirement, what *is* a specification, how to go about writing one, etc.

However, the relatively broad scope of the book has precluded pursuing many topics in great depth. For many readers, this will not be a problem, they may never need to know more on the subject – but for others this is just the start.

It is possible to write whole books upon some requirements engineering topics and, indeed, this has been done. Pointers to these books and other sources have been given within the text but for convenience, some of these, together with a few more are collected here.

There is also the matter of exposure to other perspectives. Whilst I have striven to maintain a degree of balance, some of the material presented herein can, doubtless, be regarded as biased. Alternative, general requirements engineering texts should therefore, be consulted. As it happens, there are relatively few of these and a fairly comprehensive list can be given: Davis (1993), Kovitz (1999), Jackson (1995, 2001), Kotonya and Sommerville (1997), Loucopoulos and Karakostas (1995), MacAulay (1996) and Wieringa (1996). In addition there are works, such as Thayer and Dorfman (1990) and Dorfman and Thayer (1990), that are built around the various national and international standards for software engineering.

Beyond this, a few more specialised leads may be useful. The trickier aspects of elicitation include:

- evolving requirements (Easterbrook, 1995);
- traceability (Dorfman and Flynn, 1984, Marconi, 1990);
- elicitation politics (Gause and Weinberg, 1989);
- requirements negotiation (Boehm and Egyed, 1998, Gruenbacher, 2000).

Requirements documentation, including the writing of requirements and the use of natural language, has received relatively little attention but alternative sources include: Casey and Taylor (1981), Frimer and Folkes (1982) and, of course, Kovitz (1999).

Most texts on specification are oriented towards formal methods, which have only been touched upon here. The topic may be followed up in Hall

(1990), Turner and McCluskey (1994) and Woodman and Heal (1994). Other sources tend to focus upon alternative, particular specification techniques and references are given for each technique in Part 2.

Examples of requirements documentation are curiously hard to come by, but some of the general texts (identified above) include an example. These seldom differentiate between the requirements document and the specification (Kovitz, 1999, being the obvious exception), are relatively small and usually focus upon information systems only. Examples of 'real life' specifications (particularly for larger systems) are even less common in the public domain. In my experience, requests for such documents are often rebuffed on the grounds of commercial secrecy, but there are reasons (including information from 'inside sources') to suspect that embarrassment regarding the quality of such documentation is sometimes a factor. However, a few interesting examples of large, commercial specifications have been made available, such as that provided by Heninger *et al.* (1978) and one for the NHS primary care system which can be found by following the RFA link at http://www.standards.nhsia.nhs.uk.

It is only in the last few years that requirements engineering, as a discipline, has blossomed. This is indicated by the relatively recent publication dates of most general texts and by a couple of other significant events.

In 1996 the *Requirements Engineering Journal* (currently edited by Peri Loucopolos and John Mylopolous) was founded. This provides a home for much of the current research (which, in turn, provides numerous references to prior work). Since 1994 there has been a requirements engineering special interest group within the British Computer Society (see 'http://www.resg.org.uk'). This includes useful links and notices of most relevant conferences, etc.

The sources given above may well assist in acquiring further relevant knowledge, and much can be learned from the work of others. However, requirements engineering is still, very much, a pragmatic discipline. From now on, you are likely to find that experience gained through practice is every bit as helpful as any reading.

Part 2

Technology

Techniques 8

This part of the book is about techniques; techniques that are useful to the requirements engineer and which, to a large extent, form the tool-kit that enables the job to be done.

It would be easy to get the impression that there are a bewildering array of techniques and that new ones are being invented all the time. This is not true. Many so-called techniques are but minor variations on others and no fundamentally new techniques have been invented for 30 years or more. Nonetheless, some categorisation helps provide a grasp on what there is and also provides some organisation for this part of the book.

Partly, techniques can be classified according to which of the requirements engineering tasks they help support[78]. This is particularly pertinent for separating out the information gathering or elicitation techniques; and these form the first main section. Although there is some overlap, the remaining techniques may be described as *modelling techniques* since they model, or abstract, particular aspects of a system.

Abstraction, in this context, is to capture within a model some important essence of a system (and, inevitably, to ignore other aspects!). Therefore, it provides a simplification and, hence, a vital aid to achieving understanding. As usual, there is a price to pay and, here, it is that abstraction may overlook important aspects. However, informed selection of a variety of modelling techniques can circumvent this problem.

8.1 Notations

Most techniques adopt a particular notation or language in their execution. For example, data flow modelling is a very widely used modelling technique and DFDs, which are, technically, directed graphs, are commonly used to record such models.

---

[78] See the technique vs task cross reference matrix in the section on technique selection (Section 8.4).

In some cases, the coupling between technique and notation is so tight that the name of the technique and its associated notation are used almost interchangeably. Often this matters little. If someone says that they are doing some 'data flow diagramming', we would assume, probably correctly, that they are data flow modelling.

At other times, to appreciate the distinction between technique and notation can be more important. For example, modelling a system as a FSM (see Section 12.6) is another well known technique which, like data flow modelling, also commonly uses a directed graph, the STD; different model, same notation. However, an FSM model could also be represented by a state matrix; same model, different notation.

The ability to recognise the underlying model whatever the notation and to know when there are options regarding notation, adds to the powers of the requirements engineer.

There are, in fact, very few notations in common usage:

- directed graph – 'boxes and arrows' (properly known as nodes and arcs (or edges)) – used for STDs, DFDs, etc.;
- table – a two-dimensional matrix of cells – used for state matrices, decision tables, etc.;
- representational (iconic) picture – see Section 11.2;
- Natural language (or plain text);
- structured text – where indentation is used to delimit scope.

Natural language (NL), is so important that it is often treated as a modelling technique in itself. Strictly, this is wrong, but this part of the book does provide a convenient slot and so NL is included as are brief notes on other notations (see Chapter 14).

8.2 Methods

Sometimes, the term 'method'[79] is used interchangeably with (modelling) technique. However, a method is, or should be, more than a technique. It is a way of tackling a task and will usually consist of a set of techniques with some overall, organising schema or strategy and, it is hoped, some heuristics for their application. A well known example of a method from the world of software development is SSADM (CCTA, 1990)[80].

---

[79] Methodology is also used as a synonym for method but here will be reserved for its original use – the study or use of methods.

[80] Although as mentioned earlier, the term 'method' is used quite loosely within software development. In the formal sense of a procedure that is *guaranteed* to produce a solution, most software development 'methods' are not methods at all.

Wieringa (1996) provides a thorough review of several software development methods from the requirements engineering perspective and is recommended to the methodologist. But, for the novice, it is probably more important to appreciate the overall characteristics of the requirements engineering process (as detailed in Part 1) and of the important techniques. Only then can the strengths and weaknesses of the various methods be evaluated. Indeed, it is suggested here that the weaknesses of the proprietary methods often outweigh their strengths and entirely satisfactory results can be obtained without their use.

8.3   Tools

Software tools may be developed to support one or more notations and, if they have in-built semantic rules (as well as syntactic), may be more accurately regarded as supporting a technique (although the distinction may be subtle). To support a particular method, a tool must support most, if not all, of the techniques that the method employs and also provide a degree of integration (as dictated by the method).

The availability of software tools for requirements engineering is rather volatile, with new ones continually appearing and others becoming obsolete. This topic will not, therefore, be explored in any depth, but will be mentioned for given techniques where it is important. But, a word of warning; the marketing of tools and the methods which they support is a competitive business which tends to distort the common perception regarding techniques and methods.

So, to summarise: methods comprise techniques; techniques employ notations; notations and techniques may be supported by tools, and tools can also give support at the 'method level'.

8.4   Technique selection

Technique selection may be approached from two directions; a technique is needed for a particular purpose or, for what purposes might a particular technique be useful? Part 1 of this book gives pointers in the first direction and, in this part, for each of the techniques described, indicators are given as to when they might be used.

Table 8.1 summarises this information (in both directions!). Note that the bulk of elicitation techniques are omitted since they relate *only* to elicitation but, where techniques with wider application are also useful for elicitation, this is shown. Text is also included (although it is really a notation rather than a technique) and, although it *can* be used for any purpose, only its more common areas of application are indicated.

Table 8.1

Task/ document section	Context diagram	Problem frame	Representational drawing	Throwaway prototype	Decision table	Functional decomposition	Use-case	Task action grammar	FSM	Petri net	DFD	Structure chart	ERD	ELH	Object oriented class model	DD (BNF)	Text
Elicitation				✓			✓										
Analysis:																	
PD overview	✓	✓															✓
PD structure		✓								✓			✓				
PD data model													✓		✓	✓	
I/O problem data												✓				✓	
Sub-domain behaviour					✓				✓	✓							✓
Sub-domain states									✓	✓			✓				
Requirements, functional				✓													✓
Requirements, performance				✓													✓
Constraints																	✓
Specification:																	
SS appearance			✓	✓													
I/O solution data																✓	
SS behaviour (ER actions)			✓	✓	✓	✓	✓	✓	✓	✓							✓
SS state (ER states)									✓	✓				✓			
Timing			✓						✓	✓							✓

Elicitation techniques

9

This section presents an overview of most of the commonly used elicitation techniques (references to specialist sources are given in some cases):

- background reading
- interviewing
- questionnaires
- document inspection
- task observation
- discourse analysis
- use-cases and scenarios
- brain storming
- requirements stripping

(In addition there are a number of so-called contrived techniques (such as repertory grids and card sorts – see, for example, McGeorge and Rugg, 1992) but the above provide an adequate base for most purposes.)

As previously indicated, elicitation cannot be divorced from considerations of analysis and specification, and the interplay between these activities will be discussed as appropriate. Consideration will also be given to the role that each technique can play in an overall elicitation strategy.

9.1 Background reading

Whilst seldom explicitly mentioned, this ubiquitous 'technique' often provides the analyst or requirements engineer with their introduction to the problem domain. Documents such as business plans, operational procedures, technical manuals for interfacing systems, user manuals for pre-existing systems and so on, can be valuable sources of information.

It is hoped that little needs to be said about how to read, but one point is worth highlighting. As you read, take notes. Inevitably, much of the material will be irrelevant and, once you find the 'nuggets', you do not want to lose them again.

9.2 Interviewing

Interviewing is a technique that elicits information that resides within people's heads. It is considered in some detail, and there are three reasons for this:

- It is the predominant elicitation technique.
- Several other techniques are built around interviews and share many of the same considerations.
- There are few other sources of information on the topic.

It is not by chance that interviews are the predominant elicitation technique. Their main strengths are:

- broad band communication (verbal and body language which is readily supplemented by sketched diagrams, etc., as necessary);
- inherent flexibility (different, unplanned topics can be pursued 'on the fly');
- the scope to address all types of required information.

A distinction is often drawn between the structured and the unstructured interview. The former focuses upon a pre-planned set of questions which impose a fairly rigid structure on the interview; whereas in the latter there would be only a rough idea of the topics to be pursued and reliance would be placed upon the elicitor to 'play it by ear' as the interview proceeds.

In practice, a middling course is usually followed; interviews are planned in reasonable but not excessive detail and considerable flexibility is allowed. The maxim 'better to have a plan and depart from it than have no plan at all' is, however, pertinent. Factors which affect the choice of approach are the experience of the elicitor (for the novice, a more detailed plan is recommended) and the stage of the elicitation. During the early stages, when little is known of the problem and outline requirements and problem domain description are the target, it is ineffective (if not impossible) to plan questions in great detail whereas, in the later stages, an interview could well target specific aspects very precisely.

9.2.1 Preparation

Much of the preparation for interviews is a matter of common sense and good housekeeping. An elicitation plan can be prepared (see Section 3.4) and, in the light of this, the elicitee and objective(s) for each interview can be determined in advance. Examples are: 'Interview operator of pre-existing system to establish how a particular operation is currently performed', 'Interview system manager to establish what technical constraints she would like to impose', etc.

Around the objective(s), a plan, consisting of a set of questions, grouped and ordered in a logical way, is built. As indicated earlier, the level of detail that is appropriate in any individual plan will vary.

A useful tip is to allow, within the plan, time for checking back at the end that you have covered (and understood the responses to) all the questions. If there is much outstanding then, rather than over-running, it is usually better to continue at the next interview.

When making appointments, allow for the fact that extended interviews are counter-productive (neither you nor the elicitee are likely to be able to concentrate for more than an hour). Even if you estimate that all the necessary information (from a particular elicitee) can be obtained in one interview it is best to allow for repeat interviews. Not only is it extremely useful to be able to analyse, record and then re-present your findings to the elicitee for confirmation but it is almost inevitable that further questions will arise (both from your analysis and as a result of elicitation from other parties).

Arranging interviews is a highly variable task. Depending upon the working role of the elicitee, the relationship with, and the culture of, their organisation, it may be necessary to obtain (and check) permission for interviews from various other parties (either verbally or, if at all doubtful, in writing). As part of the arrangement process, take whatever steps are necessary to let the elicitee know what it is all about. This can be quite trivial for a follow-up interview, but a considerable amount of tactful explanation may be required in the case of a first interview with someone whose job could be significantly affected.

There is not always much option regarding the location of the interview. However, a reasonable degree of privacy and freedom from interruptions are obviously desirable.

Another matter to consider in advance is the way in which elicited information will be recorded. There are, essentially, three options:

- take notes yourself;
- have a colleague take notes;
- audio or video record the proceedings.

The main problem with taking your own notes is that, unless you are prepared for frequent silences during the interview (which may well discomfort or frustrate the elicitee), you are faced with doing two things at once. Perhaps surprisingly, many elicitors (not necessarily experienced) do cope with writing down the response to one question while they ask or receive a response to the next. Inevitably this leads to a record in note form (often decipherable only by the note maker!) and there is the danger of some loss of information. Having a colleague as a scribe who can concentrate upon the note taking alleviates this problem. This may well be an ideal solution, but it is obviously more expensive (and it is important that the scribe is also technically competent, well prepared and familiar with the problem in question).

Tape recording is often seen as the simple solution, but is not the panacea it may seem. Audio recording records only audible information and will miss, say, sketches or body language. Video recording may go some way to addressing this point, but it has problems of its own, such as only 'seeing' in one direction and, possibly, inhibiting elicitees. There is also the problem that recording is indiscriminate and the relevant information must be subsequently extracted, sorted and recorded in a suitable form. With note taking, much of the selection (and, for that matter, analysis) is performed 'on the spot' and, overall, even paying for a scribe may cost no more than recording with its subsequent processing.

A common (and effective) compromise is for the elicitor to keep their own notes but audio record as well. The notes form the basis for the subsequent documentation with the tape being listened to just once as a check that nothing significant was missed (and, possibly, kept as 'evidence' in case a client denies they have changed their mind!).

9.2.2 Modus operandi

The conduct of the interview is also, to a large extent, a matter of common sense but certain guidelines are useful. Co-operation between elicitee and elicitor is critical and it is largely the elicitor's responsibility to promote this. As with all working relationships the basics are simple. Be polite (punctual!), reasonably friendly and always try and imagine the elicitee's position.

Whilst you may be the one that feels nervous, it is up to you, where necessary, to put the interviewee at ease. They may, for example, be worried about possible implications for their career. Bear in mind that their responses may be biased but, if at all possible, try not to get embroiled in such matters and stick to the 'technicalities'. If the topic of an interviewee's future is inescapable then tact may be required.

I once witnessed a novice elicitor whose opening gambit (when asked what the interview was all about – which, incidentally, they had not indicated beforehand) was, 'I'm here to make you redundant'. Oddly, the elicitee's co-operation was somewhat lacking from then on!

Obviously, this is an extreme case, but much more subtle off-putting messages can be sent and any implications like the following should be avoided:

- 'My time is more valuable than yours'
- 'I don't know what I'm doing'
- 'You don't know what you're talking about'

That said, (unless antagonised!) most elicitees are naturally co-operative and one must even be aware of the 'trying to please' syndrome. They may, with good reason, be thinking something like, 'Why on earth are they asking me about that?' but they may, not wishing to offend, simply answer the question.

In a similar vein, in order to advance their own agenda, some elicitees may say what they think you want to hear rather than what is actually the case. Again, an awareness of possible underlying motives (which include organisational politics) is another characteristic of the astute elicitor.

Even when (as recommended earlier) adequate warning of the purpose of the interview has been given, a quick reminder is a good way to open the interview. Once into the interview the guidelines are to be:

- intelligible
- tenacious
- flexible (regarding your plan)
- receptive

Express questions clearly, in plain language. Without being patronising, adjust your language to suit the elicitee. As often as not, this is simply a case of adopting their terminology and jargon (as fast as you learn it) and avoiding the introduction of any of your own.

Do not let anything escape. If a response does not entirely answer your question or does not entirely make sense to you, follow it through until it does. If this is not possible there and then, make a note and pursue it later; with someone else if necessary. However, as always, be tactful and, in the event of an inconsistency between two elicitees, remain impartial and, in due course, simply ask each one if they know why the other said something inconsistent.

It may well be that the ability to spot and follow up anomalies, such as unexpected reactions to questions (even just a raised eyebrow), is one of the factors that distinguishes the best elicitors. This factor implies that interview plans will not always be followed rigidly, and this must be the case. When plans are drawn up they are based upon various suppositions. If these prove to be untrue or if the priorities change then the strategy must be redrawn as necessary; even whilst an interview is in progress.

At the same time, do not lose sight of the required direction of the basic information flow; from the elicitee to the elicitor. Avoid putting answers into the elicitee's mouth. Questions such as, 'I think you want this – don't you?' may be acceptable for purposes of confirmation but are inappropriate for eliciting new information. Questions will obviously lead in a certain direction (as per the plan), but should lead gently and be as 'open' as possible, encouraging elicitees to wander off down alternative (perhaps unforeseen) paths where appropriate. Keep your interruptions to the minimum consistent with completing the task. Listen to what they are saying and avoid the trap of not hearing something just because you did not expect to hear it.

9.2.3 Questions to ask

Questions can be (broadly) classified into those relating to:

- the problem to be addressed;
- the process of developing a solution;
- the elicitation itself.

The first of these (which actually constitute the bulk) can only be discussed in general terms outside the context of a particular system development. Nonetheless, some consideration is given in the section on elicitation strategy (Section 3.4) and the areas to be covered are, to a large extent, determined by the target content of the requirements document and the specification (as discussed in Sections 4.8.3 and 5.4.3 respectively). The other two categories are, however, of general applicability and can be considered here in more detail.

Questions relating to the process of developing a solution are particularly pertinent during the early stages of a development and are mainly addressed to the client. They target such issues as:

- Who is actually paying for the development?
- What are the underlying reasons for wanting a system?
- What is the trade-off between delivery date and cost?
- Is there a date after which the system would be of no (or little) value?
- What is the trade-off between cost and reliability?

Most of the responses to such questions do not appear in the requirements documentation; rather they inform the project planning process and may well be reflected in a contract.

Questions about the elicitation itself (sometimes known as meta-questions – Gause and Weinberg, 1989), similarly are not reflected in the requirements documentation, but they can be of great assistance in performing the elicitation. The point of these is to ensure that elicitation is being performed effectively and some particularly useful examples (from Gause and Weinberg, 1989) are:

- Do my questions seem relevant?
- Are your answers official?
- Are you the best person to answer these questions?
- Am I asking too many questions?
- Is there anything else I should be asking you?
- Is there anything you would like to ask me?
- Is there anybody else I should see?
- Is there anybody on this project whom we don't need?

9.2.4 Summary

Interviews are the predominant elicitation technique within requirements engineering. This is largely down to their flexibility and wide scope; provided that it resides within someone's head, almost any type of information can be elicited.

Interviews do, however, have potential snags:

- lack of access to the required people (often, the most knowledgeable are the most busy and sometimes 'filters and scramblers' are interposed);
- the difficulty of recording information whilst interviewing;
- the interviewee trying to please and saying what they think you want to hear;
- the interviewer 'putting words into the interviewee's mouth' with leading questions;
- the expenses associated with tying up key staff;
- communication problems caused by different domain expertise and jargon;
- ulterior motives and organisational politics giving rise to misinformation.

But, as indicated above, there are some common sense guidelines that can ameliorate most of these problems most of the time. That said, some have a natural flair for interviewing; others must work at it!

9.3   Questionnaires

A questionnaire can be regarded as the ultimate development of the structured interview plan. Every question is pre-planned and then presented with no possibility of elaboration or deviation. It is, therefore, important that questions are carefully phrased in order to maximise comprehension and minimise ambiguity. (A pilot run of a questionnaire can help eliminate 'bugs' before the main deployment.)

Whilst the inflexibility is a constraint, it is not always of great significance and, where questions *can* be well established in advance, questionnaires provide a relatively cost effective way of eliciting information, particularly from a large population. Questions are frequently of the multiple-choice type since this aids analysis of the responses; a task which, with technology such as OCR, can even be automated.

At the cost of increasing the analysis workload, open-ended questions can also figure in questionnaires, but due account must be taken of the ability and inclination of the target population to understand and respond unambiguously. Many people prefer the face-to-face interview (perhaps because their perceived workload is lower) and it is, of course, much easier to ignore a form than the elicitor who arrives in person.

As with all other techniques, questionnaires are probably best viewed as an adjunct to interviews, to be used only under particular circumstances.

9.4   Document inspection

This 'traditional' systems analysis approach requires that the problem domain or, more often, a pre-existing, solution system is document-based. In other words, a significant amount of the problem data (see Section 2.8) must appear on documents (usually forms of some type).

Where this is not the case, this technique is obviously irrelevant (and this can present a snag for some of the older development methods where document inspection is the *only* elicitation technique that is considered!). But where it is the case (which, for commercial systems, is usual) it should not be ignored since it is a valuable and readily accessible source of information.

Eliciting the information is relatively straightforward; it is simply a case of obtaining a copy of all the documents that are input to, output from and internal to the system. However, it should not be assumed that any such documents present a comprehensive picture of the system (and they are by no means always self-explanatory); and so this technique should only be used in conjunction with other elicitation techniques such as interviews and task analysis.

The technique is particularly useful for identifying system inputs and outputs and, by implication, intermediate functions and stored data requirements. The information elicited by this means will, therefore, often be used as the basis for data analysis and allows the development of the problem domain data model (see Section 4.3.1).

The principal hazard associated with document inspection is the potential mismatch between the *documented* system and the *actual* system. It can happen that the documented system (as reflected in the various pro-formas, etc.) has certain shortcomings, and that it is only the ingenuity of the staff involved (and their 'mis-use' of the system) that enables it to function effectively. The combined use of other elicitation techniques (such as observation and interviews) helps to detect such problems.

A more insidious problem is that the traditional ways of analysing the results of document inspection (such as the development of document flow diagrams) tend to lead to a structural model of the existing system. In itself this is not a problem, but there is then the danger of the old structure (which is quite possibly defective) being carried over to a procedural specification (see Section 5.3.4) and, hence, the new system design, without due consideration.

An awareness of the issues (see Section 4.1) is the best defence here.

9.5   Task observation

Incidental observations, such as a succession of 'urgent' interruptions (of the elicitee) during a planned interview, can provide useful clues to the astute elicitor but are, by their nature, unpredictable. The only general advice that can be given is to be aware of their potential significance.

Planned observation[81] relates to the observation of someone performing a particular task and, in the requirements engineering context, it is likely to concern their interaction with some precursor system (although observed interaction can also be a valuable means of assessing a prototype of the new system).

Such observation offers certain advantages over other elicitation techniques. It provides a way of addressing the 'documented vs actual system' problem which can arise where completed documents are just inspected (observing *how* a form is completed can reveal sections which are redundant or missing) and can also be used where document inspection is not possible, i.e. for non-document based systems. Examples of the latter case would include the observation of the interaction between an operator and a machine or the recording of a telephone call between a supervisor and a clerk.

It has been demonstrated (Bainbridge, 1979) that interviewing people about how they perform tasks is subject to many limitations and inaccuracies. This is another problem that direct observation can address.

In recent years, largely as a result of the phenomenal increase in the sophistication of HMIs, the observation and recording of human machine interaction (generally known as task analysis) has received great attention from the theorists. There has been a tendency to concentrate upon how to record and analyse (rather than elicit) the information, and some formality has been introduced,

---

[81] Sometimes, in its less formal incarnations, known by the quaint name of 'sitting with Nellie'.

particularly with regard to notations. One of these – task action grammar (TAG) – is considered briefly in Section 12.2.

Observation itself, however, remains a more subjective area and largely relies (as it always has) upon the practitioner's expertise. Whilst task analysis in general is also used for other purposes (for example, ergonomics and training) its utility within requirements elicitation, specification and external design (see Section 5.2) is significant.

As has been mentioned, the pragmatics of observation remain more of an art than a science but some guidelines can be offered. A hierarchical task decomposition is widely employed and a preliminary analysis along such lines is useful in planning detailed observation sessions (as well as in the subsequent analysis and recording of the elicited information).

Deciding what to observe is often as difficult as the observation itself. Observation and the subsequent analysis is expensive in time (and, hence, money) and it is easy to get 'carried away' and end up with more information than is useful. The recommendation is to use observation parsimoniously and concentrate upon critical, interactive tasks using a sampling approach where possible.

The practicalities of task observation reflect many of the same considerations as interviewing. Objectives, personnel and location must be selected and the appropriate arrangements, including the briefing of those concerned, must be made with as much, if not more, care. As with interviews, written notes are probably still the most effective recording technique, but increasing use is being made of video recording. As with recording of interviews, this still requires subsequent analysis in order to develop a structured (and, hence, useful) record.

There are further considerations regarding the observation environment. Essentially, there is a trade-off between how faithfully the normal task environment is retained and how sophisticated (and intrusive) is the observation and recording set up. The former is seen to promote the realism of the task performance whereas the latter increases the amount of information that is captured.

Whilst observation is often taken literally as just watching the task being performed, it is also possible, in effect, to hybridise this with an interview and ask the elicitee to talk through what they are doing, and even why they are doing it. This can reveal considerably more information and may well justify the penalty of interfering further with the normal performance of the task.

It might also be noted that observees have been known to 'put on a show' and do not necessarily perform tasks in their usual manner when they know they are being observed. This may not be easy to counter, but possible strategies include:

- fully explaining the purpose of the observation
- extended observation (so that it becomes 'normal')
- covert observation (to be approached with due caution!)

Where the observed task involves the operation of some new (to the user) system (such as a prototype), the question of user learning must be given due consideration and appropriate training given. (Of course, the training itself may be the subject of observation if, as is likely, ease of learning is a matter of interest.)

9.6   Ethnography

A particular variation upon the theme of observation is known as ethnography. This term (adopted from the disciplines of sociology and anthropology) applies where, over an extended period, the observer becomes immersed within the society or culture under study. (An analogy may be drawn with the notion of investigators going 'under cover' although there are no connotations of secrecy or deception!)

Ethnography is justified upon the basis that it is only by becoming intimately involved with the workplace situation that observers can gain a full understanding of the various practices, problems, concerns, etc.

There is evidence to support this (Kotonya and Sommerville, 1997, provide some more detail and several further references) but it would seem that the practice is relatively expensive and may be cost effective only for complex and critical systems such as air traffic control.

9.7   Use-cases and scenarios

A use-case is a description of a particular interaction between the (proposed) solution system and one or more terminators (usually, potential users).

Within elicitation, the role of use-cases might be described as a secondary one. Rather than being used for the initial gathering of information about the problem domain and requirements, they serve to check client and/or user acceptance of possible external designs and to elicit the fine detail of functionality. The use-case elicitation exercise centres upon a consideration of the usage of the solution system under a certain set of circumstances (the use-case or scenario). The elicitee is 'walked-through' the selected operation(s) and the way in which they (would wish to) interact with the system is recorded (see, for example, Hooper and Hsia, 1982). This forces the elicitee to concentrate upon the specific rather than the general, and it has been shown that greater accuracy and detail can be established in this way. Prototypes (see Section 11.3) can provide excellent support for such exercises.

There are, however, some caveats. Concentrating as they do upon the interaction between the terminators and the solution system (in other words, the *functionality* of the solution system) there is a danger that the problem domain, *per se*, may not receive full consideration and premature design of the interface between the problem domain and the solution system may be encouraged. In other words, the technique is more solution than problem oriented.

Nonetheless, with caution, use-cases can play a valuable elicitation role. However, since the primary role of use-cases is, arguably, the specification of behaviour, their description is to be found alongside the other behavioural modelling techniques (Section 12.3).

9.8 Brainstorming

The rather odd name has its roots in a 'brilliant idea' rather than a disturbance of the mind. The concept is of a group of people indulging in a mental 'free for all' and engaging in some (roughly directed) free-thinking within a non-constraining environment with the aim of generating new ideas.

Since it is, essentially, a technique that increases the number of ideas (or, within the context of requirements engineering, the number of requirements) it is pertinent where the latter are particularly vague or 'thin on the ground' as may be the case for a highly novel system.

Relatively short (around one hour), intensive sessions seem to be most productive. Since they are expensive (and subject to the law of diminishing returns), they should be used sparingly; quite possibly only one session in an entire project.

Selection of personnel is critical since it is necessary to establish an appropriate culture as well as to include an adequate knowledge base. Representatives of stakeholders can be supplemented with domain experts and recognised 'off the wall' thinkers. A minimum group size of around seven seems to be necessary to instigate a 'chain reaction' of ideas; the upper limit is more arbitrary.

A talented facilitator is beneficial and has the task of encouraging the informal yet productive atmosphere in which (almost) anything goes and even the most bashful will have their say.

Some rules have been formulated which help to achieve this:

- free for all – everyone can have their say;
- no criticism – however crazy or daft the idea;
- no debate – just note it and, hopefully, use it as a springboard for more ideas.

Meeting 'in the round' is also seen as conducive and ideally the room should accommodate this (and the meeting should be free of interruptions).

It is necessary for all participants to be able to refer back to ideas generated earlier in the meeting; a common strategy is to cover the walls in flip chart paper and employ a scribe (apart from the facilitator, the only clearly defined role) to record the ideas as they come. Some sort of structuring may evolve if related ideas are grouped, but this is not a primary objective.

In some versions of the exercise, the idea generation (part one) is immediately followed by a 'weeding' procedure (part two) in which some selection of ideas (requirements) is performed. Techniques which may be applied here include simple voting and some form of criteria-based ranking or scoring. In any case, the surviving requirements are subsequently copied from the wall charts (possibly by photo-reduction) and some of the other techniques (described herein) are then used to refine the requirements.

9.9   Requirements stripping

This technique is used where there is in existence a client's requirement document or specification or, possibly, a specification for a similar, predecessor product. Individual requirements are extracted (stripped) from the original document and incorporated into a new requirements document.

The purpose of this exercise stems from the generally low quality of such original documents; they tend to be poorly structured and contain much irrelevant material. Extraction of the 'nuggets' of accurate and relevant information and their incorporation into a new, properly structured document is often by the far the best way to deal with these problems. Whilst requirements stripping does not of itself fill gaps in the originals (the other common deficiency) a good, new structure will at least help to identify areas of omission.

Requirements stripping can, in principle, be performed manually, but where the original is available in electronic form, it is now usual to use a stripping tool. These are commonly provided with requirements traceability and management tools (aka requirements databases) and greatly increase the speed with which such databases can be populated with requirements (see, for example, James, 1997). Some degree of 'intelligence' is even available in such tools and automated requirements stripping can further increase productivity.

If at all possible, it is in the developer's interest (and, quite possibly the client's as well – although they do not always see it that way) to persuade the client to abandon their original 'specification' once all the requirements have been stripped. In effect, the oracle is re-defined. Clients are not always willing to do this and the developer then faces the problem of maintaining traceability between the two documents; not only so far as the original strip is concerned, but also in the face of subsequent modifications. Even this overhead is likely to be worthwhile for the developer since using a poor original document during subsequent development will incur great costs of its own. However, where a good requirements database is used, it can handle traceability automatically and the problem largely disappears.

So, requirements stripping, particularly when a requirements database is used, provides a quick and relatively easy way of obtaining a 'first cut' list of requirements, and, to a lesser degree, problem domain description, etc.

Modelling techniques 10

The modelling of systems is a vital ingredient in software development in general and in requirements engineering in particular. Amongst the relevant modelling techniques, the most important distinction is between those that constitute an external model of the system and those that constitute an internal model. Perhaps the best distinguishing test is to ask whether the model decomposes the system in question into sub-systems. If so, it is an internal model; if not, it is an external model. As elsewhere, the importance of the distinction is reflected in a multitude of names, including those shown in Table 10.1. Note that this distinction corresponds precisely with that between external and internal design as described in Section 2.7. External models may be further classified into those that model the *appearance* of the system (representational models) and those that model an abstraction of its *behaviour*.

Table 10.1

external	internal
functional	structural
black box	clear box
behavioural	non-behavioural

10.1 Representational modelling

Representational models model the appearance of the system. At their simplest, such models are static and provide snapshots of the system appearance. Whilst a representational model could be constructed in text:

The lift panel consists of a button for each floor arranged in a vertical row with an adjacent vertical row of indicator lights.

it is usually more effective to use drawings[82].

This applies equally where the common computer screen interface is being specified. It is clear, in this case, that it is the *output* from the system that such models help to describe.

Unlike panels of buttons, the appearance of screens does, of course, usually change with time. Even paper-based representational models can capture some of this dynamism since changing appearance over time can be modelled using a time-sequenced series of diagrams – the story-board (or, as we used to call it, 'paper-prototype') approach.

More sophisticated tools (and we are talking computers here) can produce animated representational models. These models (representational prototypes) can be designed to handle *input* as well, at which point they start to model the *behaviour* (in addition to the appearance) of the system.

10.2   Behavioural modelling

Characteristically, behavioural models define the relationship between the inputs to and the outputs from the system. It should be clearly noted that the definition of the relationships (causal and timing) between input and output is tantamount to defining function. In fact, it is practically impossible to specify functionality, however loosely, without reference, however oblique, to the data that passes to and fro across the external interfaces to the system (i.e. the inputs and outputs). For example, the statement, 'The details of all aircraft within a range of 10 km are displayed' makes obvious reference to some output data (even if it is poorly defined).

Properly done, the behavioural model describes the system in terms of *what it does* which is *the* central element of specification. This type of modelling will, therefore, be examined in detail.

The relationships between input and output can be viewed (and, hence, modelled) in various ways, and the emphasis will depend upon the nature of the system in question. Simple statements of function are commonly used – for example, 'The user can move the cursor to the next input field by pressing the tab key' – but more sophisticated and more formal techniques are available.

As described in Section 5.3.3, the simplest systems to describe are those 'single shot' programs that have no memory of past events and just respond to the last input. (The example of the Fahrenheit to Celsius temperature conversion program was given – see page 149.)

However, most systems have some memory of past input and this gives rise to the notion of *state* which is, in effect, a condensation of the input history which enables the response to the next input to be predicted. Many of the well known behavioural modelling techniques fall into this state-based category.

---

[82] In which case, a more precise definition of representational modelling could be along the lines that the space dimensions of the model correspond directly to the space dimensions of the system being modelled.

10.3 Structural modelling

Whilst generally less relevant to requirements engineering, structural modelling is well developed and can take several forms. All share the characteristic that the system is modelled as a set of interrelated *components*. In other words, there is a structural decomposition of the system into some kind of sub-systems.

Frequently, this decomposition is performed upon the basis of the processing that is performed, and the sub-systems then take the form of processes. In this case, the models may be further classified depending upon whether the resultant processes run in parallel (concurrently) or sequentially. Alternative bases for decomposition are, however, possible and decomposition into objects or entities is also common[83].

Being inherently structural, these models address the question of *how* a system works (or how it will be built). As has been seen, with regard to the new, solution system, such matters constitute design constraints and are best avoided. Structural models are, therefore, largely confined to the analysis of existing systems (the problem domain or pre-existing solution systems) and the internal design task.

The distinction between process and function is not, however, always that clear (every process performs some function after all) and the somewhat grey area of decomposition by function can cause problems. As discussed in Section 12.1.1, decomposition by function can be regarded as an external (non-structural) model provided that all the resultant functions are externally visible.

In passing, it may also be noted that design is a many layered thing. During internal design, different layers of the system design can be decomposed using different approaches.

10.4 Modelling technique classification

Adding some further sub-classification to the foregoing discussion, gives the following list into which have been slotted (*in italics*) illustrative examples of some modelling techniques.

External models
    Representational
        Static
            Screen diagrams
        Dynamic
            'Throw-away' prototypes

---

[83] Note that behavioural models can also place certain requirements upon what data are stored, but they put no constraints upon the *structure* of those data.

Behavioural
Functional
Decision tables
Function statements
Use-cases
TAG
State-based
FSMs
Petri nets
VDM

Internal models
Process oriented
Communicating concurrent processes
DFDs
JSD 'nets'
Communicating sequential processes
Structure charts
Single process – procedural/algorithmic
Pseudo-code
Flow charts
Data oriented
Entity relationship modelling
Process/data combination
ELH
Object oriented class models

Representational modelling

11

Representational models (also known as iconic models) mimic the appearance of a system.

11.1 Indications for use

Whilst representational models can be rendered in text, or in three dimensions (with clay, etc.), the most advantageous notation is usually drawing. To illustrate this point, imagine the difficulty of describing a person's appearance, even to the extent required for simple recognition in a crowd. A photograph or drawing is much more effective. (This analogy, incidentally, illustrates the fact that defining appearance is rather different from defining behaviour; a photograph of a person is of little, if any, help in determining how they behave.)

Representational models are restricted to depicting the appearance of a system which, for software systems, amounts to depicting visual outputs; usually computer screens. For system definition, this is by no means the whole story but it is an essential element and representational models have a useful role to play.

Particular strengths of this technique are readily available tool support, low ambiguity, low susceptibility to error and high accessibility. The last is probably due to there being no mapping between dimensions (i.e. the horizontal space dimension on the model represents the horizontal space dimension of the real system, etc.), so the meaning is immediately obvious to nearly all.

Despite there being some middle ground a distinction may be made between static and dynamic representational models.

11.2 Static representational modelling

This is a highly effective technique which, at its simplest, is typified by screen diagrams. Perhaps just because it is so obvious, it is often not recognised as a technique, and such models have received little attention in software engineering circles. They are none the less useful for that!

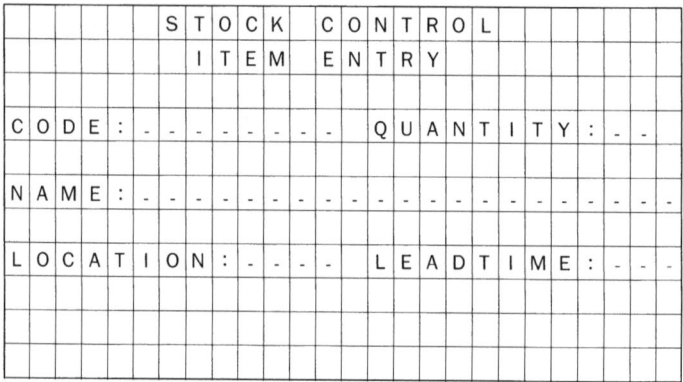

Figure 11.1

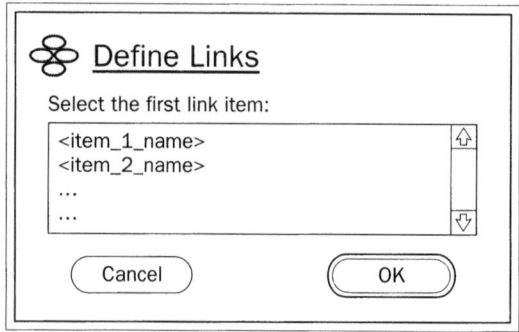

Figure 11.2

When it comes to static representational models, we are assisted by the fact that the commonest computer output device, the screen, is essentially two-dimensional. One of the earlxiest forms was the screen design form. This dates from the days when most computer terminals could display only text, and that in a fixed format of (usually) 80 columns and 25 rows. The appearance of a particular screen could be readily specified by completing such a form. Figure 11.1 shows an example for a cut-down version.

Such forms are of less relevance in the days of GUIs but a similar approach can be used for more sophisticated screens. This is illustrated in Figure 11.2.

Indeed, the technique need not be confined to screens and a dedicated hardware/software interface might be depicted as in Figure 11.3.

Whilst screens (and drawings) are essentially two-dimensional, overlapping windows create the illusion of a third spatial dimension[84]. Anything that can be

---

[84] Systems with overlapping flat objects are sometimes (rather bizarrely) described as having two and a half dimensions (2.5D).

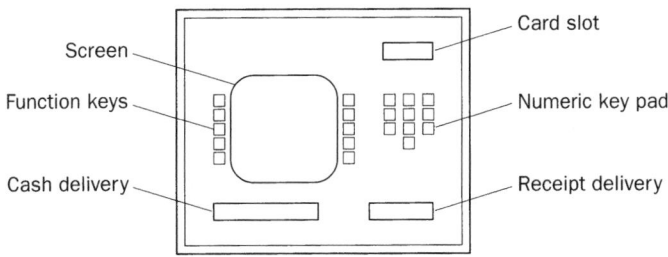

Figure 11.3

shown on a flat screen can, of course, be shown in a two-dimensional drawing but non-representational models, used in conjunction, may assist in modelling this aspect.

11.2.1 Story-boards, paper-prototypes

Computer screens also have a time dimension and it is the representation of this dynamic aspect (in a conventional specification) that is the most problematical. One solution is to represent the changes as a finite series of steps that can then be separated in space rather than in time. Of course, this is what happens with real screens anyway; the apparently dynamic screen image is actually a series of still pictures. The same is true of television and, more pertinently, of movie film. In this last case, the film itself demonstrates precisely the trick of representing the time dimension as a space dimension. Given this trick, one can concentrate upon selecting which 'frames' are the important ones to specify. This is similar to a master animator drawing the key frames and leaving the rank and file animators to produce the intermediate frames (according to well understood, if not explicit, rules).

Since digital systems are the principal concern, output is discrete (at some level) and so a 'minimal change' can be identified (e.g. output a character). In practice, rules can also be specified for proceeding from one 'key frame' to the next (e.g. 'strings of characters are output in sequence left to right'), significantly reducing the number of 'frames' which need explicit description.

Sequenced graphics have proved a cheap and effective way of modelling the changing appearance of some systems and, given their similarity to the story-board used when planning movies, they sometimes go by that name. Paper-prototype is an alternative term that I have used (see also Gomaa and Scott, 1981). However, they do have their limitations and the logical next step is some form of animation.

11.3 Dynamic representational modelling (prototypes)

Prototyping has a venerable tradition in other engineering disciplines but, within software engineering, the use of prototypes is a relatively recent phenomenon. Its adoption has had to await the availability of adequate technology since relatively powerful development platforms are required to develop prototypes cost effectively. For most systems, the technical obstacles have now been removed and we are witnessing a rapid adoption of software system prototyping.

Prototypes may be built for various purposes, but particularly pertinent to requirements engineering are those that seek to replicate the appearance of and, possibly, some of the behaviour of, a required system[85]. Despite, more or less, faithfully copying the appearance of the 'real' system, they are still models in that only part of the interface is modelled and/or the underlying functionality is missing or limited.

The term 'rapid prototyping' is often used and arose from the relatively rapid development of the prototype (as compared to the eventual product). Unfortunately, some have been misled by this name into thinking that the delivery of the final product is somehow speeded up. There is no reason to suppose that this should result (although improved requirements engineering could well lead to lower re-engineering costs).

Various classifications of prototypes have been developed (e.g. Floyd, 1984, Law, 1985, Mayhew and Dearnley, 1987 and Vonk, 1990) and a fairly conventional summary is:

- **Exploratory** prototype – an aid to eliciting or refining requirements. This is often called a **throwaway** prototype and, as that name implies, once requirements engineering (and the specification) are complete, it serves no further purpose.

- **Definitive** prototype – forms part of the definition of required behaviour (i.e. part of the specification).

- **Structural** prototype – used to evaluate possible idesign solutions, for example to check performance (hence, *performance* prototyping is one sub-class). Whilst being of most significance to the design phase, this may also be used during the requirements phase to check feasibility.

- **Evolutionary** prototype – amounts to a completely different approach to software development. By a process of gradual refinement, the 'prototype' *becomes* the product. There is no differentiation between the development of the prototype and the product, and the relevance of the requirements engineering process model used here is highly questionable. It will not, therefore, be pursued here, but no criticism of this approach should be inferred and see, for example, Ince and Hekmatpour (1987) for further information.

---

[85] There is a subtle distinction between *replicating* behaviour (i.e. behaving in the same way as the original – sometimes referred to as an iconic model) and *modelling* behaviour (i.e. producing an abstraction of that behaviour – sometimes referred to as an analytic model). Whilst reproducing (part of) a proposed system's behaviour with a prototype may be very useful, it may well be necessary to model that behaviour in a more abstract form as well (e.g. as an FSM) in order for the developer to understand it fully.

It is the first two of these that are of prime interest to requirements engineering but, as usual, the distinctions are not always that clear cut and it may well be, for example, that an exploratory prototype (which is, essentially an elicitation, and edesign tool) may, with or without prior intention, become a definitive prototype (and, hence, a specification tool).

Evolutionary prototyping was described above as constituting a completely different approach to software development. There have been advocates of the view that any sort of prototyping amounts to a completely different approach (or method). That is not a view that is shared here. As implied earlier, prototyping is not self-sufficient, but can (and should) be one of a set of techniques integrated into a coherent requirements engineering process.

The development of a prototype does, however, imply iteration. Where exploratory prototyping is used, typically to support elicitation, there is a tacit assumption that the initial prototype will be demonstrated to the user (possibly in conjunction with a use-case – see Section 12.3); the feedback so obtained will be used to refine the prototype. In practice, this happens several times over (thrice being common in small projects). However, such iteration in elicitation is nothing new and, whether or not prototyping is used, must be accommodated (as per the requirements engineering process model presented in Section 2.6).

The principal role of prototypes within requirements engineering is the modelling of user interfaces, particularly where these are relatively complex, critical and/or novel. Not only are the models more realistic than paper prototypes, but they also share that great asset of all representational models, accessibility.

It is almost an incidental advantage that prototypes can encourage involvement of potential users and commitment of clients. But there is a down side. The early appearance of a realistic prototype can lead to the erroneous belief that the project is far more advanced that it actually is and consequent frustration as the truth emerges.

11.3.1   Building prototypes

Building a prototype is, of course, a mini development project in itself and it is the time (and expense) associated with this that is, perhaps, the major drawback. As with any development, it is necessary to have an initial idea of the requirements, and the development of a preliminary specification must rely upon some of the other elicitation, analysis and specification techniques described herein.

Tool support is essential and much depends upon the tools that are selected. Whilst given suitable hardware, it is possible to build a prototype using conventional 3GLs, unless there are special circumstances (such as high safety criticality), this is seldom cost effective. In most circumstances, it is the availability of the more productive 4GLs and user interface development tools that make prototyping a practical proposition. As well as providing graphical tools for screen design, there are often associated DBMSs which allow some underlying functionality and even evolutionary development for some systems.

Also available are modelling tools with animation capability. Such computer aided software engineering (CASE) tools (often known as analyst workbenches) were originally designed to support the normal software development system modelling, but certain of these models have the potential to be executed and, hence, can form the basis of prototypes. Most are based upon FSMs and Statemate (Harel *et al.*, 1990), for example, allows animation of state charts. A behavioural FSM (see Section 12.6) model of the system is built and drawn as a state chart using the tool. A screen generator then allows simulations of the user interface to be created and these can be linked to, and driven by, the underlying model. This has the significant advantage that the system is defined in terms of the underlying model as well as by way of a dynamic representation of its behaviour; and it is guaranteed that the specification model reflects the prototype. Such prototypes have been called animated specifications (Kramer *et al.*, 1988) and tie in closely with the notion of the definitive prototype mentioned earlier. Given suitable resources, it is hard to see why non-animatable FSM-based specifications should continue to be produced.

Vonk (1990) is recommended for further information regarding prototyping within the context of requirements engineering.

Behavioural (functional) modelling **12**

Behavioural models differ from representational models in that they do not replicate or mimic the actual appearance or behaviour of the system. Instead, they are an abstraction of that behaviour.

12.1 Function statements and functional decomposition

Perhaps the simplest and most commonly used technique for defining behaviour is the function statement. Using text, these statements (as is mandatory for any behavioural modelling technique) describe the causal (and, possibly, timing) relationships between inputs and outputs. Sometimes the inputs and outputs are implicit rather than being explicitly named and, in either case, there is reliance upon their full definition elsewhere (usually in a DD).

Function statements are often presented in plain natural language, although it is recognised that careful construction is desirable and some form of structured language is often employed. Despite such tilts at formalisation, this has yet to be achieved and so the notion is best conveyed by way of examples:

- The cash machine will allow the user to change their personal identification number (PIN).
- When a call-button is pressed, that call-button is illuminated.
- Selecting the undo option reverses the last edit.
- If an invalid source file name is entered, the message 'This file does not exist' is output.

It is perhaps debatable whether such descriptive statements constitute a modelling technique. However (as is illustrated in Section 13.3.2), sets of descriptive statements *can* constitute models and function statements certainly occur in sets. Most commonly, since function statements can be constructed at various levels of abstraction, these are hierarchically ordered and are developed in a top-down fashion that is generally referred to as functional decomposition.

12.1.1   Functional decomposition

This is perhaps more of a high-order strategy than a technique, in that it may be realised using a variety of means other than function statements (for example, use-cases (Section 12.3), DFDs (Section 13.1.1.1) and structure charts (Section 13.1.2)). However, the basic idea is simple enough. The functionality of a system is defined in detail by breaking down the high-level functions into sets of lower level, more detailed functions; usually in hierarchical manner. The technique is also known as functional refinement or, confusingly, functional composition (Roman 1985).

Curiously, despite its fundamental nature and great pertinence, it is seldom recognised and described as a behavioural modelling technique. This may stem from a similarity to (and ready confusion with) a technique for *internal* design that is usually known as stepwise refinement. That is an approach to algorithm development where a statement of the *problem to be solved* is broken down into a set of tasks which, together, constitute a solution to the problem. Each task in turn is then treated as a problem in its own right and is further decomposed in a similar way until such time as a set of readily coded statements is reached.

Of course, it is perfectly legitimate, for the purposes of idesign, to structurally decompose a system along functional lines; and it is likely that all the functions in a true functional decomposition will also appear, in some form, in the corresponding structural decomposition. This only adds to the superficial resemblance, which can be striking.

In the past, stepwise refinement[86] has been actively promoted as an internal design technique; this is based upon the notion that the actual structure of the solution system *should* closely reflect the breakdown of the required functionality. This *can* work, particularly at the lower design levels, but it tends to produce poorly modularised designs and is, generally, not to be recommended.

To emphasise the distinction between functional decomposition and actual system structure, Figure 12.1 illustrates two hierarchical decompositions (functional and structural) for an electronic computer aided design (ECAD) system (used in the design of printed circuit boards). The view on the left depicts the functional structure that would be apparent to the user. The view on the right shows the structural breakdown (of the same system) that actually makes things happen.

Functional decomposition (or stepwise refinement) is not only a weak idesign approach, it is also of limited use when it comes to analysing the problem domain. However, this does not detract from its utility for *external design* and *specification* where the subject matter is, precisely, functionality.

Text is probably the commonest notation (although DFDs, see Section 13.1.1.1, are often used); this can vary from prose to relatively constrained text, even conventional programming languages. This presents some trade-off

---

[86] Confusingly, sometimes called functional decomposition!

Functional hierarchy (ECAD system)   **Structural hierarchy (ECAD system)**

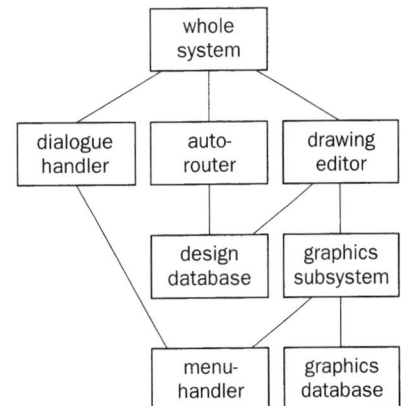

Figure 12.1

between ambiguity and accessibility, but achieving low ambiguity always relies upon the practitioner's skill. Language directed editors are desirable, but these are available only for conventional programming languages (which are less than ideal for this purpose) and so it is usually only 'dumb' word-processors that are used.

12.1.2 Description

As indicated above, the basic idea is quite simple. We start with a high-level function statement[87], for example:

> The cash machine will allow the user to change their personal identification number (PIN).

This function is then elaborated in terms of the sub-functions that must be performed in order to achieve it. For example:

> 1 The user selects the change PIN option from the main menu
>
> 2 The user's old PIN is validated
>
> 3 The user's new PIN is entered

(You may notice that, individually, these lower level function statements often involve only input *or* output. Therefore, they should, perhaps, be called 'half function' statements.)

---

[87] This introduction will use prose, but various other notations are possible and will be illustrated later.

This process can be repeated for each of the sub-functions until an agreeably unambiguous definition is reached. Taking the second sub-function as an example, this could be elaborated to:

2.1	The user is prompted to enter their old PIN
2.2	The user enters their old PIN
2.3	If the old PIN is incorrect:
2.4	The message "incorrect PIN" is displayed for 4 seconds
2.5	The system returns to the main menu display
2.6	If the old PIN is correct:
2.7	The user is prompted to enter the new PIN
2.8	etc.

Most high-level functions cannot be achieved with a linear sequence of sub-functions. It is usually necessary to introduce conditionality (as per the example above) and repetition. It is not easy to define complex sequencing in prose; the example above also illustrates how indentation may be used to add clarity. This can be taken much further and more code-like languages (even compilable programming languages) can be employed.

So, the well established structured programming elements (sequence, selection and iteration) have their place in behavioural modelling techniques as well. It is also possible to be more accommodating with regard to the dreaded 'goto' which, used with reasonable care, can make these behavioural models easier to follow.

Note that there is an inherent redundancy in this technique. The decomposed version effectively renders the original statement superfluous. However, a good case can be made for retaining such redundancy as it aids understanding of the specification.

As mentioned earlier, because of the superficial similarity between this elaboration and the elaboration of detail during idesign (decomposing systems into sub-systems, sub-sub-systems, etc.), great care is needed in order not to stray into idesign (and, thus, introduce unintended design constraints). The golden rule is to stick to those functions that are *visible to the outside world*. If this is done, the elaboration of detail (as illustrated above) continues to refer to the *whole system* and, therefore, still constitutes an *external* model.

To emphasise this point yet further, consider this alternative version of the second decomposition:

2.1	The user is prompted to enter their old PIN
2.2	The user enters their old PIN
2.3	The old PIN is checked against that held in the local copy of the user's account record.
2.4	If the PIN is incorrect:
2.5	The message 'incorrect PIN' is displayed for 4 seconds
2.6	etc.

The *mechanism* by which the old PIN is checked (statement 2.3) is certainly not apparent to the user and, unless they are intent upon fraud, it is probably not of interest either. All the user sees is the *outcome* of that check. This does not reveal how it was done, but simply implies that it was and that is all that it is necessary to specify here.[88]

The other potential problem with this technique is not knowing when to stop. A very useful guideline is 'when every input and every output have been included'.

12.2 Task analysis

Task analysis (TA) addresses the analysis or the edesign of human task performance; particularly in the context of HMI. Whilst it has application in such areas as staff training, here, it is the relevance to requirements engineering that is important. Arguably, three, non-exclusive roles may be identified:

- During elicitation and analysis, TA can be used to study and record the activity of (implicitly, expert) users within the problem domain.

- The insight and guidelines provided can assist in the edesign of the HMI.

- The notations that have been developed may be seen as useful for documenting behaviour in the specification.

Task analysis starts with the goals that people wish to achieve. Tasks are the high-order mechanisms by which such goals may be achieved; operations are the interaction (behaviour) that realises the task. Whilst this is slanted towards the user rather than the system perspective, parallels may be identified with relevant requirements engineering concepts; requirements (goals), functions (tasks) and terminator interaction (operations).

A particular, popular variation on TA is hierarchical task analysis (HTA) (Annett and Duncan, 1967). This explicitly recognises that goals may be broken down into hierarchies of sub-goals (and sub-sub-goals, etc.), organised by some suitable plan or strategy. (If this starts to sound rather like functional decomposition (see Section 12.1.1), well, yes.)

As in other areas, much of the published work on TA concentrates upon the notations that have been developed to record the outcome of the analysis. Both diagrammatic and textual notations have been developed. The first resemble process structure charts (see Section 13.1.2); the latter often resemble the structured text used in functional decomposition (see Section 12.1.1) and use-cases (see Section 12.3). (Although TA certainly pre-dates use-cases.)

---

[88] It may well be that the client (the bank) are interested in how such checks are made, but that should be specified separately. If they also wish to specify the interleaving of the user interaction and the internal checks that may well constitute a design constraint. (The internal PIN read could be made before or after the user enters their version.)

A particularly interesting aspect has been the development of a relatively formal interface description language. Derived from BNF (see Section 14.3.4), task action grammars (TAGs) adopt the notion that complex definitions can be built up from a 'dictionary' of simple tasks by way of a set of rules or schemas. Although originally intended more as a tool for cognitive psychology, clearly, this has potential for the precise specification of system behaviour.

Despite the potential, TA cannot currently be regarded as a mainstream requirements engineering technique and so only a very brief overview has been presented here; for a broader and more detailed introduction (and numerous further references) see Diaper (1989).

12.3   Use-cases and scenarios

A use-case is a description of a particular interaction between the (proposed) solution system and one or more terminators. The notion may be conveyed with a simple example:

1   The user presses the call-button for the desired direction of travel
2   The relevant button is illuminated
3   The lift stops at the user's floor and the button is un-illuminated
4   The lift doors open
5   The user enters the lift
6   The user presses the desired send-button
7   The lift travels to the requested floor (possibly stopping at other floors en route)
8   The lift stops at the requested floor
9   The lift doors open
10   The user leaves the lift

The notion of use-cases (or, at least, scenarios) has been around for some time (see, for example, Hooper and Hsia, 1982), but it is since their description by Ivar Jacobson *et al.* (1992) that use-cases have become very popular. They have also become closely associated with object oriented approaches to analysis and specification, but there is no particular rationale for this and use-cases can fit comfortably with other approaches such as those described here.

Seasoned professionals may have noticed parallels with older 'technology', notably the notion of a transaction (as used in functional testing), functional decomposition (see Section 12.1.1), task scripts, flow-charts and, even, TAGs (see Section 12.2). Be that as it may, use-cases seem set to predominate in the immediate future.

12.3.1   The role of use-cases

Within the object oriented culture, use-cases are presented as, primarily, an analysis and specification technique. Analysing the uses to which the new system will be put is seen as tantamount to developing the requirements which it must meet. Indeed, it seems to be the case that clients and potential users do find use-cases readily accessible and so they can aid communication between client/user and developer.

This suggests that use-cases also serve as a means of *eliciting* information and, whilst it is clearly necessary to elicit some information before use-cases can be developed, there seems to be a good case for their use in 'follow-up' elicitation[89]. On the other hand, they can be regarded as simply providing 'ordinary' elicitation records that feed understanding into the analysis and specification processes.

The more widely promoted role is to regard refined use-case definitions as a means of specification, even to the extent that they should form the entire specification. This is unfortunate as use-cases have their limitations (see, for example, Kovitz, 1999, and Jackson, 2001) and should be seen as just one of a number of available techniques.

Essentially, use-case based specification is specification by example (rather than by rule – see Section 5.3.5). The consequences are incompleteness and, arguably, lack of a high-level abstraction of behaviour. Given only a set of use-cases, it may be very difficult to determine whether behaviour has been specified completely and coherently.

The notion that use-cases can be used to 'reverse-engineer' requirements must also be treated with caution. The development of detailed interaction scenarios may well reveal hitherto unrealised requirements; this is implicit in the feedback loop from specification to analysis that appears in some requirements process models. However, as an analysis approach, use-cases cannot be relied upon to reveal or record all requirements. For one thing, use-cases only deal with actors (i.e. those who directly interface with the solution system), but there are other stakeholders who may well have requirements of their own; for another, use-cases assume discrete episodes of interaction, but some systems exhibit continuous behaviour. More selective use, in a supporting role, may, therefore, be deemed appropriate.

It may also be noted that use-cases operate at a relatively low level of abstraction; right down at the i/o level. This kind of detail (specific user prompts and responses[90]) and its determination is often regarded as part of HMI design. Use-cases may, therefore, also be regarded as a technique for documenting HMI designs.

12.3.2 Scenarios

The term 'scenario' pre-dates use-case and has been used more or less interchangeably by some, but other, subtly different, meanings have been ascribed, including the milieu within which a use-case may be performed. Some

---

[89] We have already seen that there is an intimate intertwining of elicitation and analysis and so it may be no surprise that some techniques 'cross over'.
[90] Often comprising solution data, see Section 2.8.

vagueness still persists, but it is now usually taken to indicate an *instantiation* of a use-case (where particular values are applied) or a *particular route* through a use-case. Simple use-cases, such as the introductory example, are linear and have only one route but, as we will see, most use-cases have alternate routes; it is in those circumstances that one particular route would comprise a particular scenario[91].

12.3.3   Identifying use-cases

The difference between a requirement and a function has already been examined (Section 5.2). One may equally ask, 'what is the difference between a use-case and a function?' One may equally well answer, 'not a lot'. Functions such as:

- call the lift to a selected floor
- add details of a new boat
- set the maximum tokens per place

can all be seen as ready candidates for use-cases. Identifying potential use-cases may therefore be approached in a very similar manner to the abstraction of functions from requirements[92].

This still leaves two important matters to consider:

- the level at which functions (or requirements) are mapped to use-cases;
- degree of coverage.

As is shown in Section 1.6.1, functions (of the solution system) can be stated at various levels of abstraction. This makes the identification of 'functions' that might be represented as use-cases, somewhat problematical.

As a further example, consider this stated function:

The system allows the user to enter and edit details of boats.

This could equally well presented as three separate (sub)functions:

The system allows the user to enter details of a new boat.
The system allows the user to edit details of an existing boat.
The system allows the user to delete an existing boat.

So, do we map one high-level function to one use-case or three lower level functions to three separate use-cases? Unfortunately, there is no simple rule,

---

[91] Software testing aficionados may recognise a parallel with selecting paths during path testing.
[92] Although, as hinted at earlier, there is a tendency for use-case based approaches to bypass the listing of requirements and pick use-cases directly from the problem domain.

but the general guideline is to keep use-cases simple and, for the above example, most practitioners would probably opt for the three separate use-cases.

There is, then, the question of coverage; how much of the required functionality should be described with use-cases? The obvious answer might seem to be 100%, but this is not necessarily the best bet. Use-cases are by no means the only option for functional specification and, for some areas, alternatives (as described in this book) can prove more versatile, succinct and unambiguous.

Particularly where an application has repetitively similar functional areas, it may be deemed unnecessary to provide use-cases for the entire user interaction. Provided that the full functionality is specified at the 'logical' level (see Section 5.2), it may be sufficient to provide 'sample' use-cases to establish the general style of interaction.

An associated question is the level of detail required in an individual use-case. As with functional decomposition (see Section 12.1.2), a useful guideline is to stop when all inputs and outputs have been documented.

Also shared with functional decomposition is the danger of straying into internal design. The same guideline applies; avoid including any actions or operations that are not apparent to the outside world (in this case, the actors).

12.3.4 Mapping use-cases to actors (or functions to terminators)

Most solution systems have interfaces with several external systems. Hitherto, these external systems have been referred to as terminators but, within the use-case community, they are customarily called 'actors'. Actors are frequently human but other data-processing systems (software or hardware) can also be considered as candidates for use-case development. (A degree of anthropomorphism may be required to imagine how, say, a card reader would like to interact with the system controlling an ATM, but this can still be productive.) The emergent guideline is that representative interaction of every class of actor should be considered for use-case enquiry. Note also that an actor is, in effect, a *role*; the same individual could perform the role of two different actors[93]. Whilst actors are not necessarily humans, they are always represented as labelled 'matchstick men', or, alternatively, with the stereotype <<actor>>. Each use-case (function) may involve one or more actors (terminators)[94] and the use-case diagram shows how the actor(s) map to the use-cases, the latter being shown as labelled 'sausages'. Lines connect the relevant actors to the relevant use-cases and arrows show where one use-case makes use of another. For example, in Figure 12.2, the enter-boat-in-race use-case will use select-from-list to select the required boat and race.

A context diagram (see Section 13.1.1.7) is a fairly obvious starting point for deriving the use-case diagram. (In this light, it may occur to you that the

---

[93] Not quite like the theatre, where the same actor could perform in more than one role!
[94] If this sounds familiar, it may be because much the same point was raised in Section 5.1.1.

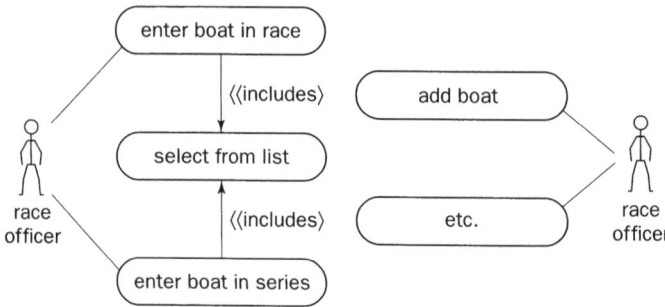

Figure 12.2

use-case diagram resembles a first-level DFD. There are, indeed, parallels; the actors are equivalent to terminators and the use-cases are equivalent to the principal functions (or processes). The main difference is that (although these are often implicit) the lines do not represent data flows; rather, they are akin to the calls shown on structure charts (see Section 13.1.2) or the collaboration links shown on UML class diagrams (see p. 315). It is also the case that only functions that interact directly with the outside world are shown; however, as mentioned in Section 13.1.1.2, this is to be considered advantageous if DFDs are used for specification purposes and so the differences may not be that significant.)

12.3.5   Documenting use-cases

The use-case itself is documented with text or with UML activity diagrams. The text may be at varying levels of 'formality'. At the one extreme, there is plain text, for example:

> If the user wishes to enter a boat into a race, they first select the 'race' button. They are then presented with a scrolling list of races (in date order) and can select the required race. They are then presented with the details of the race (including a scrolling list of current entries). To add a new entry the user must select the 'add entry' button. A list of boats (restricted to those that are eligible to enter the race and are not already entered) is then presented and the user may select the required boat. The display then reverts to the race details.

At the other extreme, a stylised specification language might be used[95]:

---

[95] See also Section 12.2 on task analysis.

select	< race button
display	> race list
select	< race
display	> race details
select	< add button
display	> boat list
select	< boat
display	> race details

(In both of the above cases, reliance may well be placed upon a DD to define 'race details', etc.)

Often, as per the introductory example, an intermediate, 'semi-formal' text (just like that introduced for functional decomposition – see Section 12.1.1) is used. That will be adopted for the remaining examples.

The alternative to text is the UML activity diagram (*not* the same as the use-case diagram!). These are said to be a specialisation of STDs (see Section 12.6.2, which you may care to read first if you are not familiar with these) and, similarly, use a directed graph notation. However (apart from decision nodes) only one type of node is used and this can represent states, events (triggers) and responses; a more realistic parallel may, therefore, be drawn with flow-charts. Figure 12.3 shows an example[96].

In a simple linear example such as this, activity diagrams appear to offer no advantages over text (indeed, the diagram requires more effort and can accommodate less text). However, they can show explicitly where flow branches because of conditionality (one branch or the other is followed), or where parallel actions can occur (the, so-called, 'fork'n'join'). In the next example (Figure 12.4), having entered a valid sail number, the other details may be entered in any order.

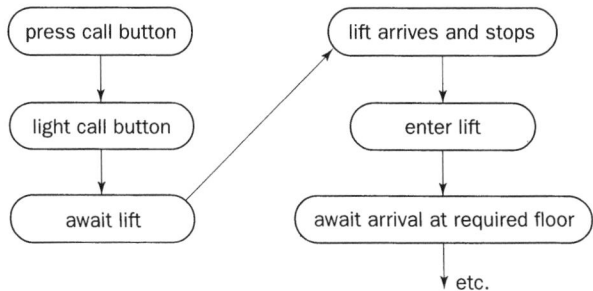

Figure 12.3

---

[96] This use-case does not correspond to any of those shown in the preceding use-case activity diagram (Figure 12.2).

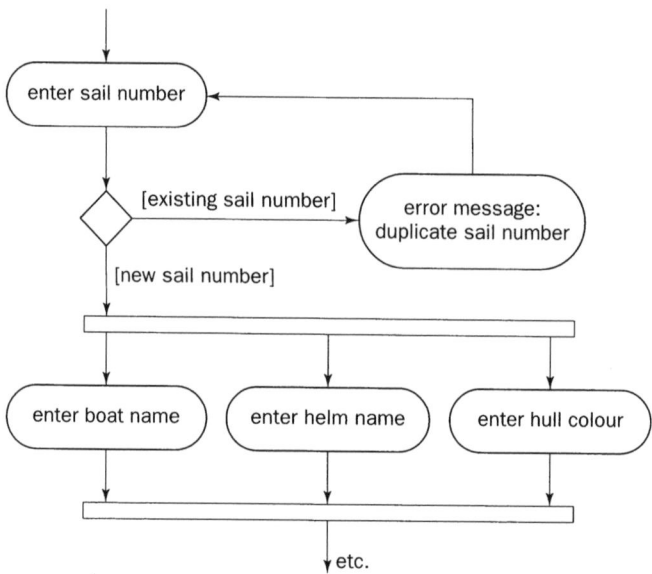

Figure 12.4

Despite the fact that branching logic can be modelled, most authorities recommend that, where possible, this should be avoided. A simple *thread* of inter-action is followed and where (as is usual) branches arise, just one is followed. So, for example, the difficulty of modelling branching interaction illustrated in Section 12.1.2 would be avoided by having a use-case of 'change PIN, all entries valid' and, if necessary, another use-case 'change PIN, old PIN invalid', etc. Defining the thread of interaction is, therefore, straightforward and the simple notations shown above suffice.

12.3.6 Types of use-case

Focusing upon linear use-cases gives rise, in part, to various different types of use-case. Alternate (secondary) courses of action become subordinate to the basic or primary cases.

12.3.6.1 Primary use-cases

For each use-case it is usual to concentrate upon the 'mainstream' interaction first. This can be justified upon the basis that it is usually the most important to the actor(s) and will represent the great bulk of the eventual, actual usage. It is typically the case that 20 per cent of the functionality accounts for 80 per cent of the usage[97]. Less usual situations or variants can then be considered separately.

---

[97] This is another example of the strangely ubiquitous 80/20 rule of thumb, sometimes known as Pareto's Law.

12.3.6.2 Secondary use-cases
Secondary use-cases may be discovered by asking questions such as:

- Is there another way of accomplishing this task?
- Does the actor have a choice of next steps?
- What errors might arise during the task?

Secondary use-cases may be documented in their entirety, or you may just document how they differ from the primary case[98]. For the latter purpose, two alternates are particularly useful:

- **include** (previously known as 'uses') use-cases – may be viewed as general purpose sub-routines that can be incorporated into various primary use-cases. For example, in the YRR application, there may be several points at which the user must select something from a scrolling list. To avoid repetition, the way in which this is performed could be described in an include case which can then be referenced as required with the key word 'include' (e.g. – Include select-item-from-list);

- **extend** (aka **alternate**) use-cases – are the usual way of dealing with exceptions or errors but can be used for any variation where there is *additional* interaction. For example, when the user attempts to add a new boat, they may enter a boat-class and sail-number that are already in use (an exception), or they may decide to enter optional details such as the helm-name.

12.3.7 Completing the documentation

Regardless of the technique used for describing the interaction, it is also necessary to define the circumstances or state of the solution system under which each use-case can occur, and the state of the system upon completion of the use-case. This may be done with statements of *pre-conditions* and *post-conditions*. For example, for the use-case enter-boat-in-race we may well state:

Pre-conditions:
> Details of the relevant boat have already been entered
> Details of the relevant race have already been entered
> The boat is not already entered in the race

Post-condition:
> The boat is entered in the race

Beyond this, it is usual to include a brief description of the use-case, name the actors that are involved and name any secondary use-cases that are used.

---

[98] Whilst not advocated by most authorities, another option is to use more complex use-cases (with branches and loops) and incorporate the alternatives into the primary.

So, although the documentation guidelines are quite flexible, a complete use-case might look something like this:

ENTER BOAT IN RACE
Allows the user to enter a boat into a race.
Actors
Race officer
Secondary use-cases
Select from list
Pre-conditions
Details of the relevant boat have already been entered
Details of the relevant race have already been entered
The boat is not already entered in the race
Post-condition
The boat will be entered in the race
Flow of events

1   The user selects the race-button

2   A scrolling list of races is displayed

3   Include Select-from-list (race)

4   The race details are displayed

5   The user selects the add-button

6   A scrolling list of boats is displayed (this is restricted to boats that are eligible to enter the selected race)

7   Include Select-from-list (boat)

8   The race details are re-displayed (with the selected boat added)

12.3.8   Support materials

In addition to the above, it is also possible (and often helpful) to include or to reference any relevant representational drawings, such as screen layouts (see Section 11.2). Whilst paper-based use-case descriptions are often an adequate basis for use-case elicitation, the approach has obvious synergistic links with prototyping. On the one hand, a prototype can support the use-case approach by providing a realistic environment for the user. On the other, walking through use-cases provides a good mechanism for obtaining client or user assessment of a prototype.

12.3.9   Subsequent synthesis

Where there are links between use-cases, the activity diagram summarises these. However, this goes only some way towards showing the overall integration of what can appear to be a set of stand-alone use-cases. Together they provide numerous snapshots of system behaviour, but in what ways may they be linked?

In order to describe fully the behaviour of the system, a higher level abstraction of the behaviour may well be needed.

There are various ways in which this can be approached; one is illustrated by the ATM change PIN example in Section 12.1.2, and the last example in Section 12.3.5 shows how two potential use-cases have been integrated with the introduction of branching logic. Another approach is to use a FSM to model the pre- and post-condition states of every use-case and hence define the way in which they are related.

Regnell *et al.* (1995) describe an (input/output) data flow based integration technique (the synthesised usage model) for developing a specification from use-cases.

12.3.10   Summary

Whilst they seem to owe much to earlier techniques of documenting inter-action between the system and its terminators, use-cases may be characterised as being more linear, less hierarchical and, perhaps, less comprehensive. Partly as a result of this, they provide a relatively easy and accessible way of describing the interaction between the solution system and its terminators (often human users). As well as contributing to specifications, they can assist in the elicitation of re-quirements (although there are some caveats regarding their usage in either role).

An advantage of use-cases is that, by their nature, they concentrate upon external interfaces and, hence, provide external, behavioural models. There is, as usual, some danger of introducing internal (hidden) functions, but since there is an emphasis upon inputs and outputs this is less so than with some techniques.

Considerable flexibility is allowed in their application and construction, and this may be seen to contribute to a lack of rigour. The application of suitable guidelines seeks to address this matter; see, for example, Cox *et al.* (2001).

Further details upon usage may be found in Cockburn (2001), Fowler and Scott (2000) and Schneiderman (1998).

Also of interest may be the notion of task scripts (Graham, 1996). These re-semble use-cases but, amongst other things, seek to address their potential pro-liferation by introducing a higher level generification.

12.4   Decision tables

Decision tables provide a mechanism for defining the relationships between conditions and resultant outcomes by way of rules.

12.4.1   Indications for use

Within requirements engineering, the scope of decision tables is limited, but they have an obvious use in specifying the relationships between the inputs to and the outputs from the solution system (i.e. the i/o relationships). There is a size constraint in that simple i/o relationships are easily handled in other ways, whereas very complex ones (more than, say, 64 rules) may be too cumbersome, even using linked tables.

From the requirements specification perspective, one of the most important advantages of decision tables is that they are inherently non-procedural. The relationships between the imposed conditions (inputs) and required outcomes (outputs) are specified without any hint as to how the system might eventually achieve this. It is a purely black-box definition that avoids introducing any design constraints.

A further advantage concerns the almost guaranteed completeness of the table. It is a simple, mechanical matter to fill in the conditions such that all possible combinations of input conditions are covered. Whilst optimisation does provide some opportunity for subsequent error, even then, the outcome compares very favourably with textual definitions of complex decisions.

I well recall the building of a configuration management tool that required complex decisions to be made regarding file access rights. (These depended upon the status of the file, who wanted access, the type of access required, any current access, and so on.) Errors had propagated through the entire development process and were only detected during final testing. Even the first attempts at correction failed, and it was not until a decision table was used to re-define the rules that the problem was solved.

It takes some expertise to create decision tables, but this is easily acquired. Non-specialists such as users rarely experience any difficulty in appreciating their meaning; this promotes the full understanding that is required in order to check the accuracy of a specification. Whilst tool support is, in principle, straightforward, there is, curiously, little on the market[99].

12.4.2   Description

Simple i/o relationships are readily defined using function statements (Section 12.1). For example, consider the control of a boiler that heats a hot water tank. The required operation may be described thus:

> If the system is switched on and the tank temperature is less than the thermostat setting, then the boiler should be on. Otherwise, the boiler should be off.

However, when multiple inputs (either simultaneous or, more often, in the form of an input-history) must be considered, such statements can become hard to understand (and hence, error prone).

Consider now, a slightly more complex, but very common, system for domestic heating. This is fully pumped and has a three-way valve controlling the

---

[99] JM Software supply a PC-based tool that includes C code-generation.

flow to the hot water tank, or to the radiators, or to both. There is a thermostat for the hot water tank and another for the room. The required operation could be described along these lines (and I have attempted to make this clear!):

> If hot water only is selected, then the three-way valve is set to the hot water position (A), the boiler and the pump are both switched on only when the tank temperature is below the tank thermostat setting.
>
> If heating only is selected, then the valve is set to the heating position (B), the pump runs continuously and the boiler is switched on only when the room temperature is below the room thermostat setting.
>
> If the hot water and heating are both selected, and both of the thermostat settings exceed their ambient temperatures, then the boiler will be on, the pump will be running and the valve will be in the central position (C). If neither thermostat setting exceeds its ambient temperature, the boiler is turned off but the pump remains on and the valve is set to position B. If only the hot water tank thermostat setting exceeds its ambient temperature then boiler and pump are both on and the valve is set to position A. If only the room thermostat setting exceeds its ambient temperature then boiler and pump are both on but the valve is set to position B.
>
> If neither heating nor hot water are selected then boiler and pump are turned off and the position of the three-way valve is irrelevant.

In cases like this a decision table (Table 12.1) can help to clarify the situation.

This example also illustrates the basic structure of a decision table. As can be seen, using double lines, the matrix is divided into four sections, named as in Table 12.2. The condition statements are simply a list of the *independent variables* (inputs) that are of interest; the condition entries show the possible

Table 12.1

	1	2	3	4	5	6	7	8	9	10	11	12	13	14	15	16
heating	on								off							
hot water	on				off				on				off			
tank thermostat	un		ov		un		ov		un		ov		un		ov	
room thermostat	un	ov	un	ov	un	ov	un	ov	un	ov	un	ov	un	ov	un	ov
boiler on		✓	✓	✓		✓		✓			✓	✓				
pump on	✓	✓	✓	✓	✓	✓	✓	✓			✓	✓				
three-way valve	B	B	A	C	B	B	B	B	A	A	A	A	–	–	–	–

ov(er) = thermostat setting over ambient temperature, un(der) = thermostat setting under ambient temperature,
A = hot water position, B = heating, C = both.

Table 12.2

condition statements (or condition stub)	condition entries
action statements (or action stub)	action entries

Table 12.3

Table title	Decision rules							
	1	2	3	4	5	6	7	8
Condition stub			Condition entries					
Action stub			Action entries					

values of those variables; the action statements describe the possible actions (outputs); and the action entries indicate when those actions will occur.

Each column[100] in the right-hand part of the table defines a combination of conditions and the associated action(s) and is known as a *rule*. These may be numbered for easy reference. It is also good practice to include the title of the table as shown in Table 12.3.

An alternative approach for the lower part of the table is to just describe the resultant action under each column (thus making the action stub redundant). This is appropriate where there is no (or slight) commonality between the actions. With the vertical rule table (as shown in Table 12.3), this usually requires actions to be written vertically in order to make them fit and so, for this variant, the horizontal version of the table may be preferred, as per Table 12.4 (note the blank action stub – shaded).

12.4.3 Types of decision table

Decision tables are often classified upon the basis of the independent variables. If all the independent variables are binary (i.e. can take only one of two values,

---

[100] It is quite possible (although less common) for the whole table to be rotated through 90°, in which case a rule will, of course, be represented by a row.

Table 12.4

example table			
	Condition 1	Condition 2	Condition 3	
1	true	yes	on	Action 1
2			off	Action 2
3		no	on	Action 3
4			off	Action 4
5	false	yes	on	Action 5
6			off	Action 6
7		no	on	Action 7
8			off	Action 8

such as true/false, yes/no – as in the example given above), the table is known as a limited entry table. When the variables may take more than two values, the table is known as extended entry. (Sometimes this name is reserved for tables where *all* the variables are multi-valued and then, where there is a mix of binary and multi-valued, the table is known (not surprisingly) as mixed entry.)

12.4.4 Number of rules

The maximum number of rules (i.e. columns in the right part) for a table is readily calculated by multiplying together the number of values that each variable (condition) can take. For example, a table with three binary conditions would have eight rules. This would, of course, be a limited entry table, and for such a table with n conditions the number of rules is always 2^n. A table with two tri-valued variables and one binary variable would have 18 rules ($3 \times 3 \times 2$).

It can be useful to calculate the number of rules in advance of drawing the table because, as you may have guessed, tables with many rules are not so easy to follow and so, to a large extent, the advantage of clarity is lost. (A maximum of 64 rules may be used as a rule of thumb, but linked tables may help address this problem – see later.)

12.4.5 'Optimisation'

It often happens that one or more rules actually have the same outcome. This occurs where, given certain values for some of the variables, the values of some other variable(s) are irrelevant. There are several examples of this in the heating system table (Section 12.4.2), as can be seen in, say, rules 9 and 10. In effect, there are redundant rules and the table can be simplified or *condensed* by

Table 12.5

central heating	1	2	3	4	5	6	7	8	9
heating	on						off		
hot water	on				off		on		off
tank thermostat	un		ov		–		un	ov	–
room thermostat	un	ov	un	ov	un	ov	–	–	–
boiler on		✓	✓	✓		✓		✓	
pump on	✓	✓	✓	✓	✓	✓		✓	
3-way valve	B	B	A	C	B	B	A	A	–

combining such rules and marking the 'doesn't matter' entries with a dash. Table 12.5 is a condensed version of the original example, Table 12.1.

As demonstrated above, looking for rules with the same outcome and combining them can usually achieve useful simplification. If necessary, the columns and rows must be shuffled around in order to facilitate this process, but do not lose sight of the aim which is to make the definition as foolproof as possible.

Such simplification is often referred to as *optimisation*, but this should not be taken too literally as, sometimes, the odd redundant rule may allow a more logical (and easy to follow) ordering of the rules. (In fact, the above table could be condensed further, as there are still rules with identical outcomes, and you are invited to try this and compare the results for intelligibility.)

12.4.6   The 'else' rule

The else rule may be regarded as a special case of optimisation and should be used where a variety of condition mixes all result in the same outcome. It is then easier to specify only the significant cases and to lump together all other cases in one 'if no other rules apply use this one' rule – the else rule. Table 12.6 shows this applied to the classification of triangles by the length of their sides A, B and C. (Un-simplified this would have 2^6 (64) rules.)

12.4.7   Linked tables

If it appears that a table will have too many rules to be manageable or intelligible, it does not necessarily mean that the technique must be abandoned. It may well be possible to partition the decision process such that the outcome of one or more rules in a top-level table is to refer to a further table.

In practice, the central heating example is probably too simple to justify this treatment but it can be used for illustrative purposes as shown in Tables 12.7 and 12.8 (and so on). In effect, a hierarchy of relatively simple tables has been created.

Table 12.6

triangle	1	2	3	4	5	else
A = B	Y	Y	N	N	N	
B = C	Y	N	Y	N	N	
A = C	–	–	–	Y	N	
A + B > C	–	Y	–	–	Y	
B + C > A	–	–	Y	–	–	
A + C > B	–	–	–	Y	Y	
Equilateral	✓					
Isosceles		✓	✓	✓		
Scalene					✓	
Not a triangle						✓

Table 12.7

central heating (primary table)	1	2	3	4
heating	on		off	
hot water	on	off	on	off
	see **both** on table	see **heating** on table	see **h/w** on table	pump and boiler off

Table 12.8

both on table (heat and h/w on)	1	2	3	4
tank thermostat	un		ov	
room thermostat	un	ov	un	ov
boiler on		✓	✓	✓
pump on	✓	✓	✓	✓
3-way valve	B	B	A	C

ov(er) = thermostat setting over ambient temperature,
un(der) = thermostat setting under ambient temperature,
A = hot water position, B = heating, C = both.

Further examples of the use of decision tables may be found in the lift control case study requirements document (Section 16.2.1.4) and in Gildersleeve (1970) and Johnston and Davis (1970).

12.5   State-based techniques

All these models are explicitly based upon the notion of state (see Section 5.3.3). In other words, the solution system 'remembers' what has happened in the past, at least in so far as is necessary to determine its future responses. The most commonly used state-based modelling technique (and, probably, the one with most variations) is the finite state machine.

12.6   Finite state machines

12.6.1   Indications for use

Finite state machines (FSMs) model the behaviour of a system in terms of the causal relationships between inputs and outputs and, hence, have a major role to play in behavioural specification. Whilst it is possible to execute FSM models, with the exception of concurrent FSMs (see later), they do not impose a modularisation upon the system and may be regarded as relatively implementation free. At the same time, they provide quite rigorous and, hence, unambiguous descriptions. Moderate expertise is required in the construction and interpretation of FSM models, but this is unlikely to prove problematical for most practitioners, clients or users.

The commonly used notations are directed graphs and tables. There is some good tool support available for the former.

12.6.2   Description

Finite state machines (also known as finite state automata) can usefully model systems that:

- can be viewed as having a number of distinguishable stable states;
- change from being in one state to another in response to external stimuli.

A very simple example is a table lamp. It can be in one of two states (on or off) and it moves from one to the other in response to being switched on or switched off. Using a common notation, this can be depicted as a directed graph (see Figure 12.5). A node represents each state and the change between

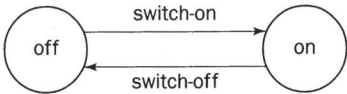

Figure 12.5

states (known as a transition) is shown as an arc (arrow). Not surprisingly, such a graph is known as a 'state transition' diagram (STD).

The external stimuli (commonly known as events or triggers) can also be shown, in this case, as labels adjacent to the relevant transition. Usually, each transition is not named but the associated trigger is. Since the same trigger may be valid for more than one state, there is the potential for some confusion, but note that *for any given state* there can be only one transition *from* it associated with any trigger.

Whilst the basic notation shown above is often adequate, it may well be useful to show *outputs* from the system, usually known as actions. Figure 12.6 models the operation of a simple (and rather unfriendly!) automatic teller (cash) machine (ATM) and includes examples of actions which are shown as rectangular boxes. (Note that PIN = 'Personal Identification Number'.) When reading Figure 12.6, bear in mind that a transition starts and ends at a state; in this case, there are eight transitions shown.

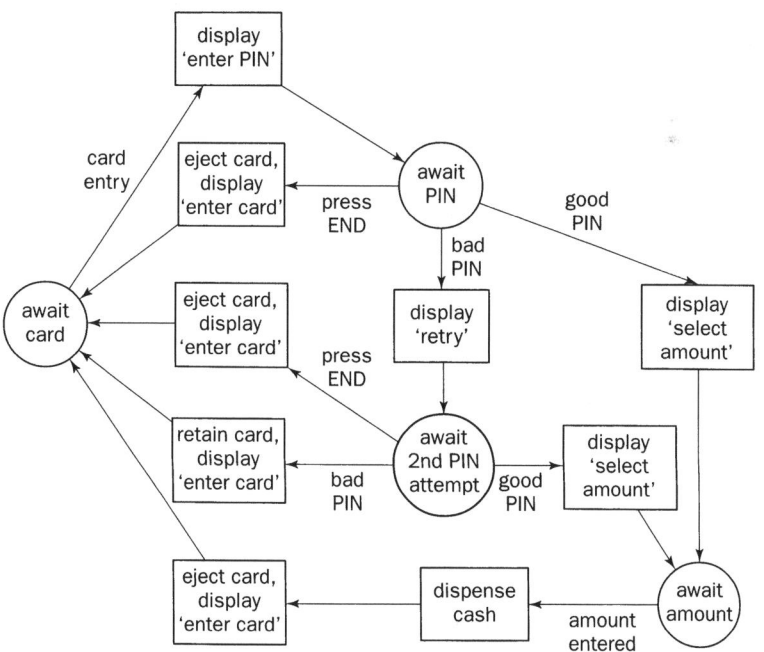

Figure 12.6

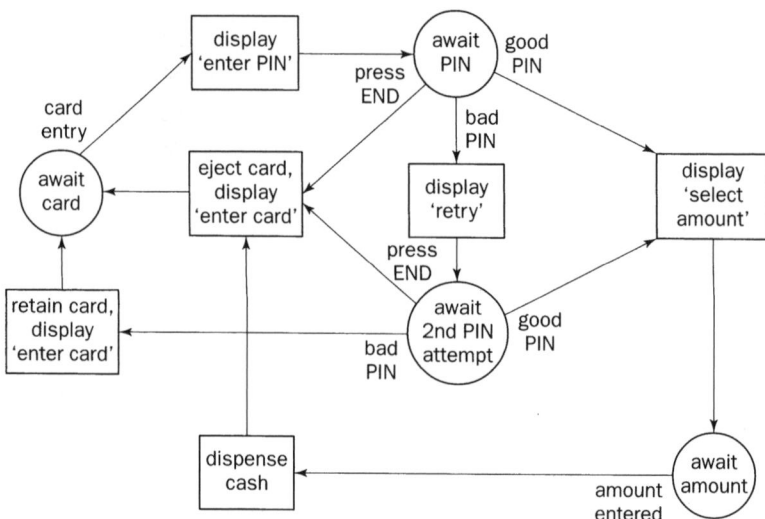

Figure 12.7

A somewhat 'condensed' version can be produced if transitions are allowed to 'merge'[101]. Note that the logic of this version (Figure 12.7) is identical to that of Figure 12.6 (and there are still eight transitions).

Having introduced the basic concept, it is now possible to give further consideration to the characteristics of FSMs.

12.6.3   Design rules for FSMs

- A transition always starts from and ends at a state.
- A transition always has *one* associated trigger.
- A transition *may* have one or more associated actions.
- The same trigger may be valid in more than one state (but will obviously be associated with a different transition in each state).

12.6.4   Design guidelines for FSMs

- If a state has no incoming transition it is unreachable. Therefore, it must be a *start* state and can only be entered once. (It makes sense to have only one start state.)
- If a state has no outgoing transition it is unleavable. Therefore it must be a *stop* state and it too can only be entered once. (Conceivably, there could be one or more stop states.)

---

[101] This is considered bad practice by some authorities, but it is hard to see why.

- Conceptually, systems may often be regarded as operating continuously (as in the examples above). In this case, start or stop states may not be shown.

- Transitions that return directly to the same state are allowed but, unless they have an associated action (like error trapping), they are useless.

12.6.5 Features of FSMs

- Finite state machines are, conceptually, 'flat'. In principle, a transition can go from any state to any other state. (This is fundamentally different from a hierarchy, where the permitted paths are constrained.)

- A state represents the state of the *whole system*. There is no structural sub-division of the system.

- The system can be in only one state at a time and will stay in that state indefinitely unless there is a trigger.

- Transitions cannot be 'partial'; no 'intermediate' situation is recognised. Once a transition has started, no outside event can prevent its completion. (Transitions can, therefore, usually be regarded as instantaneous.)

- Such systems (those which respond to external events) are often referred to as event driven systems and are by no means rare; most computer-based systems are readily viewed in this way[102].

12.6.6 Non-deterministic FSMs

The FSMs so far considered are known as deterministic. In any given state, the trigger alone determines which will be the next state reached. Sometimes, however, it is useful to be able to take account of other information and allow a transition to branch at a decision point. Such an FSM is known as non-deterministic. (Note the difference between a branching transition (where there is fan-out) and the *merging* of transitions (fan-in) described earlier (which is still deterministic).)

Incorporation of decisions requires an extension to the STD notation. Decision points are usually shown as diamonds and their use is illustrated in an amended (but still logically identical) version of the ATM, Figure 12.8. Note that decision boxes are never essential; the same logic can always be depicted with non-branching transitions (deterministic FSMs) but, as in the ATM example, more states are required. A judgement must be made as to which version gives the least cluttered and clearest diagram.

---

[102] However, where the concern is with systems that are 'vague' and do not have a limited number of readily identifiable states (e.g. people, the economy, the weather) this approach may not be very helpful. As with all modelling, the FSM technique is just a way of *viewing* systems; whether or not the system is 'really' an FSM scarcely arises. Provided that the model is useful (generally, in this context, if it closely mimics the apparent behaviour of a system) then fine.

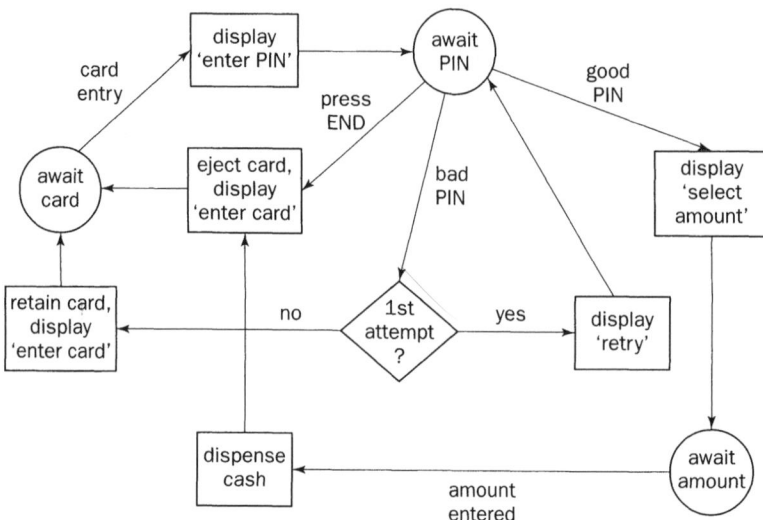

Figure 12.8

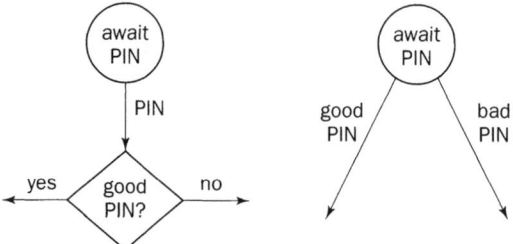

Figure 12.9

Note also that this mechanism is not intended for making decisions about triggers. Whilst the two fragments shown in Figure 12.9 are equivalent, the one on the left exhibits poor style (at best!).

If not triggers, then it follows that the FSM must have some other data upon which to base a decision. This is indeed the case; non-deterministic FSMs are characterised by the fact that they store data, known as state variables (in addition, that is, to the knowledge of which state they are in). In the non-deterministic version of the ATM (Figure 12.8), it is implicit that it is 'remembering' how many attempts have been made at entering the PIN. Indeed, we should make this explicit by showing the actions that set and reset the number of attempts, as in Figure 12.10.

If FSMs are new to you, and yet the STD notation (particularly with decision boxes) is starting to seem familiar, it may well be that they remind you of flow-charts. In fact, non-deterministic STDs *are* a type of flow-chart. Unfortunately, not all types have such a good rationale and, coupled with the effect of

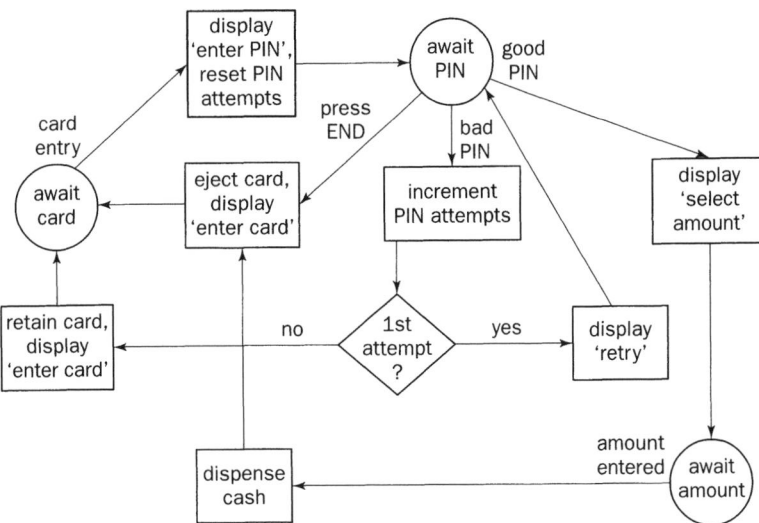

Figure 12.10

widespread misuse, flow-charts in general have fallen into disrepute. This should not, however, be seen as an indictment of the 'proper' flow-chart (the STD) which has a major role in requirements engineering.

12.6.7   Variations in notation

As is often the case, rival versions of the STD notation have been developed. They are, however, logically equivalent and Figure 12.11 illustrates a couple

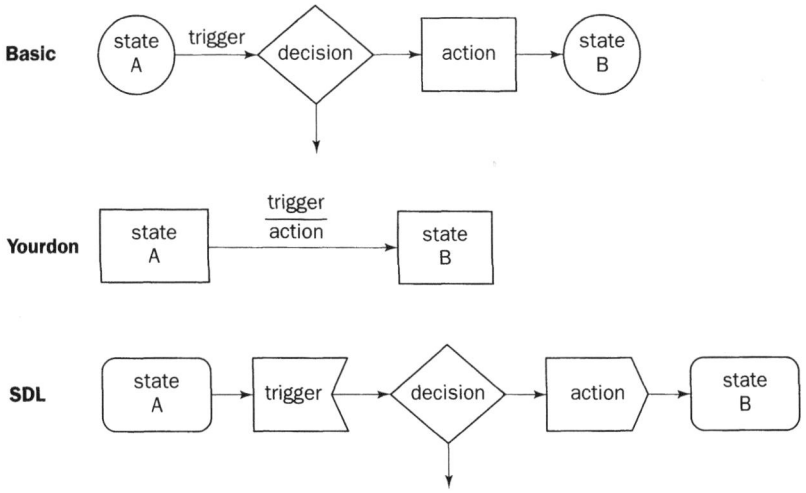

Figure 12.11

of the common alternatives. Note that the Yourdon version is deterministic (and, hence, does not support decisions) and the specification and description language (SDL) 'output' is simply an action that produces an output. SDL
also supports plain rectangles for actions that produce no output (i.e. those that
operate upon state variables). The Yourdon notation is set out in Yourdon
(1989a); SDL is described in Rockstrom and Saracco (1982). It has a published
international standard and has been widely used within the telecommunica-
tions industry.

12.6.8   Timers

Since they respond only to external stimuli, it is impossible for a 'pure' FSM to
behave spontaneously. Modelling a clock (or counter or timer) or even a simple
time delay is not possible. Because this is limiting, the notion of a timer has
been added. This is simply a special sort of action that will produce an output
after a determined time delay. This output can then be used as a trigger elsewhere in the FSM. Figure 12.12 illustrates a simple 'time-out' for entering the
PIN on the ATM. Note that the dashed arc does *not* represent a transition.
Rather, it represents the passage of the trigger signal; in fact, a data flow. Since
this is a regular cause of confusion it is recommended that the novice omit such
arcs entirely. The connection between the timer action and the timer trigger is
then established entirely by the identical name.

12.6.9   Concurrent FSMs

Since an FSM can only be in one state at a time and can only respond to one
trigger (input) at a time, difficulty can arise when attempting to model more
complex behaviour (e.g. systems that may have to handle simultaneous input).
In such cases, the system may be better modelled as two or more concurrent
FSMs.

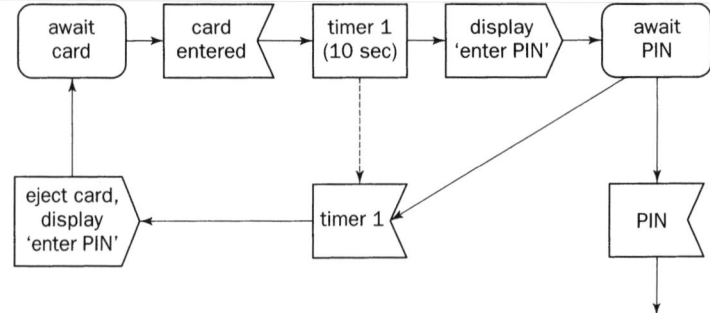

Figure 12.12

Unless they communicate with each other, concurrent finite state machines are, effectively, independent systems (and the notion of concurrency is redundant). The mechanism for inter-FSM communication has, in fact, already been introduced in the context of timers. It can be achieved by an action in one FSM generating an output signal that is seen as a trigger by another. Here is a brief description of the operation of a fairly sophisticated fire alarm:

> The alarm receives signals from two sources: an infra red (IR) heat detector and a smoke detector. The infra red heat detector signals are either negative or positive. Two consecutive positive signals trigger the alarm. Smoke detector signals are 'positive only' and if two signals are received within 10 seconds, the alarm will also be triggered. A reset signal resets the alarm.

As per Figure 12.13, this system could be modelled as three concurrent FSMs (incorporating a timer).

It is surprisingly tricky to model this behaviour accurately without using concurrent FSMs; you may care to try it. It must, however, be appreciated that the concurrent FSM model has introduced a structural decomposition of the system into sub-systems and, as previously discussed, this may be considered undesirable in a specification.

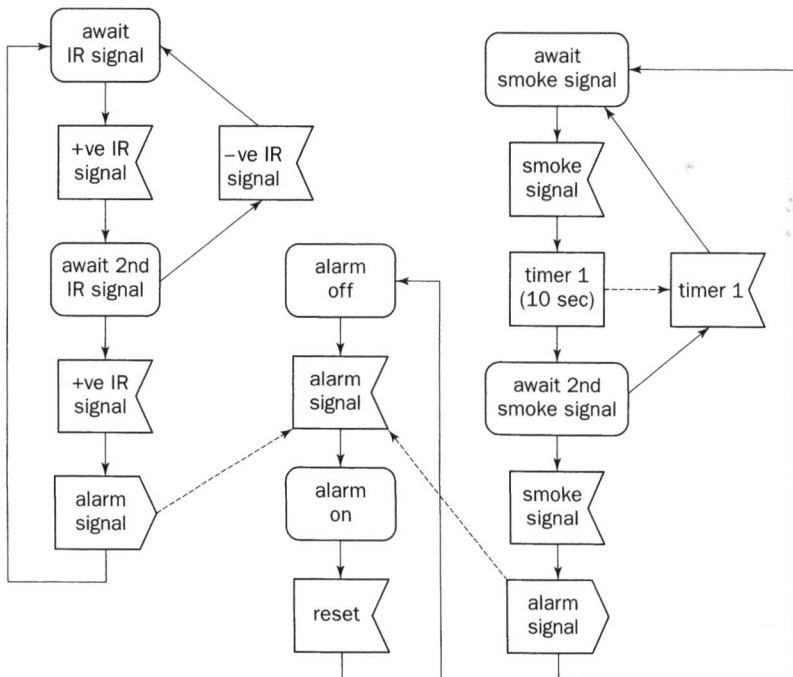

Figure 12.13

Table 12.9

	Press play	Press fast forward	Press rewind	Press record	Press stop	End of tape
1 Stopped						
2 Playing						
3 Recording						
4 Fast forwarding						
5 Rewinding						
6 Fast play (forward)						
7 Fast play (reverse)						

12.6.10   State transition matrices (STMs)

The STD is not the only available FSM notation and a common alternative is to use a table. Such a table is known as a state transition table or state transition matrix (STM) (or, sometimes, just state matrix (SM)).

The basic notion is very straightforward; a matrix of states vs triggers is plotted. Table 12.9 shows an STM for a simple video cassette recorder (VCR). As can be seen, the states are listed down the left-hand side of the table and the triggers are listed across the top. (There is no convention for this and it can be done either way around.)

The next step is to fill in the body of the matrix and this is where the transitions are recorded. For each cell, the next state (resulting from that combination of current state and trigger) is entered. This effectively defines the transition. Where there is no transition (i.e. in the current state that particular trigger has no effect) the cell is left blank. The completed matrix for the VCR is shown in Table 12.10.

You may have noticed that as yet, the SM has included no information about actions. Sometimes, this is not a problem as actions may be regarded as implicit but, where necessary, actions can be shown. Two variations on the state matrix can be distinguished, dependent upon whether actions are associated with a transition (the Mealy model) or with entering a state (the Moore model)[103].

---

[103] In case it is ever important to recall which is which, just remember that 'Moore is less' (the Moore model has fewer actions).

Table 12.10

	Press play	Press fast forward	Press rewind	Press record	Press stop	End of tape
1 Stopped	2	4	5	3		
2 Playing		6	7		1	1
3 Recording					1	1
4 Fast forwarding	2		5		1	1
5 Rewinding	2	4			1	1
6 Fast play (forward)	2		7		1	1
7 Fast play (reverse)	2	6			1	1

The latter might sound a bit unlikely, but it is often the case that, no matter how a particular state is reached, it is necessary to perform the same action prior to entering it. In this case, the action performed upon *entering* the state is shown by adding a single 'action' column to the state matrix. If the message display only is considered, the simple ATM can be depicted as a Moore model, see Table 12.11.

For this particular system, however, this model does not handle all the actions. Ejecting or retaining the card and dispensing cash cannot be shown

Table 12.11

	Card entry	Good PIN	Bad PIN	Press END	Amount entered	ACTION
1 Await card	2					Display 'Enter card'
2 Await PIN		4	3	1		Display 'Enter PIN'
3 Await 2nd PIN attempt		4	1	1		Display 'Re-try'
4 Await amount				1	1	Display 'Select amount'

Table 12.12

	Card entry	Good PIN	Bad PIN	Press END	Amount entered
1 Await card	2 Display 'Enter PIN'				
2 Await PIN		4 Display 'Select amount'	3 Display 'Re-try'	1 Eject card, Display 'Enter card'	
3 Await 2nd PIN attempt		4 Display 'Select amount'	1 Retain card, Display 'Enter card'	1 Eject card, Display 'Enter card'	
4 Await amount				1 Eject card, Display 'Enter card'	1 Dispense cash, Eject card, Display 'Enter card'

because these do depend upon the *source* of the transition (as well as its destination). We therefore need a Mealy model and, for this, it is necessary to show the actions within the body of the matrix. One way is to show the next state *and* the action in each cell. Alternatively, the whole matrix can be duplicated; one copy showing the next states and the other the actions. The first version might appear as in Table 12.12. State matrices have the advantage over STDs where there is a tendency for each trigger to be valid in a number of states (as, for example, in Table 12.12). Where the opposite applies (each trigger is valid only in one state) the state matrix will have many empty cells. Such sparse matrices waste space, tend to be large and, consequently, can be hard to follow.

12.6.11 State charts (aka state diagrams)

Despite their good points, the FSMs considered so far (sometimes referred to as 'pure' FSMs) have limitations, notably their inherent 'flatness'. Any pair of states may be linked by a transition and so, of itself, the technique imposes no large scale structure; a problem which may become serious with large FSMs[104].

To tackle this, and other shortcomings, David Harel (1987) developed various extensions to the model together with an enhanced notation which he called

---

[104] Although I well recall drawing very large STDs on A0 paper and still finding them readable and useful models.

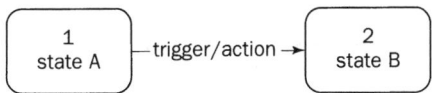

Figure 12.14

state charts (SCs). The basic notation owes much to STDs and is illustrated in Figure 12.14.

States are shown as SDL style boxes and, as well as having the usual name label, they can be numbered to aid easy reference. Trigger names are placed on the transition arcs and, optionally, may have an associated action separated by a '/' (in much the same style as Yourdon, see Figure 12.11). However, to avoid clutter, actions are often listed separately in a table.

12.6.11.1 Conditions
The first new feature to consider is the condition. Conditions are the given, neater, alternative to decision diamonds and, where needed, are shown in brackets[105] after the trigger name as shown in Figure 12.15.

12.6.11.2 State hierarchy
However, the most obvious elaboration provided by SCs is the introduction of the super-state. The super-state 'contains' other states and provides a dimension of hierarchy to help address complexity.

The depiction of super-states is simple enough and is shown in Figure 12.16.

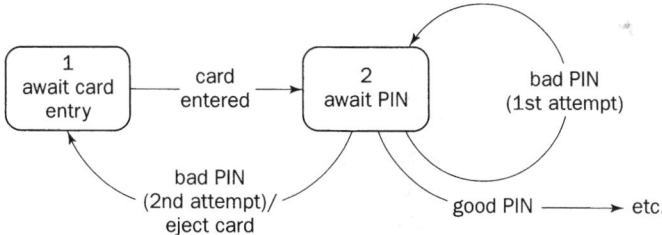

Figure 12.15

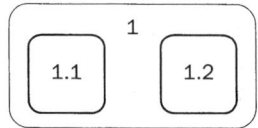

Figure 12.16

---

[105] Some sources use round brackets '( )'; some use square brackets '[ ]'.

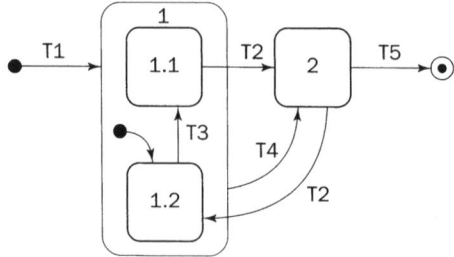

Figure 12.17

There is, however, a need for some additional conventions to handle the resultant transitions. Just before looking at these, this is a convenient point at which to introduce the notation for start and stop states:

Figure 12.17 illustrates the essential mechanisms for depicting the transitions to and from sub-states.

This should be interpreted thus:

- the start trigger (T1) causes entry to state 1 and sub-state 1.2;
- when in state 1 (either sub-state 1.1 or 1.2), T4 causes entry to state 2;
- when in state 1.1, T2 causes entry to state 2;
- when in state 1.2, T3 causes entry to state 1.1;
- when in state 2, T2 causes entry to state 1.2;
- when in state 2, T5 causes entry to the stop state.

(Note, by the way, that the system cannot simply be in state 1, it must also be in one of the sub-states.)

12.6.11.3 History

A useful addition to the above is the history mechanism. When returning to a super-state, it is quite common to want to return to the sub-state that was last held (when in that super-state). The notation for expressing this is illustrated in Figure 12.18. This should be interpreted as: when re-entering state 1, go to the

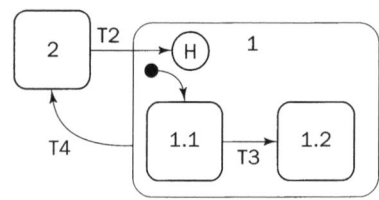

Figure 12.18

sub-state that was most recently held. (The start symbol indicates which sub-state pertains when entering state 1 for the first time.)

12.6.11.4 Developing state hierarchy

The concept of and the notation for representing super- and sub-states (and the associated transitions) are all very well, but there remains the matter of how these may be applied. The state hierarchy may be developed in two ways. Given a 'flat' STD, it is often possible to recognise groups of states which share common responses to certain events. It is then possible to cluster those states within a super-state and, hence, reduce the number of transitions. For example, the two charts in Figure 12.19 are logically equivalent.

Such clustering of states is an artifice. The super-state does not correspond to any structure in the modelled system and so there may be no meaningful name that can be attached to it. All that is gained is some clarity in the diagram; not a lot in the example below, but consider the example shown in Figure 12.20 (from the YRR case study) which, even with the omission of the trigger labels, may be regarded as rather heavy going.

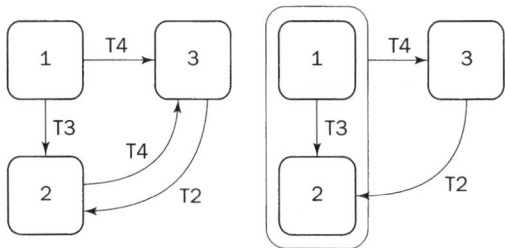

Figure 12.19

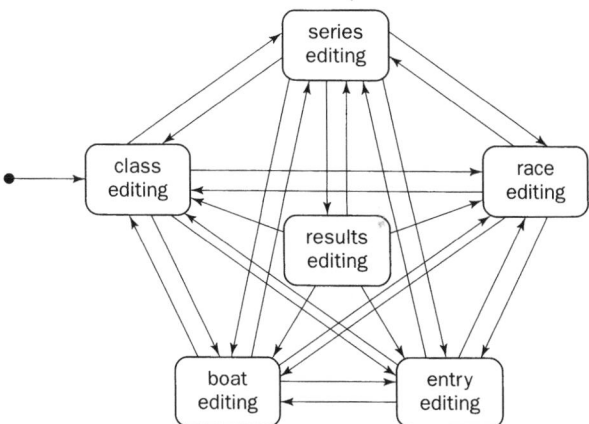

Figure 12.20

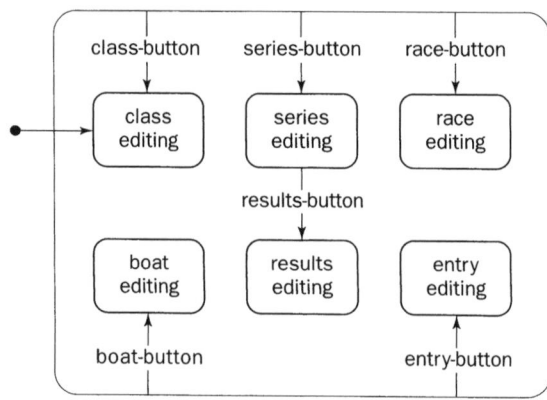

Figure 12.21

The equivalent clustered version (Figure 12.21) introduces one super-state but eliminates most of the transitions.

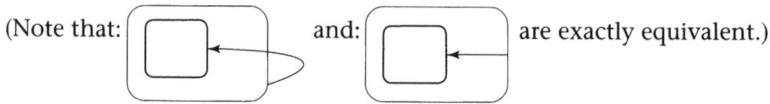

(Note that: ▢ and: ▢ are exactly equivalent.)

The other, possibly more significant, application of state hierarchy is to reflect the inherent structure of the system; in other words, where the super-state corresponds to some part of the system logicality (i.e. an area of functionality). To pursue the above example, each of the states shown corresponds to an editing screen (class editing, boat editing, etc.), and within each there are various sub-states (await boat name entry, await sail number entry, etc.) which are logically associated. It, therefore, makes sense to group these and, in such cases, it is possible, and appropriate, to assign a meaningful name, such as 'class editing', to the super-state.

It is also possible (and often appropriate) to employ this mechanism in a top-down manner. The high-level areas of functionality (the super-states) can be identified first; the detailed operation of each can then be devised, at least to some extent, independently. Section 5.7.4 provides a fairly extensive example of this approach. (And this approach may be viewed as an incarnation of the principle of functional decomposition (see Section 12.1.1).)

Apart from state hierarchy, state charts provide or accommodate various other useful features.

12.6.11.5   Internal triggers and transient states

Triggers are generally regarded as originating from outside the FSM; they are events in the operating environment to which the machine may respond. We have, however, already encountered a couple of exceptions; the triggers generated by timers and by concurrent FSMs. State charts generalise this notion to allow the generation of triggers by what might be termed internal processes.

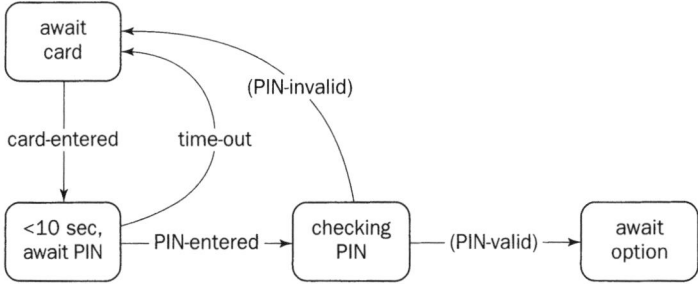

Figure 12.22

There is but a fine line between internally generated triggers and conditions. Perhaps in reflection of this, internally generated triggers (but, curiously, not time-out signals) are, like conditions, shown in brackets. The example state chart fragment in Figure 12.22 (for the simple ATM) includes a timer and a self-terminating, 'transient' state. As may be seen, transient states (such as 'checking-PIN') are often tantamount to processes, and there is some danger of straying into internal design and introducing unnecessary design constraints. Be warned.

12.6.11.6 Concurrency

State charts support the notion of concurrent FSMs, placing the concurrent machines within a super-state but separated by dashed lines. Interaction between the concurrent machines is confined to the passing of triggers (as shown below) and the possibility of one machine testing conditions (state variables) that are set in another. The fire alarm example given in Section 12.6.9 could be depicted as in Figure 12.23.

More extensive examples of SCs are given in the case studies (notably in Section 18.2) and much more information regarding their principles and application may be found in Ian Horrocks's excellent book (Horrocks, 1999).

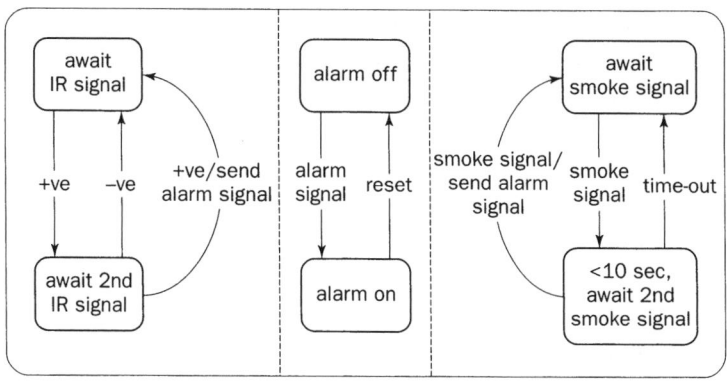

Figure 12.23

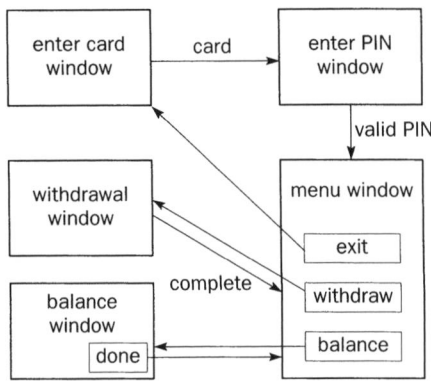

Figure 12.24

12.6.12 Windows navigation diagrams

These diagrams are described in Page-Jones (1999) and may be regarded as a special case of the SC where each state corresponds to a window of a GUI. Also shown are buttons that can be used to move to another window. Figure 12.24 shows an example based upon a simple ATM.

12.6.13 R-nets

Sometimes it is of interest to examine how a system will respond to a particular input in each of its states. This is pertinent to testing and safety considerations. For example, consider a power plant control system; a good question might be, 'Are there any circumstances under which pushing this button would be dangerous?'

This means considering the effect of a particular input in all states of the system. Provided the states have been listed down the y-axis, this corresponds to a *column* of an SM (see Section 12.6.10). A graphical notation to represent this model has been developed by Alford and Burns (1976).

12.6.14 Finally

Do not forget that (within specifications) FSMs describe only the way in which systems *appear* to behave. Davis recommends the following 'health warning':

> Dear designer: I don't care how you design the system but, when it is all done and I observe it as a black box, I want it to behave externally as if it were designed as the finite state machine shown.
> Signed, the Requirements Writer.

> (Davis, 1993, p. 221)

Notwithstanding the above, it can be seen as a definite bonus if a behavioural model is easy to implement (if only for the purposes of simulation). This is certainly the case with FSMs; and options include nested case (switch) statements (switch on state and then on trigger) and the definition of SMs as constant, two-dimensional arrays.

12.7 Petri nets

Like FSMs, Petri nets are a type of abstract virtual machine that is useful for modelling system behaviour in specifications[106].

12.7.1 Indications for use

Whilst receiving considerable attention from the theorists, Petri nets have, to date, seen little use within requirements engineering. Although they do not have *very* wide applicability, this is puzzling given the scarcity of alternatives and the neatness with which some systems can be modelled.

The usage considerations are similar to those for FSMs and Bastide and Palanque (1995), for example, advocate their use for the general specification of event driven systems, including the human interfaces. However, they are of particular benefit where there is some form of concurrency or parallelism and where process or event synchronisation is critical. Other significant differences are rather lower accessibility and relatively poor provision of tool support.

12.7.2 Description

Various versions and extensions to Petri nets have been proposed[107] but, for the purpose in hand, a straightforward treatment is entirely adequate. I will, therefore, consider only synchronous, multi-token nets.

The graph-based notation is simple, consisting of just four elements:

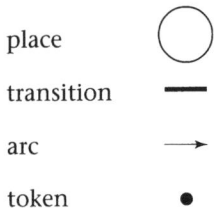

place

transition

arc

token

The first three are used to construct nets as in the example shown in Figure 12.25 (which has been contrived to illustrate various points).

As with STDs, there are certain design rules:

- an arc always connects a place to a transition (in either direction); never a place directly to another place nor a transition directly to another transition;

- each place and each transition should have at least one incoming and at least one outgoing arc;

- there is no upper limit to the number of arcs that can connect to a place or a transition.

The actual layout of the diagram is arbitrary and clarity is the watchword.

---

[106] In fact, FSMs are a special case of Petri nets.
[107] Murata (1989) provides an good overview.

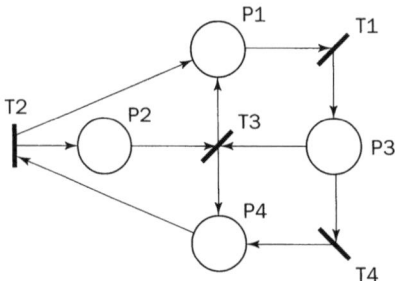

Figure 12.25

Tokens are then used to indicate which places are active and (in the version described here) it is quite possible for an active place to contain more than one token.

inactive place: ⭕   active places: ⭕ ⭕

The location of tokens within a net constitutes its *marking*. I will also adopt the convention of referring to places as 'incoming' or 'outgoing', with reference to a particular transition, depending upon the direction of the connecting arcs thus:

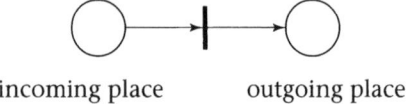

incoming place   outgoing place

The rules governing the operation of the net can now be stated:

- If all its incoming places are active, a transition will 'fire'.
- When a transition fires:

  all its incoming places lose a token; and

  all its outgoing places gain a token.

As mentioned earlier, the assumption will be made that the net is synchronous; i.e. every transition will fire (if, by the first rule, it can) at the same time and in a regular manner. It may help to imagine a 'firing cycle' or clock pulse.

In practice, when executing a net, it is necessary to examine every transition and decide which can fire *before* performing the firing operation upon any of them. This is because the firing of one should not affect another *in the same cycle*.

The execution of the example net will now be examined where initially (Figure 12.26) there is a token in place P4 (which constitutes the initial marking). On the first cycle, only T2 can fire and, as it does, it consumes the token on P4 and produces tokens on both its outgoing places, P1 and P2, resulting in

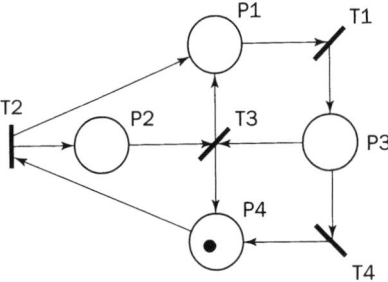

Figure 12.26

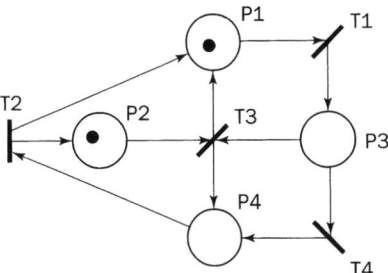

Figure 12.27

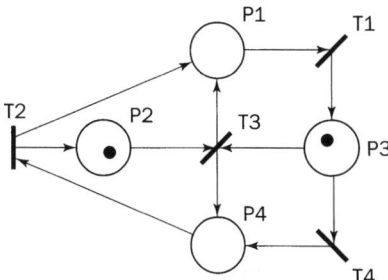

Figure 12.28

Figure 12.27. On the next cycle (Figure 12.28) T1 can fire (but not T3 because P3 is inactive). And on the next cycle (Figure 12.29) T3 and T4 can fire.

Note that (whilst not all authorities would agree on this convention) the single token on P3 has been taken as capable of triggering T4 *and* (in conjunction with P2) T3. Also, P4 gains 2 tokens; one from T3 and one from T4.

So far, Petri nets have provided no more than a little intellectual exercise. Let us now look at their application within requirements engineering. Perhaps the biggest stumbling block for the newcomer is 'what do places and tokens represent?'. The answer 'whatever you like' may not immediately appear very helpful but is not far removed from the truth. Some examples should elucidate.

Figure 12.30 shows a Petri net model of the operation of a simple photocopier. This incorporates one new feature; sources and sinks for tokens. These

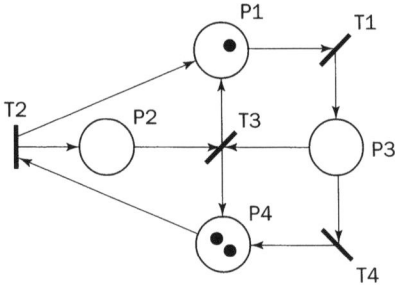

Figure 12.29

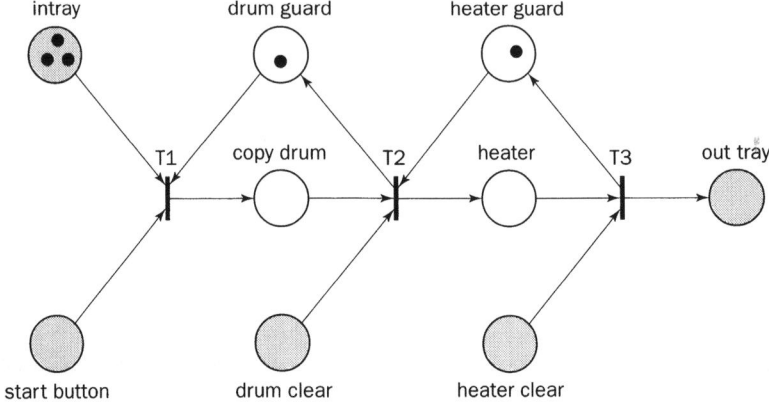

Figure 12.30

are highly pertinent for specification purposes, as they can represent connections between the system being modelled and the outside world (in other words, input and output). They are usually represented in the diagram as shaded places. Their use should become apparent as the operation is described, but note: sources will have no incoming arcs; and output places have no outgoing arcs, but do not accumulate tokens, they simply absorb them.

As indicated in Figure 12.30, some places represent parts of the photocopier (intray, copy drum, etc.). Others represent the sources of signals, for example 'drum clear' which is a signal indicating that a sheet of paper has cleared the copy drum. The guard places are rather different in that they do not correspond to anything physical, but provide a logical mechanism for guarding against two sheets of paper entering the same section of the machine simultaneously (and hence jamming it!).

Tokens are also used for more than one purpose. Some represent sheets of paper passing through the copier whilst others represent signals (e.g. start button pressed) or, in the guard places, logical conditions.

As can be seen, the photocopier can only start to operate (T1 can fire) if there is paper in the intray, the start button is pressed and the drum guard has a token

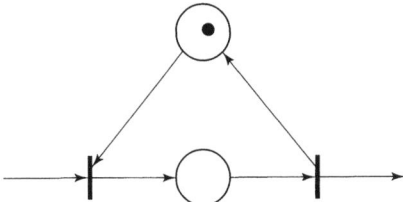

Figure 12.31

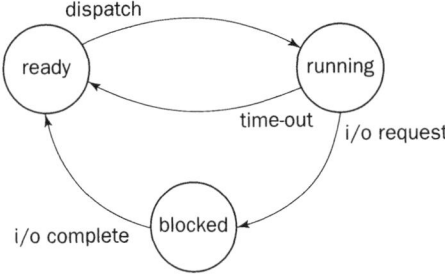

Figure 12.32

(which, as will become apparent, corresponds to the copy drum being vacant). Under these circumstances, a token (representing a sheet of paper) appears in the copy drum, the intray loses a sheet, the start button press is 'used-up' and the copy drum guard place becomes vacant. This last occurrence prevents another token (sheet of paper!) entering the copy drum until such time as it is empty and the drum guard has been replaced (i.e. T2 has fired). You may like to follow through a few cycles of this machine to see how it progresses.

The guard place mechanism is commonly required in order to prevent more than one token entering a particular place. The 'guard place triangle' (Figure 12.31) is worth remembering. Note that, as in Figure 12.31, the guard place needs a 'seed' token (which forms part of the initial marking of the net).

The next example illustrates an instance where a Petri net displays advantages over other techniques (in this case, the FSM). The STD (Figure 12.32) shows the widely used model of the progress of a job through the job scheduler of a computer operating system.

This is fine as far as it goes but it models the state of only *one* job. A more realistic problem is modelling the possible state of all jobs in the system (and the interaction between them). Before examining the Petri net version in Figure 12.33, you may like to have a go at devising one of your own. (Hint, since only one job at a time can be running, a guard place is required.)

The model could be easily extended with the addition of a source of new jobs (which would feed into the 'ready' place) and a sink for completed jobs but, as it stands, it is equivalent to the original, STD version.

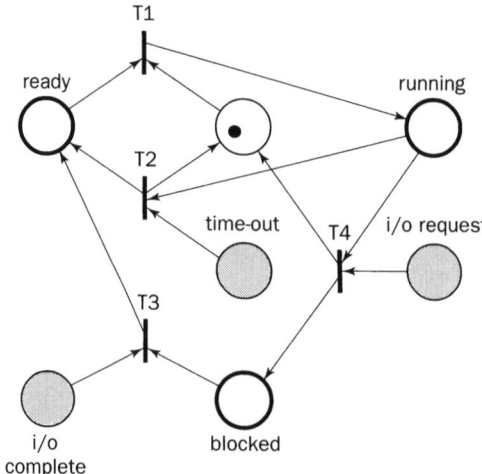

Figure 12.33

The places corresponding to the original three states of jobs are shown in bold, but note that it is now possible for several jobs (indicated by tokens) to be ready or blocked. The guard place (with its seed token) ensures, however, that only one job can be running. There are two possible exits for a running job (time-out or i/o request) and both of these transitions (T2 and T4) replace the token in the guard place. We can dispense with 'dispatch' since the logic will automatically move a job (token) from ready to running whenever possible.

A few further elaborations of the Petri net notation are worth mentioning. As with FSMs, it is often useful to be able to model the action of timers. With synchronous Petri nets, this is trivial since a string of transitions and places will delay a token by as many cycles as required (see Figure 12.34).

This can, however, be cumbersome if many cycles are required and the following shorthand (Figure 12.35) is therefore suggested as equivalent.

It is then sometimes useful to be able to check whether there is a token anywhere within a timer and the following equivalents (Figure 12.36) are also suggested.

A second elaboration is the notion of *weighted* arcs. These simply indicate that for a transition to be enabled, there must be more than one token in the

Figure 12.34

Figure 12.35

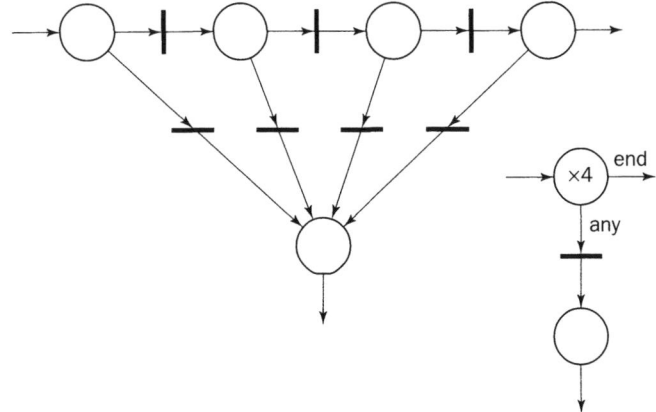

Figure 12.36

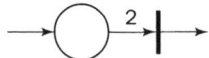

Figure 12.37

designated input place (and more than one will be consumed when the transition fires). The specific number is usually indicated by a number on the arc, as shown in Figure 12.37.

One further extension that is sometimes useful is the *inhibitor* arc. Again, the idea is simple; the presence of a token inhibits transition firing whereas the absence of a token enables firing (and, of course, no token is consumed upon firing). Inhibitor arcs are usually shown as dashed lines with a circle rather than an arrow head (Figure 12.38).

In passing, the difference between the nets in Figure 12.39 might be noted. That on the left operates only if both incoming places are active whereas that

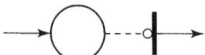

Figure 12.38

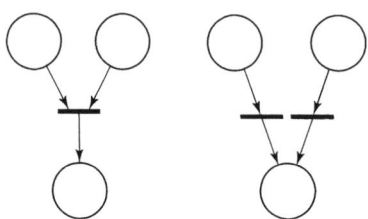

Figure 12.39

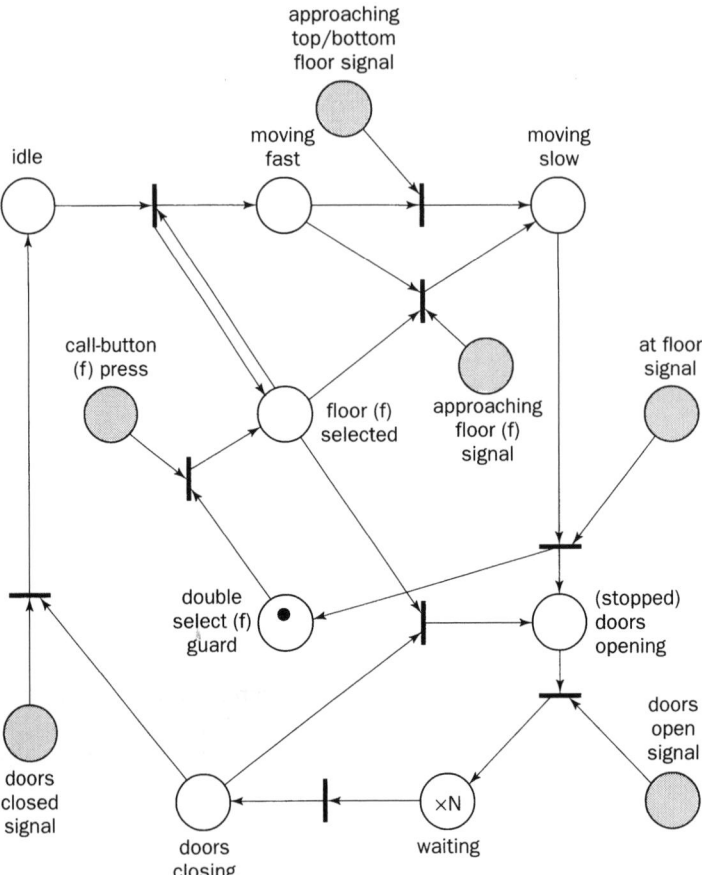

Figure 12.40

on the right operates if either incoming place is active. You may like to think of these as 'and' and 'or' logic gates. (The guard place mechanism provides a kind of 'not' gate if you want to pursue this idea.)

As a final example of Petri nets, Figure 12.40 models part of the behaviour of a lift similar to that described in the case study (see Chapter 16). There are a couple of points to note:

- It is quite possible for a transition to remove a token and replace one *in the same place*. This is useful for 'referencing' a token without consuming it. Check that you can see where and why this is done.

- Only one 'floor selected' place is shown and this is taken to represent all the floors. (Showing all floors separately would be possible but confusing.)

Internal modelling   **13**

13.1 Process oriented techniques

These abstractions model the system in question as a set of communicating sub-systems with the emphasis upon the processing that they perform.

13.1.1 Communicating concurrent processes

In this version, the sub-systems (processes) are viewed as running in parallel (concurrently). This type of model appears to be quite intuitive and has been evident in the world of hardware engineering from its earliest days. For example, a radio might be modelled as a 'block' diagram, Figure 13.1, where the blocks (nodes) represent the sub-systems and the arrows (directed arcs) represent the communication between them.

13.1.1.1 Data flow diagrams
Since its adoption by the computing community, the graphical notation for this kind of model has been standardised somewhat and, since software systems communicate *only* by passing data, the graphs have become known as DFDs. As a result, the technique is often known as 'data flow diagramming' but, strictly speaking, the technique is data flow analysis and DFDs are merely the most commonly used notation.

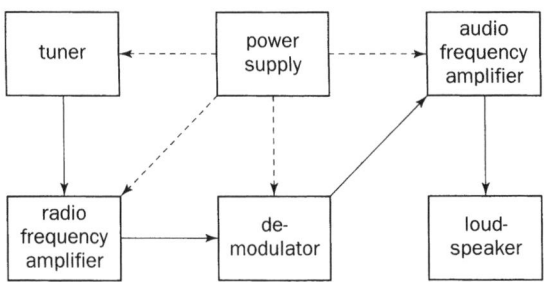

Figure 13.1

13.1.1.2   Indications for use

Over the past 25 years, data flow analysis has probably been the most widely used modelling technique in software development. It can be used for:

- analysis of the problem domain or a pre-existing system;
- specification of the solution system (but if structural specification (see Section 5.3.4) is to be avoided, only processes corresponding to external functions may be included);
- internal design of the solution system.

Unfortunately, the caveat for the second usage is often ignored and this can contribute to the undesirable practice of proceeding directly from the first to the third (see Section 4.3).

It may also be argued that an over-emphasis on data flow analysis has led to an under-emphasis on other useful modelling techniques, particularly in the area of specification. Since it develops a model which is essentially internal and it does not model causal relationships (behaviour) well, data flow analysis is not a strong specification technique. Since this book does not cover the idesign phase, it is, therefore, the role of data flow analysis within analysis that will be the focus.

Largely because of the reliance upon good labelling, the development of DFDs requires significant expertise, and the temptation to model inappropriate aspects can easily lead to ambiguity and errors. However, the subsequent interpretation of (good) DFDs is widely intuitive and so, overall, the technique scores moderately well for accessibility. Good tool support is widely available which is just as well since, otherwise, modification of diagrams can be very tedious.

13.1.1.3   Technique description

The two essential elements are:

- processes (aka transformations (since they transform data) or functions (since they correspond to something that the system does));
- the data flows between the processes.

These are commonly depicted using a directed graph (Figure 13.2) where the nodes (bubbles) represent the processes and arcs (arrows) represent the flow of data between them.

Of themselves, the symbols mean little and the importance of the labelling cannot be over-emphasised. The names of processes are normally chosen to

Figure 13.2

give a succinct indication of what they *do*. They are usually, therefore, in the form of a function statement (see Section 12.1) and centre upon a transitive verb and its object. Good examples of process labels might be:

- validate user request;
- calculate contribution;
- sort transactions;
- obtain pressure reading;
- display average speed.

The main exception is where the label is the name of the sub-system itself. In particular, this may be appropriate at the higher levels where the role of the system or person or the name of the department that performs the process can appear. For example:

- inertial guidance sub-system;
- pay-roll section;
- sales office;
- weigh-bridge sub-system.

Such names are really a convenient shorthand for 'perform all the functions of the inertial guidance sub-system', 'do everything that the pay-roll section does', etc.

Note that names should be as precise as possible. The catch-all name, 'process data' adds nothing; the one thing the reader already knows is that the bubble represents a process that processes data!

The names of data flows should reflect the fact that they are pieces of information and, hence, should centre upon a noun. Good examples are:

- user request;
- validated user request;
- contribution;
- unsorted transactions;
- pressure reading.

As with process names, they should convey a reasonable amount of information, but there is a trade-off against obscuring the diagram with too much text. As a minimum, every data flow should be uniquely identified and a DD entry (see Section 14.5) should be used to flesh out the definition.

Naming errors are often symptomatic of deep-seated logical errors. Examples of common errors include:

- data flows that are really conditions, e.g. 'if pressure valid';
- data flows that are really processes, e.g. 'output results';
- processes that are really states, e.g. 'system initialised';
- processes that are really data, e.g. 'sorted results'.

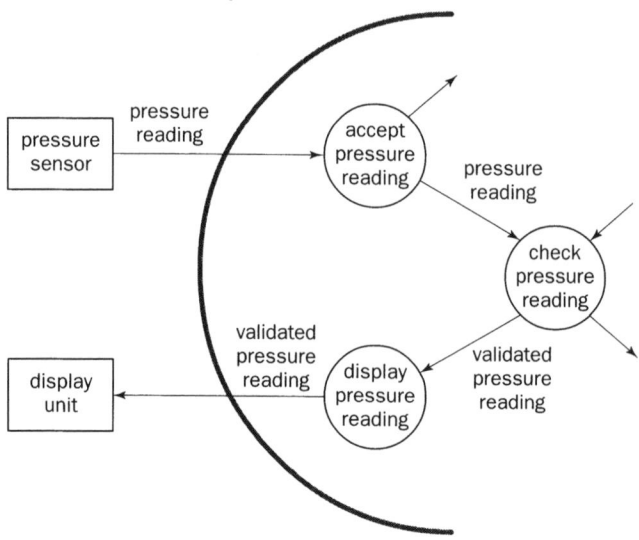

Figure 13.3

External systems (which can include users) may also be shown and are known as terminators. These can be divided into:

- sources (which supply data);
- sinks (which consume data).

(Although quite often, of course, a terminator can do both.)

A graphical distinction is drawn between sub-systems (processes) that are internal to the system in question and those systems (terminators) that are external. This is illustrated in Figure 13.3. The position of the system boundary is not usually shown explicitly but here the thick, grey line indicates where it must lie.

A further node symbol (a pair of horizontal parallel lines) is used to represent data stores. These are distinct from processes in that they are passive repositories of data (usually corresponding to a file or database) and perform no data transformation. (Note that only data stores *within* the system are shown – external data stores are assumed to reside within terminators and are never accessed directly.)

Bringing all these elements together, a fragment of a DFD for a customer support system might appear as in Figure 13.4.

There are some variations in notation. Unfortunately, the two commonest use almost opposite symbols for internal and external sub-systems/processes, but the equivalents are shown in Figure 13.5. As can be seen, the SSADM version of the process box is divided into three sections. The large bottom section contains the descriptive name of the process; the top left section is used for a reference number and the top right to indicate the agent, i.e. the person,

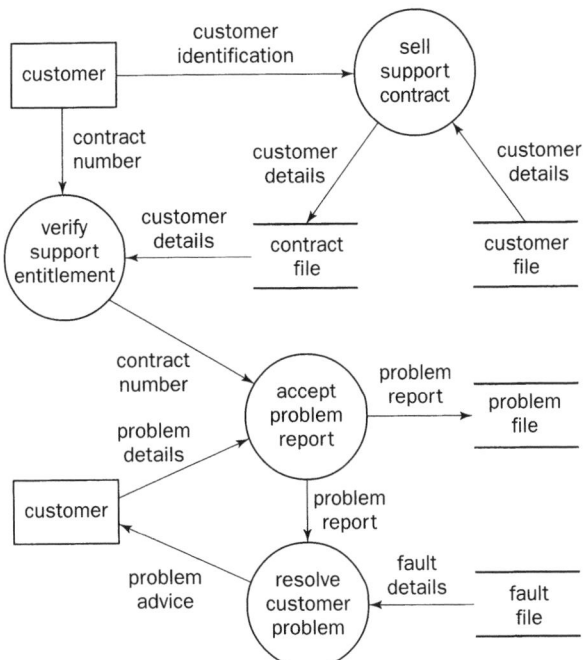

Figure 13.4

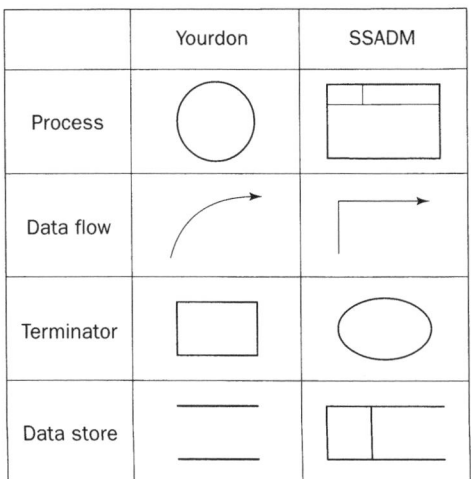

Figure 13.5

department or machine that performs the process. The last is only shown when it is of interest and would be omitted when the purely logical operation of the system in under consideration. The small box on the left of the SSADM type data store is also used for a reference number.

13.1.1.4 Validation

Certain rules can be applied to check the validity of DFDs:

- Data cannot flow directly between data stores (stores are passive).
- By convention, data flows between terminators are not shown (since they do not directly affect the system).
- Processes and data stores usually have at least one input *and* at least one output. (This is not mandatory but exceptions are rare and should always be treated with suspicion.)

However, most problems with DFDs stem from more fundamental problems, in particular:

- 'processes' that are not processes;
- 'data flows' that are not data flows.

Good naming (see above) is the key to avoiding these problems and, if a good name cannot be devised, it may well mean that an attempt is being made to incorporate some aspect that DFDs cannot readily model.

13.1.1.5 Limitations

Whilst the data stores that appear within DFDs imply some sub-division of the data storage, this, is at, best only high-level and may well be spurious, often owing more to some pre-existing system than to the logical way of storing the data. Alternative, complementary techniques are available for the analysis and design of data structures (see Section 13.3).

Data flow diagrams do place some constraints upon the ordering of process execution (a process cannot proceed until all its input data are available) but do not completely define:

- when processes execute;
- whether processes execute.

Given the high profile of the technique, such issues have attracted much attention and have led to many 'refinements' and extensions. Some of these have fallen prey to the temptation to try and model too much at once (which completely defeats the point of abstraction). Most of the remainder are of more relevance to idesign (e.g. the introduction of a control process introduces a design constraint and, for specification purposes, the same information can be modelled in a more external way using behavioural models – see Chapter 12) and so will not be considered further here. There are also certain heuristics for achieving good modularisation. However, again, this relates to the use of the technique for idesign and so will not be considered further here.

13.1.1.6 Levelling

One refinement that is worth examination is the notion of levelling. Data flow diagrams can easily grow too big to digest. Useful size guidelines are that they should fit onto one A4 sheet and that they should not contain more than about nine process bubbles.

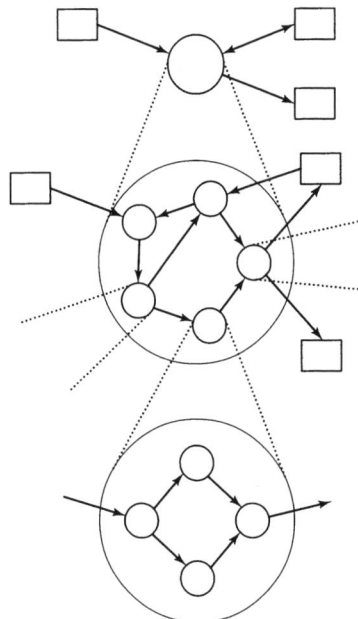

Figure 13.6

To address the problem of modelling large systems we can resort to a *hierarchy* of DFDs. Each process bubble at one level is decomposed into sub-processes at a lower level as is illustrated in Figure 13.6. Certain rules apply when levelling:

* The boundary data flows *must match* from 'parent' to 'child' level.

* Data stores are placed at the lowest *possible* level (i.e. such that all accessing processes are within that level).

Levelling can be very helpful but it is not without its hazards. It is often advocated that levelled DFD sets be developed in a top-down manner (i.e. start at the highest level and work down). Whilst this is often a helpful way in which to *present the results* of applying the technique, it is by no means always the best way to *develop* the model. Partly this is because it may not match well with the thought processes of the analyst/designer, but it also presupposes that the knowledge necessary to *define the system boundary completely* (for the top-level diagram) is available *before* 'lower level' detail has been investigated. In practice, iterative switching between development of DFDs at several levels often works best.

The question of when to stop decomposing also arises. The conventional guidelines are, at best, vague and it may be more helpful to consider the issue of concurrency. Data flow diagrams present an essentially concurrent processing model; once a level is reached at which processing is, perforce, sequential, sequential processing models (see Section 13.1.2) may well be more appropriate. In any event, such considerations relate far more to idesign than to

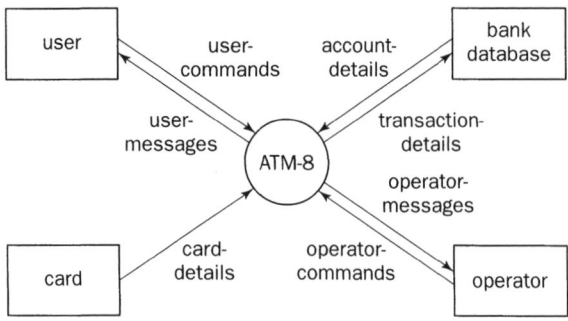

Figure 13.7

requirements engineering, where only high-level data flow modelling (during requirements analysis) is usually effective.

13.1.1.7 Context diagram

The top level DFD (where the solution system is shown as one bubble) is known as a context diagram. This is significantly different from all other levels of DFD in that the system in question is not decomposed (no internal processes or data stores are shown). It is, therefore, a purely external (rather than internal) model, and it follows that it is the one type of DFD that unquestionably figures in requirements specification (as opposed to analysis or idesign). In line with the comments about 'top-down' (see above), it will often be more appropriate to regard a fully defined context DFD as an *end point* in analysis rather than (as is more usual) a starting point. Figure 13.7 shows an example context DFD for the ATM-8 system.

Note that any DFD is of decidedly limited meaning without definitions of the data flows. Selected entries for Figure 13.7 are shown below. Note how much additional information these provide:

user-commands	::= display_balance | withdraw_cash | end_session | user_PIN;
user-messages	::= "enter card" | "enter PIN" | "invalid PIN, please re-enter" | "enter amount" . .
account-details	::= sort_code, account_number, balance, account_PIN, PIN_attempts, lost;
transaction-details	::= sort_code, account_number, amount, date, time;
card-details	::= sort_code, account_number;
account_number	::= ^{8}{digit}^{8};
amount	::= ^{1}{digit}^{8}; (* units are .01 of base currency *)
balance	::= ^{1}{digit}^{6}, ".", ^{2}{digit}^{2};
date	::= day, "/", month, "/", year";
day	::= "1" . . "31";
month	::= "1" . . "12";

year	::= "1990" . . "2099";
lost	::= boolean; (* a card is lost if reported lost (by the user) *)
account_PIN	::= PIN;
user_PIN	::= PIN;
PIN	::= ^{4}{digit}$^{4;}$ (* Note, each digit must be different *)
sort_code	::= ^{6}{digit}$^{6;}$ (* Uniquely identifies the card's home bank *)

13.1.2   Communicating sequential processes

In common with the object class abstraction, this model was developed for software systems in particular. The majority of 'real world' systems process in parallel. This does not apply only to natural systems (for example, an animal can see and hear at the same time); it is also the case that most man-made systems, such as production lines and offices, have multiple processes operating in parallel.

Most computers, on the other hand, process sequentially and so modelling the ordering of those processes is of interest. That said, there is now a strong trend towards parallel processing, either at the hardware level or, more commonly, at some abstract machine level. The necessity of modelling process sequencing is, therefore, fading. Since it is also of great relevance only to idesign (which is largely beyond the scope of this book) it will be examined only briefly (see, for example, Budgen, 1994, for further information if required).

The usual notation for modelling communicating sequential processes is the tree diagram or structure chart (SC), the main alternative being pseudo-code (see Section 14.3.2). With but minor variations in syntax, SCs are used for (at least) five different purposes:

- program (process) structure charts (this section);

- algorithm definition (see Section 13.2);

- functional definition (see Section 12.1.1);

- data structure charts (an alternative to, say, BNF – see Section 14.3.4);

- ELHs (see Section 13.4.1).

(And so, it is important to be clear which pertains in any given situation!)

At its simplest, the process structure chart models just the *calling hierarchy*. At each level, the processes (aka modules, sub-programs or procedures) are shown below their calling process(es), and the connecting lines represent the calls that are made. (In this context, it may be useful to think of a call as temporarily handing over the processor to the sub-process or module.) An example is given in Figure 13.8. The natural language interpretation of Figure 13.8 would be:

Module A can call modules B, C and D; module B can call modules E and F; module C can call modules F, G and H.

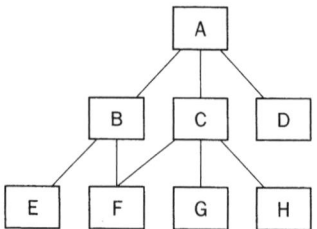

Figure 13.8

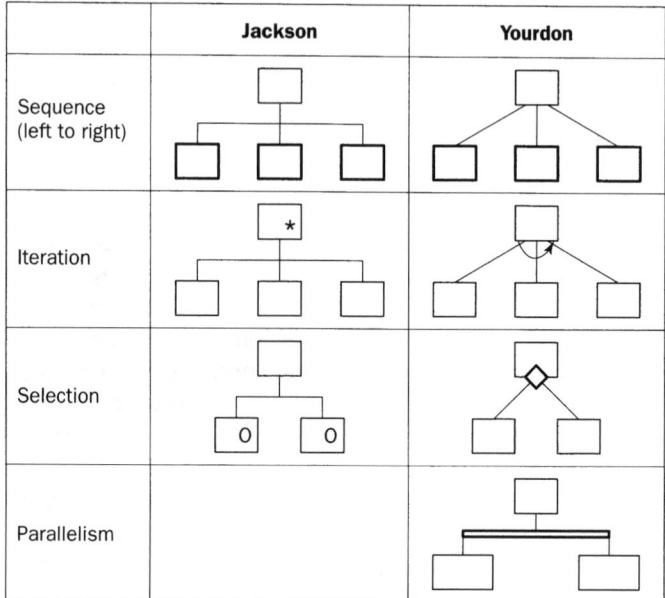

Figure 13.9

The notation must be somewhat elaborated to allow the possible *sequencing* of the calls to be defined. The constructs provided are derived from the principles of structured programming (Dijkstra, 1965) and Figure 13.9 shows the two most common notation variants.

Using these constructs, arbitrarily complex execution sequences can be defined. For example, Figure 13.10 shows an SC for an electronic dashboard system.

Figure 13.10 is interpreted as meaning that: the top-level module dashboard calls speed-and-distance which, in turn, calls display-distance which, in turn, calls get-distance. Speed-and-distance then calls display-speed which, in turn, calls calculate-speed. Control is returned to dashboard which then calls trip-display which, in turn, calls get-driver-selection before calling either display-trip-speed or display-trip-distance. The entire process is then repeated indefinitely.

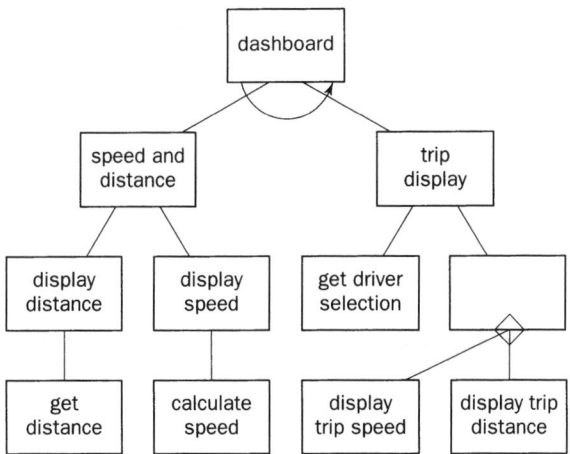

Figure 13.10

A further elaboration (data couples) allows the data flows between modules to be shown as well (these generally correspond to the parameters or arguments of the call). However, the addition of this information can lead to cluttered diagrams and the benefits of abstraction may be compromised.

The fact that data flows *can* be shown on program SCs nevertheless highlights the relationship with DFDs. Both feature processes prominently and, for a DFD and an SC of the same system (and at the same level), the 'leaf' processes (i.e. those which have no further processes 'hanging off them') on SCs should correspond to the process bubbles on the DFD. Program SCs, however, may well have additional, high-level 'control' processes that determine the execution sequence of the leaf processes. Since communicating sequential process models are highly internal (showing not only the modularisation of the system but also the calling sequence), they are primarily of use in idesign.

However, the same notation can be used to model the sequencing of only the externally observable functions. Despite the great superficial similarity (which generates the potential for serious confusion), the underlying model is fundamentally different and is examined in Section 12.1.1.

13.2 Algorithmic techniques

Occasionally, the problem domain may impose a particular algorithm upon the application. Examples might include the calculation of tax or the calculation of the handicaps for yachts according to their various dimensions. Equally rarely, even where not imposed by the problem domain, the client may decide that a particular algorithm must be used; this would be a design constraint.

Generally, however, the determination of the algorithms to be used within applications is left to the low-level internal design phase and so algorithm definition has but a small role to play within requirements engineering. Where algorithms must be defined, the most widely adopted techniques are SCs (see Section 13.1.2) and pseudo-code (see Section 14.3.2).

13.3 Data structure oriented techniques

Data structure modelling, or data analysis, as it is often called, concerns the structure of static data.

13.3.1 Indications for use

Data structure modelling is of most significance for information systems (see Section 4.5.1.7), but it may well be relevant for other types of application as well.

Data structure models of *problem domain* data may well be produced during analysis; during idesign, models of the *solution system* data structure must be developed.

There is an important, if sometimes subtle, distinction between models of problem domain data and models of data contained within the solution system (see Section 2.9), but it is often the case that the solution system will *contain a data model of the problem domain*. Presumably for this reason, solution system data structure models are also commonly found in specifications. This is not really necessary and may be considered undesirable since, as structural models, they constitute design constraints.

That said, the underlying rationale of data modelling is very well developed (Codd, 1970), and so there is little room for variance in the resultant models. It may, therefore, be argued that data analysis models, even though structural, scarcely impose design constraints, since they represent the *only* rational way of modelling the logical structure of the stored data. That such models are often found in specifications may, therefore, be considered excusable if not warranted.

The utility of data analysis varies considerably from one application to another. Some domains contain significant amounts of data whereas others contain very little. However, of greater relevance is the *complexity* of the data structure. Where this complexity is high, data analysis plays a vital role; where it is low (even though the *quantity* of data may be high) data analysis is not so vital.

Whilst the models are essentially simple, many users (and quite a few practitioners) have difficulty in understanding them. It is not clear why this should be the case. However, for the expert there is little opportunity for error and, coupled with the technique's inherently low ambiguity, this produces models that are good at highlighting gaps in knowledge. As with most structural modelling techniques, tool support is readily available.

13.3.2 Entity attribute relationship modelling

The first fundamental concept in data modelling is the entity. This may be defined as something of interest *which has associated information*. Entities arise from the problem domain and correspond to both tangible and abstract items. For example, for a customer support system, entities could well be: customer, contract, fault etc.

As mentioned in the previous section, it is as well not to lose sight of the fact that there are two versions of each entity: there is the thing that actually exists in the problem domain; and then there is any *model* of that thing that we may choose to create within a solution system. The latter is defined *entirely* in terms of its stored data; the former may have many other properties as well (which this technique ignores!).

When performing data analysis, the usual starting point is to trawl through the elicitation records picking out candidate entities. It is sometimes suggested that this is simply a case of identifying all the nouns in the elicitation records, but by no means all nouns correspond to entities! Common exceptions are terminators (i.e. systems with which the new, solution system may interact), agents (i.e. the person, department or machine that performs some process) and reports (which are often *lists* of entities). The best way to identify true entities is to ask the question 'what relevant information is associated with this entity?'. If you cannot think of any then it may well not be an entity (in the data analysis sense).

The pieces of information that are associated with each entity are usually known as attributes (aka data items or fields) and it is recommended that, when drawing up the initial entity list, just to check their validity, one or two attributes of each entity are noted. To extend the customer support system example, the following attributes may be identified on a first pass:

customer	company-name, contact-name, address, telephone number . .
contract	contract-number, start-date, expiry-date . .
problem	date-reported, seriousness, description . .

It may not be apparent yet that an entity (potentially) represents a whole set of items of the same type. So, whilst we may talk about *the* customer entity (note the singular), we anticipate that there will be many customers. Each actual customer is an *instance* of the customer entity. They all have the *same attributes* but the *values* of those attributes may well differ. For example, every instance of customer has a telephone number but they all have different telephone numbers.

It is essential that each instance of an entity can be uniquely identified and, to this end, we must specify a key. A key is simply one or more attributes, the values of which will never be the same for two instances of an entity. Often a 'naturally occurring' attribute (or set of attributes) will form a suitable key, but sometimes it is more convenient to add an attribute for the specific purpose of forming a key. So, the above example might become (keys are underlined):

customer	<u>company-name</u>, contact-name, address, telephone number . .
contract	<u>contract-number</u>, start-date, expiry-date . .
problem	<u>problem-id</u>, date-reported, seriousness, description . .

Table 13.1

	customer	contract	problem
customer	X	=======	=======
contract	takes out	X	=======
problem	reports	X	X

The final, and most problematical, matter for consideration is the *relationships* between (instances of) entities. There are two approaches to this: the first is simply to think about which entities are related; the second is to examine where one entity contains a copy of the key of another entity. The final outcome should be the same either way, and the latter approach is examined within the context of normalisation in the next section.

The 'thinking about it' approach can be aided with the use of an entity/ entity cross reference matrix (EECRM). This simple tool is merely a means to an end, but it can help ensure that no relationships are overlooked. For the three example entitles considered above, the EECRM would be as shown in Table 13.1.

Table 13.1 was generated by plotting the entities along the horizontal *and* vertical axes, blanking out the top right corner (but not the diagonal because an instance of an entity may be related to another instance of the same entity) and then considering whether the potential relationships represented by the blank cells exist or not. If not, a cross is entered, otherwise a tick or (as here) a label for the relationship.

So far, text has been used for recording the data structure and this is, indeed, the normal notation. For recording the relationships, however, resort is often made to a graph. There are variations but a simple version for the example used so far is shown in Figure 13.11.

There is a potential snag with the model depicted in Figure 13.11 in that there are two ends to each relationship (link); using a single label ignores this. For example, whilst a customer *takes out* a contract, from the contract viewpoint, it is *taken out by* a customer. It is also the case that some relationships are optional whereas others are mandatory (and this may depend upon which viewpoint is taken).

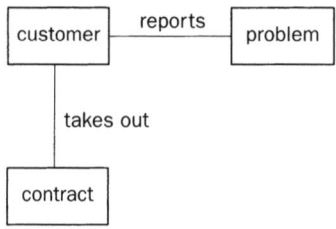

Figure 13.11

Yet more information that might be added concerns the *order* of the relationship; how *many* instances of entity A might be related to how many instances of entity B. Three possibilities are usually recognised:

- one to one;
- one to many;
- many to many.

Version 4 of SSADM (CCTA, 1990) introduces a greater formalisation of the textual notation for specifying relationships and this incorporates all of the above considerations. It is of the form:

> Each <entityA> [may | must] <relationship> [one and only one | one or more than one] <entityB>

and there must be two statements for each relationship, representing the views from either end.

> Applied to the foregoing example, this would result in the following entity relationship statements:
>
> Each contract must be taken out by one and only one customer
> Each customer may take out one or more than one contract
> Each customer may report one or more than one problem
> Each problem must be reported by one and only one customer

Whilst this makes it clear that data structure models can readily be recorded using only text, there are extensions to the graphical notation which accommodate these additional features. Figure 13.12 is an extended version for the customer support system.

Appropriately, this is known as an entity relationship diagram (ERD). The ERD in Figure 13.12 uses the SSADM notation, but there are variations and a comparison with the other widely used notation is summarised in Figure 13.13.

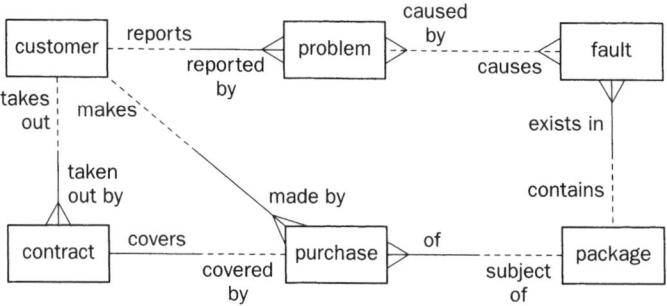

Figure 13.12

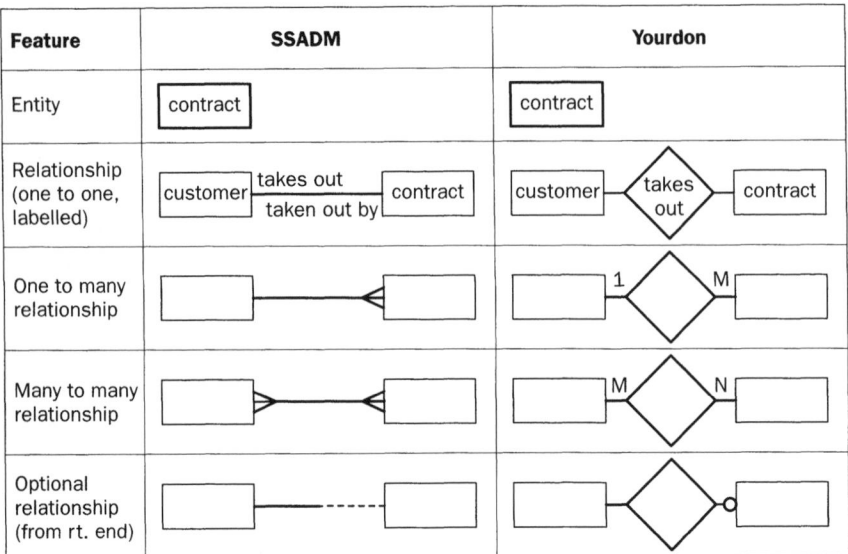

Figure 13.13

Note, however, that ERDs only model the *relationships* between entities and should always be accompanied by lists of attributes and keys for each entity. (Occasionally this information is shown on the ERD by squeezing it into the entity boxes (as is shown in Figure 13.15), but things can become rather crowded!)

This is by no means the whole story on data analysis and further informa-tion may be found in, for example, Connolly *et al.*, 1999, Date, 1999. However, as with other internal modelling techniques, during the analysis phase there is no profit in pursuing the model beyond the point at which this aspect of the problem domain is fully understood. More detailed elaboration is pertinent to implementation and can be deferred to the idesign phase.

13.3.3   Normalisation

13.3.3.1   Indications for use
An alternative (or complementary) approach to data analysis employs the data normalisation rules. This technique is usually applied in 'computerisation', i.e. where there is a pre-existing, paper-based system that the solution system will replace. It can also be used to check the results of data analysis (described in the previous section). Normalisation is also used extensively during the idesign of systems with complex databases but the emphasis here is upon its use in analysis.

13.3.3.2   The technique
The starting point is also the problem domain data but, in this case, as it is documented in a pre-existing system. The relevant paperwork is examined and a 'first cut' data model is extracted. Initially, the emphasis is upon identifying attributes rather than entities.

Imaginary Systems Ltd			Order number	
Customer name			Date	
Phone number			Order taken by	
Address...			....	
....			....	
....			....	
Package name	Code	Price	Quantity	Total
			Grand total	

Figure 13.14

For example, it may well be that for the customer support system (introduced in the preceding section), there is a pre-existing paper-based system. One of those pieces of paper might be a form (see Figure 13.14) that is completed when a customer purchases one or more package.

It is a relatively simple matter to extract an initial list of potential attributes (stored data items) from such a form. For example, the form in Figure 13.14 contains package-name, code, price, etc. Further elicitation from the users will probably be required to confirm those attributes and, in this case, for example, it may be that, even though the form records who takes the order, the solution system is not required to store order-taken-by. Similarly, whilst there are line totals and a grand total, these can always be calculated if quantity and price are stored, so it may be decided that totals should not be stored either.

It is also usual to proceed upon the initial assumption that the form represents an entity and that a suitable name will have to be invented (this does not normally appear, as such, on the document). So, continuing with the above example (and with a little rationalisation of the names) we could arrive at the following:

ORDER
<u>order-number</u>
order-date
customer-name
customer-address
customer-phone
     package-name
     package-code
     package-price
     quantity

Where the presumed entity has been named ORDER, its key attribute is order-number and the indentation indicates a group of attributes that may be repeated on the form (and, therefore, in the entity).

It is usual to perform this operation upon a selection of forms (or similar documents). This inevitably introduces considerable duplication of attributes, but the guideline is to analyse as many forms as are necessary to ensure that every attribute appears at least once.

From this starting point, we are now in a position to normalise the data. The objective is to convert the data into their most logical form. Ultimately, this will ensure that all potential operations upon those data are, indeed, feasible and (as a free bonus) it ensures that the data occupy the minimum amount of space.

There are, in fact, six levels of data normalisation (see Codd, 1970) but, for most practical purposes, the third level is adequate. In order to convert the data into third normal form (TNF) we must ensure that it complies with the first three normalisation rules:

1   An entity may contain no repeating (groups of) attributes.

2   Every non-key attribute must depend upon every attribute of the key.

3   Every non-key attribute must depend upon no attribute other than the key attribute(s).

This is often condensed into the mnemonic rule, 'Every non-key attribute must depend upon the key, the whole key and nothing but the key'. Whilst this covers rules 2 and 3 quite well, it ignores rule 1 and so a better, if less memorable, version might be, 'There shall be no repeating attributes and every non-key attribute must depend upon the key, the whole key and nothing but the key'.

In order to make the data comply with these rules, it is usually necessary to shift attributes from the provisional entity they happen to be in to the one where they logically belong. This process will be examined using the ongoing example:

ORDER
order-number
order-date
customer-name
customer-address
customer-phone
      package-name
      package-code
      package-price
      quantity

The rules should be applied in order and so, in consideration of rule 1, the repeating attributes must be removed. Any group that is removed is placed in a new entity, the key of which consists of a *copy* of the original key *plus* an attribute 'promoted' from the group. In this case, a new entity (called ORDER-LINE) is created and package-code is the obvious choice for the new, additional key element:

ORDER
<u>order-number</u>
order-date
customer-name
customer-address
customer-phone

ORDER-LINE
<u>order-number</u>
<u>package-code</u>
package-name
package-price
quantity

Since no repeating attributes remain, rule 2 can now be considered: 'Every non-key attribute must depend upon every attribute of the key'. Rule 2 can apply only to entities with compound keys (in this case ORDER-LINE), and each non-key attribute in turn is examined to see whether it depends upon *both* of the key attributes.

It is at this point that the precise interpretation of 'depends upon' is significant. A useful guideline is that it is equivalent to 'is uniquely determined by'.

Package-name is dependent upon (uniquely determined by) package-code alone. It should therefore be removed from the ORDER-LINE entity and placed in a new entity whose key is a *copy* of the *relevant* attribute from the original key. Package-price should be treated in the same way, but quantity depends upon order-number *and* package-code and so remains *in situ*:

ORDER
<u>order-number</u>
order-date
customer-name
customer-address
customer-phone

ORDER-LINE
<u>order-number</u>
<u>package-code</u>
quantity

PACKAGE
<u>package-code</u>
package-name
package-price

The data are now in second normal form and so we move on to rule 3: 'Every non-key attribute must depend upon no attribute other than the key attribute(s)'. Every non-key attribute of each entity is examined and the transgressors, in this case, are customer-address and customer-phone which depend only upon customer-name. Those two attributes are, therefore, removed and placed in another new entity, and a *copy* of the attribute that they *do* depend upon is taken with them and forms the new key:

ORDER
<u>order-number</u>
order-date
customer-name

ORDER-LINE
<u>order-number</u>
<u>package-code</u>
quantity

PACKAGE
<u>package-code</u>
package-name
package-price

CUSTOMER
<u>customer-name</u>
customer-address
customer-phone

The data are now in TNF and, when this process is performed upon a comprehensive set of documents, the chances are that all the relevant entities and attributes will be identified. (In fact, there will often be duplicate entities but these are easily recognised and merged.)

This model is equivalent to an ERD and converting it into that form is a mechanical process. Wherever an attribute appears in two entities, this indicates a link (relationship) between that pair of entities. As a result of the normalisation, it follows that all those relationships are of order 'one to many'. Furthermore *one* of the duplicated attributes will always be a *single* key and this is at the 'one' end of the link. This fragment of the data model can, therefore, be converted into an ERD as shown in Figure 13.15.

13.3.4   Data structure charts

Structure charts, along the lines of those described in Section 13.1.2, can also be used to model the structure of data. Such an approach does not support the logical analysis of data structures (as is the case with ERDs and normalisation described in the previous sections), but it may be seen as an alternative to BNF-like approaches (see Section 14.3.4) for describing i/o streams and file structures.

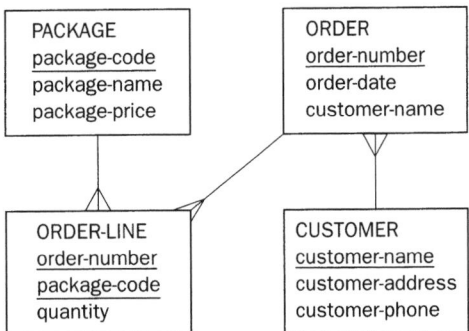

Figure 13.15

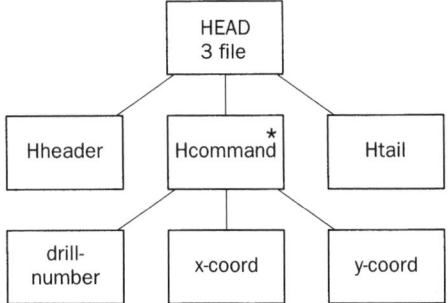

Figure 13.16

Figure 13.16 is a small example drawn from the drill file case study. (The BNF equivalent is given in Section 17.1.2.2 and you may well conclude that it provides a more succinct definition!)

13.4   Process/data combination

The techniques examined so far concentrate upon modelling either the processing that takes place or the data that is processed. Sooner or later, it can be advantageous to take a more integrated view. But there is one caveat; the abstractions are inevitably more complex.

13.4.1   Entity life history

13.4.1.1   Indications for use
The entity life history (ELH) or entity state history (ESH) is not a very widely used model. However, it appears (in a rather different form) in a couple of well known analysis/design methods, SSADM (CCTA, 1996) and JSD (Jackson, 1983).

Within SSADM, ELH modelling plays a relatively subservient role. It necessarily follows on from data analysis (see Section 13.3.2) and data flow modelling (see Section 13.1.1). Entities are taken from the ERD and the events (processes) that affect those entities are taken from the DFDs. An ELH modelling the sequencing of the processes that affect it is then developed for each entity. The role of ELH modelling is to act as a cross-check and a form of integration between the other models rather than as an end in itself.

Within JSD, ELHs model the sequencing of significant events within the problem domain (rather than processes). An event may be defined as a discrete happening within the problem domain and, in this context, an entity is simply something that generates or responds to events (and correspondence with the 'stored data' notion of an entity would be coincidental). Within JSD, ELH modelling plays a central role; it is, in fact, the starting point. Using, presumably, the elicitation records as input, events are identified and listed, as are the entities associated with those events. Not surprisingly, the technique is indicated for systems where the events are significant and where the possible ordering of those events must be clearly understood.

13.4.1.2 Description

Despite these differences, the models have much in common as both show the possible sequencing of processes or events that affect each entity. A similar, graphical notation is used and this is often referred to as a structure chart (SC). As previously mentioned, with but minor variations in syntax, SCs are used for (at least) five different purposes:

- program SCs (see Section 13.1.2);
- algorithm definition (see Section 13.2);
- functional definition (see Section 12.1.1);
- data SCs (see Section 13.3.4);
- ELHs (this Section).

There is some potential for confusion here, and so note that the ELH models the potential sequences of processes or events applied to a *particular* entity[108].

The basic notation is covered in Section 13.1.2 and will not be repeated here, but a couple of examples should help illustrate the application of the technique. Note that the top box always contains the name of the entity; the other boxes indicate the relevant events.

The first example (from the YRR system) encapsulates such points as:

- A boat cannot be entered into a race before it has been added.
- A boat cannot be entered into a race after it has been deleted.
- A boat can have its details edited or can be entered into a race any number of times whilst it exists.

---

[108] The entity may be an entity from the problem domain or an entity from the solution system (see Section 2.9).

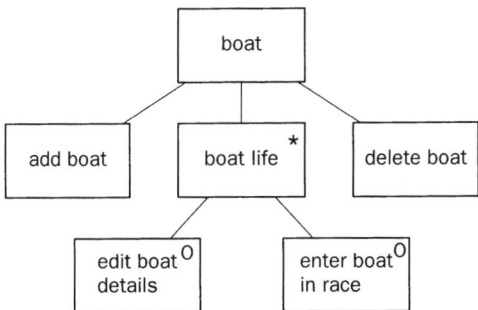

Figure 13.17

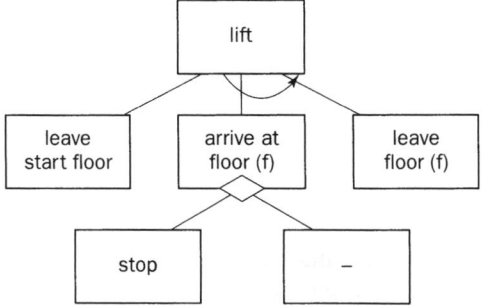

Figure 13.18

These are illustrated in Figure 13.17.

With events such as 'add' and 'delete', it might be (correctly) deduced that this is a model of a solution system entity. So, for the second example, consider a problem domain entity, an actual (hardware) lift (and, just by way of variation, the alternative notation is used) – see Figure 13.18. Not the most exciting life perhaps, but that's lifts for you.

There are other ways of modelling event sequencing (see Section 5.3.3). Particularly for specification purposes, they may sometimes be considered preferable as they do not necessarily decompose the system into entities.

13.4.2 Object oriented modelling (OOM)

Object oriented modelling is very widely documented elsewhere (see for example Booch, 1991, Coad and Yourdon, 1991, Fowler and Scott, 2000, Jacobson *et al.*, 1996, Shlaer and Mellor, 1988, etc.). Thus, just the essentials are covered here, sufficient to support Section 4.4 on OOA.

Unfortunately, there have been many variations in object oriented notation and terminology. Standardisation is now underway and so the widely promoted unified modelling language (UML) is illustrated below, but some alternative terminology is also indicated.

13.4.2.1 Indications for use

Object oriented modelling is a relative newcomer, but it has been widely adopted as an analysis and idesign technique in recent years. The underlying principle requires that the system in question be modelled as a set of intercommunicating objects. An object, in this context, is an abstraction of some thing that models its stored data *and* the operations that can be performed upon those data. (You may initially find it helpful to view OOM as a combination of the communicating concurrent processes model (see Section 13.1.1) and the data structure model (see Section 13.3) although, as will be seen, there is rather more to it than that.)

The models are inherently structural and so the role of OOM in specification is limited. Its role in idesign is very significant and OOD is seeing widespread adoption. Object oriented analysis is now strongly promoted as an approach to analysis, based on the notion that the objects within the model can be drawn from the problem domain. As indicated in the section on analysis (Section 4.1), this is a debatable point but, given the widespread promotion, it is as well to be familiar with the approach. The technique appears to be moderately accessible and there is good tool support available for the common, graphical notations.

13.4.2.2 Objects and classes

An object consists of its stored data (operands or attributes) and the operations (methods or services) that it can perform using those data. It is important that the defined operations are the *only* way in which the object's data may be accessed. It follows that only the object's own operations 'know' (or need to know) the structure of those data and that access to the data is controlled. This is a realisation of the principle of encapsulation or information hiding. It helps ensure that related parts of the system are considered in juxtaposition, thereby minimising 'traffic' around the system and, hence, limiting the ramifications of (inevitable) changes. Encapsulation may be pictured as in Figure 13.19 where the object's operations are shown as 'wrapping up' its attributes (the arrows represent the (indirect) data flows).

An example object from the ATM problem domain could be the device that actually dispenses the cash. One of its attributes might be how much cash it

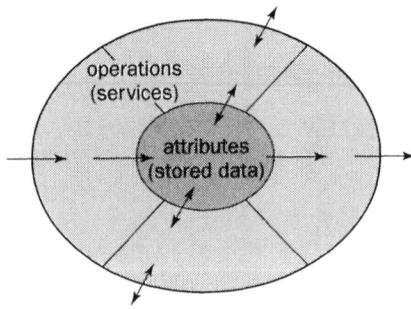

Figure 13.19

contains and operations could include, 'dispense <quantity> cash' and 'has cash been taken?'

Whilst an ATM would probably have only one cash dispenser, it is frequently the case that a problem domain will contain several (or many) objects of the same type. Another example from the ATM domain could be the customer – presumably there will be many customers. Each will have the same attributes (e.g. user-PIN) and each will have the same operations (e.g. 'provide user-PIN'), but the *values* of the attributes will not (necessarily) be the same.

A set of objects of the same type are said to form a class. The identification of individual objects (or instances) is usually subordinate to the task of identifying and defining (in terms of their operations and attributes) object classes.

13.4.2.3 Object relationships

Identifying and defining classes of object is only part of the story; to achieve the desired understanding, the relationships between those classes and objects must be explored.

Object oriented modelling recognises several types of inter-object (or inter-class) relationship:

* specialisation/generalisation;
* association;
* aggregation/composition (whole/part);
* collaboration links (message connection – use of operations/services).

Specialisation/generalisation

This type of relationship embodies the notion of the sub-class and super-class. It may be the case that two classes of object share some, but not all, of their characteristics (attributes and operations). Examples are commonplace, one being, say, the buttons in the lift system. Lift buttons come in two varieties: there are the call-buttons (outside the lift) that call a lift to a floor; and the send-buttons (inside the lift) that send it to a floor. Both types of button will have operations of 'press' and 'check-press' (and, possibly 'unpress') and both will have an attribute of 'floor-id'. However, call-buttons will have an additional attribute of 'direction', whereas send-buttons will have an additional attribute of 'lift-id'. So, there is some commonality but some individuality. Within object orientation, this can be modelled with a super-class 'button', which contains the shared characteristics, and sub-classes for each specialisation as shown in Figure 13.20.

Note:

* Sub-classes can only *add* to the characteristics of their parent (super-) class; nothing can be taken away.
* In this case, the sub-classes add only attributes, but it could equally well be operations or both.
* The small triangle on the link line is used to indicate that the relationship is a specialisation.

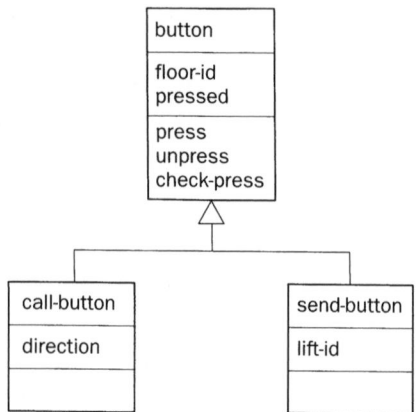

Figure 13.20

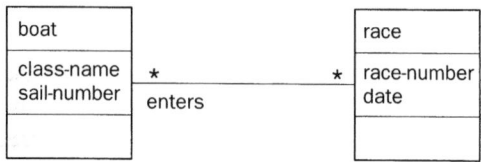

Figure 13.21

By analogy with living organisms, the sub-classes are often said to *inherit* the characteristics of their super-class. This principle of inheritance allows much duplication across similar classes to be avoided.

There is a recognised concept of multiple inheritance but this is seldom used. Whilst a class may have any number of sub-classes, each usually has only one super-class.

Associations

Associations capture the transient relationships that can exist between objects. These are practically identical to the entity relationships that are described in Section 13.3.2. For example, in the YRR application, a boat might be associated with a race by way of entering it.

The relevant notation is a plain line connecting the object classes. This may have an indication of the order of the relationship ('*' is used to indicate 'zero or more') and it may be named. Both these features are illustrated in Figure 13.21.

Aggregation/composition (whole/part)

Sometimes one object is made up of other, component objects; for example, a lift has a door. This could be modelled as an association but UML provides alternate notation for modelling these relatively permanent whole/part relationships as an aggregation or composition. The distinction between these two is determined by the relative lifetimes of the objects. If when the assembly is destroyed, its components can survive, then it is an aggregation; if when the

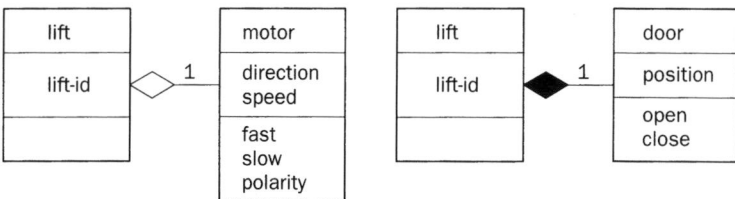

Figure 13.22

assembly is destroyed, its components 'die' as well, then it is a composition. The notation is simple enough, and is shown in Figure 13.22 (aggregation on the left, composition on the right). (It can sometimes be difficult to decide whether a particular relationship should be modelled as an association or an aggregation. In such cases Bray's Law may be pertinent – given the facts and expertise, the harder it is to choose between design alternatives, the less it matters which you choose.)

Collaboration links (message connection – use of services)
The operations (or services) that each object provides are there for the use of the other objects. An object requests an operation by sending a message to the other object, and there may well be a consequential response or reply. This is the object oriented equivalent of a procedural call, and messages can have associated parameters.

Whilst this may appear similar to a conventional data flow model, there is a significant paradigm shift required which can prove problematical for those experienced in structured analysis or design. Instead of passing data to procedures so that they can operate upon them, objects are 'asked' to provide data or perform a service. For example, one would not pass a list to a sort routine in order to sort it, but would ask a list object to sort itself.

The collaboration links may be shown as plain lines accompanied by short, named arrows indicating the particular operations that are used. Brackets after the name indicate that parameters often accompany the messages but these may not be explicitly named. Figure 13.23 is a small example from the lift controller problem.

As mentioned at the beginning of the section, this is but a brief overview of OOM. There are numerous sources for more detailed information, including the references given at the start.

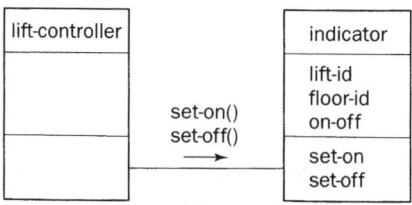

Figure 13.23

Text-based definition **14**

Much can be (and, elsewhere, has been) said about the various modelling techniques described above. Whilst such models do indeed figure large in much analysis and idesign documentation, it is easy to gain the impression that requirements documents and specifications can be constructed using almost exclusively those modelling techniques. This turns out *not* to be the case.

The various types of models can each be used for particular purposes, but none defines everything that is needed and, indeed, there are some important elements (for example, performance requirements) that are not well addressed by *any* modelling techniques.

This goes some way towards explaining the curious fact that whilst requirements engineering textbooks and courses (and research) often concentrate upon modelling techniques, such models contribute little to most actual requirements documents and specifications[109]. This obviously raises the question of what techniques *are* being used. The usual answer is that the majority of requirements and specification documents utilise text.

However, this does not exactly answer the question because, as discussed previously, text is *not* a modelling technique. Rather, it is a *notation* and, as such, may be used only to *record* a model that is due to some technique. For example, the following is a fragment from a textual specification for the simple ATM:

> The system can exist in any one of three states; 'Await card', 'Await PIN' or 'Await amount'. When idle, it is in the 'Await card' state and if a card is entered it displays the message 'Enter PIN' and then assumes the 'Await PIN' state. Whilst in this state, if the 'END' button is pressed . . .

In this case, the underlying model is clearly a FSM as illustrated in Figure 14.1.

So, is text simply used as a notation to record the sorts of models that have been described earlier? As it turns out, no; whilst fragments of such models may sometimes be recognised, there are other ways, apart from those modelling techniques, of describing systems. Not only do these other mechanisms exist, but they also make a vital contribution to requirements documents and specifications.

---

[109] An (unpublished) survey of my own, in 1992, found that around 80% of specifications in the UK make little or no use of such modelling techniques.

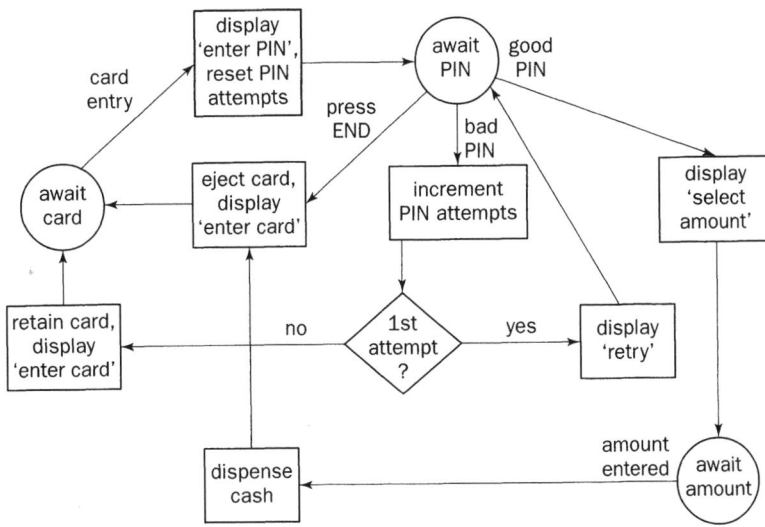

Figure 14.1

14.1 Formality of text

Text can appear in a wide variety of forms. All share the distinguishing characteristic of being a string of characters, but there is considerable variation in syntactic complexity. At the highest level, there is natural language (NL), 'ordinary' English or prose, where the grammar is so complex that it defies formal description.

The lower levels of complexity are typified by the multitude of computer programming languages, but there are other examples, such as machine control languages and, even, the code used in knitting patterns. At the extreme there are highly restricted grammars, such as predicate calculus and BNF. All have a role to play, and we will come to some of the more constrained types of text later (Section 14.3) but, first, prose.

The highly complex rules which make natural language so powerful may be widely understood, but they are ill-defined. So too are many of the words that form the massive lexicon. The consequence is that making sense of NL depends upon having a vast store of background knowledge to allow context dependent interpretation. The result is ambiguity, the bête-noir of requirements engineering. However, even with prose, much can be done to ameliorate this problem.

14.2 Natural language

Writing prose is, at once, the most important and the most difficult documentation skill. It is not the only documentation technique and, for any particular purpose, not always the best. However, it is uniquely flexible and may, at the very least, be regarded as the fall back. There is virtually no thought, no information that cannot be communicated via good writing, and it is an inescapable fact that good documentation requires good writing.

Within requirements engineering, NL often receives a bad press. Whilst it is acknowledged to be a uniquely powerful notation, this is often viewed as being more than offset by its potential for vagueness, ambiguity and verbosity. All too often, NL *is* associated with a decline into loose, woolly, ambiguous and poorly structured description. But this is not inevitable. An awareness of precisely when and how to use NL allows its power to be exploited whilst minimising, if not eliminating, its shortcomings.

Widespread poor usage of NL has been widely cited as a justification for its abandonment in favour of more formal techniques. However, this has had the unfortunate effect of distracting attention from addressing the problem of poor usage. Indeed, this is doubly unfortunate; not only are there often very good reasons to use NL, but also many of the 'replacement' techniques (such as DFDs, use-cases and so on) employ text and actually depend upon good NL usage anyway!

It takes many years to learn to use language and yet more to learn to use it well. We start young, of course, and most of us achieve reasonable competence, but few can write really well. Here, it is competence in technical writing that is in question. The skill required is rather different from that for writing good literature, but it is no more common or easier to acquire.

So, the bad news is that producing good writing is difficult. It probably requires a certain aptitude, certainly requires a lot of practice and, to be blunt, many will never achieve it. There are severe limits to the help that this book (or any other) can provide.

However, there is some good news in that, without redefining the language itself, all can improve. This is partly a matter of style and partly a matter of appreciating the ends and means of NL usage. Useful guidelines and examples can be provided for both these matters. And there is some more good news. Whilst *writing* good technical prose may be difficult, the ability to interpret it accurately (read it!) is very common and so one good writer can accurately disseminate information to many.

14.2.1 Ambiguity

Ambiguity is widely cited as the Achilles heel of NL. There is some truth in this, but careful usage can go a very long way towards ameliorating the problem. Examples of ambiguity arise everyday; here is an example from some instructions I recently received: 'Do not hesitate to cancel the race if there is any doubt about poor weather'. Taken literally, this means that if I am certain that there will be poor weather I should not cancel. Probably not what was intended! One of my favourites comes from a course I once attended: 'The following rules are strictly forbidden.' Surely it does not mean what it says (or does it?).

The above examples are quite easy to spot, but the hazard is that we may not always guess the intended meaning correctly. Sometimes it is of little consequence; at other times it can be disastrous.

Here is a more software oriented example: 'When all items have been entered, the total price is displayed.' This implies that the total price is not displayed until all items have been entered. They may have meant that, but it seems a little unlikely. We could clear up any doubt by stating that, 'When, and only when, all items have been entered, the total price is displayed'. And, if that is not what was meant, we could have said, 'The total price is displayed and is updated as each item is added.'

Once you are alert to such potential problems, they are really not difficult to avoid. As per the list below, the question to pose continually is, 'Are any reasonable misinterpretations possible?'

14.2.2 Style guidelines

The following are partly derived from Ben Kovitz's splendid book (Kovitz, 1999).

14.2.2.1 The naming rules
A few simple rules can help no end.

1 Designate or, wherever possible, formally define all terms that might cause problems (see Sections 14.4.1 and 14.4.2).

2 As far as is sensible, adopt the terminology of the problem domain. By all means clarify the meaning of existing terms, but do not invent new terminology (including acronyms!) just for the sake of it.

3 Never use the same term for different things. If this already happens in the problem domain, you must invent new terms or number them. An example is provided by the YRR case study; in the problem domain, the word 'class' is used for both 'boat-class' and 'race-class'. These new terms were coined to fix the problem. Examples also occur in this book with terms such as edesign and idesign and entity(1) and entity(2) (see glossary entries).

4 As far as is sensible, always use the same term for the same thing. If duplicates already exist, show the equivalence in the DD.

14.2.2.2 Write for the reader
Assume that the reader is intelligent and co-operative, but constantly ask:

• Is there an easier to understand, alternative expression?
• Are you overloading the reader with too much information at once?
• What is more important, and what is less important to them?
• Is it too abstract without illustration?
• Is it too disconnected without an underlying principle?
• Are any reasonable misinterpretations possible?
• Is there any benefit to the reader in this part?
• What is the feel – formal, stuffy, rambling etc?
• Is the document boring?

14.2.2.3 Select technology carefully

- Use lists (like this!), tables, etc. Lists, sorted and unsorted, are perceived by clients, users and developers alike as a good thing. Clearly it makes sense to number sorted lists. Where references need to be made, unsorted lists can be numbered as well, but otherwise bullet points serve well.
- Allow form to follow content (avoid up-front policy decisions).
- Do not force fit (you do not *have* to use any particular technique).
- Use pre-defined contents lists only as a guide.

14.2.2.4 Organise carefully

The basic principle is:

a place for every thing and every thing in its place.

And there are some serious advantages to be gained from adopting this principle:

- Accidental duplications will be sorted to the same place – where they will be obvious and can be eliminated.
- Omissions will be apparent from the places that contain nothing.

This still leaves the big problem of deciding upon the ordering of the places, but see also Sections 4.8.3 and 5.4.3 on document content and structure.

One further heuristic is to present the general before the particular. Suppose, for example, that a system is required to monitor various sensors; each provides different data but they share common physical characteristics. Present the common characteristics first, and then present the characteristics that are peculiar to each one.

14.2.2.5 Provide navigation clues

- A detailed contents list, cross-references and an index are all useful.

14.2.2.6 Reinforcement, not repetition

- A trade-off – avoid redundancy in general (it can lead to inconsistency and excess bulk) but selective use of overviews, examples etc. can aid understanding.

  Here is an example of where *not* to replicate:

  To exit from the boat details entry screen the user may select quit to return to the main menu or cancel to return to the edit menu.

  ...

  To exit from the race details entry screen the user may select quit to return to the main menu or cancel to return to the edit menu.

This problem is easily avoided. Any common characteristics should be extracted and presented first (the general before the particular), leaving only those unique characteristics to be dealt with separately.

14.2.2.7 Avoid decoy text

Decoy text is Ben Kovitz's (1999) term for text that serves no useful purpose. Remember that there is no minimum word limit for technical documents. Decoy text includes:

- Metatext – text that describes the text. e.g. 'This document is the requirements document for the SkiHi lift controller system' (which should be clear from the title).

- Generalities – e.g. 'All requirements should be testable.' We already know that is a good principle, but is it feasible? And what if it is not?

- Inclusions – do not copy from other documents – reference them.

- Duckspeak – meaningless padding and tautologies. e.g. 'The lift request validation function will validate lift requests.'

14.2.2.8 Layout and fonts

- Use consistently.

- Avoid clutter – use white space.

14.2.2.9 Read what you write

It is rare for the first draft of any text to be particularly good. (The previous sentence is, actually, the third version; it originally started as, 'It is rare for the first attempt at writing . . .', but, for reasons that are hard to pin down, I prefer the revised version.) So, critically examine what you are writing; consider the guidelines that are given above (and any others that you find useful) and, if you do not like it, try changing it. Back when documents were hand-written or typed, such changes were extraordinarily laborious but, thanks to electronic text processing, there really is no excuse now!

14.3 'Unnatural' language

Despite the usefulness of NL, more formal, text-based notations are sometimes advantageous. The principal options are introduced in the following sections. There is a continuum from every day NL, through more constrained text (often called structured English), to languages that are based upon, or closely resemble, executable programming languages (often called pseudo-code) and mathematical notations.

14.3.1 Structured English

Replicated below is the example from Section 12.1.1 (functional decomposition). This is representative of the style that many would call structured English:

2.1	The user is prompted to enter their old PIN	
2.2	The user enters their old PIN	
2.3	If the old PIN is incorrect:	
2.4		The message 'incorrect PIN' is displayed for 4 seconds
2.5		The system returns to the main menu display
2.6	If the old PIN is correct:	
2.7		The user is prompted to enter the new PIN
2.8		etc.

Sentences more or less follow the usual grammatical constructions, but tend to be terse. The structured programming constructs for selection and repetition may be incorporated, by using indentation to show the scope of conditions and loops. A very similar style is often found in the documentation of use-cases.

14.3.2 Pseudo-code

For many years pseudo-code (sometimes shortened to p-code) has been widely used in the low-level idesign of algorithms that implement procedures and methods. However, it is equally useful for specifying behaviour. As an example, here is a rather more 'codey' version of the last example:

```
1   output_message ('enter old PIN')
    input (<user pin>)
    if <user_pin> ≠ <stored_pin> then
        output_message ('incorrect PIN')
        wait (4 seconds)
        goto 1
    else
        output_message ('enter the new PIN')
    etc.
```

As can be seen, this takes formalisation a step further. The syntax may be more precisely defined, and (as a reflection of its origins) there is more widespread adoption of the essential structured programming constructs of sequence, selection and iteration (looping). There have been attempts to standardise pseudo-code, but these are not widely adopted; many organisations have their own, usually quite flexible, in-house style.

Within requirements engineering, a potential problem with p-code is a tendency to go beyond the specification of externally observable behaviour and to incorporate descriptions of the internal workings (in other words, drift into premature idesign). This is not really a problem with p-code *per se* (and it is not unique to p-code) and, provided one remains alert to the hazard, it is easily avoided.

14.3.3 Programming languages

It is a small step from p-code to some compilable languages, and these can also be used to describe behaviour in quite an external way. More common within requirements engineering, however, is the adoption of code-like constructions for data definition. All the common computer languages provide mechanisms for data declaration, and most allow the definition of data types as well. Whilst it has little to do with coding, the same, or similar, constructions can be used for the definition of 'external' data (i.e. problem and solution data – see Section 2.8) that exist within the problem domain and/or form the inputs to and outputs from the solution system.

14.3.4 Backus Naur form (BNF)

Backus Naur form (Naur, 1960, Scowen, 1983) provides a well defined grammar which can help in the production of precise and concise definitions. It is particularly useful for defining syntax. Syntactic definitions are built in a hierarchical manner (either 'top down' or 'bottom up'). At the lowest level are terms (known as terminals, literals or primitives), which are taken to be of self-evident meaning. A terminal is defined literally and is shown enclosed in double quotes, e.g. "A" represents the character A[110].

More complex terms (known as non-terminals) are represented simply as character strings and are defined by way of a defining expression thus:

    non-terminal   ::= defining expression;

where the '::=' sign can be interpreted as 'is defined as' and the semi-colon terminates the definition. The defining expression is constructed from terminals and other, defined non-terminals linked, where necessary, with various logical symbols. A trivial example is:

    my-name   ::= "Ian";

The logical symbols that may be used in the defining expression are shown in Table 14.1.

To see how BNF works in practice, imagine the definition of an interface between a robot arm and its control system. It has been determined that the interface is effected as a dialogue between the control system and the robot arm, and that each exchange is initiated by the control system. We might then define:

    dialogue   ::= {exchange};
    exchange   ::= command, {command}, response;

---

[110] Actually, this is not the original notation but is a common alternative. In the original notation, terminals are shown in plain text and non-terminals are enclosed in angle brackets <>.

Table 14.1

Symbol	Meaning
,	is followed by ('and')
|	exclusive 'or'
{a}	0 or more occurrences of **a** (repeat)
[a]	0 or 1 occurrences of **a** (optionality)
( )	delimits a group

This should be interpreted as: a dialogue consists of zero or more exchanges and each exchange consists of one or more commands followed by a response.

Command and response also require definition:

```
command      ::= instruction, {parameter} ";";
response     ::= ok | not-ok;
```

This should be interpreted as: a command consists of an instruction followed by zero or more parameters and terminated with a semi-colon and a response is either ok or not-ok. The new non-terminals now require definition:

```
instruction  ::= ROT_C | ROT_A | OPEN | CLOSE | etc . . . ;
parameter    ::= integer | real;
ok           ::= "0";
not-ok       ::= "1";
```

and so on:

```
real         ::= integer | fraction | integer, fraction;
fraction     ::= ".", integer;
integer      ::= digit | digit, integer;
digit        ::= "0" | "1" | "2" | . . | "9";
ROT_C        ::= "100";
ROT_A        ::= "101";
. . . etc.
```

Note how the definition is elaborated in more and more detail, until we can express it in terms of terminals such as single characters. For the given example, this would not be the whole story (it would probably be necessary to define the physical incarnation of the signal represented by the digit '0' and so on) but we have certainly moved a long way in the right direction. Another feature of BNF has also been illustrated. Recursive definitions are perfectly in order (as in the definition of 'integer', above).

BNF also supports the notion of the comment, which is usually shown enclosed in brackets and asterisks thus: (* comment *). A comment is an informal definition which is most often used to ascribe meaning to a defined term. For example:

```
ROT_C    ::= (* rotate 1 degree clockwise *);
ROT_A    ::= (* rotate 1 degree anti-clockwise *);
```

This is tantamount to a *designation* (see Section 14.4.1); and sometimes the syntax and semantics are defined separately thus:

```
ROT_C    ::= "10";
         ::= (* rotate 1 degree clockwise *);
```

This combination of a syntactic definition and semantic designation is the only way in which the same term should ever have a double definition.

The ellipsis, '. .', used above in the definition of 'digit', is not standard BNF, but is a commonly used extension of obvious meaning. One other particularly useful extension defines limits to the number of repeats.

```
string    ::= {character}^6;
```

means that a string consists of up to six characters, whereas

```
name      ::= ^4{character}^8;
```

means that a name consists of between four and eight characters.

The addition of extensions and other amendments to the original syntax has resulted in numerous variations on the BNF theme, and these are often known collectively as BNF-like languages. However, they share the same basic principles and, provided that the syntax is defined, they can make a valuable contribution to requirements documentation. Table 14.2 includes some useful extensions and common alternative symbols. (As a matter of interest, the following internet site (as at 04/01) includes BNF definitions of various common computing languages: http://cui.unige.ch/db-research/Enseignement/analyseinfo/AboutBNF.html.)

14.3.5 Predicate calculus

Predicate calculus provides another language for the formal definition of data types and values. In fact, it goes far beyond this in that it also supports the expression of logical statements about data, the relationships between data and the effects of operations upon those data.

As with all definitions, designations are a good place to start and the following mechanism may be used:

```
designation    ≈ designated term
```

Table 14.2

Symbol	Meaning
::=	is defined as
:= or =	is defined as (alternative notations)
,	is followed by ('and')
+	is followed by (an alternative notation)
I	exclusive 'or'
{a}	0 or more occurrences of **a** (repeat)
^{n}{a}	**a** is repeated at least n times
{a}^{m}	**a** is repeated up to m times(inclusive)
^{n}{a}^{m}	**a** is repeated between n and m times (inclusive)
[a]	0 or 1 occurrences of **a** (optionality)
. .	indicates a contiguous range (as in 'a' . . 'z')
( )	delimits a group
(* *)	delimits a comment
/* */	delimits a comment (an alternative notation)
;	terminates a definition

And here is an example of such a designation:

a particular type of boat $\approx$ Boat_class

Formal definitions may be built upon such designations, together with certain pre-defined base types, such as integers and booleans. For the construction of data definitions, predicate calculus provides four constructs:

- sets;
- sequences;
- composites (very similar to records);
- maps (which are used to represent associations).

Herewith, an example of each (by convention, types start with an upper case character, variables with lower case):

boats   = Boat-set   /* the boats within the club are a set of Boats */

Sail_number   = digit*   /* sail_number is a sequence of digits */

inv-Sail_number(sn) $\underline{\Delta}$ $1 \leq \text{len(sn)} \leq 6$ /* of length between 1 and 6 */

```
Boat ::                                    /* a boat has a sail-number and a
       sail-number : Sail_number          boat_class */
       boat-class : Boat_class
Race-entry        = Boat-set ⁻ᵐ Race-set  /* a race entry type is in the map
                                              of boats to races */
```

Predicate calculus can, however, do far more. Boolean expressions, known as predicates, may be used to define constraints and relationships and can even construct formal proofs of correctness.

A predicate is a composed of local variables and operators and (separated with a dot '•') is preceded by a declaration of those variables. For example:

$$\forall \ b, r, s \ \bullet \ (Series\_entry \ (b, s)) \land (Series\_race \ (r, s)) \Rightarrow (Race\_entry \ (b, r))$$

This should be read as: 'for all values of b, r and s, it is the case that, if b is an entry in series s and r is a race in series s, then it follows that b is an entry in race r'. Such an expression could be employed as a formal definition of the fact that entering a series automatically enters a boat in every race in that series.

Within software development, predicate calculus is mainly used within the so-called formal methods, and the topic is pursued a little further in Section 5.5.2.1. Even there it is a case of but scratching the surface of a large subject, but references for further reading are provided.

However, reading (as opposed to writing) specifications in predicate calculus is relatively easy given only the meanings of the special symbols. The list is given in Section 5.5.2.1.

14.4 Means and ends

It is important to have expertise in the various forms of text, but this scarcely addresses the question of what to do with that text. We need to explore further how best that expertise may be applied.

All technical documentation may be viewed as a matter of description or definition. (But it is a fine line between definition and description – one dictionary definition of definition is 'accurate description'). A rough distinction may be made in that definition is taken to indicate a higher degree of precision, characterised by the use of:

- quantification;
- standard constructions (definition mechanisms);
- defined terms.

Michael Jackson (1995) goes further and identifies four types of description:

- designation;
- (formal) definition;
- refutable description;
- rough sketch.

14.4.1   Designation

Designation may be regarded as the definition of fundamental terms. It is the means by which you ascribe relatively precise meaning to the terms that you will use to refer to phenomena of interest. As such, designations can be seen as the foundations upon which all other descriptions are built. Designations take the form of a **recognition rule** that will enable a reasonably informed reader to recognise an instance of the designated phenomenon. For example:

> call-button   ::= (* a press button situated in the foyer outside the lift that can be pressed in order to summon a lift *);

Most ordinary, dictionary 'definitions' are designations; close examination reveals that they always rely upon a common understanding of other terms and, ultimately, tend to be circular. For example[111]; 'object – any thing which can be seen, touched or perceived by any of the senses'. This clearly presumes an understanding of various other terms including 'thing'. But, upon checking, we find that 'thing' is defined as 'any material object'!

There is not a great deal that can be done about this particular problem, but some awareness of the options may help with the forming of designations. The simplest way to designate a term is by *equivalence*; simply stating that it means the same as some other (usually, more widely known) term. For example; **gloaming** – twilight, **parsimonious** – mean.

Explaining the difference between the term in question and something similar can extend this idea. For example; **expensive** – very costly. This approach leads on to the particularly useful, and widely used, definition principles of *classification* and *discrimination*. A class containing the item in question is named and the characteristics that distinguish that item from the rest of the class are described[112]. For example; **sea-dog** – a sailor with many years' experience. The class is 'sailor', the discriminator being that they have 'many years' experience'. The call-button example (above) also adopts this mechanism; a call-button is a type of press button with certain distinguishing characteristics.

Another useful, definition mechanism is the 'sum of parts' or 'component list'. Where the thing in question is an assembly of some kind, it may be defined simply in terms of its constituent parts. This is often the case for data, for example; **boat-details** – the boat's class, sail number, handicap and owner's name.

Finally, we can resort to designation by example, for example (!); **going** – the condition of some thing (e.g. the path was rough going). Here, a (vague) equivalence definition has been beefed-up with an example of usage. Examples,

---

[111] The following and several other definitions are taken from the *Heinemann English Dictionary* (1993).

[112] Definition by *classification* and *discrimination* is long established and can be traced back to the ancient Greeks. You may have noticed that this mechanism resembles the object oriented class/sub-class notion (see pp. 315–16). Because of this, and because of its ancient roots, I refer to it as the 'classic' definition mechanism.

generally, can be most helpful in conveying meaning (although as stand-alone definitions they lack comprehensiveness).

Whatever mechanism is used, designations are inherently informal and inevitably rely upon some pre-existing common understanding. You may feel a little uncomfortable with informality being introduced at the 'foundations' of all description, but it is unavoidable. I could, of course, designate some of the terms in the recognition rule; I could explain what I mean by a 'press button', a 'foyer' and so on but, ultimately, I must rely upon some pre-existing, shared knowledge. Where to stop is a matter of judgement, the guideline being, when you are confident that there will be too little misunderstanding to cause significant problems.

As Michael Jackson points out, there is a big difference between naming things that already exist (typically within the problem domain) and naming things (typically within the solution system) that, as yet, do not (Jackson, 1995). In the first case, we are simply attaching labels to entities or concepts that have a well established existence in their own right. In the latter case, we are attempting to create and convey new concepts, and we run the risk of delivering only vague notions. Even more care is, therefore, needed when designating envisioned phenomena.

There are no rules regarding the construction of recognition rules and lengthy explanations are sometimes required. In practice, however, a few constructions generally suffice and, to summarise, we have various definition mechanisms available, including:

- equivalence (means the same as . . .);
- qualified equivalence (similar to but different in some given way);
- classic (classification + discrimination);
- sum of parts;
- example.

Good designations are vital, but it is a principle of good definition that their number be kept to the minimum. Wherever possible, phenomena (terms) should be formally defined instead.

14.4.2 (Formal) definition

Although the principles can be applied in NL, formal definitions benefit from formal notations and three possibilities were introduced in Section 14.3:

- predicate calculus;
- programming languages;
- BNF.

Relatively few mechanisms are needed (or known), and some can be seen as formalisations of the designation mechanisms described in the previous section. One of the simplest is definition of the phenomenon in terms of its component parts. For example, the stored entity 'boat' might be defined (in BNF) as:

boat   ::= boat-name + sail-number + boat-class-name + helm-name;

where all the elements on the right have been designated. Another mechanism can be applied where the phenomenon is one thing or another. For example:

race-class   ::= boat-class | race-class-name;

Rather more complex are formal definitions of relationships. Suppose it is the case that if a boat enters a series then it is, perforce, entered into every race in that series. We may designate a race entry and a series race (in predicate calculus, see Section 14.3.5) thus[113]:

boat b is entered in series s $\approx$ series-entry (b, s)
race r is part of series s $\approx$ series-race (r, s)

We could also designate a race entry thus:

boat b is entered in race r $\approx$ race-entry (b, r)

But there is an alternative; using the previous designations, we could construct a formal definition of race-entry:

$$\forall\ b,\ r,\ s \bullet (series\text{-}entry\ (b,\ s)) \wedge (series\text{-}race\ (r,\ s)) \Rightarrow (race\text{-}entry\ (b,\ r))$$

This can be read as: for any boat, race and series, if the boat is entered in the series and the race is part of the series, the boat will be entered in the race.

Note that neither designations nor formal definitions can be described as true or false since we are simply stating what we mean by the terms. They can, however, be poorly written, lack clarity and, hence, be open to misunderstanding.

It may also be noted that not all useful information is amenable to formal definition. In the YRR case study, it is stated that the helm is *likely* to be the owner. The interface designer could use this information to make the HMI more efficient, but it cannot be formally defined.

14.4.3 Description

Designations and definitions are a means to an end; they provide the building blocks but they cannot, of themselves constitute useful descriptions.

This is perhaps a good point at which to reflect briefly upon what (within the realm of requirements engineering) must be described. Fundamentally, we

---

[113] It just so happens that with predicate calculus (as opposed to NL and BNF) it is the convention to put the designated term to the right of the designation.

have the problem domain, the requirements (effects that are required to be produced within the problem domain) and the behaviour of the envisioned solution system. This may be generalised to descriptions of:

- systems in terms of their components or sub-systems;
- the relationships between (sub)systems in terms of the shared phenomena (often data flows);
- system behaviour in terms of functions and, ultimately, relationships between inputs and outputs.

There is, as yet, no comprehensive mapping between these various elements to be described and the mechanisms that may be used. However, a few useful constructions may be identified, some of which we have already seen:

- the classic designation mechanism (Section 14.4.1);
- definition in terms of component parts (also in Section 14.4.1);
- the function statement (Section 12.1).

Others, such as a relationship statement and an attribute statement, may be postulated, but this is the subject of future work.

14.4.4 Refutable description

Provided that terms have been carefully designated or defined, we are in a position to construct refutable descriptions; in other words, descriptions, statements or assertions that (unlike designations) are demonstrably false (or not!). You might imagine that this is the case with any description, but it is not so. Unless we are careful, various interpretations are possible and the matter of correctness is obfuscated by questions such as 'it depends what you mean by . . .'.

Provided that I have designated 'boat-class' and 'PY handicap', the following may be regarded as a refutable description:

A boat-class always has an associated PY handicap.

Simply identifying a boat-class without a PY handicap can refute it.

On the other hand, if I do not carefully define what I mean by 'enter', the following statement may not be refutable:

A boat cannot enter the same race twice.

It may well be that an actual boat cannot physically enter a particular race twice but, if I mean that an entry cannot be made into some data processing system twice, then I may (or may not) be wrong. (And does this exclude it being entered thrice?)

Unfortunately, despite the fact that they may constitute a large part of a requirements document, little more advice can be offered regarding the construction of refutable descriptions; it is very much an art. However, some of the style guidelines in Section 14.2.2 (such as, 'are any reasonable misinterpretations possible?') are highly pertinent, and the case studies in this book may be seen as examples of good practice.

14.4.5   Rough sketches

Generally, it is not possible to start with refutable descriptions. In the early stages of analysis we have only a rough idea of what we are talking about but, in order to develop these ideas and gain understanding, we need to document them. This is the role of the rough sketch.

Unfortunately, much documentation never progresses beyond the rough sketch. I have seen many a 'specification' where only the 'overview' was ever written. Some developers have grown so used to this that they do not appreciate how damaging it can be.

Like elicitation notes, rough sketches are, then, to be regarded as temporary or work in progress. They may be refined into precise descriptions, or they may exist alongside precise descriptions as these are developed. They may be kept to aid traceability, or they may be discarded but, in any case, they have a very limited role in the final documentation.

14.5   Data dictionary

As we have seen (Section 14.4.1), one of the most important aspects of description, is a common understanding of the meaning of terms. It is fair (and only practical) to assume that your readers will know what you mean by most everyday words but, within any problem domain, there will appear many specialist terms, and some commonplace words can take on a specialist meaning. To avoid problems, any such terms should be defined. (The glossary – see p. 394 – is an embodiment of this principle.)

Amongst the many things that require definition are the data that are associated with the problem and its solution. This includes entities and their attributes, as well as the inputs and outputs associated with the solution system. It is common practice to gather all these definitions in one place and such a collection is usually called a data dictionary (DD). In fact, it is almost as common to include the definitions of other elements (such as terminators and relationships). The name 'glossary' may, therefore, be preferred. Several examples of DDs may be found in the case studies.

Part 3
Case studies

This section provides, more or less complete, requirements documentation for the main case studies that have been used throughout this book.

To save space and avoid unnecessary repetition, there is an elicitation plan only for the first, elicitation notes for the first two and 'document details' (authorship, change history, content, etc.) have been omitted in all cases. The principal documents (the requirements document and specification) are, however, provided for each case.

Within the parameters of good documentation, different styles and technology have been deliberately adopted in the examples, in order to convey some of the 'natural variation' that can occur. The danger remains that each example illustrates just one way in which particular problems might be addressed. There are many alternatives that could be regarded as equally good, and so you should not be tempted to follow any examples slavishly.

It is also the case that examples are constrained in size and number and may not match closely with any real-life problems. Nonetheless, examples can prove very helpful when it comes to applying the general principles and guidelines, and so here they are.

The yacht racing results (YRR) case study　**15**

15.1　Elicitation plan

Only the plan for the first of a series of (imaginary) interviews is given here.

> Interview with primary contact, sailing secretary of Dartchurch sailing club, Dave Rowntree. To be held at their place on 6/6/00.
>
> From phone conversation, we know they are after a 'cheap' (!) PC-based system to calculate results of yacht races.
> Establish basic problem.
> Establish role of DR – is anyone else involved?
> Investigate financial aspects.
> How (in outline !) does it work now?
> What are the current problems?
> What are they looking to achieve?

15.2　Elicitation notes

Notes for just one of a series of (imaginary) interviews are given here. A move to simulate the poorly ordered and presented nature of such notes has been made, but there is some compromise towards comprehensibility!

Interview with David Rowntree, sailing secretary, Dartchurch sailing club (DSC) 6th June.

Basic scenario - They have an old spare PC, reckons they could use it to help work out race results. Currently all done by hand.

DR well experienced in the process (frequently worked out results, etc. himself). Probably knows as much as anyone here but Jim Lock bit of a technical whizz if needed.

Cagey about money side - really wants to know "how much it would cost?". Advised that after today's session, we'll give quotes for basic system and "all singing" one.

Current system:-

Sailors enter boats on race sheet prior to race (at least 1 hour).

The "OOD" (Officer of the Day!) takes race sheet out on "committee boat" to start race (or sheets - one per race and they often have several starting one after the other). Some "race officers" (proper name for OOD!) allow entries at the start (not really allowed but it's up to them). At end of race RO enters finish times of boats on race sheet. (No start time per boat - all start at same time.) Details on sheet are:- boat name, sail number, class, helm name (the helm is the one sailing it). Mostly optional - only really need sail number and class.

Back at club, RO works out results and enters on results sheet (see attached copy). (May leave it to class captains (CCs).) Easy for OD (one design classes) tedious for handicap classes (which are?!). Some races for one type of boat, others for different types! For 2nd sort, finish times adjusted by handicaps. For ODs, just put in finishing order. (So don't actually need finish times for those (!) - just positions.)

Handicap is a multiplier for elapsed time (ET = finish time – start time). Based on RYA (Royal Yachting Association) lists (copy on race notice board). RO can refer to list but usually knows. Example - start at 12:00, finish at 13:14:22 (to nearest second, note!) - elapsed time = 1:14:22. Convert to seconds – 4462, then elapsed time = finish time × 1000/handicap. (And there's another, similar, way of doing it - worry about that later!)

Results are written up on results sheet and posted on race notice board. May be right after race (more or less) or may be a week later (if RO is lax) (avoiding delays is a potential plus here).

Boats may not finish a race - could be DNF (did not finish) or RTD (retired). (What's the difference? - we needn't worry!)

Quantities:- about 200 boats in club. Each class, 2 or 3 races per week, about 10 boats per race (max, say 30). 7 classes of boat but some classes are "open". (Same as handicap classes!) Different classes of boat may enter handicap races. (Eh?????) So, some classes of race are for one class of boat (the OD classes), others are for several classes of boat (handicap classes). Actually about 20 classes of <u>boat</u>. (7 classes of <u>race</u>!!)

Interested in system printing out race entry forms with race details. ROs can then enter results into system and it will print out result sheets.

(There are some "oddities" regarding the race results sheet:-

DARTCHURCH SAILING CLUB

RACE RECORD SHEET

DATE ....   Series ....   Cup ....   WIND ....   START ....

CLASS ....   COURSE ....

YACHT	OWNER	Recall	Finish			Elapsed time			PYN	Corrected time			Place	Points	Overall		NOTES
		no.	hr	min	sec	hrs	min	sec		hr	min	sec			Place	Points	

Figure 15.1

"Recall no." is just another name for "sail number"
The "PYN" column is used for PY <u>and</u> TMF handicaps
The corrected time is seconds (not hrs, mins and secs)
The "overall" column isn't used.

Otherwise, it's just fine!)
   And there are <u>series of races</u> but out of time - follow up next
week 10:00 Thursday - same place.

15.3   Requirements document

15.3.1   Problem domain description

15.3.1.1   Introduction
The YRR program is required to assist in the calculation of the results of sailing races. All data regarding boats, races, etc., is entered by the user of the system, and the system will produce results sheets for the races and for series of races.

15.3.1.2   Problem frame
This is a simple information system and is shown in Figure 15.2.

15.3.1.3   Boats
Each boat has a:

- boat name;
- boat class name;
- sail number;
- helm (i.e. the person who usually sails it).

15.3.1.4   Classes
Within yacht racing, the term 'class' is used loosely. There are actually two meanings:

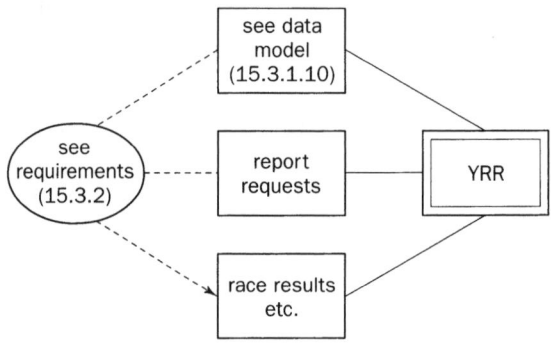

Figure 15.2

- A boat class is a type of boat (all boats of the same class are, within specified limits, the same). Each boat class will have a:
  - boat class name;
  - handicap type;
  - handicap value.
- A race class indicates the types of boat that may enter a race. Races are either one-design or handicap. In one-design, all competing boats are of the same boat class, and the race class name *will be* a boat class. In handicap races, different boat classes may enter, and the race class name will not be the same as any boat class. Each race class will have:
  - a race class type ('one-design' or 'handicap');
  - a race class name;

  and for handicap race classes only a:

  - handicap type;
  - minimum handicap;
  - maximum handicap.

15.3.1.5 Handicaps

Handicaps are used to adjust race times (see Section 15.3.1.7). There are two handicap systems (or handicap types); PY and TMF. For each type, any given boat may have a handicap value.

- PY handicap values consist of a four digit integer and the corrected time is defined as:

  corrected time ::= elapsed time × 1000 / PY handicap value

- TMF handicap values consist of a three digit decimal (e.g. .977) and the corrected time is defined as:

  corrected time ::= elapsed time × TMF handicap value

In either case, the corrected time is rounded to the nearest second (.5 is rounded up).

15.3.1.6 Races

In one-design races, competing boats race 'level'. That is, they start at the same time and their finishing order determines the result. In handicap races, boats of different classes may compete. They also start at the same time, but their finishing times are adjusted using their handicaps in order to determine the results. Each race has a:

- race class name;
- race date;
- start time.

It may also have a:

- race name;
- a course.

15.3.1.7 Race outcome calculation

For each race that it enters, a boat will have a result which may be:

- DNS   did not start;
- OCS   on course side (i.e. wrong side) of line at start;
- DNF   did not finish;
- RTD   retired after starting;
- DSQ   disqualified;

or it will finish the race.

For one-design races, each finishing boat will have a finish position (1st, 2nd, 3rd, etc.)

For handicap races, each finishing boat has a finish time. For each boat, an elapsed time, in seconds, is calculated as the difference between the race start time (all boats in a race have the same start time) and the boat's finish time. The elapsed times are then adjusted by the boats' handicaps (see 'handicaps' above) to give the corrected times; these are then used to work out the positions, the lowest time being 1st, etc. Where corrected times are equal, boats tie for the place, as shown in Table 15.1.

15.3.1.8 Race series

A race may be part of a series, a series consisting of two or more races for the same race class. For each series, there is a 'number of races to count' which is usually about two thirds of the number of races in the series (but is actually entered by the user). Each series has a:

- series name;
- race class name;
- number of races;
- number of races to count.

Table 15.1

corrected time	place
3234	1st
3255	2nd =
3255	2nd =
3378	4th

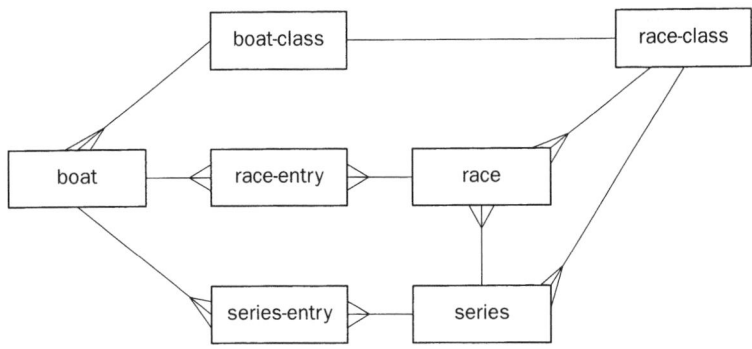

Figure 15.3

15.3.1.9   Series outcome calculation

To calculate the outcome of the series, boats are awarded points for each race in the series. Each finishing boat is given points equal to their position (i.e. the first boat gets one point, the second boat gets two points, etc.). Boats that entered but did not finish a race (DNS, OCS, etc.) are awarded one point more than the number of boats that enter the *series* (i.e. the number of boats that have a result, other than DNS, for at least one race in the series).

Each boat's lowest scores for the 'number of races to count' are aggregated. For example, if 7 out of 10 races count, a boat's lowest 7 are totalled and the rest are discarded. The boats are then placed in ascending order of points, and the boat with the lowest score wins and so on. In the event of a tie, the boat with the highest number of first places (or, if still a tie, second places, etc.) is favoured.

15.3.1.10   Data model

The data model is shown in Figure 15.3.

15.3.1.11   Data dictionary

boat	::= boat-name, boat-class-name, sail-number, helm-name;
boat-name	::= {alphanumeric}^{25};
boat-class-name	::= ^{1}{alphanumeric}^{10};
sail-number	::= ^{1}{digit}^{6};
helm-name	::= {alphanumeric}^{25};
boat-class	::= boat-class-name, handicap-type, handicap-value;
handicap-type	::= "PY" | "TMF";
handicap-value	::= ^{3}{digit}^{4};
race-class	::= race-class-type, race-class-name, [handicap-type, minimum-handicap, maximum handicap];

race-class-type	::= "one-design" | "handicap";
race-class-name	::= boat-class-name | $^1\{$alphanumeric$\}^{25}$;
minimum-handicap	::= handicap;
maximum-handicap	::= handicap;
race	::= race-class-name, race-date, start-time, [race-name, course];
race-date	::= day, ":", month, ":", year;
start-time	::= hour, ":", minute;
race-name	::= $^1\{$alphanumeric$\}^{25}$;
course	::= $\{$alphanumeric$\}^{25}$;
race-entry	::= boat-class-name, sail-number, race-class, race-date, race-time, [result];
result	::= "DNS" | "OCS" | "DNF" | "RTD" | "DSQ" | race-position | finish-time;
race-position	::= $^1\{$digit$\}^3$;
finish-time	::= hour, ":", minute, ":", second";
elapsed-time	::= $^1\{$digit$\}^5$; (* in seconds*)
corrected-time	::= $^1\{$digit$\}^5$; (* in seconds*)
race-outcome	::= race, $\{$boat-name, sail-number, [handicap-value, finish-time, elapsed-time,] position$\}$; (* handicap-values and times are only shown for handicap races *)
series	::= series-name, race-class-name, number-of-races, number of-races-to-count;
series-name	::= $^1\{$alphanumeric$\}^{25}$;
number-of-races	::= $^1\{$digit$\}^2$;
number-of-races-to-count	::= $^1\{$digit$\}^2$;
series-entry	::= boat-class-name, sail-number, series-name;
boat-class-list	::= $\{$boat-class$\}$;
boat-list	::= $\{$boat$\}$;
series-list	::= $\{$series$\}$;
series-outcome	::= series $\{$race-number, race-date $\{$boat-name, sail-number, points$\}$, total-points, series-position$\}$;
total-points	::= $^1\{$digit$\}^3$; (* total points, after discards, in the series *)
series-position	::= $^1\{$digit$\}^3$;
day	::= "01" . . "31";
month	::= "01" . . "12";
year	::= "1900" . . "2999";
hour	::= "00" . . "23";
minute	::= "00" . . "59";
second	::= "00" . . "59";
alphanumeric	::= "a" . . "z" | "A" . . "Z" | "0" . . "9" | "-" | "'" | "." ;

15.3.2   Requirements

15.3.2.1   Data entry and output

R1   Subject to the constraints detailed below, the user can enter, amend and delete details of: boat-class, boat, race, series, race-entry, series-entry.

R2   A boat cannot be entered into the system unless it has a boat-class and sail-number.

R3   A boat may only be entered into a one design race (or series) if its boat-class matches the race-class.

R4   A boat may only be entered into a handicap race (or series) if its handicap-type matches that of the race and its handicap-value is within the (inclusive) range specified by the minimum and maximum handicaps.

R5   A boat that enters a series is automatically entered into every race in the series.

R6   If a boat's details are amended, this will not automatically affect the outcome of any races where the boat's result has already been entered, but the user may opt for the race (or series) outcome to be recalculated.

R7   The outcome for races and series should be available (for reports) as soon as the relevant data are entered, but for incomplete series, the outcome will be shown without any discards being made.

R8   Upon command from the user, the system will produce the following reports (content as defined in the DD):

R8.1   boat-class-list

R8.2   boat-list

R8.3   series-list

R8.4   series-details

R8.5   series-outcome

R8.6   race-outcome

R9   All reports will be output to screen and may also be printed upon user request.

15.3.2.2   Performance

Speed

R10   The system should respond to all user input within one second and, subject to printer speed, should produce a series outcome report for a series with 10 races and 50 boats entered within five seconds.

Capacity

R11 The system should handle at least the following capacities:

R11.1   99 boat classes

R11.2   999 boats

R11.3   999 races

R11.4   999 series

Reliability

R12 This is not a critical system but it should be available at least 20 hours per week and, subject to usual back-up practice, should not lose data.

Usability

R13 To save user effort, wherever possible, the most likely values for data should be presented during data entry, for example:

- where boat-details are being entered, it is likely that a boat will have the same class as the last one entered;

- where races are being added to a series, it is likely that all races in the series will have the same start-time.

R14 All data should be validated as soon as practicable after entry, and the user should be advised of any errors.

R15 A WIMP type interface is required.

15.3.2.3   Platform

R16 The system should operate upon a JCN compatible PC under the Fenestra 99 operating system.

15.4   Specification

[Note: to save space, document details (change history, etc.) have been omitted and the requirements and the DD have not been copied from the requirements document.]

The YRR system is intended to assist in the calculation of the results of sailing races. All necessary data regarding boats, race entries, etc., is entered by the user and, upon request, various reports about race entries, results, etc., are produced. It is a single user system and will operate under Fenestra 99. A description of the problem domain and a list of requirements are to be found in the YRR requirements document.

15.4.1 The user interface

There is only one interface to YRR, that to the user. The interface adopts a WIMP style. The detailed operation is described for the 'classes' window; the other option windows (boats, races, etc.) operate in a similar way.

15.4.1.1 Invocation and the main window

Once YRR has been installed upon the target machine it may be invoked by the usual Fenestra 99 mechanisms (see *Fenestra 99 User Manual*). Upon invocation, the user is presented with the main YRR window (see Figure 15.4). Generally, the main window will be overlaid with option windows (see figure) in the position indicated by the dashed line.

15.4.1.2 The data location window

Upon invocation, YRR will check whether it has an existing data store. If not the data location window is laid over the main window as shown in Figure 15.5.

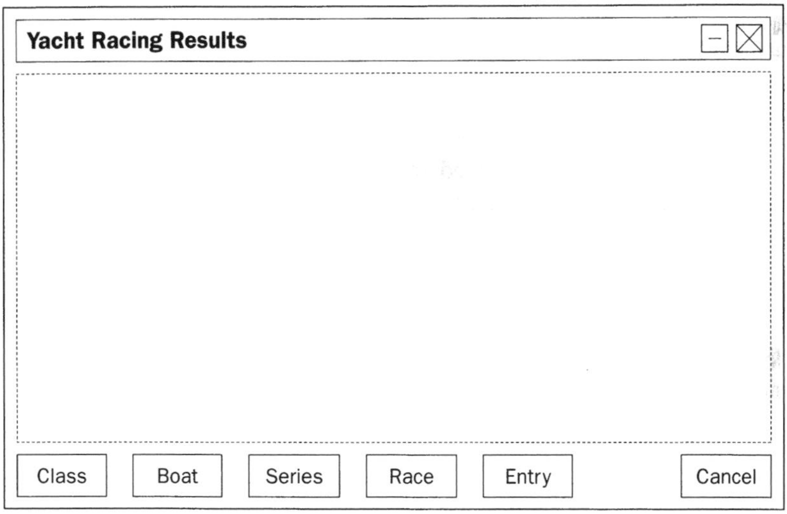

Figure 15.4

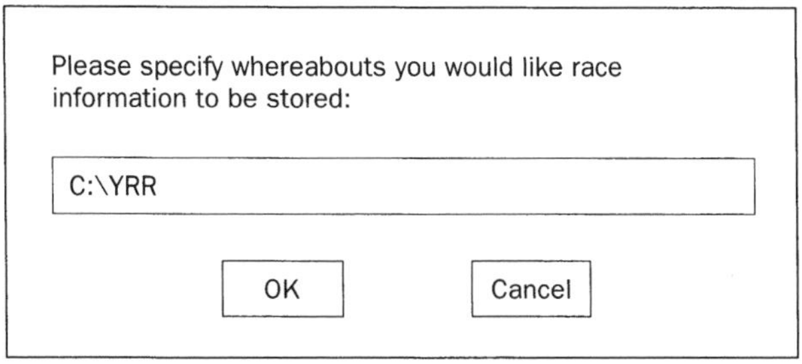

Figure 15.5

Dialogue:

1   if desired

        the user overwrites the default (i.e. C:\YRR) data location

     the user selects either:

        cancel

           exit program

or   ok

        if the data location is valid

           the data location window is removed

        else

           message: invalid data location, please re-enter

           goto 1

15.4.1.3 Option navigation

The user can select their required option by clicking on the buttons at the bottom of the main window. This will cause the option window to be displayed, overlaying (and centred upon) the main window and overlaying any other visible windows. Option windows are of fixed size and fixed location (relative to the main window) such that the main window option buttons are always visible.

The five option windows are:

- class
- boat
- race
- series
- entry

and the user may opt to move from any option window to any other option window at any time.

There is also a results window (see Figure 15.6) but this can only be accessed via the series window (see Section 15.4.1.7).

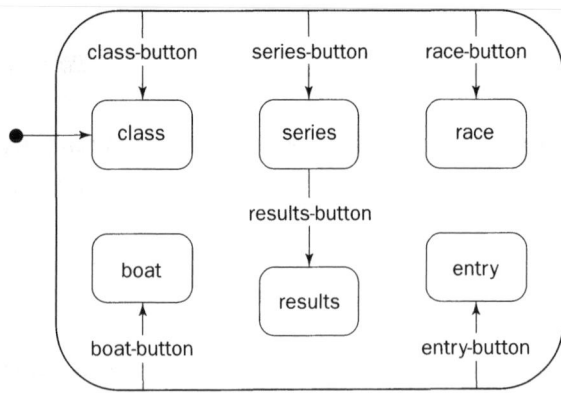

Figure 15.6

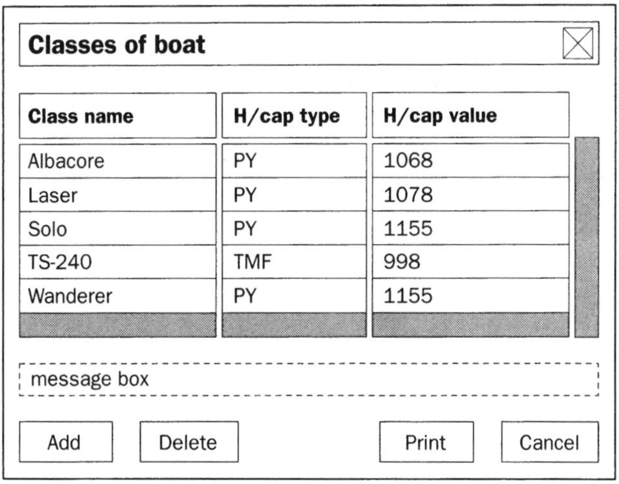

Classes of boat

Class name	H/cap type	H/cap value
Albacore	PY	1068
Laser	PY	1078
Solo	PY	1155
TS-240	TMF	998
Wanderer	PY	1155

message box

| Add | Delete | | Print | Cancel |

Figure 15.7

Normally, the option windows will simply overlay each other with the most recently selected option being on top. The user may, however, choose to close a window by clicking the close-button in the top right corner.

If, during an invocation of the application, a window is closed and then re-opened, it will retain the same appearance unless editing within another window has affected its content. In particular:

- If a series is deleted, then all races for that series will have been deleted.
- If the races window is showing a particular series, then a change of selected series in the series window will be reflected in the races window (and similarly for the results window).

15.4.1.4 Class
This option allows the user to edit details of boat classes.

Figure 15.7 The classes window

- This drawing is to scale (within an acceptable tolerance of +/– 10%).
- Six lines for classes are always displayed: unused lines are 'greyed out'.
- The last line is kept blank (greyed out) to allow for additions (see below).
- If more than five classes are entered, the scroll bar (on the right) becomes active.
- Column width may be adjusted by picking and dragging the column separators.
- There is a minimum column width of one character.
- Entries may be sorted by any column. The required sorting column is selected by clicking on its heading (e.g. 'Class name').
- The message box is visible only when a message is on display.

Class editing

The usual WIMP type editing mechanisms may be used (e.g. highlight and delete, paste, over type, etc.). A field entry is invalid if it does not comply with the type definition (given in the DD) or, in the case of the class name, if it is not unique.

Editing of a field (i.e. one column of one row), is terminated by:

- pressing the return or enter key (which also moves the cursor down one row);
- pressing the tab or shift/tab keys (which also moves the cursor forward or back one field);
- clicking to move the cursor out of the field.

An attempt to terminate entry of invalid field data or a complete entry (row) will result in an error message and the cursor will be constrained to the relevant, invalid field.

Possible error messages for class editing:

- No more classes may be added (maximum 99).
- The class name must be letters, digits, -, ' or . (max 25 characters).
- The class name must be unique.
- The handicap type must be PY or TMF.
- The handicap-value must be three or four digits (no decimal point required).
- This class cannot be deleted as it is in use.

Messages are displayed until a valid entry is completed, or another message over-writes, or 'Cancel' is selected.

The 'Cancel' button may be selected to 'undo' editing of the current entry. If it is a new entry then no entry will be added. If an existing entry is being edited then it will revert to the previous values.

To add a class entry, the last (greyed out) line is over-written (and, upon completion, a new, blank (greyed out) line will be created). The user may either move the cursor to this line, or click the 'Add' button which will automatically scroll to this last (blank) line and place the cursor in the first field.

To delete a class entry the user must highlight the whole line (either by click and drag or by clicking just to the left of the class name). They can then click the 'Delete' button (or type cntrl x).

If the handicap type or value for a particular class is changed and there are one or more boats assigned to that class, any of which have one or more race entries, then a pop up window appears:

```
┌─────────────────────────────────────────┐
│                                          │
│   Do you want this handicap change to:   │
│                                          │
│   take effect now  ☐                     │
│                                          │
│   be backdated to  │ <date> │   ☐        │
│                                          │
└─────────────────────────────────────────┘
```

The user may, optionally, over-write the default date (today) and then click the 'now' box or the 'backdate' box. All races on or after the chosen date will then have their results (re)calculated according to the new handicap.

To print the class listing, the user clicks on the 'Print' button. The report is headed:

Classes of boats   **< date>**

(where <date> is the current system date). Below this, the column (field) headings are printed (and, if the report extends over more than one page, are repeated at the top of subsequent pages) followed by the classes, listed as displayed.

15.4.1.5 Boats

This option allows the user to edit details of boats.

The boats window

The boats window is similar to the classes window (see above) but is wider (approx. seven inches), is headed 'Boats' and displays columns (fields) under the headings:

Boat name, Class, Sail number, Helm

Boat editing

Boat entry editing is similar to class entry editing. Both the boat name and helm name fields are optional and may be left blank. The most significant difference concerns entry of the 'class' field. Whenever this field is selected, a scrollable, 'drop down' menu appears, listing five of the registered class names (in alphabetical order) and centred upon the name of the class of the *previous entry in the boats list*. An example is given in Figure 15.8.

(If there is no previous entry (i.e. it is the first boat in the list) then the first five classes (padded out with blanks if necessary) are listed). The user may then scroll up and down the list as necessary and select the required entry by clicking upon it. If the required boat class is not registered, the user must select the classes option (from the main window) to add the boat class, before proceeding with the boat entry. (Alternatively, they must cancel the boat entry.)

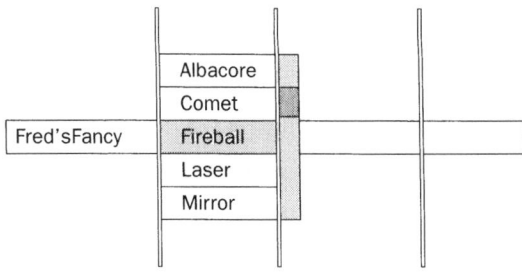

Figure 15.8

Possible error messages for boat editing:

- The boat name must be letters, digits, -, ' or . (max 25 characters).
- The sail number must be digits (max six).
- The sail number must be unique (within the class).
- The helm name must be letters, digits, -, ' or . (max 25 characters).
- This boat cannot be deleted as it is entered in races.

15.4.1.6   Series

This option allows the user to edit details of series (of races).

The series window

The series window is similar to the classes window (see above) but is headed 'Series' and displays columns (fields) under the headings:

Series name, OD/H, Class, #Races, #RTC

It also has an additional 'Results' button (at the bottom of the window). This allows the user to view (and print), but not edit, the results of the currently selected series (see Section 15.4.1.7).

Series entry editing

Series entry editing is similar to class entry editing but with certain exceptions.

- The OD/H column accepts entries of 'OD' (or 'od') or 'H' (or 'h') and indicates whether the series is one design or handicap.
- If the series is one design, then the selection of race class operates in exactly the same way as the selection of boat class for a boat (see p. 351).
- If the series is handicap, then the user enters their chosen race class name.
- The #RTC column shows the number of races to count. This must be less than or equal to the number of races (#Races) and, if the #Races has been entered first, a default equal to two thirds (rounded to the nearest integer) of #Races is displayed (but may be overwritten if required).

Possible error messages for series editing:

- The series name must be letters, digits, -, ' or . (max 25 characters).
- The series name must be unique.
- The OD/H entry must be OD or H.
- The race class must be letters, digits, -, ' or . (max 25 characters).
- The number of races must be between 2 and 99.
- The number of races to count cannot exceed the number of races.
- Warning – if this series is deleted, all its race details will be lost.

15.4.1.7   Series results

This option allows users to view and print the results of series.

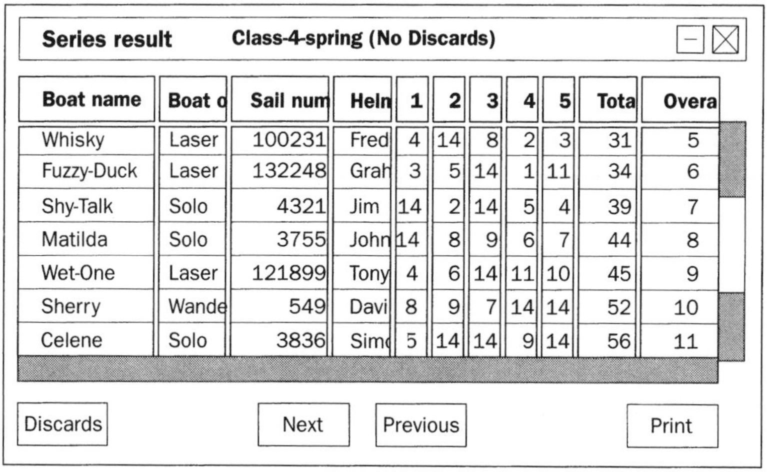

Series result	Class-4-spring (No Discards)									⊟ ⊠

Boat name	Boat c	Sail num	Heln	1	2	3	4	5	Tota	Overa
Whisky	Laser	100231	Fred	4	14	8	2	3	31	5
Fuzzy-Duck	Laser	132248	Grah	3	5	14	1	11	34	6
Shy-Talk	Solo	4321	Jim	14	2	14	5	4	39	7
Matilda	Solo	3755	John	14	8	9	6	7	44	8
Wet-One	Laser	121899	Tony	4	6	14	11	10	45	9
Sherry	Wande	549	Davi	8	9	7	14	14	52	10
Celene	Solo	3836	Sim	5	14	14	9	14	56	11

Discards		Next	Previous		Print

Figure 15.9

The series results window

This window (Figure 15.9) displays the columns under the headings:

Boat name, Boat class, Sail number, Helm, {Points}, Total, Overall

- There are as many points columns as there are races in the series. These are headed '1', '2', etc. and show the points awarded for each race.
- The Discards button allows the user to toggle between showing the results with the discards applied (i.e. only totalling best (lowest) points for the number of races to count) or with no discards (i.e. all races totalled).
- The title bar displays the currently selected series and whether or not discards are applied.
- This window (only) has a horizontal (as well as vertical) scroll bar.

Series results editing

Columns can be re-sized and the entries re-sorted as described for the class window. However, it is not possible, in this window, to edit the values that are displayed. The Next and Previous buttons allow the user to scroll through series of races (which are in the order currently sorted in the series window).

The user may select a race within this window (by drag-highlighting or clicking the left end of the relevant row). If the Entry option is then selected (from the main window) this will allow the entries for that race to be edited (see p. 355). The Print button allows the results to be printed as displayed (except that all entries will be printed).

15.4.1.8   Race

This option allows the user to set up details of races.

The races window

The races window is similar to the classes window (see above) but is wider (approx. seven inches), is headed 'Races' and displays columns (fields) under the headings:

OD/H, Race class, Race date, Start time, Race name, Course

The user may select to show:

- all races that do not belong to a series;
- races in the currently selected series (as selected in the series window – the default being the first race as currently sorted).

The selection is made from a drop down menu that appears in the races window title bar:

Races	Non-series races	☒
	Selected races	

If the user picks 'selected series', it is the name of the actual series that is then displayed in the title bar (otherwise, 'Non-series races' is displayed).

Race editing

Race entry editing is similar to class entry editing but with certain exceptions.

- The date and course fields are optional; and can be left blank.

If races for a selected series are being shown, then:

- All races inherit their type (OD or H) and their class from the series to which they belong (these fields can be changed only in the series window).
- The number of races listed is always the number of races in the series.
- The races are always listed in date order (if dates are not entered, the order is immaterial).
- The race name column defaults to showing the race number (within the series) which cannot be edited. The first (top) race is number 1 and the others are numbered consecutively.
- Once the time for a race has been entered, all others *below* it in the list will default to the same time (but can be over-written).

When non-series races are being displayed, then:

- The race class is entered for each race in the same way as for a series (see p. 352).

  Possible error messages for race editing:

- The race name must be letters, digits, -, ' or . (max 25 characters).
- The race name must be unique.

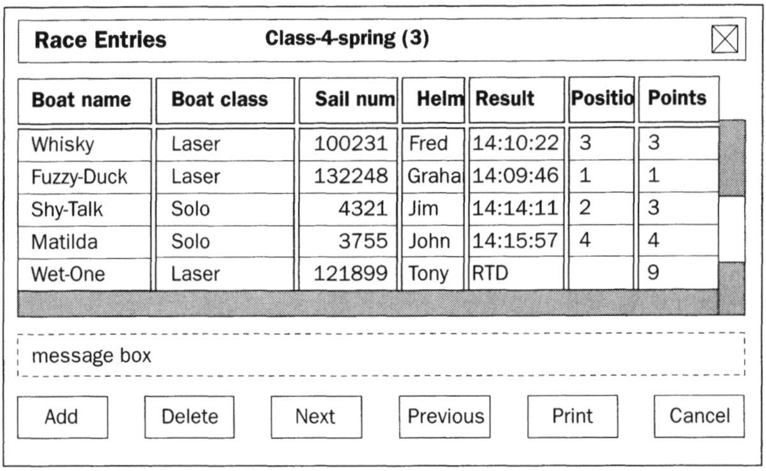

Race Entries		Class-4-spring (3)					⊠
Boat name	**Boat class**	**Sail num**	**Helm**	**Result**	**Positio**	**Points**	
Whisky	Laser	100231	Fred	14:10:22	3	3	
Fuzzy-Duck	Laser	132248	Graha	14:09:46	1	1	
Shy-Talk	Solo	4321	Jim	14:14:11	2	3	
Matilda	Solo	3755	John	14:15:57	4	4	
Wet-One	Laser	121899	Tony	RTD		9	

message box

Add	Delete	Next	Previous	Print	Cancel

Figure 15.10

- The OD/H entry must be OD or H.
- The race class must be letters, digits, -, ' or . (max 25 characters).
- Warning – if this race is deleted, all its race details will be lost.

15.4.1.9   Entry

This option allows the user to enter boats into races and enter their results. It is also used to enter boats into series of races because, if the selected race is a member of a series, then an entry is taken to apply to all races in the series.

The race entry window

The race entry window (Figure 15.10) displays columns (fields) under the following headings:

Boat name, Boat class, Sail number, Helm, Result, Position, Points

This window displays entries for the currently selected race, the default being the first race in the currently selected series or, if non-series races are selected (see p. 352), the first non-series race. For a non-series race, the title bar displays the race name; for a series race it displays the series name and race number (as per the example above). The Next and Previous buttons allow the user to scroll through the races in the currently selected series (or non-series races).

Race entry editing

Race entry editing is similar to class entry editing but with certain exceptions:

- If the race is a one design race, all entries default to the relevant class name (which cannot be edited).
- Boats may be entered by boat name, by helm name or by class and sail number.

- If the boat name does not unambiguously identify a boat that is eligible for the race (non-unique boat names are allowed), a drop down list of the sail numbers of possible entries is displayed and the user must select accordingly.
- Entry by helm name operates in the same way.
- During entry of the result field, the system will complete any alpha entries (DNS, OCS, etc.) as soon as they are recognisable.
- For a one design race, the result must be alpha entries (as above) or must be a position (1 to 999).
- For a handicap race, the result must be alpha entries or be a finish time (HH:MM:SS). (Note, a finish time that is earlier than the race start time will be interpreted as relating to the following day.)
- If entries are sorted by result or position, numbers (lowest at the top) will head the list followed by any alpha entries (in alphabetical order).
- Position and points column entries cannot be edited; these are calculated by the program.

Possible error messages for entry editing:

- The entered boat class and sail number are not recognised.
- The result must be a position (1 to 999).
- The result must be a time (HH:MM:SS).
- Are you sure? This finish time is >100% above/below average.

The lift controller case study

16

Note that this case study is entirely fictional and doubtless over-simplifies real lift systems.

16.1 Elicitation notes

Notes for just one of a series of (imaginary) interviews are given here. A move to simulate the poorly ordered and presented nature of such notes has been made, but there is some compromise towards comprehensibility!

Client - skyhi elevator co. Contact (technical) Jason Hukins 01202 489345, X 4783. I/v 15/6.

Previous s/w contractor unsatisfactory. (Late and buggy!) Full h/w details available. Looking for full spec by 1/10. Will pay instalment for spec and negotiate for the rest (Andy can cover this - needs to contact Geoff Shepperd (finance director).) H/w all to hand - full specs available (got copies). Interface blocks all operate at 0-5 V (20 mA) - direct port connection no prob.

Max 4 lifts per controller, max 20 floors. One lift per shaft (next generation won't be !). All lifts, same # of floors.

Requirements:-
All lifts (if >1) to be used approximately equally.

Lift only reverses direction if no outstanding lift calls in current direction (lift send-button inside lift, lift call-button outside lift !)

Must not change motor polarity whilst moving ! (It'll blow.)
In emergency, stop all motors (if poss.).

Lift calls should be serviced by the lift that will get there soonest (approx.). Tricksy to predict - could pick up more calls on the way.

Services calls in the order it gets there - not the order they are made.

Indicators: -
Light for each floor - one set in each lift + one set on each floor
(all switch together - can treat as one set).
Switch on basis of nearest floor so one off, one on when about
half way between.

Sensors: -
3 sets for each floor - warning either side + at. Go hi (5 V) when
lift present (i.e. 20 cm either side). If stopping, send slow signal
to motor within 0.3 secs of warning and stop 0.2 +/- 0.1 secs
after at signal. (Stop delay has to be configurable.) Top and
bottom floors only have one set of warning sensors. (Obviously?)

Lift must always stop when arriving at top or bottom !
Lift normally moves at 1.2 m/sec. In slow mode, 0.3 m/sec. Takes
approx. 1 sec to slow (i.e. about 0.75 m) and moves about 0.15 m
between stop signal and actually stopping.
   Lift will stop at a floor if there is a lift-send or a lift call *and*
moving right way or if top/bottom. - **R**

Doors: -
Doors cycle every time it stops. (Note - cannot *cancel* a
request.)
   Controller only needs to send open/close signal - doors
handle the rest. Door sensors (just the one pair per lift) go hi
when shut/open. *Never move lift with doors open!* -**R**
   Also one block sensor per door but connects direct to door
controller - we don't need to worry.
   If lift call or send request while doors open or closing, open
again and restart wait. (Wait is 4 secs +/- 0.5.) -**R**
   Note max pins - each lift fast, slow, direction (3 out) + sensors, (#floors x 3) –2 (all in) + indicators (#floors, out) + doors,
close/open + closed/opened (2 out, 2 in).
   To start lift go straight to fast, to stop must go to slow first
(except in emergency? - he'll check). -**R**
   Next wed - 10:00 - ring on Tue to confirm.

16.2 Requirements document

16.2.1 Problem domain

16.2.1.1 Overview

A software-based system is required to control lifts (elevators) manufactured by
Skyhi Lifts. Lifts are constrained to shafts (one lift per shaft) and are moved up
and down by winding motors (one winding motor per lift).

   Users can call a lift to a floor by pressing buttons outside the lift (call-buttons)
and can send lifts to a floor by pressing buttons inside the lift (send-buttons).
There are indicators to show the users the current floor of each lift.

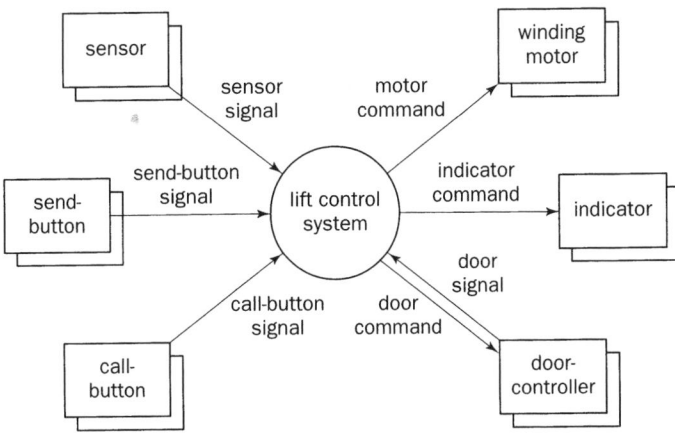

Figure 16.1

Context diagram (Figure 16.1)

All signals to and from the lift system components are via electric cables. All signals operate upon a hi/lo basis where hi is within the range 3–5 V and lo is < 1 V. Maximum draw-down current is 20 mA. All input signals (i.e. from the terminators to the control system) may take up to 10 milliseconds to stabilise within the specified ranges.

16.2.1.2   Problem frame

The problem frame is shown in Figure 16.2. (It may be supposed that there is also a relationship between users and the door mechanism, since the doors can

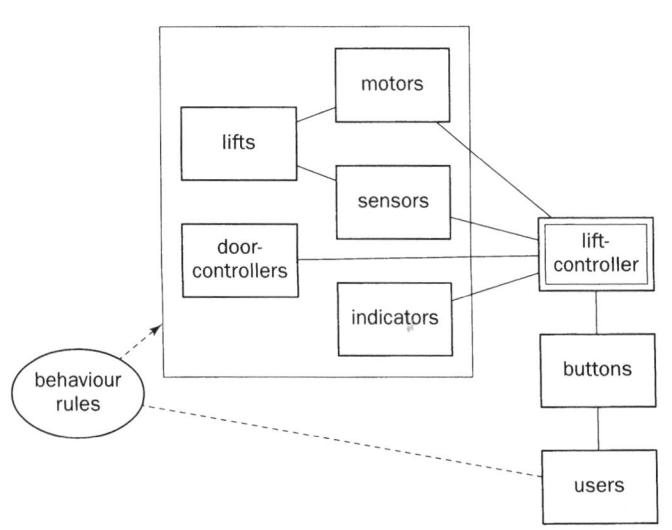

Figure 16.2

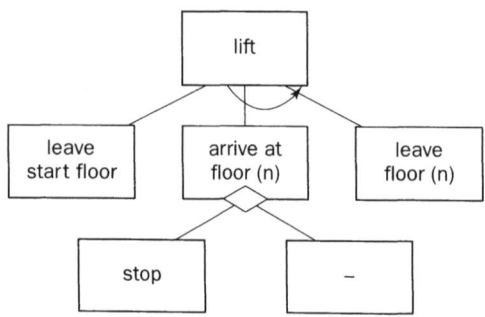

Figure 16.3

sense if a user is obstructing closure and will re-open. However, this is handled entirely by the door-controller and so is beyond the scope of the lift-controller.)

16.2.1.3   Lifts
A lift is constrained to move vertically up and down in its lift shaft. It follows that when a lift leaves a floor, the next floor it arrives at will be an adjacent floor or, possibly (if it reverses direction between floors), the same floor. This is illustrated in Figure 16.3.

16.2.1.4   Winding motors
Winding motors each have three control lines; slow, fast and polarity – which operate as per the decision table below (Table 16.1).

In fast mode, the motor moves the lift at 1.2 m/sec (+/– 10%). In slow mode, at 0.3 m/sec (+/– 10%). The motor mechanism itself ensures a gradual acceleration and deceleration as per Table 16.2.

16.2.1.5   Buttons
Whilst pressed, buttons produce a hi signal (when released, a lo signal). Within each lift there is a set of send-buttons, one for each floor. On each floor, outside

Table 16.1

slow	hi				lo			
fast	hi		lo		hi		lo	
polarity	hi	lo	hi	lo	hi	lo	hi	lo
wind up fast	✓				✓			
wind down fast		✓				✓		
wind up slow			✓					
wind down slow				✓				
stop							✓	✓

Table 6.2

	time	distance
rest to fast	2 sec	1.2 m
fast to slow	1 sec	0.75 m
slow to rest	1 sec	0.15 m

(All figures are subject to a tolerance of +/− 20%.)

the lifts, there is a set of call-buttons. This set consists of two buttons for each floor (one up call-button and one down call-button), except for the bottom floor, which has an up call-button only, and the top floor, which has a down call-button only. (There may actually be more than one set of call-buttons on each floor but, if so, they are linked and will appear to the controller as one set.)

16.2.1.6 Indicators
Indicator sets consist of one indicator light for each floor that the lift system services. For each lift there is a set of indicators inside it and a set on each floor outside it. For each lift, the two are linked and will appear to the controller as one set.

16.2.1.7 Sensors
Sensors detect the presence of a lift. When a lift is within 20 cm vertically (either side) of the sensor's nominal position it sends a hi signal; otherwise a lo signal. Each lift shaft has a set of sensors for each floor. For each floor (except top and bottom), there is a proximity-sensor (aka the 'at-sensor') at the nominal floor position, an above-sensor 1.5 m above (the nominal floor position) and a below-sensor 1.5 m below. The top floor has proximity- and below-sensors only and the bottom floor proximity- and above-sensors only.

16.2.1.8 Door-controllers
The doors on each lift have their own, in-built controller which handles door cycling (i.e. opening, waiting and closing), including re-opening when obstructed. (Through a mechanical linkage, the doors on the floor that the lift is on are automatically operated together with the doors of the lift itself.)

Doors will commence cycling upon receipt of a cycling signal (i.e. the door cycle line is sent hi for at least 0.1 seconds). A door controller sends a hi signal when the doors are closed; otherwise it is lo.

16.2.1.9 Users
Users are members of the general public. The majority of their characteristics (e.g. comfort under vertical acceleration, ability to reach and press buttons, time to enter/leave lifts, etc.) are already accommodated by the given hardware (including the door-controller).

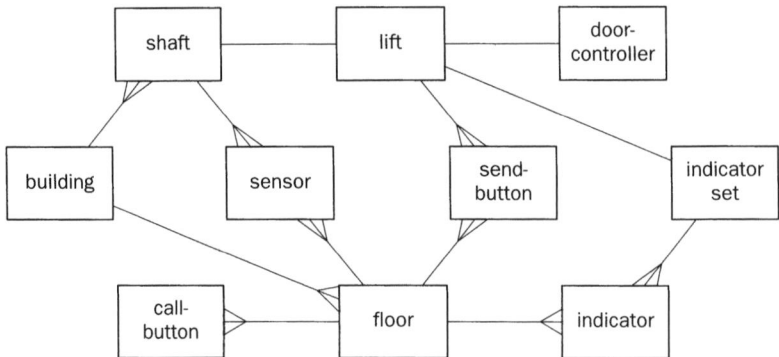

Figure 16.4

Additionally, it has been determined that, typically:

- Users report mild annoyance after a 20 second wait for a lift.
- If, from the indicators, it appears that, in response to a call-button request, no lift will arrive for at least 30 seconds, 50% of users will use the stairs for up to two floors.

16.2.1.10 Summary of sub-domain relationships
There are the following:

- many floors to each shaft;
- one lift to each shaft;
- one door controller to each lift;
- three sensors (above, at, below) per floor per shaft, except for top (at, below) and bottom (above, at) floors;
- one indicator set per lift;
- one indicator per floor per indicator set;
- one send-button per lift per floor;
- two call-buttons (one up, one down) per floor, except for top (down only) and bottom (up only) floors.

16.2.1.11 Entity relationship diagram
This is shown in Figure 16.4 above.

16.2.1.12 Data dictionary

building	::= number-of-floors, number-of-lifts;
floor	::= floor-id;
shaft	::= lift-id;
hi-lo	::= hi | lo;
hi	::= /* signal is "hi", i.e. 3 to 5 volts */;

lo	::= /* signal is "lo", i.e. < 1 volt */;
on-off	::= on | off;
on	::= /* device is "on" (e.g. a button is pressed) */;
off	::= /* device is "off" */;
lift	::= lift-id, direction, position;
direction	::= "up" | "down";
position	::= floor-id;
door-controller	::= lift-id;
door-command	::= hi-lo;
	::= /* "hi" starts lift door opening */
door-signal	::= hi-lo;
	::= /* "hi" indicates that door is closed */
sensor	::= lift-id, floor-id, sensor-type, on-off;
sensor-type	::= "above" | "at" | "below";
sensor-signal	::= hi-lo;
indicator-set	::= {indicator};
indicator	::= lift-id, floor-id, on-off;
indicator command	::= hi-lo;
call-button	::= floor-id, direction, on-off;
send-button	::= lift-id, floor-id, on-off;
send-button-signal	::= hi-lo;
call-button-signal	::= hi-lo;
winding motor	::= lift-id;
motor-command	::= slow, fast, polarity;
slow	::= hi-lo;
fast	::= hi-lo;
polarity	::= hi-lo;

16.2.2 Requirements

16.2.2.1 Safety

R1 The lift is never to be allowed to move above the top floor or below the bottom floor. (There is an emergency shut down system that will stop the motor if the lift goes above the top floor or below the bottom floor (by more than 10 cm), but this shut down system is beyond the scope of the control system.)

R2 The lift is not to be stopped from fast mode but should always be switched to slow mode for at least one second before stopping.

R3 The motor polarity is not to be changed whilst the lift is moving. (This could wreck the winding gear.)

R4 The lift is never to be moved with the doors open.

R5 With the stop-delay correctly configured (as below) the lift will stop within +/− 1.5 cm of the floor being serviced.

16.2.2.2 Call servicing

R6 A call is established by pressing a send-button (inside the lift) or a call-button (outside the lift) for the relevant floor and, in the case of call-buttons, for the relevant direction. (Duplicate calls are ignored.)

R7 Calls are cancelled only when serviced by a lift.

R8 To service a send-button call, the relevant lift must stop at that floor. A call-button call may be serviced by any lift that is travelling in the correct direction stopping at that floor.

R9 A lift will stop at a floor if:

R9.1 there is a send-button call for that floor or

R9.2 there is call-button call and the lift is moving in the right direction or

R9.3 if it is the top or bottom floor

Where there is more than one lift:

R10 Send-button calls must be serviced by the relevant lift.

R11 Call-button calls should be serviced by the lift that is likely to arrive there soonest. (It is appreciated that this cannot be guaranteed because the selected lift might be requested to service a new call whilst en route.)

R12 Each lift should be used an approximately equal amount.

R13 A lift will reverse direction only when stopped at a floor.

R14 A lift will reverse direction only if it has no outstanding calls in its current direction of travel.

R15 For each lift, one indicator at a time should be illuminated, that being the one for the floor that the lift is (approximately) nearest to.

16.2.2.3 Configuration

R16 The service technician must be able to set:

R16.1 number of lifts

R16.2 number of floors

R16.3 stop signal delay, for each lift (in the range 0.10 to 0.40 seconds)

16.2.2.4 Performance

R17 The maximum number of lifts is four, the minimum one.

R18 The maximum number of floors is 20, the minimum two.

16.2.2.5 Reliability

R19 The control system should not violate any safety requirements. Non-safety critical control errors (e.g. lift sent to wrong floor) should not occur more than once per week of operation.

16.2.2.6 Physical environment

R20 The control system must fit within a volume of $1 \times 0.5 \times 0.5$ m.

R21 The control system must operate over a temperature range of 0–40°C.

R22 RF emissions must comply with BS50081–2.

16.3 Specification

[Note, only the system behaviour section of the specification is given. To save space, the various standard, 'wrapper' parts (see Section 5.4.3) and replicated requirements are omitted.

Included (in call-outs) are indications of whereabouts the various requirements are addressed by the edesign. This is not usual (indeed, for some requirements it is virtually impossible since their realisation can be very 'diffuse') but may prove illuminating.]

16.3.1 Hardware interfaces

16.3.1.1 Ports and pins
The control system interfaces with the hardware via 32 pin ports.

- Port 1 is left spare.
- Ports 2 and 3 are allocated to call buttons.
- Starting with port 4, each lift is assigned 4 ports to be referenced as ports 4n, 4n+1, 4n+2, 4n+3, where n is the lift number (starting at 1).

Table 16.3 shows the pin allocations.

16.3.1.2 Event responses
Events occur when the following signals go hi:

- below-sensor-signal (l, f)   – lift (l) is 150 cm (+/– 20 cm) below floor (f)
- at-sensor-signal (l,f)   – lift (l) is at (+/– 20 cm) floor (f)
- above-sensor-signal (l)   – lift (l) is 150 cm (+/– 20 cm) above floor (f)
- door-sensor-signal (l)   – door is closed
- send-button-signal (l, f)   – request to send lift (l) to floor (f)
- call-button-signal (f, d)   – request for any lift to call at floor (f) and then proceed in direction (d)

and when the following signal goes low:

- door-sensor-signal (l)   – door is opening/open/closing

16.3.1.3 Signal de-bouncing
In order to allow for stabilisation, all input signals will be handled as below.

Table 16.3

Port	Purpose	Pin 0	Pin 1	Pin 2	Pin 3	...	Pin 29	Pin 30	Pin 31
1	spare								
2	up call buttons	floor 0	floor 1	floor 2	floor 3	etc. (to 20)	unused	unused	unused
3	down call buttons	unused	floor 1	floor 2	floor 3	etc. (to 20)	unused	unused	unused
4 (4n)	lift (1) sensors	unused	at 0	above 0	below 1	etc. (to 10)	above 10	unused	unused
5 (4n+1)	lift (1) sensors	below 11	at 11	above 11	below 12	etc. (to 20)	unused	unused	unused
6 (4n+2)	lift (1) indicators + motor	floor 0	floor 1	floor 2	floor 3	etc. (to 20)	motor slow	motor fast	motor polarity
7 (4n+3)	lift (1) send buttons + door	floor 0	floor 1	floor 2	floor 3	etc. (to 20)	unused	door sensor	door com'nd
8 (4n+1)	lift (2) sensors	unused	at 0	above 0	below 1	etc. (to 20)	above 10	unused	unused
etc.									

(Note, floor 0 is the bottom (ground) floor.)

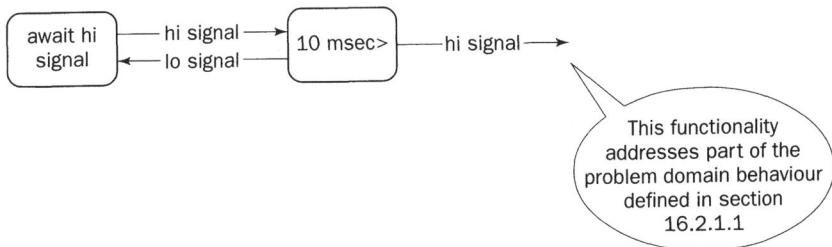

await hi signal
hi signal
lo signal
10 msec>
hi signal
This functionality addresses part of the problem domain behaviour defined in section 16.2.1.1

16.3.1.4 Lift behaviour

Most of the responses to sensor signals and the door signal are captured in the following state chart (Figure 16.5) showing the emergent behaviour of a *single* lift[114].

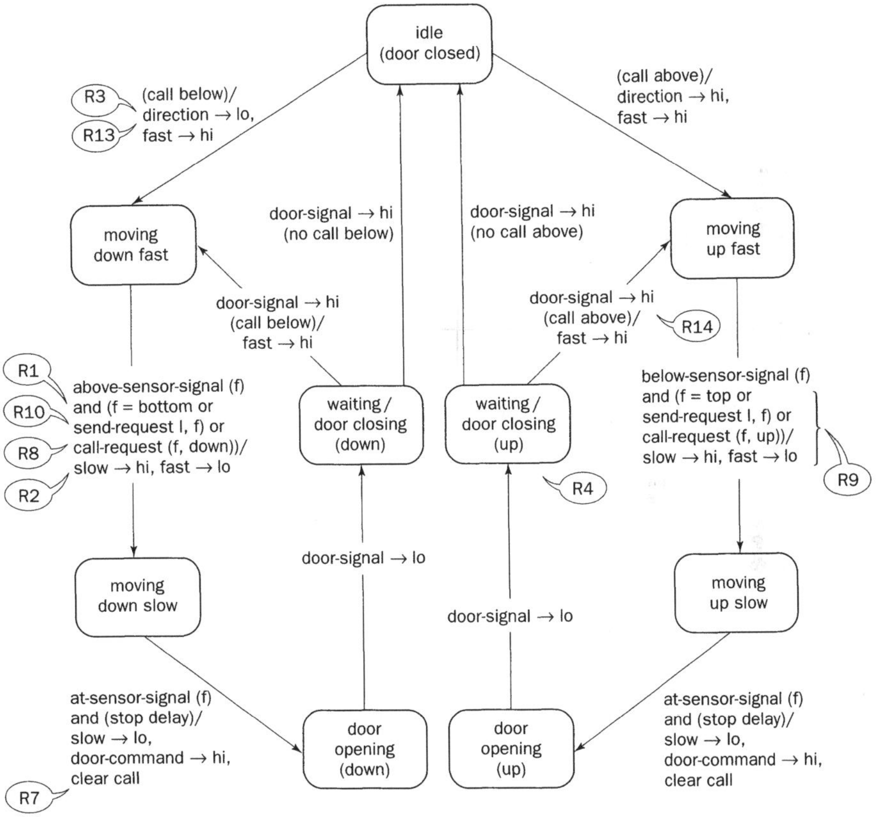

idle (door closed)
R3
R13
(call below)/ direction → lo, fast → hi
(call above)/ direction → hi, fast → hi
moving down fast
door-signal → hi (no call below)
door-signal → hi (no call above)
moving up fast
door-signal → hi (call below)/ fast → hi
door-signal → hi (call above)/ fast → hi
R14
R1
R10
R8
R2
above-sensor-signal (f) and (f = bottom or send-request l, f) or call-request (f, down))/ slow → hi, fast → lo
waiting / door closing (down)
waiting / door closing (up)
below-sensor-signal (f) and (f = top or send-request l, f) or call-request (f, up))/ slow → hi, fast → lo
R9
R4
door-signal → lo
moving down slow
door-signal → lo
moving up slow
at-sensor-signal (f) and (stop delay)/ slow → lo, door-command → hi, clear call
R7
door opening (down)
door opening (up)
at-sensor-signal (f) and (stop delay)/ slow → lo, door-command → hi, clear call

Figure 16.5

---

114 [It may be observed that the given edesign is fairly simplistic. It would be possible, indeed, desirable, for the controller to check upon the progress of lifts by taking account of sensor signals going from hi to lo as well. For example, when a lift leaves floor(f) and goes upwards, the at-floor(f) sensor should go lo, followed by the above-floor(n) going lo before the below-floor(f+1) sensor goes hi. Any departure from this sequence would indicate a fault which could be reported. Further, from the known speeds of the lifts, it would also be possible to check that signals occur within expected time windows. Such sophisticated behaviour can be incorporated into finite state machine models but this is left to the reader as an exercise.]

In addition, the indicators are operated as per the following state charts:

above-sensor-signal (f)/
indicator (f) → hi,
indicator (f + 1) → lo

moving
down fast

moving
up fast

below-sensor-signal (f)/
indicator (f) → hi,
indicator (f − 1) → lo

R15

R6

Send-button-signals cause calls (above or below) to be allocated to the appropriate lift.

Where there is more than one lift, call-button-signals are handled in the following way:

R10

- Allocate the call to the lift with the shortest response time.

R8+R11

- If lifts have equal response times, then select one of those lifts randomly.

Response time for each lift is calculated as:

R12

(1.2 * floor-height (metres) * number-of-floors-to-travel) +
(number-of-stops-en-route * (waiting-time (seconds) + 8))

16.3.2   User interface

The user interface hardware (button panels and indicator panels) are preexisting and so are not defined here. From the user perspective, the emergent behaviour of the system is reflected in the following use-case:

LIFT JOURNEY
User calls lift and travels to required destination floor.
Actors
    User
Pre-conditions:
    None
Post-condition:
    The user will be at their required destination floor
Interaction

   1 The user arrives outside a lift door and presses the relevant callbutton

   2 A lift arrives and the door opens

   3 The user enters the lift

   4 The user presses the send-button for the required destination floor

   5 The door closes, the lift travels to the destination floor (possibly stopping at other floors en route) and the door opens

   6 The user exits the lift

Figure 16.6

16.3.3 Technician interface

R16

The service technician can configure:

- number of lifts;
- number of floors;
- stop signal delay, for each lift (in the range 0.10 to 0.40 seconds).

Figure 16.6 illustrates (approximately to scale) the configuration panel which consists of a 30 character display and four buttons (left, right, up, down). There is also a key operated switch which must be switched to on in order to be able to change configuration.

The sequence of operation is depicted in the state chart (Figure 16.7).

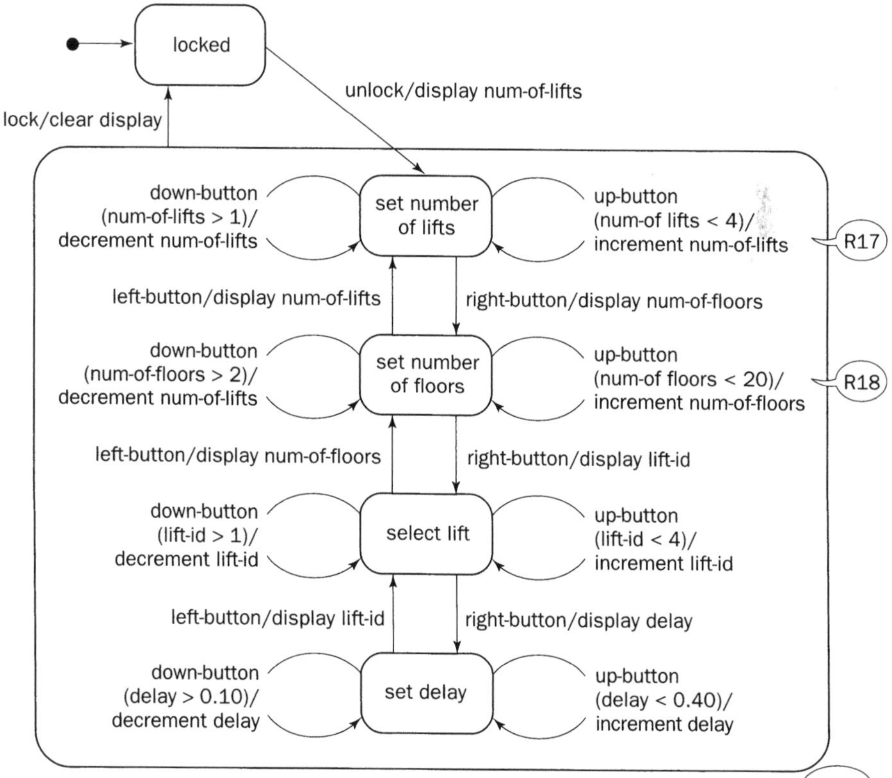

locked

unlock/display num-of-lifts

lock/clear display

down-button
(num-of-lifts > 1)/
decrement num-of-lifts

**set number
of lifts**

up-button
(num-of lifts < 4)/
increment num-of-lifts

R17

left-button/display num-of-lifts

right-button/display num-of-floors

down-button
(num-of-floors > 2)/
decrement num-of-lifts

**set number
of floors**

up-button
(num-of floors < 20)/
increment num-of-floors

R18

left-button/display num-of-floors

right-button/display lift-id

down-button
(lift-id > 1)/
decrement lift-id

select lift

up-button
(lift-id < 4)/
increment lift-id

left-button/display lift-id

right-button/display delay

down-button
(delay > 0.10)/
decrement delay

set delay

up-button
(delay < 0.40)/
increment delay

Figure 16.7

R17

Table 16.4

current number of lifts (n)	1		2 .. 3		4	
button pressed	↑	↓	↑	↓	↑	↓
'NUMBER OF LIFTS = ', n	✓		✓	✓		✓
'MAX LIFTS = 4'					✓	
'MIN LIFTS =1'		✓				

The decision table (Table 16.4) defines the technician messages that may be output whilst in 'set number of lifts' state. The other states should operate in a similar and consistent manner.

The F2K drill file translation case study

17

Whilst loosely based on real-life applications, this case study is fictional (and simplified). It is included as being representative of a large class of, mainly commercial, 'off-line' transformation applications. As will become apparent, the specification of such systems can be relatively straightforward.

17.1 Requirements document

17.1.1 Introduction

This application concerns the machines that drill the holes in printed circuit boards (PCBs). The drill machines are controlled by data files containing control instructions. The client uses a PCB computer aided design (CAD) package, known as 'PISA', which produces drill control files in the format required by their Frankenstein, HEAD3 drilling machine. However, they are acquiring a new drilling machine, the Karaoke Mk3, that requires a different file format and, therefore, a program, to be known as F2K, is required to convert files from HEAD3 to Karaoke format.

17.1.2 Problem domain description

The system is UNIX-based, input and output being from/to UNIX files. Input and output files are both sequential text files consisting of a stream of ASCII characters. File terminators, etc., are as specified in the UNIX manual (ref.1).

17.1.2.1 Problem frame
This is a transformation problem whose frame is shown in Figure 17.1.

17.1.2.2 HEAD3 (input) file format
All fields are separated by one space character (which is not shown in the following definitions). No fields, apart from the name and comment fields, contain space characters.

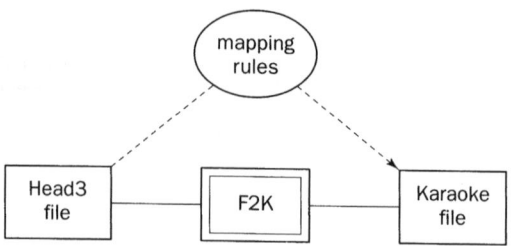

Figure 17.1

HEAD3-file	::= Hheader, [1]{Hcommand};
Hheader	::= Hboard-name, Hversion, Hdate, offset-x, offset-y, Hcomment;
Hboard-name	::= """, {character}[32], """;
Hversion	::= [3]{digit}[3];
Hdate	::= dd, mm, yy;
offset_x	::= coord;
offset_y	::= coord;
Hcomment	::= """, {character}[128], """;
Hcommand	::= drill-number, x-coord, y_coord;
drill-number	::= [3]{digit}[3];
x-coord	::= coord;
y-coord	::= coord;
coord	::= [8]{digit}[8];
dd	::= [2]{digit}[2];
mm	::= [2]{digit}[2];
yy	::= [2]{digit}[2];
digit	::= "0" .. "9";
character	::= /* any printable ASCII character */

17.1.2.3   Karaoke (output) file format

Karaoke-file	::= Kheader, {Kcommand}, Ktail;
Kheader	::= marker, Kdate, Kversion, Kboard_name, offset-x, offset-y
marker	::= Kname;
Kdate	::= dd, mm, yyyy
Kversion	::= [2]{digit}[2], ".",[2]{digit}[2];
Kboard-name	::= Kname;
offset_x	::= coord;
offset_y	::= coord;
Kname	::= """, {character}[256], """;
yyyy	::= [4]{digit}[4];
Kcommand	::= drill-command	hole_command;
drill_command	::= "drill", drill-number;

Table 17.1

Hfile	Kfile	Mapping rule (if not a straight copy)
Hheader	Kheader	
Hboard-name	Kboard-name	
Hversion	Kversion	Insert "0" at front and "." before last 2 digits
Hdate	Kdate	Prefix H yy with "20", unless operator has indicated otherwise, in which case "19"
offset_x	offset_x	
offset_y	offset_y	
Hcomment	marker	
Hcommand	Kcommand	
drill-number	drill-command	Whenever the Hcommand drill-number is different from the previous Hcommand drill-number, create a K drill-command; ""drill "drill-number"
	hole-command	
x-coord	x-coord	
y-coord	y-coord	
	depth	Always set depth to "60"
	Ktail	
	hole-count	To be calculated by summing number of holes
	"XXXXX"	Simply append constant string

hole_command	::= x-coord, y_coord, depth;	
depth	::= $^2\{digit\}^2$;	
Ktail	::= hole-count, "XXXXX";	
hole-count	::= $^4\{digit\}^4$;	

17.1.2.4 File mapping
This is shown in Table 17.1.

17.1.3 Requirements

17.1.3.1 Functional

R1 The input file, in Head2 format, is to be converted to produce an output file, in Karaoke3 format, according to the mapping given in Table 17.1.

R2   Input file errors are to be detected and as many errors as possible to be reported at the individual field level of detail.

R3   The program (F2K) to be invoked (from UNIX) by the operator.

R4   The operator to supply:

R4.1   the address of the input file

R4.2   the address of the output file

R4.3   the century

17.1.3.2 Performance

R5   A 50 Kb input file to be converted in less than 10 seconds.

R6   The only limit on file size to be machine capacity.

17.2   Specification

Input and output file interfaces are as defined in the requirements document.

17.2.1   The operator interface

The operator is provided with a UNIX command line interface, as defined in the UNIX manual (ref.1). F2K is invoked by typing its name and path. The following dialogue ensues (output from F2K is indicated by '>', input from the operator is indicated by '<'; input and output messages are shown in quotes and variable fields are enclosed in '<>'):

```
1   >   'Enter name and path of input file'
    <   <input-file-path>
    possible errors:
            >   'File not found' – go to 1
            >   'You do not have read permission for this file' – go to 1
2   >   'Enter name and path of output file'
    <   <output-file-path>
    possible errors:
    >   'Directory not found' – go to 2
    >   'You do not have write permission for this directory' – go to 2
    >   'File already exists – do you wish to overwrite? (enter "y" or "n")'
        <   'n' – go to 2
        <   'y' – proceed    (any other input is ignored)
    >   'Enter "y" to retain default century (20—) or "n" for 19—'
    <   'y' or 'n'                    (any other input is ignored)
    >   'Input file is <input-file>,
        Output file is <output-file>,
        Century is <century>,
        Enter "y" to start translation, "n" to abort'
```

< 'n' – go to 1
< 'y' – proceed   (any other input is ignored)

F2K will then attempt the translation and will terminate with:

'Translation successful'

or

'Translation unsuccessful – n errors detected'

17.2.2 Input file error reporting

Input file errors are output to stderr (which may be redirected by the operator using the standard UNIX mechanisms if required). When encountering an error, F2K will attempt to check the remainder of the input file and report any further errors up to a maximum of 20.

The following error messages may be produced:

- 'Header <field-name> invalid'
- 'Command number <n>, <field name> invalid'

where n is the number of the command (counted sequentially from the start) and field-name is one of:

- board-name
- version
- date
- offset_x
- offset_y
- comment
- drill-number
- x-coord
- y-coord

The Petri net diagram tool case study

18

18.1   Requirements document

A software tool, Petool, is required to allow the editing and execution of Petri nets. Petool will support synchronous nets with multiple tokens per place but only single arc weighting.

18.1.1   Petri nets

A general description of Petri nets may be found in Section 12.7 of this book.

18.1.2   Problem frame

This is mainly a workpiece problem, but the system is also required to control the execution of Petri nets. The combined workpiece and control frame diagram is shown in Figure 18.1.

18.1.3   Data model

The data model is shown in Figure 18.2.

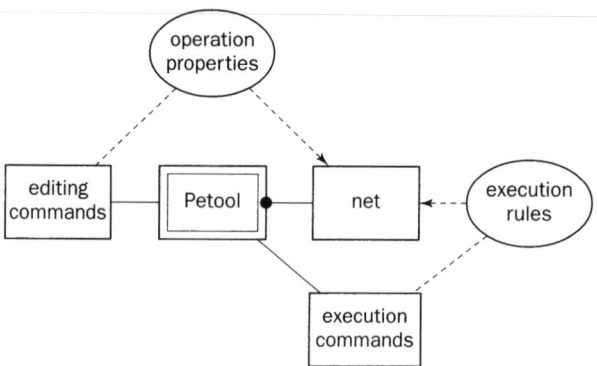

Figure 18.1

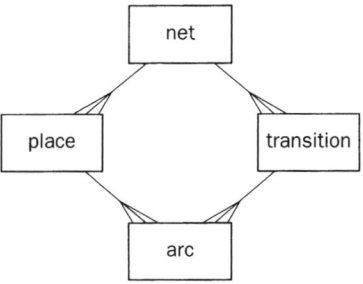

Figure 18.2

18.1.4   Data dictionary

net	::= [net-name], file-address, cycle-time, {place}, {transition};
place	::= [place-name], initial-token-number, current-token-number, token-capacity, overflow, {arc};
arc	::= /*arrow connecting a place to a transition (or vice-versa) */;
transition	::= [trans-name], {arc};
net-name	::= label;
place-name	::= label;
trans-name	::= label;
label	::= [1]{alphanumeric}[20];
alphanumeric	::= "a" .. "z" | "A" .. "Z" | "0" .. "9" | "-" | "'" | "." | "/";
file-address	::= /* as determined by operating system */
cycle-time	::= "0.1" .. "5.0";
	::= /* the period, set by the user, for one transition firing cycle */
initial-token-number	::= "0" .. "99";
current-token-number	::= "0" .. "99";
token-capacity	::= "0" .. "99";
overflow	::= boolean;
boolean	::= /* true or false */

18.1.5   Requirements

18.1.5.1   Functional

Drawings

R1   Petool provides for the creation, editing, saving, copying, execution and deletion of (diagrams of) Petri nets.

R2   Each net drawing is to be saved to (retrieved from) a user designated file.

Editing

R3   Drawings are created interactively, on screen, using mouse, menus and keyboard.

R4   Subject to the constraints given below, individual drawing elements may be added (at a fixed size), moved and deleted.

R5   The following drawing elements are accommodated:

   R5.1   places

   R5.2   transitions

   R5.3   arcs

   R5.4   tokens

R6   Conventional representation is to be supported, along these lines:

   Place: ◯   Transition: ▭   Arc: ⟶

R7   Tokens may be represented as dots (within places) or just their number may be indicated.

R8   Places and transitions may have attached labels.

R9   Arcs must connect a place to a transition, or vice versa (unconnected arcs are not allowed).

R10   An initial marking may be established by allocating tokens to places.

R11   Places have a minimum of 0 tokens and a maximum token capacity may be set by the user (the default being the given capacity limit).

R12   The user can choose whether a place, upon reaching its maximum token capacity, will 'overflow' (and lose additional tokens) or if it will become 'full'.

R13   The current number of tokens at a place is always visible.

R14   Places and transitions may be moved (probably by 'click and drag'). Any associated labels and tokens are automatically moved and the connectivity of any attached arcs is maintained.

R15   The deletion of a place or a transition results in the deletion of all connected arcs.

Execution

R16   Only synchronous execution is supported.

R17   Execution speed is determined by the user and may be changed during execution.

R18   It is possible to start, suspend, resume and end net execution.

R19   Execution will automatically stop when no transitions are enabled or when any place becomes full (in the latter case, all full places will be highlighted).

R20   Currently enabled transitions (i.e. where all incoming arcs connect to places with at least one token) are differentiated (probably by colour).

18.1.5.2   Performance

Speed

R21   Petool should respond to net editing commands within 0.5 seconds.

R22   Petool should complete save, copy and retrieve commands within five seconds.

R23   Execution speed can be varied between 0.1 and five seconds per firing cycle.

Capacity

R24   Petool will accommodate at least:

    R24.1   10 nets

    R24.2   30 places per net

    R24.3   50 transitions per net

    R24.4   99 arcs per net

    R24.5   99 tokens per place

Usability

R25   File handling and drawing operations should, wherever reasonable, follow the conventions adopted by established drawing utilities. (It may be assumed that users are familiar with the concepts and notation of Petri nets.)

18.2   Specification

[This specification is a logical specification. It does not specify the physical details of the inputs and outputs which are left to the HMI designers (or implementers).] Figure 18.3 defines the possible transitions between the top level states of 'drawing-loaded' and 'drawing-not-loaded'.

Triggers (events):

new	::= /* user command to create a new drawing file */;
open	::= /* user command to open an existing drawing file */;
close	::= /* user command to close currently open drawing file */;
save	::= /* user command to save currently open drawing file */;
save-as	::= /* user command to save current drawing to a new file. (This is the (only) way in which copying of drawings is realised) */;
quit	::= /* user command to terminate execution of the application */;

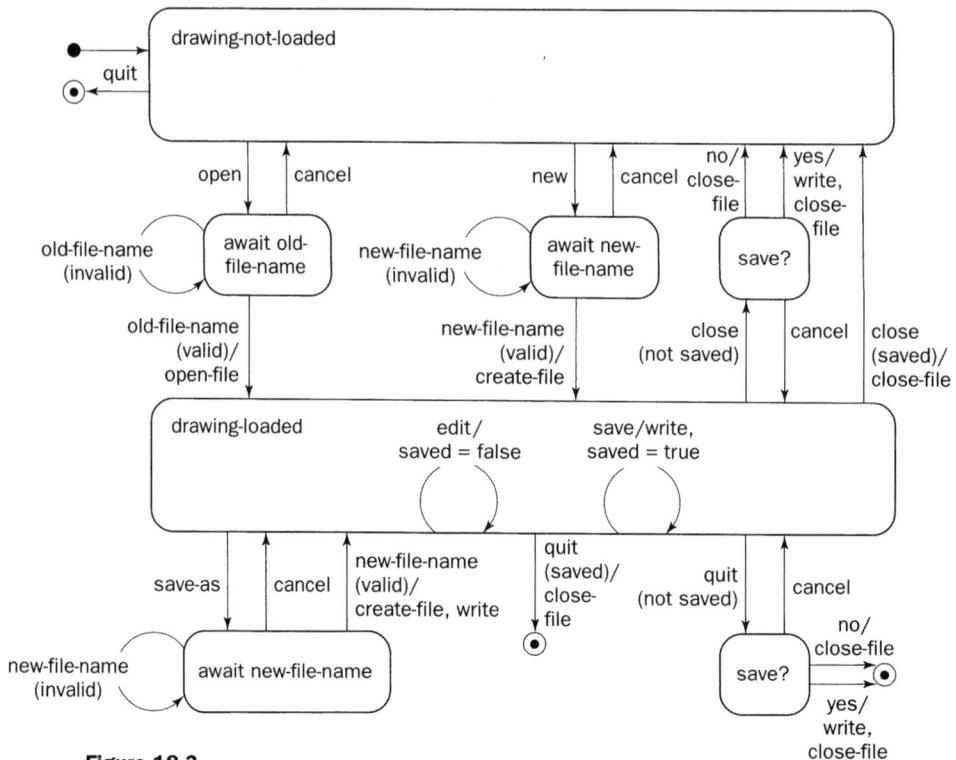

Figure 18.3

cancel	::= /* user command to cancel current action */;
no	::= /* user command to reject offered option */;
yes	::= /* user command to accept offered option */;
edit	::= /* represents any editing command (detailed later) */
new-file-name	::= /* user entered name for a new file. To be valid it must comply with operating system constraints upon file names and must not already exist */;
old-file-name	::= /* user entered name for an existing file. To be valid it must already exist */;

Actions (responses):

create file	::= /* create and open a new drawing file with the given name */;
open-file	::= /* open an existing drawing file with the given name */;
close-file	::= /* close currently open drawing file */;
write	::= /* overwrite currently open drawing file to reflect edits since last save */;

When a drawing is loaded, the two main areas of functionality, editing and executing Petri nets, are available. Figure 18.4 defines transitions between those modes and gives more detail of the behaviour when in the executing mode.

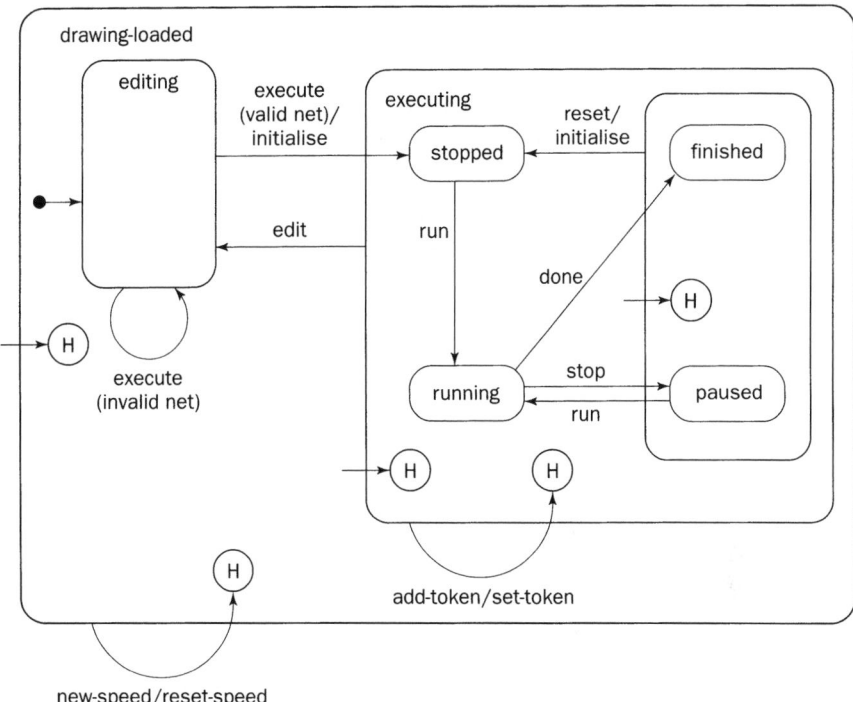

Figure 18.4

Triggers (events):

execute	::= /* user command to enter execution mode. Note that in this context, a valid net is an executable net, i.e. there must be at least one connected and enabled transition */;
edit	::= /* user command to enter editing mode */;
new-speed	::= /* user command to change the execution speed (cycle time-delay) of the net */;
add-token	::= /* user command to add a token to a particular place */;
run	::= /* user command to start (or continue) execution of the net */;
stop	::= /* user command to suspend execution of the net */;
reset	::= /* user command to return a net to its initial marking */;
done	::= /* occurs when the net cannot execute further, either because there are no more enabled transitions or because a place has reached its token limit and is set to not overflow */;

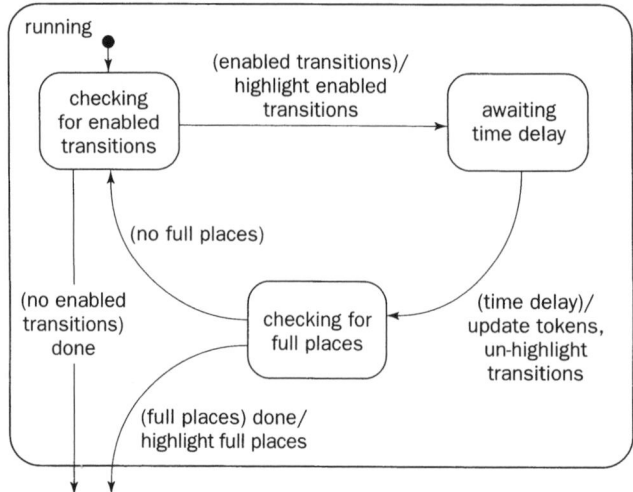

Figure 18.5

Actions (responses):

reset-speed   ::= /* set the execution speed (cycle time-delay) of the net to new value */;

set-token   ::= /* add a token to the current total (not the initial marking) of a particular place */;

initialise   ::= /* reset the net to its initial marking */;

Further detail of the 'running' state is shown in Figure 18.5. (The effects of the given actions are deemed to be self-evident.)

The operation when in editing mode is shown in Figure 18.6. (Note that an object may be a place, a transition or an arc.)

Triggers (events):

select-place   ::= /* user command to select an existing place as the current object. (It is anticipated that this will probably be implemented by way of mouse click.)*/;

select-transition   ::= /* as above but for transition */;

select-arc   ::= /* as above but for arc */;

deselect   ::= /* user command to de-select currently selected object. (It is anticipated that this will probably be implemented by way of mouse click on empty space.)*/;

select-object-type-to-add ::= /* user command to enter adding mode and select a particular type of object to add */;

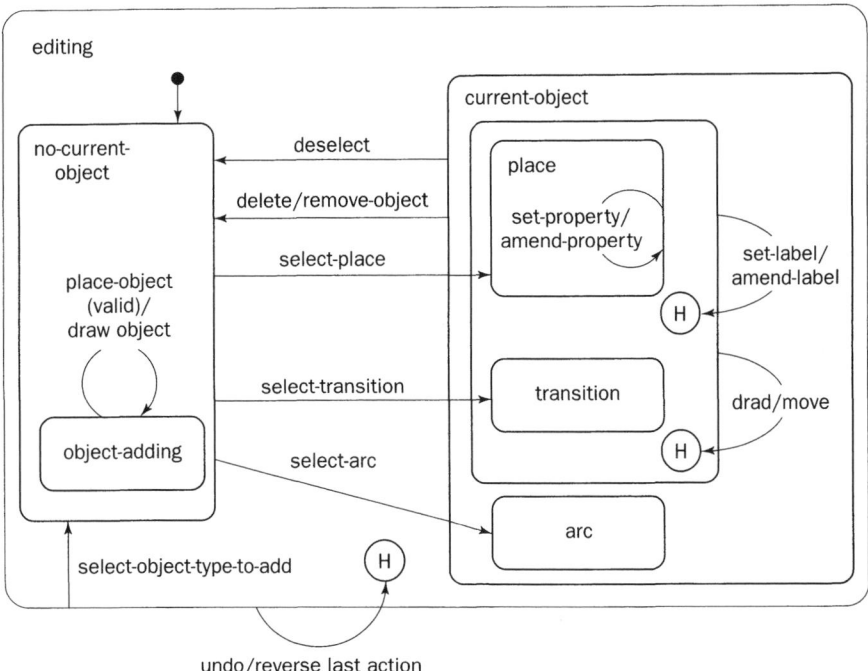

Figure 18.6

place-object	::= /* user command to place a particular object in the current drawing. Only arc placements may be invalid as both ends must be placed, one on a place and the other on a transition */;
set-property	::= /* represents a family of user commands that enable the initial-number-of-tokens, maximum-number-of-tokens and overflow of a place to be set */;
set-label	::= /* entry by the user of a (new) value for the label of a place or transition */;
drag	::= /* user command to move an object. (As determined by R14, probably by 'click and drag') */;
undo	::= /* user command to undo last command */;

Actions (responses):

| draw-object | ::= /* draw specified type of object at specified location */; |
| remove-object | ::= /* remove specified object from drawing. In the case of places and transition, any connected arcs will also be removed */; |

amend-property	::= /* amend the specified place property to the new given value */;
amend-label	::= /* amend the specified label to the new given value */;
move	::= /* move the specified place or transition to the new given location. Any attached arcs will be moved to retain attachment */;
reverse-last action	::= /* in so far as possible, reverse the effect(s) of the last action */;

References

19

Abbott R, Moorhead D (1981) Software Requirements and Specification, *Journal of Systems and Software*, Vol. 2, pp. 297–316.

Alexander I (1999) Against Fashion in Engineering, *Requirements quarterly (Newsletter of the BCS RE sig.)*, Issue 16 (Feb. 1999), pp. 7–8.

Alford M W, Burns I F (1976) R-Nets: A Graph Model for Real-time Software Requirements, *Symposium on Computer Software Engineering*, New York, Polytechnic Press, pp. 97–108.

Annett J, Duncan K D (1967) Task analysis and training design, *Occupational psychology*, No. 41, pp. 211–21.

Ashworth C, Slater L (1993) *An Introduction to SSADM version 4*, New York, McGraw-Hill.

Babich W A (1986) *Software Configuration Management*, Wokingham, Addison-Wesley.

Bainbridge L (1979) Verbal Reports as Evidence of the Process Operator's Knowledge, *International Journal of Human Computer Studies*, Vol. 51, No. 2, pp. 213–38.

Balzer B, Goldman N (1981) Principles of Good Software Specification and their Implications for Specification Language, *Proceedings of National Computer Conference*, AFIPS, Arlington, VA, USA, pp. 393–400.

Bastide R, Palanque P (1995) A Petri Net Based Environment for the Design of Event Driven Systems, *Proceedings of the 16th International Conference on the Application and Theory of Petri Nets*, Springer-Verlag, Berlin, Germany, pp. 66–83.

Beizer B (1990) *Software Testing techniques*, Princeton, NJ, Van Nostrand-Rheinhold.

Boehm B (1981) *Software Engineering Economics*, Hemel Hempstead, Prentice Hall.

Boehm B, Egyed A (1998) Software requirements negotiation: some lessons learned, *Proceedings of the Third International Conference on Software Engineering, Forging New Links*, Los Alamitos, CA, USA, pp. 503–6.

Booch G R (1991) *Object-Oriented Design with Applications*, New York, Benjamin-Cummings.

Brown D (1997) *Object Oriented Analysis: Objects in Plain English*, New York, Wiley.

Budgen D (1994) *Software Design*, Wokingham, Addison-Wesley.

Casey B E, Taylor B J (1981) Writing Requirements in English: A Natural Alternative, *IEEE Software Engineering Standards Workshop*, Washington, DC, IEEE Computer Society Press, pp. 95–101.

CCTA (1996) *SSADM (Version 4+) Reference Manual*, NCC Blackwell.

Checkland P (1981) *Systems Thinking; Systems Practice*, New York, Wiley.

Chen P (1976) The Entity-Relationship Model; Towards a Unified View of Data, *ACM Transactions on Database Systems*, Vol. 1, No. 1, pp. 9–36.

Coad P, Yourdon E (1991) *Object Oriented Analysis*, Old Tappan, NJ, Prentice Hall.

Cockburn A (2001) *Writing Effective Use Cases*, Harlow, Addison-Wesley.

Codd E F (1970) A Relational Data Model for Large Shared Data Banks, *Communications of the ACM*, Vol. 13, No. 6, pp. 377–87.

Connolly T, *et al.* (1999) *Database Systems: A practical approach to design, implementation and management*, Harlow, Addison-Wesley.

Cotterell M (1995) *Software Project Management*, Thomson.

Cox K, Phalp K, Shepperd M (June 2001) Comparing Use Case Writing Guidelines, *REFSQ 2001 Seventh International Workshop on Requirements Engineering: Foundation for Software Quality*, Interlaken, Switzerland.

Date C J (1999) *An Introduction to Database Systems*, Harlow, Longman.

Davis A M (1988a) A Comparison of Techniques for the Specification of External Behaviour of Systems, *Communications of the ACM*, Vol. 31, No. 9, pp. 1098–115.

Davis A M (1988b) A Taxonomy for the Early Stages of the Software Development Life Cycle, *The Journal of Systems and Software*, Vol. 8, pp. 297–311.

Davis A M (1993) *Software Requirements: Objects, Functions and States*, Hemel Hempstead, Prentice Hall.

DeMarco Tom (1978) *Structured Analysis and System Specification*, Harlow, Prentice Hall.

DeMarco Tom (1982) *Controlling Software Projects*, Harlow, Prentice Hall.

Diaper D (Ed.) (1989) *Task Analysis for Human Computer Interaction*, New York, Ellis Horwood.

Dijkstra E W (1965) Programming Considered as a Human Activity, *Information Processing 65: Proceedings of IFIP Congress*, North-Holland, pp. 213–17.

Dix A (Ed.) (1998) *Human–Computer Interaction*, Harlow, Prentice Hall.

Dorfman M, Flynn R F (1984) ARTS – An Automated Requirements Traceability System, *Journal of Systems and Software*, Vol. 4, No. 1, pp. 63–74.

Dorfman M, Thayer R (1990) *Standards, Guidelines and Examples on Software Requirements Engineering*, IEEE Computer Society Press Tutorial.

DTI/NCC (1986) *STARTS – Software Tools for Application to Large Real-Time Systems*, NCC.

Easterbrook S (1995) Managing Inconsistencies in an Evolving Specification, *2nd IEEE Symposium on Requirements Engineering*, pp. 48–56.

Easterbrook S, Chechik M (2001) A framework for multi-valued reasoning over inconsistent viewpoints, *Proceedings of the 23rd International Conference on Software Engineering*, Los Alamitos, CA, pp. 411–20.

Fagan M E (1999) Design and code inspections to reduce errors in program development, *IBM-Systems-Journal*, Vol. 38, Nos. 2–3, pp. 258–87.

Faulkner C (1998) *The Essence of Human Computer Interaction*, Harlow, Prentice Hall.

Finkelstein A, Potts C (1986) Structured Common Sense: The Elicitation and Formalization of System Requirements, in *Software Engineering '86*, P Brown and D Barnes (Eds), Stevenage, Peter Peregrinus.

Flowers S (1996) *Software Failure: Management Failure*, New York, Wiley.

Floyd C (1984) A Systematic Look at Prototyping, in *Approaches to Prototyping*, R Budde *et al.* (Eds), Berlin, Springer-Verlag, pp. 1–18.

Fowler M, Scott K (2000) *UML Distilled* (2nd edition), Harlow, Addison-Wesley.

Frimer M, Folkes M (1982) *Standards Document: Software Requirements Specification*, Advanced Technology Laboratories, draft 2, Bellevue, Washington.

Gause D C, Weinberg G M (1989) *Exploring Requirements: Quality Before Design*, Dorset House.

Gibson C F, Jackson B B (1987) *The Information Imperative: Managing the Impact of Information Technology on Business and People*, New York, Lexington Books.

Gildersleeve T R (1970) *Decision Tables and their Practical Application in Data Processing*, Hemel Hempstead, Prentice Hall.

Glass R (1998) *Software Runaways*, Harlow, Prentice Hall.

Goldsmith S (1993) *A Practical Guide to Real-Time Systems Development*, Hemel Hempstead, Prentice Hall.

Gomaa H, Scott D (1981) Prototyping as a Tool in the Specification of User Requirements, *Fifth International Conference on Software Engineering*, Washington, IEEE Computer Society Press, pp. 333–42.

Graham I (1996) Task scripts, use cases and scenarios in object oriented analysis, *Object Oriented Systems*, Vol. 3, No. 3, pp. 123–42.

Gruenbacher P (2000) Collaborative requirements negotiation with EasyWinWin, *Proceedings of 11th International Workshop on Database and Expert Systems Applications*, Los Alamitos, CA, USA, pp. 954–8.

Hall A (1990) Seven Myths of Formal Methods, *IEEE Software*, pp. 11–19.

Harel D (1987) Statecharts: A visual formalism for complex systems, *Science of Computer Programming*, Vol. 8, pp. 231–74.

Harel D *et al.* (1990) STATEMATE: a working environment for the development of complex reactive systems, *IEEE Transactions on Software Engineering*, Vol. 16, No. 4, pp. 403–14.

Heitmeyer C L (1985) Requirements Specification in the Military Message System Project, *Third International IEEE Workshop on Software Specification and Design*, Washington, DC, IEEE Computer Society Press, pp. 98–100.

Heninger K L *et al.* (1978) Software Requirements for the A-7E Aircraft, *Naval Research Laboratory Memorandum Report 3876*, Washington, DC.

Hirschheim R A (1983) Participative Development: 'Assessing Participative Systems Design: some Conclusions from an Exploratory Study', *Information and Management*, Vol. 6, No. 6, pp. 317–27.

HMSO (23/6/1999) *Select General Committee on Environment, Transport and Regional Affairs Memorandum*, London, Stationery Office.

Hooper J W, Hsia P (1982) Scenario-based Prototyping for Requirements Identification, *ACM Sigsoft Software Engineering Notes*, Vol. 7, No. 5, pp. 88–93.

Horrocks I (1999) *Constructing the User Interface with Statecharts*, Harlow, Addison-Wesley.

Howes N (1987) On Using the User's Manual as the Requirements Specification, in *Tutorial: Software Engineering Project Management*, R Thayer and M Dorfman (Eds), IEEE Computer Society Press.

Humphrey W S (1989) *Managing the Software Process*, Harlow, Addison-Wesley.

Ince D C, Hekmatpour S (1987) Software Prototyping – Progress and Prospects, *Information and Software Technology*, Vol. 29, No. 1, pp. 8–14.

Institute of Electrical and Electronics Engineers (1984) IEEE Guide to Software Requirements Specifications, *IEEE/ANSI Standard 830-1984*, New York (also published in Thayer and Dorfman, 1990).

Jackson M A (1975) *Principles of Program Design*, New York, Academic Press.

Jackson M A (1983) *System Development*, Hemel Hempstead, Prentice Hall.

Jackson M A (1995) *Requirements & Specifications: A Lexicon of Software Practice, Principles and Prejudices*, Wokingham, Addison-Wesley.

Jackson M A (2001) *Problem Frames: Analyzing and Structuring Software Development Problems*, Harlow, Addison-Wesley.

Jacobson I *et al.* (1992) *Object Oriented Software Engineering: A Use-case Driven Approach*, Wokingham, Addison-Wesley.

Jacobson I *et al.* (1996) *Object Oriented Software Engineering: A Use-case Driven Approach* (Revised Printing), Harlow, Addison-Wesley.

James L (1997) Automatic requirements specification update processing from a requirements management tool perspective. *International Conference and Workshop on Engineering of Computer-Based Systems*. Los Alamitos, CA, pp. 2–9, IEEE Computer Society Press.

Johnston F J J, Davis J C (1970) *Decision Tables in Data Processing*, Manchester, NCC.

Kaner C, Falk J, Nguyen H (1993) *Testing Computer Software*, Princeton, NJ, Van Nostrand Rheinhold.

Kaposi A, Myers M (1990) Quality Assuring Specification and Design, *Software Engineering Journal*, Vol. 5, No. 1, pp. 11–26.

Kelly M (1996) *Configuration Management: the Changing Image*, New York, McGraw-Hill.

Kotonya G, Sommerville I (1997) *Requirements Engineering; Processes and Techniques*, New York, Wiley.

Kovitz B (1999) *Practical Software Requirements; A Manual of Content and Style*, Greenwich, CT, Manning.

Kramer J, Ng K, Potts C, Whitehead K (1988) Tool Support for Requirements Analysis, *Software Engineering Journal*, Vol. 3, No. 3, pp. 86–96.

Lano K, Haughton H (Eds) (1994) *Object-Oriented Specification Case Studies*, Hemel Hempstead, Prentice Hall.

Law D (1985) *Prototyping: A State of the Art Report*, Manchester, NCC.

Lehman M M, Belady L A (1985) *Program Evolution*, London Academic Press.

Levene A, Mullery G (1982) An Investigation of Requirement Specification Languages: Theory and Practice, *IEEE Computer*, Vol. 15, No. 5, pp. 50–59.

Loucopoulos P, Karakostas V (1995) *System Requirements Engineering*, New York, McGraw-Hill.

MacAulay L (1996) *Requirements Engineering (Applied Computing)*, Berlin, Springer Verlag.

Maiden N, Rugg G (1996) ACRE: selecting methods for requirements acquisition, *Software Engineering Journal*, Vol. 11, No. 3, pp. 183–92.

Maiden N, Ncube C (1998) Acquiring COTS software selection requirements. *Proceedings of the Third International Conference on Requirements Engineering*, Los Alamitos, CA, USA, pp. 241–49.

Marconi (1990) *Requirements Traceability Management – User Guide*, Marconi Underwater Systems Ltd, Doc No. 300/HD/01501/000.

Mayhew P J, Dearnley P A (1987) An Alternative Prototype Classification, *The Computer Journal*, Vol. 30, No. 6, pp. 481–84.

McGeorge P, Rugg G (1992) The uses of 'contrived' knowledge elicitation techniques, *Expert Systems*, Vol. 9, No. 3, pp. 149–54.

MIL-STD-498 (1985) SFW DID 08, SPAWAR 10-12, 2451 Crystal Drive (CPK-5), Arlington, VA 22245-5200.

Mullery G P (1979) CORE – a Method for Controlled Requirements Expression, *Fourth International Conference on Software Engineering*, Washington DC, IEEE Computer Society Press, pp. 126–35.

Murata T (1989) Petri Nets: Properties, Analysis and Applications, *Proceedings of the IEEE*, Vol. 77, No. 4, pp. 541–80.

Mylopoulos J, Chung L, Nixon B (1992) Representing and Using Non-functional Requirements – A Process Oriented Approach, *IEEE Transactions on Software Engineering*, Vol. 18, No. 6, pp. 483–97.

Naur P (Ed.) (1960) Revised Report on the Algorithmic Language ALGOL 60, *Communications of the ACM*, Vol. 3, No. 5, pp. 299–314.

Page-Jones M (1999) *Fundamentals of Object-Oriented Design in UML*, Harlow, Addison-Wesley.

Parnas D *et al.* (1990) Evaluation of Safety Critical Software, *Communications of the ACM*, Vol. 33, No. 6, pp. 636–48.

Phalp K, Cox K (2000) Picking the right problem frame – an empirical study, *Empirical Software Engineering Journal*, Vol. 5, No. 3, pp. 215–28.

Polya G (1957) *How To Solve It*, Princeton, NJ, Princeton University Press.

Potts C (1993) Software Engineering Research Re-visited, *IEEE Software*, pp. 19–27.

Regnell B *et al.* (1995) Improving the Use-case Driven Approach to Requirements Engineering, *Proceedings of the 2nd IEEE International Symposium on Requirements Engineering*, Los Alamitos, CA, USA, pp. 40–47.

Rockstrom A, Saracco R (1982) SDL-CCITT specification and description language, *IEEE Transactions on Communications*, Vol. 30, No. 6, pp. 1310–18.

Roman G C (1985) A Taxonomy of Current Issues in Requirements Engineering, *IEEE Computer*, Vol. 18, No. 4, pp. 14–23.

Schneider G, Winters J P (1998) *Applying Use-cases; A Practical Guide*, Harlow, Addison-Wesley.

Schneiderman B (1998) *Designing the User Interface: Strategies for Effective Human–Computer Interaction*, Harlow, Addison-Wesley.

Scowen R S (1983) *An Introduction and Handbook for the Standard Syntactic Metalanguage*, NPL Report DITC 1983.

Shlaer S, Mellor S (1988) *Object Oriented Systems Analysis: Modelling the World in Data*, Harlow, Prentice Hall.

Silberschatz A *et al.* (2001) *Operating System Concepts*, New York, Wiley.

Sklaroff J, Smith C (1988) Writing Quality Software Specifications: the Engineer's Challenge, *Proceedings of the 1988 IEEE Southern Tier Technical Conference*, IEEE New York, NY, USA, pp. 167–76.

Sutcliffe A (1998) Scenario-based requirements analysis, *Requirements Engineering*, Vol. 3, No. 1, pp. 48–65.

Thayer R, Dorfman M (Eds) (1990) *System and Software Requirements Engineering*, Los Alamitos, CA, IEEE Computer Society Press.

Turner J, McCluskey T (1994) *The Construction of Formal Specifications*, McGraw Hill.

Turski W M, Maibaum T S E (1987) *Specification of Computer Programs*, Harlow, Addison-Wesley.

Vonk R (1990) *Prototyping: the Effective Use of CASE Technology*, Hemel Hempstead, Prentice Hall.

Wallace R *et al.* (1987) *A Unified Methodology for Developing Systems*, New York, McGraw-Hill.

Ward P, Mellor S (1985) *Structured Development for Real-time Systems*, Hemel Hempstead, Prentice Hall.

Wasserman A *et al.* (1986) Developing Interactive Information Systems with the User Software Engineering Methodology, *IEEE Transactions on Software Engineering*, Vol. 12, No. 2, pp. 326–45.

Wieringa R J (1996) *Requirements Engineering; Frameworks for Understanding*, New York, Wiley.

Wirth N (1974) On the composition of well-structured programs, *Computing Surveys*, Vol. 6, No. 4, pp. 247–59.

Wood J, Silver D (1995) *Joint Application Development*, New York, Wiley.

Woodman M, Heal B (1994) *Introduction to VDM* (2nd edition), New York, McGraw-Hill.

Yeh R, Zave P (1980) Specifying Software Requirements, *Proceedings of the IEEE*, Vol. 68, No. 9, pp. 1077–85.

Yourdon E (1989a) *Modern Structured Analysis*, Harlow, Prentice Hall.

Yourdon E (1989b) *Structured Walk-throughs* (2nd Ed), Harlow, Prentice Hall.

Yourdon E, Argila C (1996) *Object Oriented Analysis & Design*, Harlow, Prentice Hall.

Bibliography

20

Alavi M, Wetherbe J C (1982) Reducing Complexity in Information Requirements Planning, *Systems Objectives & Solutions*, Vol. 2, No. 3, pp. 143–58.

Alford M W (1977) A Requirements Engineering Methodology for Real-Time Processing Requirements, *IEEE Transactions on Software Engineering*, Vol. 3, No. 1, pp. 60–69.

Anger F D *et al.* (1990) Temporal Consistency Checking of Natural Language Specifications, *Applications of Artificial Intelligence*, Vol. 1293, pp. 572–80.

Basili V R, Perricone B T (1984) Software Errors and Complexity: an Empirical Investigation, *Communications of the ACM*, Vol. 27, No. 1, pp. 42–52.

Bell T E, Thayer T A (1976) Software Requirements: Are they really a Problem? *Second International Conference on Software Engineering*, Washington DC, IEEE Computer Society Press, pp. 61–8.

Bethke F J *et al.* (1981) Improving the Usability of Programming Publications, *IBM Systems Journal*, Vol. 20, No. 3, pp. 306–20.

Biewald J *et al.* (1980) Real-time Features of EPOS: Formulation, Evaluation and Documentation, *IFIP/IFAC Real-time Programming Workshop*, Oxford, Pergamon Press, pp. 95–100.

Bruno G *et al.* (1988) A Knowledge Based System Approach to the Development of a System Functional Requirement Specification Processor, *IEEE COMPSAC '88*, pp. 387–94.

Bubenko J (1994) Facilitating 'Fuzzy to Formal' Requirements Modelling, *Ist IEEE Symposium on Requirements Engineering*, pp. 154–7.

Celko J *et al.* (1983) A Demonstration of Three Requirements Language Systems, *ACM SIGPLAN Notices*, Vol. 10, No. 1, pp. 9–14.

Chandrasekharan M *et al.* (1985) Requirements Based Testing of Real-Time Systems: Modelling for Testability, *IEEE Computer*, Vol. 118, No. 4, pp. 71–80.

Coad P, Yourdon E (1990) Object Oriented Analysis, *System and Software Requirements Engineering*, IEEE Press, pp. 272–89.

Cooper J W, Hsia P (1982) Scenario Based Prototypes for Requirements Identification, *ACM SIGSOFT Workshop on Rapid Prototyping*, New York, ACM Press, pp. 17.1–17.11.

Cox H (Oct 1973) The Constitution of an Adequate Software Specification, *Organisation and management of computer based control and automation projects*, IEE, London, pp. 35–41.

Cunningham R J *et al.* (1985) Formal Requirements Specification – The FOREST Project, *Third IEEE International Workshop on Specification and Design*, Washington DC, IEEE Computer Society Press, pp. 186–91.

Davis A M (1990) The Analysis and Specification of Systems and Software Requirements, in *System and Software Requirements Engineering*, R Thayer and M Dorfman (Eds), IEEE Computer Society Press, pp. 119–44.

Davis J S (1989) Identification of Errors in Software Requirements Through Use of Automated Requirement Tools, *Information & Software Technology*, Vol. 31, No. 9, pp. 472–6.

Dumas J (1988) *Designing User Interfaces for Software*, Hemel Hempstead, Prentice Hall.

Flynn D J, Warhurst R (1994) An Empirical Study of the Validation Process within Requirements Determination, *Information Systems Journal*, Vol. 4, No. 3, pp. 185–212.

Gilmore D (1994) Does the Notation Matter, *NATO ISI Series, Series F, Computer & System*, pp. 107–17.

Hadlock F *et al.* (1989) Automated Inference of Flow Diagrams from Natural Language Specifications, *Proceedings of Second Florida AI Research Symposium*, Orlando, FL, pp. 230–37.

Heitmeyer C L, McLean J D (1983) Abstract Requirements Definition, *IEEE Transactions on Software Engineering*, Vol. 9, No. 5, pp. 580–89.

Heninger K L (1979) Limits to Specifications: Why Not More Progress?, *ACM Software Engineering Notes*, Vol. 4, No. 3, pp. 15–16.

Heninger K L *et al.* (1980) Specifying Software Requirements for Complex Systems: New Techniques and their Application, *IEEE Transactions of Software Engineering*, IEEE, Vol. 6, No. 1, pp. 2–13.

Hester S D, Parnas D L, Utter D F (1981) Using Documentation as a Software Design Medium, *The Bell System Technical Journal*, Vol. 60, No. 8, pp. 1941–77.

Hoffman D (1989) Practical Interface Specification, *Software – Practice and Experience*, Vol. 19, No. 2, pp. 127–48.

Hsia P, Yaung A (1988) Another Approach to System Decomposition: Requirements Clustering, *IEEE COMPSAC '88*, Washington DC, IEEE Computer Society Press, pp. 75–82.

Hsia P, Davis A, Kung D (1993) Status Report: Requirements Engineering, *IEEE Software*, Vol. 10, No. 6, pp. 75–9.

Huff S L, Madnick S E (1978) An Approach to Constructing Functional Requirements Statements for System Architectural Design, *Center for Information Systems Research, MIT School of Management, Technical Report 6*, Cambridge, MA.

Jackson D, Rinard M (2000) *The Future of Software Analysis*, in *The Future of Software Engineering*, A Finkelstein (Ed.), ACM Press.

Kaindl H (1993) The Missing Link in Requirements Engineering, *ACM Sigsoft Software Engineering Notes*, Vol. 18, No. 2, pp. 30–9.

Kimbler A, Regnell B, Weeslen A (1995) Improving the Use-case Driven Approach to Requirements Engineering, *2nd IEEE Symposium on Requirements Engineering*, pp. 41–7.

Lauber R J (1982) Development Support Systems, *IEEE Computer*, Vol. 15, No. 5, pp. 36–46.

Lubars M, Potts C, Richter C (1992) A Review of the State of the Practice in Requirements Modelling, *IEEE Software*, pp. 2–14.

Maybury M T (1991) Generating Natural Language Definitions from Classification Hierarchies, *Advances in Classification Research, 53rd Annual ASIS Meeting*, Ontario, pp. 99–106.

Mills H *et al.* (1986) *Information Systems Analysis and Design*, Academic Press, Orlando, Fl.

Monk A, Curry M, Wright P (1994) Why Doesn't Industry Use the Wonderful Notations We Researchers Have Given Them, *NATO ASI Series F Computer & System Sciences*, pp. 185–8.

Palmer J D, Liang Y, Wang L (1991) Classification as an Approach to Requirements Engineering, *Advances in Classification Research, 53rd Annual Meeting ASIS*, Ontario, pp. 129–36.

Payne S G, Green T R G (1986) Task Action Grammars: a Model of the Mental Representation of Task Languages, *Human Computer Interaction*, Vol. 2, No. 2, pp. 93–133.

Peterson J L (1977) Petri Nets, *Computing Surveys*, Vol. 9, No. 3, pp. 223–52.

Roman G C (1982) A Rigorous Approach to Building Formal System Requirements, *IEEE COMPSAC '82*, Washington DC, IEEE Computer Society Press, pp. 417–23.

Ross D T, Schoman K E (1977) Structured Analysis for Requirements Definition, *IEEE Transactions on Software Engineering*, Vol. 3, No. 1, pp. 6–15.

Taylor B (1980) A Method for Expressing the Functional Requirements for Real-time Systems, *Proceedings of the IFAC/IFIP Workshop, Schloss Retzhof*, Leibnitz, Austria, Pergamon Press, pp. 111–20.

Teichrow D, Hersey E H (1977) PSL/PSA: A Computer Aided Technique for Structured Documentation and Analysis of Information Processing Systems, *IEEE Transactions on Software Engineering*, Vol. 3, No. 1, pp. 41–8.

Thayer R, Dorfman M, Bailin S (Eds) (1997) *Software Requirements Engineering*, Los Alamitos, CA, IEEE Computer Society Press.

Wasserman A, Stinson S (1979) A Specification Method for Interactive Information Systems, *Proceedings of Specifications of Reliable Software*, IEEE, NY, USA, pp. 68–79.

Zave P (1984) The Operational Versus the Conventional Approach to Software Development, *Communications of the ACM*, Vol. 27, No. 2, pp. 104–18.

Glossary

21

ABSTRACTION – a view or MODEL (generally of a SYSTEM) that is simplified by considering only the aspects relevant to a particular purpose and ignoring the rest.

AGENT – the SYSTEM (human or machine) that executes or performs a PROCESS.

ANALYSIS (PROBLEM ANALYSIS, REQUIREMENTS ANALYSIS, SYSTEMS ANALYSIS) – the task which, through study of a PROBLEM DOMAIN, enables the achievement of understanding of and the documentation of, the characteristics of that domain and the problems (requiring solution) that exist within that domain.

(Note, the term 'analysis' often attracts other meanings, notably as in object oriented analysis where it usually refers to the high-level, architectural design of the SOLUTION SYSTEM *after* the required SOLUTION SYSTEM behaviour has been established.)

ANALYSIS DOCUMENT – see REQUIREMENTS DOCUMENT.

ANIMATED SPECIFICATION (EXECUTABLE SPECIFICATION) – (part of) a SPECIFICATION that can be executed and, hence, doubles as a DEFINITIVE PROTOTYPE or, possibly, allows automated implementation of the specified SYSTEM.

APPLICATION – a software product or generic type of software product.

ATOMIC REQUIREMENT – a single, individual requirement. (A poorly defined concept – best avoided.)

ATTRIBUTE – **1** a qualitative characteristic or property of some thing. **2** a STORED-DATUM (of an ENTITY).

AVAILABILITY – the proportion of time that a SYSTEM is operating correctly or, at least, usably.

BEHAVIOUR – what a SYSTEM does. For a predictable SYSTEM this may, ultimately, be defined in terms of the INPUTS and OUTPUTS and the relationships between them.

BEHAVIOURAL – concerning BEHAVIOUR.

BUSINESS APPLICATION (BUSINESS SYSTEM) – an application that specifically assists in the running of a business. Usually an INFORMATION SYSTEM and often handling financial information.

CLIENT REPRESENTATIVE (CUSTOMER REPRESENTATIVE) – for GENERIC PRODUCTS, the person appointed (normally from within the DEVELOPER's organisation) to represent the viewpoint of potential CLIENTS or USERS.

CLIENT (CUSTOMER) – the person or organisation with the authority to commission and accept (and, often, pay for) the SOLUTION SYSTEM.

COMMERCIAL APPLICATION – see BUSINESS APPLICATION.

COMMERCIAL CONSTRAINT – a CLIENT imposed constraint regarding the time to delivery or cost of a product (or similar such matters).

COMMISSIONED PRODUCT – a product that is custom-built for the express purposes of a single CLIENT.

CONCEPTUAL DESIGN – see EXTERNAL DESIGN.

CONSTRAINT (DESIGN CONSTRAINT) – a REQUIREMENT which, for a given FUNCTIONALITY, limits the options regarding the INTERNAL DESIGN or implementation of a SYSTEM.

CONTEXT DIAGRAM – a DATA FLOW DIAGRAM of the OPERATING ENVIRONMENT which depicts the SOLUTION SYSTEM and each of its TERMINATORS as separate PROCESSES.

DATA ANALYSIS – a technique for modelling the structure of the data contained within a SYSTEM (usually the PROBLEM DOMAIN or the SOLUTION SYSTEM).

DATA DICTIONARY – a list of definitions relating to a particular SYSTEM or development; sometimes restricted to definitions of DATA only.

DATA FLOW – a DATUM that is passed from one SYSTEM to another.

DATA FLOW ANALYSIS – a technique for modelling a SYSTEM as a set of processes or subsystems together with the data that flows between those processes.

DATA FLOW DIAGRAM – a diagram depicting a model due to DATA FLOW ANALYSIS.

DATA-ITEM – see DATUM.

DATUM (DATA-ITEM, FIELD) – a piece of information.

DEFINITIVE PROTOTYPE – a PROTOTYPE that is used to specify required appearance or behaviour (of the SOLUTION SYSTEM).

DELIVERABLE – the documented output or product from a task or phase of the software development process.

DESIGN – invention. There are two varieties, see EXTERNAL DESIGN and INTERNAL DESIGN.

DESIGN CONSTRAINT – see CONSTRAINT.

DESIGN PHASE – the task, stage or phase of the software development process during which the INTERNAL DESIGN of the SOLUTION SYSTEM is performed. (Generally, follows the REQUIREMENTS ENGINEERING phase.)

DETERMINISTIC FINITE STATE MACHINE – a FINITE STATE MACHINE model with no stored data or decisions; the next STATE is, therefore, determined solely by the current STATE and the TRIGGER.

DEVELOPER – the person or organisation that undertakes to build and deliver the SOLUTION SYSTEM.

DOMAIN KNOWLEDGE – expertise regarding the PROBLEM DOMAIN.

EDESIGN – see EXTERNAL DESIGN.

ELICITATION – see REQUIREMENTS ELICITATION.

ELICITATION NOTES (ELICITATION RECORD) – relatively unprocessed (raw) notes recorded during REQUIREMENTS ELICITATION.

ELICITEE – a person from whom information is obtained during REQUIREMENTS ELICITATION.

END USER COMPUTING – the use of sophisticated high-level languages and development packages to enable those with little software development expertise to build computer applications for their own use.

ENGINEERING APPLICATION – typically, software that is used as a design tool or to control machines.

ENTITY – 1 a distinguishable (type of) thing in the PROBLEM DOMAIN which is of interest because of its associated data. 2 the data model of an ENTITY(1) that will be stored in the SOLUTION SYSTEM. Defined in terms of its STORED-DATA.

EVENT DRIVEN SYSTEM – a SYSTEM that responds to external stimuli (and remains dormant in the absence of such stimuli).

EVENT RESPONSE – the way in which a SYSTEM, in a particular STATE, responds to a particular event or INPUT – much the same as an IO-RELATION.

EVOLUTIONARY PROTOTYPE – a PROTOTYPE that is intended to be developed into the SOLUTION SYSTEM.

EXPLORATORY PROTOTYPE – a PROTOTYPE developed solely for the purpose of investigating possible EXTERNAL DESIGN or INTERNAL DESIGN strategies.

EXTERNAL DESIGN (EDESIGN) – the invention of the external appearance and BEHAVIOUR of a SYSTEM.

FINITE STATE MACHINE – see Section 12.6.

FUNCTION – a useful piece of BEHAVIOUR – may often be regarded as a service that is provided by the SOLUTION SYSTEM.

FUNCTIONAL – pertaining to FUNCTION.

FUNCTIONAL DECOMPOSITION – breaking down FUNCTIONS into smaller, ('lower level') FUNCTIONS that produce the required effect (generally in the context of EXTERNAL DESIGN).

FUNCTIONALITY – the sum total of a SYSTEM's FUNCTIONS. (Since engineered systems are designed to produce only useful behaviour, FUNCTIONALITY and BEHAVIOUR are often used interchangeably.)

GENERIC PRODUCT – a product that is intended for multiple sales on the open market.

HUMAN MACHINE INTERFACE – the INTERFACE between the SOLUTION SYSTEM and the USER(s).

ICONIC MODEL – see REPRESENTATIONAL MODEL.

IDESIGN – see INTERNAL DESIGN.

INDIVIDUAL REQUIREMENT – see ATOMIC REQUIREMENT.

INFORMATION SYSTEM – a particular type of APPLICATION; one that provides information (reports) about some domain, possibly only in response to queries.

INPUT – a DATA FLOW that passes from its OPERATING ENVIRONMENT to the SOLUTION SYSTEM.

INSTANCE – a unique, individual instance of an ENTITY.

INTERFACE – the boundary between one SYSTEM and another.

INTERNAL DESIGN (IDESIGN) – the decomposition of a SYSTEM into its component subsystems for the purposes of realising its construction; the invention of the internal structure and mechanisms of the SOLUTION SYSTEM.

IO-RELATION – short for INPUT/OUTPUT-RELATION; the causal and timely relationships between the INPUT and OUTPUT of a SYSTEM.

KEY – one or more ATTRIBUTES of an ENTITY, the values of which uniquely identify each INSTANCE of that ENTITY.

LIFE-CYCLE MODEL – see PROCESS MODEL.

LITERAL – see TERMINAL.

META-QUESTIONS – questions used during REQUIREMENTS ELICITATION which relate to the REQUIREMENTS ELICITATION process itself.

METHOD – a procedure for addressing or accomplishing some task or problem. See also SOFTWARE DEVELOPMENT METHOD. (It may be noted that 'method' is used quite loosely within software development. In the formal sense of a procedure that is guaranteed to produce a solution, most software development 'methods' are not methods at all.)

METHODOLOGY – the study of methods or a body of methods.

MODEL – see ABSTRACTION.

MODELLING TECHNIQUE – see TECHNIQUE.

NON-BEHAVIOURAL REQUIREMENT – see PERFORMANCE REQUIREMENT.

NON-DETERMINISTIC FINITE STATE MACHINE – a FINITE STATE MACHINE model which incorporates stored data and decision boxes and, hence, branching TRANSITIONS; the next STATE cannot, therefore, always be determined by the current STATE and the TRIGGER alone.

NON-FUNCTIONAL REQUIREMENT – see PERFORMANCE REQUIREMENT.

NON-TERMINAL – a term, used in a definition, which is itself further defined elsewhere (see also TERMINAL).

OBJECT (OBJECT CLASS) – an encapsulation of data and the services that manipulate that data.

OPERATING ENVIRONMENT – that part of the universe that can affect or can be affected by the SOLUTION SYSTEM; i.e. its SUPER-SYSTEM. (Often, similar to the PROBLEM DOMAIN but, strictly, only that part of the PROBLEM DOMAIN that interacts directly with the SOLUTION SYSTEM.)

OUTPUT – a DATA FLOW that passes from the SOLUTION SYSTEM to its OPERATING ENVIRONMENT.

PAPER-PROTOTYPE – see STORY-BOARD.

PARENT SYSTEM – a SUPER-SYSTEM that contains the SYSTEM in question.

PERFORMANCE REQUIREMENT (NON-BEHAVIOURAL REQUIREMENT, NON-FUNCTIONAL REQUIRE-MENT) – a REQUIREMENT relating to the way in which FUNCTIONS are performed. (Commonly, four sub-types: speed, capacity, reliability and usability.)

PETRI NET – see Section 12.7.

PRECURSOR SYSTEM (PRE-EXISTING SYSTEM, CURRENT SYSTEM) – a unique, pre-existing, pos-sibly manually operated SYSTEM which fulfils a similar role to, and is intended to be replaced by, the SOLUTION SYSTEM.

PREDECESSOR SYSTEM – an existing, possibly competitive, product which fulfils a simi-lar role to the SOLUTION SYSTEM.

PRIMITIVE – see TERMINAL.

PROBLEM ANALYSIS – see ANALYSIS.

PROBLEM DOMAIN (APPLICATION DOMAIN) – that part of the universe within which the problem (that requires solution) exists.

PROCESS – a SYSTEM or SUB-SYSTEM that receives INPUT and/or produces OUTPUT.

PROCESS MODEL (LIFE-CYCLE MODEL) – a model of the various tasks that need to be per-formed during software development and the relationships between those tasks. May also include the associated DELIVERABLES.

PROTOTYPE – a realistic, dynamic model of (part of) a SYSTEM – see Section 11.3.

RAPID PROTOTYPE – a prototype that is built rapidly.

REPRESENTATIONAL MODEL (ICONIC MODEL) – a model (such as a sketch) that mimics the appearance of some SYSTEM.

REQUIREMENT – 1 an effect that the CLIENT wishes to be brought about in the PROBLEM DOMAIN. 2 similarly – a condition or capability that must be met by the SYSTEM to solve a problem or achieve an objective.

REQUIREMENTS ANALYSIS – see ANALYSIS.

REQUIREMENTS DOCUMENT (ANALYSIS DOCUMENT) – the DELIVERABLE from ANALYSIS; the document that records the description of the PROBLEM DOMAIN and the REQUIRE-MENTS to be met by the SOLUTION SYSTEM.

REQUIREMENTS ELICITATION – the process of discovering and collecting information about the PROBLEM DOMAIN and potential REQUIREMENTS to be met by the SOLUTION SYSTEM.

REQUIREMENTS ENGINEERING – investigating and describing the PROBLEM DOMAIN and REQUIREMENTS and EDESIGNING and documenting the characteristics for a SOLUTION SYSTEM that will meet those REQUIREMENTS – see also, the whole book!

REQUIREMENTS GATHERING – see REQUIREMENTS ELICITATION.

REQUIREMENTS SPECIFICATION – possibly the documentation of requirements, but used here synonymously with SPECIFICATION (1).

SCENARIO – see Section 12.3.2.

SOFTWARE DEVELOPMENT METHOD – a set of TECHNIQUES and an organising schema for performing a significant part of the software development process.

SOFTWARE LIFE-CYCLE – see PROCESS MODEL.

SOLUTION SYSTEM (NEW SYSTEM, APPLICATION, MACHINE) – the new SYSTEM that may be developed or acquired in order to solve the problems in the PROBLEM DOMAIN.

SPECIFICATION – 1 the invention and definition of a BEHAVIOUR (and, possibly, appearance) of the SOLUTION SYSTEM such that it will produce the required effects in the PROBLEM DOMAIN. 2 the DELIVERABLE that records the specified BEHAVIOUR of the SOLUTION SYSTEM.

SPECIFIC REQUIREMENT – see ATOMIC REQUIREMENT.

STAKEHOLDER – someone who has an interest (potential gain or loss) in a system development. This includes the CLIENT, the USER and the DEVELOPER.

STATE – a mode of existence of a SYSTEM (represented by the aggregate of the values of its STORED-DATA).

STATE MATRIX – a table defining the STATES, TRIGGERS and TRANSITIONS for a FINITE STATE MACHINE.

STEPWISE REFINEMENT – an INTERNAL DESIGN technique that a creates a structure for a SOLUTION SYSTEM by decomposing it in a top-down, hierarchical manner.

STIMULUS (TRIGGER, EVENT) – an INPUT which causes a SYSTEM to change STATE and/or produce a particular OUTPUT.

STORED-DATUM – a DATUM that is stored within the SOLUTION SYSTEM.

STORY-BOARD – an ordered set of representations of a SYSTEM which depict its changing appearance over time.

SUB-SYSTEM – a subordinate SYSTEM which forms part of a larger SYSTEM.

SUPER-SYSTEM – the SYSTEM of which the SYSTEM in question is a SUB-SYSTEM.

SYSTEM – a set of interconnected elements constituted to achieve some given or supposed objective.

SYSTEM REQUIREMENTS SPECIFICATION (SRS) – see SPECIFICATION, but may also be a combined SPECIFICATION and REQUIREMENTS DOCUMENT.

TASK ANALYSIS – see Section 12.2.

TECHNIQUE – a prescribed way of modelling a SYSTEM or performing a task – see also Chapter 8.

TERMINAL – a word or term, the meaning of which is deemed to be self-evident.

TERMINATOR – a SUB-SYSTEM (sub-domain) of the OPERATING ENVIRONMENT – an external SYSTEM that interfaces with the SOLUTION SYSTEM. Sometimes (at the considerable risk of confusion with the concept ENTITY) referred to as an external entity.

THROWAWAY PROTOTYPE (EXPLORATORY PROTOTYPE) – a PROTOTYPE developed for the purpose of clarifying or validating the REQUIREMENTS for or EXTERNAL DESIGN of the SOLUTION SYSTEM – see Section 11.3.

TRANSFORMATION – see PROCESS.

TRANSITION – 1 the change from one STATE to another of a FINITE STATE MACHINE. 2 a logic 'gate' controlling the execution of a PETRI NET.

TRIGGER – an INPUT that initiates a TRANSITION in a FINITE STATE MACHINE.

USE-CASE – see Section 12.3.

USER – a human TERMINATOR. Someone who will or may interface directly with the SOLUTION SYSTEM.

USER INTERFACE – see HUMAN MACHINE INTERFACE.

VALIDATION – ensuring that the correct FUNCTIONALITY for the SOLUTION SYSTEM has been determined (highly pertinent to REQUIREMENTS ENGINEERING).

VERIFICATION – ensuring that the SOLUTION SYSTEM, as constructed, complies with the SPECIFICATION and produces the correct FUNCTIONALITY (less pertinent to REQUIREMENTS ENGINEERING than VALIDATION).

VIEWPOINT – a particular perspective upon a SYSTEM or a system development. Within the context of ELICITATION, a VIEWPOINT may be more or less equivalent to a STAKEHOLDER, within the context of ANALYSIS or SPECIFICATION, the equivalent of a TERMINATOR.

Abbreviations

ADT	abstract data type
aka	also known as
API	application programmer interface
ATM	automatic teller machine
BNF	Backus Naur form
CAD	computer aided design
CASE	computer assisted software engineering
CBA	cost benefit analysis
CORE	controlled requirements expression
COTS	commercial off the shelf
CRC	cooperative requirements capture
CRS	client requirements specification
DBMS	database management systems
DD	data dictionary
DFD	data flow diagram
ECAD	electronic computer aided design
edesign	external design
EECRM	entity/entity cross reference matrix
ELH	entity life history
ER	event response
ERD	entity relationship diagram
ESH	entity state history
FIFO	first in first out
FRQ	floor request queue
FSM	finite state machine
GUI	graphical user interface
HCI	human computer interface
HMI	human machine interface
HTA	hierarchical task analysis
idesign	internal design
i/o	input/output
JAD	joint application design
JSP	Jackson structured programming
JSD	Jackson system design
mtbf	mean time between failures
NL	natural language
OCR	optical character recognition

OOA	object oriented analysis
OOD	object oriented design
OOM	object oriented modelling
OOS	object oriented specification
OOSE	object oriented software engineering
PCB	printed circuit board
p-code	pseudo-code
PD	problem domain
PDOA	problem domain oriented analysis
PIN	personal identification number
PRL	problem requirements list
RTSA	real-time structured analysis
SA	structured analysis
SC	state chart or structure chart
SCRU	speed, capacity, reliability, usability
SDL	specification and description language
SM	state matrix
SRS	system requirements specification
SS	solution system
SSADM	structured systems analysis and design methodology
STD	state transition diagram
STM	state transition matrix
TA	task analysis
TAG	task action grammar
TBD	to be determined
TNF	third normal form
UML	unified modelling language
URS	user requirements specification
VCR	video cassette recorder
VDM	vienna development method
WIMP	Windows, icons, mouse [or menu], pointer
YRR	yacht race results

Index